OTTO SKORZENY

OTTO SKORZENY

THE DEVIL'S DISCIPLE

STUART SMITH

OSPREY PUBLISHING
Bloomsbury Publishing Plc
PO Box 883, Oxford, OX1 9PL, UK
1385 Broadway, 5th Floor, New York, NY 10018, USA
E-mail: info@ospreypublishing.com
www.ospreypublishing.com

OSPREY is a trademark of Osprey Publishing Ltd

First published in Great Britain in 2018

A catalogue record for this book is available from the British Library.

ISBN: HB 978 1 4728 2945 0; eBook 978 1 4728 2946 7; ePDF 978 1 4728
2947 4; XML 978 1 4728 2948 1

18 19 20 21 22   10 9 8 7 6 5 4 3 2 1

Maps by Bounford.com
Index by Zoe Ross
Originated by PDQ Digital Media Solutions, Bungay, UK
Printed and bound in Great Britain by CPI (Group) UK Ltd, Croydon
CRO 4YY

Front cover: SS-Sturmbannführer Otto Skorzeny, c. 1944. (Popperfoto/
Getty)

Osprey Publishing supports the Woodland Trust, the UK's leading woodland
conservation charity. Between 2014 and 2018 our donations are being spent
on their Centenary Woods project in the UK.

To find out more about our authors and books visit **www.ospreypublishing.
com**. Here you will find extracts, author interviews, details of forthcoming
events and the option to sign up for our newsletter.

Contents

Acknowledgments   7

Prologue   8

Maps   11

1. The Knowledge of Pain   18

2. Accidental Soldier   30

3. Thugs in Field Grey   41

4. The Liberator of Mussolini   57

5. Special Ops and High-Value Targets   82

6. Miracle Weapons   98

7. The Stauffenberg Plot – July 1944   109

8. The Scherhorn Affair   124

9. The SS Changes Tack   134

10. Operation *Panzerfaust*: Budapest, October 1944   149

11. Everything on One Card: Operation *Greif*   162

12. Operation *Greif*: Mission and Aftermath   179

13. Implosion: The Schwedt Bridgehead   197

14. Skorzeny's Last Stand   220

15. Trial and Errors   236

16. Escape from Darmstadt   255

17. Apocalypse Soon: Preparing for World War III   261

18. Neo-Nazis and Colonel Nasser: Skorzeny's Wilderness Years   283

19. The Years of Plenty   295

20. Ghosts of the Past: Skorzeny's Last Years   305

Epilogue: Man and Myth   319

Glossary   326

Note on the Waffen-SS   329

Bibliography   331

Notes   340

Index   376

Acknowledgements

Above all, I must thank my editor, Jeremy Dronfield, for skilfully corseting the unwieldy original manuscript into a more focused and, mercifully, shorter book. Along the way, Jeremy provided invaluable insight into sources, copyright issues and miscellaneous factual debates – the benefits, in short, of his own experience as a published author.

Beyond that, my thanks to: Dave Trott, who (unknowingly) provided the germ idea for this book, with his reflections on Skorzeny's part in the Gran Sasso raid. Chris Wood, who encouraged me to write the book in the first place. Stephen Foster, for his judicious appraisals over the occasional glass of see-through red. Runi Phillips, for her invaluable help in translating the original German. Karol Griffiths, for meticulously dissecting the original manuscript. Maxine Taylor, for pointing me to the right literary agent. Andrew Lownie, the agent in question, for efficiently steering the book to publication. Osprey/Bloomsbury's editorial team, for their sympathetic and long-suffering compliance with my legion requests for alterations to the copy.

And finally, but not least, to: Hilary, my wife, and Todd (sadly no longer with us), who mutely (in Todd's case) and uncomplainingly (in my wife's) provided support during the long, lonely hours consumed in writing a book.

Prologue

12 September 1943: Gran Sasso, central Italy

The Propaganda Kompanie cameraman panned across the white peaks and jagged ridges looming above, and the grassy, rock-strewn slopes. He filmed the exterior of the Hotel Campo Imperatore, and Luftwaffe paratroopers and SS commandos posing and grinning. They were rightly pleased with themselves, and the Propaganda Kompanie men encouraged them to play up for the camera. One blond, boyish paratrooper was singled out for a close-up: 'Take off your helmet! Look to the sky!'

They had reason to smile. In a daringly planned and well-executed operation, this small team of a hundred men had landed in gliders, seized the mountain-top and the hotel from a large detachment of Italian guards – without firing a shot – and rescued former dictator Benito Mussolini from captivity. If the Führer's strategy went to plan, this would scupper the rebel Italian government's peace deal with the Allies. It would also play brilliantly in the next edition of *Die Deutsche Wochenschau*, the official state newsreel – hence the heavy Propaganda Kompanie presence.[1]

Even in flickering monochrome on cinema screens, the mountain setting looked spectacular. The troops resembled supermen. Mussolini, done up tight in a long winter overcoat and dark fedora, walked out of the hotel towards the camera among a crowd of soldiers. They grinned. Il Duce grinned. At his right elbow, guiding him, was a tall, imposing German officer in a pale uniform, moustached, with a long scar disfiguring the left side of his face; he was evidently conscious of the camera's eye. The clipped voice of the narrator identified him as SS-Hauptsturmführer Skorzeny, commander of the lightning strike which had just liberated 'Der Duce'. To Skorzeny's satisfaction, his name was correctly pronounced, a matter to which he attached great importance.

Mussolini's rescue was a gift for the producers of *Die Deutsche Wochenschau*.[2] As each week passed, their job – which was to depict the Third Reich's magnificent performance in the war – was getting harder. Allied aircraft were firebombing cities in the heart of the Reich, and German forces were being pushed back on all fronts. Just a few weeks earlier, they had lost the Battle of Kursk, and would never again be able to take the offensive on the Eastern Front. In this same edition of the newsreel, the propagandists continued the increasingly difficult task of conjuring from the relentless, grinding retreat a heroic defence of civilisation against the Communist barbarian horde.[3] Luckily they had other things to counterbalance it – such as Operation *Achse* (*Axis*), Germany's lightning seizure of control in Italy. It had been triggered by the Fascist government deposing Mussolini and plotting to sell him to the Allies in exchange for favourable peace terms. On cinema screens, the taking of Rome by German forces looked like a victory. Against that background, the heroic rescue of Mussolini – throwing a spanner in the traitors' works – was a propaganda triumph for the Führer. It helped to distract from the fact that the Allies, having taken North Africa and Sicily, had just landed on the Italian mainland at Salerno.

The newsreel rolled on. With Skorzeny sticking to Mussolini's side (and the camera's lens), the group of officers and men walked to the waiting getaway plane. The aircraft brought in for the task was an ultra-lightweight Fieseler Fi 156 Storch, chosen for its ability to take off from extremely short improvised runways; indeed, it was such an eager flyer that in a good headwind it could hover. At the controls was Luftwaffe Hauptmann Heinrich Gerlach, personal pilot to Generaloberst Kurt Student, commander of the Luftwaffe's airborne arm, XI. Fliegerkorps, and the man in overall command of this operation. Gerlach had been specially selected for the mission, and after circling overhead for a while had executed a superb landing on a strip of ground only 35 metres long.

The little Storch could only take one passenger. This should pose no problem; after all, there was only one important man on that mountain-top. Gerlach would fly Mussolini to Rome while the rest of the German team departed by cable car and truck.

SS-Hauptsturmführer Otto Skorzeny didn't see it that way; in his mind there were two important men who needed to get to Rome, and he was one of them. Was he not the mastermind and leader of the operation? In fact, he was neither, but he had a special role and was determined to make the most of it. In this moment he had the eye of the world on him, and he'd be damned if he would step aside. Skorzeny was more conscious of the cameras on him than any other man on that mountain except for Mussolini. He wanted to be seen personally bringing Mussolini to freedom. German military men had a name for this kind of thirst for glory: *Halsschmerzen* – 'sore throat' – an allusion to the Ritterkreuz (Knight's Cross), which was worn around the neck. Glory and romance drove Otto Skorzeny – and an acute sense of his own image. On this day, despite being an SS officer, he was wearing the romantic golden tan tropical kit of the Luftwaffe, a service he greatly admired and in which he had once briefly served.

Skorzeny informed Gerlach that he was coming aboard. Away from the camera, a brief and angry discussion took place between the two. Given the extremely short take-off strip, having Skorzeny's weight in the plane was an invitation to disaster. Skorzeny invoked the name of the Führer, who had appointed him Mussolini's guardian; it was more than his life was worth to let the prize out of his sight. He exhorted and threatened, and soon got his way.

Back on screen, Skorzeny smilingly helped a distinctly anxious-looking Duce into his seat and strapped him in. Mussolini, himself an experienced pilot, knew they were courting disaster. The engine started, and Skorzeny squeezed himself into the luggage compartment. Gerlach held the Storch on its brakes and ran the engine up to full power. Surrounded by cheering, waving commandos, the plane lurched forward, bouncing on the uneven ground as it lumbered towards the edge of the precipice.

The newsreel cut away an instant before it reached the brink. The men on the ground gasped as the Storch shot over and dropped instantly out of sight, plummeting into the void, taking with it Otto Skorzeny's hopes of glory and Adolf Hitler's scheme for a strategic solution in Italy. The engine howled, strained … and after a horrible pause the fragile plane reappeared in the distance, struggling, slowly climbing away, shrinking to a dot as it banked away westward.

There could hardly be a more apt symbol of Otto Skorzeny's life thus far – and to come – than the fall and flight of that little plane.

Maps

1. The Gran Sasso Raid, 12 September 1943   12
2. Projected advance of 6. Panzerarmee, 16–18 December 1944   13
3. Fölkersam's assault on the Warche Brück, Malmédy,
    21 December 1944   14
4. The Schwedt Bridgehead, early February 1945   15
5. The final campaign in Germany, showing extent of the Alpenfestung,
    April–May 1945   16

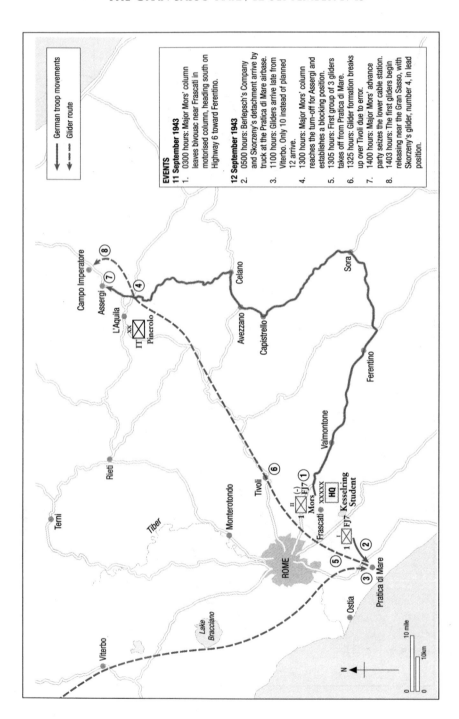

German troop movements

Glider route

EVENTS

11 September 1943

1. 0300 hours: Major Mors' column leaves bivouac near Frascati in motorised column, heading south on Highway 6 toward Ferentino.

12 September 1943

2. 0500 hours: Berlepsch's Company and Skorzeny's detachment arrive by truck at the Pratica di Mare airbase.

3. 1100 hours: Gliders arrive late from Viterbo. Only 10 instead of planned 12 arrive.

4. 1300 hours: Major Mors' column reaches the turn-off for Assergi and establishes a blocking position.

5. 1305 hours: First group of 3 gliders takes off from Pratica di Mare.

6. 1325 hours: Glider formation breaks up over Tivoli due to error.

7. 1400 hours: Major Mors' advance party seizes the lower cable station.

8. 1403 hours: The first gliders begin releasing near the Gran Sasso, with Skorzeny's glider, number 4, in lead position.

Projected advance of 6. Panzerarmee, 16–18 December 1944

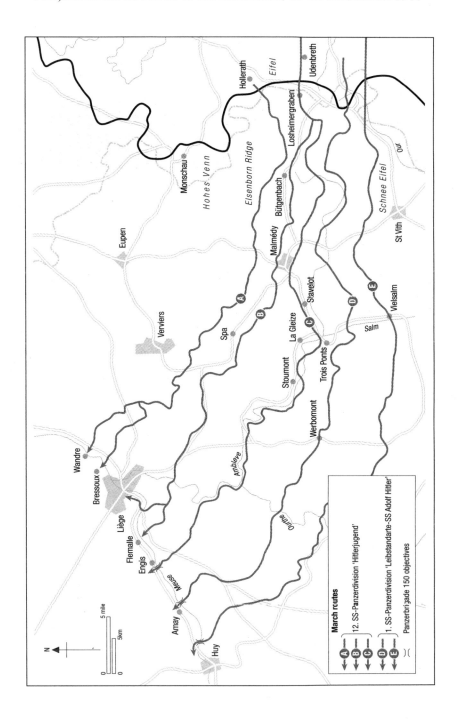

Fölkersam's assault on the Warche Brück, Malmédy, 21 December 1944

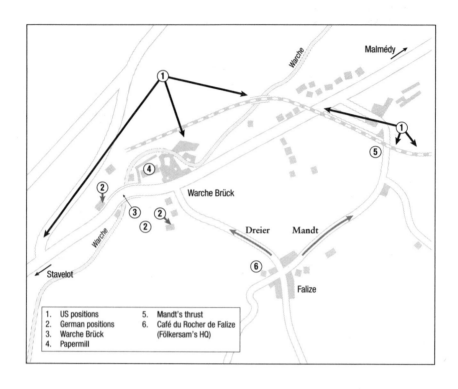

1.	US positions	5.	Mandt's thrust
2.	German positions	6.	Café du Rocher de Falize
3.	Warche Brück		(Fölkersam's HQ)
4.	Papermill		

THE SCHWEDT BRIDGEHEAD, EARLY FEBRUARY 1945

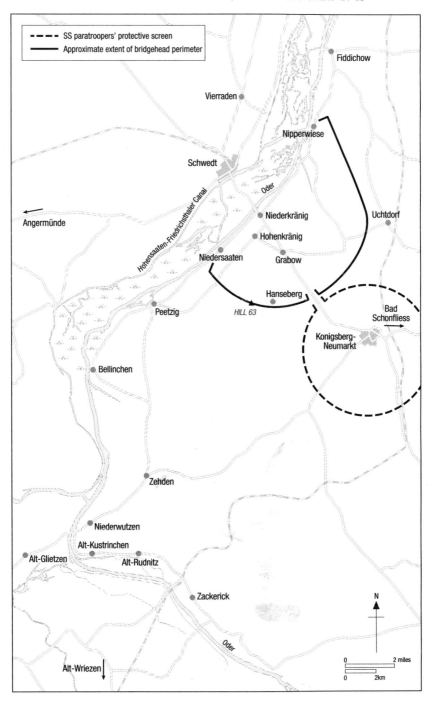

- - - SS paratroopers' protective screen
——— Approximate extent of bridgehead perimeter

Fiddichow

Vierraden

Nipperwiese

Schwedt

Oder

Niederkränig

Uchtdorf

Angermünde

Hohenkränig

Niedersaaten

Grabow

Hanseberg

Peetzig

HILL 63

Bad
Schonfliess

Konigsberg-
Neumarkt

Bellinchen

Zehden

Niederwutzen

Alt-Kustrinchen

Alt-Glietzen

Alt-Rudnitz

Zackerick

N

Oder

0 _____ 2 miles
0 ____ 2km

Alt-Wriezen

THE FINAL CAMPAIGN IN GERMANY, SHOWING EXTENT OF THE ALPENFESTUNG, APRIL–MAY, 1945

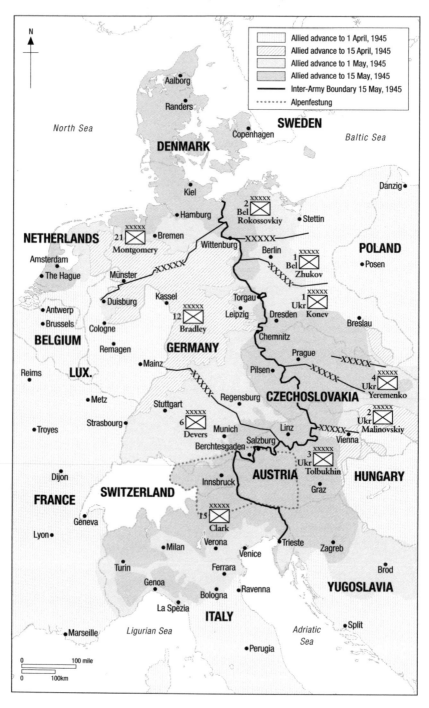

1

The Knowledge of Pain

Otto Skorzeny was born into a once great empire just as it entered its twilight. He grew up in its crepuscular radiance, his life shaped by a belief that his homeland's greatness could be restored through courage, conflict, and the purging of bad influences. In that respect, he was like millions of other young Austrians and Germans; but in most other ways Otto Skorzeny was a one-off.

In 1908, the year Skorzeny came into the world, Emperor Franz Josef of Austria-Hungary celebrated his diamond jubilee, marking 60 years' inglorious reign over Europe's greatest empire. Vienna, the Skorzeny family's home city, cosmopolitan fin de siècle capital, was the centre of a sprawling patchwork quilt stretching from the borders of Italy and Switzerland to the Ukraine and the northern marches of the Christian Balkans; but like its monarch, the empire was backward-looking and well past its best. Beneath a crust of feudal traditions, the magma of nationalism was welling. In this jubilee year, Austria-Hungary annexed Bosnia-Herzegovina, thus opening up one of the cracks that would lead to the eruption of World War I and eventually the empire's implosion.

Not that anyone would have dreamt of such a nightmare in the serene Vienna of 1908 where, on 12 June, a baby was born into the prosperous middle-class Skorzeny family. Otto was the third child and second son of engineer and architect Anton Skorzeny, who at 38 years old presided over the successful construction business he had built up in his twenties. The family name was a fairly unusual one, originating in the east Pomeranian village of

Skorzęcin[*]. There were military connections on both sides of the family; Anton served as a reserve artillery officer in World War I,[1] while his wife, Flora (*née* Sieber Steiner-Hardt), came from an old military family which for generations had patrolled the far-flung borders of the empire, apparently without distinction.[2]

The defeat of the Central Powers in 1918 brought the Austro-Hungarian Empire to an end, and Otto spent the second half of his childhood in the embittered, economically dysfunctional rump state that remained. It was a challenging world in which to build a life. But Otto Skorzeny relished a challenge, and had a way of coming out on top, even if he had to face adversity to get there.

Unlike his father, the young Otto was little concerned with traditions, but did share a passion for technology and engineering, which he saw as the key to the future. At school he found 'realistic' subjects like mathematics and science 'quite easy', but disdained the humanities and wasn't a prolific reader.[3] However, he proved a competent linguist; French, which was seen as more sophisticated than German, was the preferred language in Viennese bourgeois households of the time, while English (which he spoke with a British accent) and Spanish came to him quite easily in later life.

Like his father and his elder brother Alfred (born 1900), Otto trained to be an engineer. Having entered Vienna's Technische Hochschule (Technical University) in 1926, he passed the first examinations in the winter of 1928–29, putting the initial, mainly theoretical, stage of his training behind him, and embarking on the three-year practical engineering course, which he preferred.[4]

No amount of practicality could guarantee a viable job in post-war Austria. Right from the start, the new republic was a failed state. The ethnic German population had been the empire's most ardent supporters – unsurprisingly since they monopolised most positions of power and influence within it. Now, not only had they lost the war – with all the material privations that involved – but they also found themselves being punished for having started it.

The victorious Allies had sought to rationalise the political geography of a Europe which had just experienced the collapse of four enormous empires: Russian, German, Austro-Hungarian and Ottoman. They did so by invoking 'ethnic self-determination'. The great difficulty was in deciding whether this should be based on racial characteristics, common language, cultural and religious values, or all these things combined. Looking at the ethnic kaleidoscope

[*]   Now in Poland

19

of post-war Europe, it was clear that no standard blueprint could suffice. The resulting states would be artefacts, defined arbitrarily by the victors.

Worse, the Versailles peace treaty seemed, to German minds, vindictive: if ethnic self-determination was the supreme principle of statehood, why were Germany and Austria forbidden from combining into a single *Grossdeutsch* (Greater Germany) state? Most Germans regarded this as calculated Allied hypocrisy, designed to subjugate them while they paid off colossal reparations for a war they did not admit to starting.

The shrunken boundaries of Austria ensured that many factories supplying the domestic market were deprived of raw materials, while the natural resources that remained were frequently denied processing plants. The former free-trade area of 54 million people was now a mosaic of competing protectionist states.

There were political problems too. Austria's new democracy had shallow roots. That might not have mattered if it had been supported by a prosperous, confident middle class. It wasn't. Austria's middle class was weak, disaffected and disproportionately impoverished by the break-up of the empire. People's savings were ravaged by inflation (the money that would have bought a small house before the war had, by 1922, been reduced to the value of a postage stamp).[5] Many businesses were undercapitalised, and a vast army of professionals – military officers, bureaucrats, lawyers, accountants, doctors, architects and civil engineers – found themselves redundant. Even before the Great Depression, many middle-class people had written off the republic. Efficient authoritarian rule – preferably bringing Anschluss (unification with Germany) in its wake – became an increasingly attractive alternative for them.

As a schoolboy, Otto Skorzeny showed no susceptibility to these radical ideas. There was no foreshadowing of his later enthusiasm for Fascism. Politics in the Skorzeny household were conventionally right-wing – nostalgia for the empire and the lost business opportunities it represented, and dislike of the post-war regime, but little more. Indeed, their reaction to adversity seems to have been dignified resignation. Skorzeny recalled that he was 15 before he had his first (post-war) taste of butter: 'My father told me there was no harm in doing without things; it might even be a good thing not to get used to a soft life. And he was right.'[6]

At university, however, Skorzeny's political attitudes changed. Despite his flair for engineering, he did only the minimum work to get by. But if not highly motivated academically, he was very active athletically. He was a massive young man – 6 feet 4 and heavily built – with good physical coordination, and an enthusiastic sportsman, especially in sports that involved machines or weapons. It was this that brought him closer to politics.

In 1927, in his second year at the Technische Hochschule, he became immersed in the activities of the Schlagende Verbindung: the duelling society. Built around ritualistic duels with the Schläger sword (in which the object was to gain and inflict impressive facial scars, not to kill one's opponent) and gargantuan drinking sessions, such societies were a fixture of German and Austrian universities, and membership constituted a rite of passage for a certain kind of macho student. Otto Skorzeny excelled at duelling; by the time of his graduation he had fought 14 Schläger duels.[7] The expectation of personal injury was high – and indeed, desired. Skorzeny's success made him a target for those who wished to test their mettle. During his tenth duel, in 1928, he received a severe slash from ear to chin on the left side of his face, forming the scar which became his trademark; it was stitched up on the spot without anaesthetic. For the Schlagende Verbindung, handling pain and injury was a more important test of character than winning. In later years, Skorzeny liked to characterise his prowess as a kind of Spartan preparation for warfare:

> I was to be grateful for the self-discipline we learned in our student clubs. I never felt so bad under fire as I did at eighteen when I had to fight my first duel, under the sharp eye of my fellow students. My knowledge of pain, learned with the sabre, taught me not to be afraid of fear. And just as in duelling you must fix your mind on striking the enemy's head, so, too, in war. You cannot waste time feinting and sidestepping. You must decide on your target and go in.[8]

Many leading Nazis bore duelling scars – or *Schmisse* – as badges of honour, social status and manhood. They were frequently belittled; Himmler claimed to have one, though it looked more like a shaving mishap, while the enemies of SS-Obergruppenführer Ernst Kaltenbrunner claimed he had come by his in a car accident. Skorzeny's scar was never subject to doubt, and his prowess as a duellist was outstanding.

Like his scar, Otto Skorzeny acquired his politics in student clubs. Austro-German student associations were originally a product of the nationalistic fervour stirred up during the Napoleonic Wars. By the 1920s many had acquired a reactionary ethos dressed up as ardent patriotism. Skorzeny, like many other duellists, became a member of Vienna's Markomannia Student Society – named after the Marcomanni, an ancient Germanic tribe of the Danube region which had resisted Roman conquest.

Many of its members – especially the duellists, with their culture of martial machismo – developed close affiliations with shady paramilitary organisations then beginning to flourish. Austria was polarised politically; parties on the left found inspiration in the fledgling Bolshevik state of Russia; the right increasingly looked to unification with Germany. A Marxist putsch in 1927 was brutally suppressed by government forces, but not before the insurgents managed to terrify Vienna's bourgeoisie. One important outcome was the formation of the paramilitary Academic Legion in Austrian universities in 1928. Acting on a sense of patriotic duty, Skorzeny joined it.[9]

The Legion was a thinly disguised chapter of the most powerful Austrian paramilitary force of the time, the Heimwehr (Home Guard). Enforcing state security and order was difficult for the right-leaning coalitions that ruled Austria from the mid-1920s onwards, due to a cap imposed on the armed forces by the 1919 Treaty of St Germain. They had little option but to accept the support of paramilitaries, which were hostile to the concept of parliamentary democracy and for the most part recruited from disgruntled war veterans. During this period the Austrian Nazi Party with its paramilitary Sturmabteilung (SA) wing was weak and divided compared with the Heimwehr, which rapidly assimilated the student groups. By the time of his graduation in December 1931, Skorzeny was a Heimwehr platoon leader and deputy company commander.

His association didn't last long. Walter Pfrimer, leader of the Heimwehr's radical, pan-German wing, attempted to turn the Heimwehr into a parliamentary party and play the politicians at their own game. Skorzeny saw this as a 'tragic' move, and 'by 1930, I and most of my comrades regarded it as a signal to sever our connection ... We were determined to have nothing to do with party politics and not allow ourselves to be the tools of party politicians.'[10] Pfrimer's initiative miscarried badly at the ballot boxes. When Pfrimer embarked on a last-ditch 'March on Vienna', in the style of Mussolini's ascent to power in 1922, the result was a fiasco.

Under Pfrimer's successor, Prinz Ernst Rüdiger von Starhemberg, the Heimwehr reluctantly formed a coalition government with the ruling Christian Social Party, and, as part of a deal with Britain and France, abandoned support for Anschluss. This left the Nazi Party as the only significant standard-bearer of pan-German ideals. Many middle-class Austrians who had no interest in the details of Nazi ideology now turned to the party, believing that political union with Germany was the only way of delivering them from their economic plight.

* * *

After completing his thesis on 'The Calculation and Construction of a Diesel Engine' and graduating as a mechanical engineer on 31 December 1931, Otto Skorzeny confronted the challenge of making a career for himself. He welcomed the rise of the Nazis. So did his father, Anton, who liked the idea of a Nazi government because it would be 'good for the economy'.

Anton's initial enthusiasm would wane rapidly after the murder of Chancellor Dollfuss by Nazi gunmen in yet another unsuccessful putsch in 1934.[11] But while his father drifted away from the Nazis, Otto Skorzeny moved closer. He joined the Nazi Party on 1 May 1932, inspired – he claimed – by a speech Josef Goebbels had given in Vienna.[12] Shortly afterwards, on 19 June, Dollfuss banned the party, driving it underground.

The party took on new disguises,[13] including cultural, sports and social clubs, the chief among them being the Deutschen Turnerbund 1919 (German Gymnastic League 1919), which Skorzeny joined. Although the government banned the party as a political organisation, they failed to suppress its specialist paramilitary organs, whose survival was partially guaranteed by their autonomous funding. Skorzeny remained a party member, and in February 1934 he joined its most elite organisation, the Schutzstaffel (SS).[14]

Although Nazism appealed mainly to the dispossessed lower middle class, Skorzeny's background in the university-educated Viennese bourgeoisie is entirely characteristic of an SS recruit at this time. The National Socialist emphasis on quick, decisive solutions to apparently complicated, intractable problems provided exactly the kind of credo that appealed to many young adults – educated ones among them – whose employment opportunities were minuscule.

Skorzeny, a cunning operator, did better career-wise than most. After graduation, while engaging in right-wing politics in his spare time, he started working in a garage as a glorified mechanic. Within a couple of years his situation improved dramatically, with a junior partnership in Meidlinger Gerüstbau, a small but successful construction and scaffolding company. He owed his step-up to marriage; in May 1934 he wed the company owner's 19-year-old daughter, Margareta Schreiber ('Gretl'), after a four-year relationship.[15] The honeymoon was 'sporty', involving a motorcycle and sidecar tour of some of Italy's principal sights: Bologna, Venice, Ravenna, Pisa, Florence and – a portentous choice – the Abruzzi, near Gran Sasso. (His touristic knowledge of this part of Italy would later influence his selection for the Mussolini rescue operation.)

In 1937, Otto and Margareta divorced.[16] In January of that year, he had bought a majority share in the now flourishing scaffolding company – a business relationship that would survive to the end of the war.[17] It is hard not to read this cynically, as if Margareta had served her purpose in helping him onto the economic ladder and could now be discarded.

* * *

By 1937 the political temperature in Vienna was feverish. Underground Nazi propagandists busily and skilfully played upon economic dispossession, political uncertainty and anti-Semitic prejudice, mixing them into a cocktail that many middle-class Austrians found intoxicating. Despite comprising a minority of Vienna's population, Jews dominated the professions (university dons, lawyers and doctors) as well as the industrial, mercantile and financial classes and many skilled trades, a fact which was ripe for anti-Semitic propaganda. Contradictorily but seductively, the Jews were portrayed as masters of world capitalism, Bolsheviks intent on revolution, and rootless carpetbaggers denying middle-class Viennese folk their rightful station in life. This paradoxical racial doctrine was one that Otto Skorzeny, as an active and ambitious member of the SS, unquestionably embraced.[18]

The pre-war Austrian SS differed greatly from the SA in purpose, scale and membership. The SA was a streetfighting organisation, mainly composed of unemployed, thuggish working-class men, whose primary purpose was to protect the party's own political meetings while intimidating other people's. The SS, by contrast, was essentially a party police force, and mostly middle class. Its members usually had jobs, often in the professions and the civil service, and their preoccupations tended to be more cerebral: particularly the amassing of police intelligence by covert means. The architect of the SS, Heinrich Himmler, wanted to create an elite, like the Roman Praetorian Guard; therefore, SS membership was restricted, to about one-tenth of the SA's. By early 1938 the Austrian SS had no more than 7,000 members.

While political machinations in Germany had caused the fortunes of the Austrian SA to wane, the SS steadily gathered momentum as the preferred instrument of an increasingly powerful Nazi regime in Berlin. The head of the SA, Ernst Röhm, had been liquidated and the SA emasculated in the Night of the Long Knives in 1934.* The Austrian SA survived in strength, but Berlin's money was channelled to the Austrian SS, who provided Berlin with priceless intelligence as Hitler limbered up for his final confrontation with the Austrian government.

---

*   A bloody purge, carried out by the SS between 30 June and 2 July 1934, to eliminate Hitler's political opponents.

A pivotal figure at this time – and a key player in Skorzeny's own future – was Ernst Kaltenbrunner, who became head of the Austrian SS in 1936. Kaltenbrunner's background resembled Skorzeny's. Born into a family of lawyers, the 6-foot 7-inch, granite-featured colossus gained a law doctorate but found his progress blocked by the Depression. Disillusionment and increasingly extremist convictions drew him to the Heimwehr; then, for much the same reason as Skorzeny, he turned to the Nazis, becoming a member of the party and the SS in 1932.

Skorzeny and Kaltenbrunner had been acquainted through the student society network (Kaltenbrunner was a member of the Arminia fraternity based in Graz), their relationship going back to at least 1929.[19] So well acquainted, indeed, that by 1938 Skorzeny was a frequent guest at Kaltenbrunner's Vienna home.[20]

While Kaltenbrunner covertly built up the Austrian SS, Hitler was manoeuvring himself into position to annex the country. The balance of power had changed in Austria. Chancellor Kurt von Schuschnigg led a Fatherland Front coalition that was on the point of implosion. There had been no elections since 1933, and the country was being ruled by emergency decree – which scarcely enhanced its moral authority. Isolated internationally, Schuschnigg was under pressure to seek an accommodation with the Nazis.

Complicating the situation for Hitler, the Austrian Nazi Party was attempting to pursue its own agenda, encouraging the threat of German military intervention, but not the reality. Austrian Nazis hoped to stage their own independent accession to power. This was not part of Hitler's plan at all. In these circumstances, close collaboration between the Austrian SS (which remained loyal to the Führer) and Hitler's agents on the ground in the German embassy would be critical. Legally, German forces could only enter Vienna by invitation, after an internal revolution had been effected. Annexation could then be completed.

It was Schuschnigg himself who precipitated the crisis, by calling a national plebiscite on the question of Austrian independence. The date was set for Sunday 13 March 1938, and a massive pro-independence campaign began. Jewish organisations, having witnessed the treatment of Jews in Germany since 1933, threw their weight behind the campaign. Popular opinion – even among those who broadly sympathised with Nazi ideology – tended towards independence. Schuschnigg endeavoured to ensure a 'Yes' vote by barring people aged under 24 from voting, on the principle (not admitted publicly) that the most enthusiastic Nazis were generally below that age.

Otto Skorzeny denounced the plebiscite as 'bizarre' and the government that called it as lacking 'any popular basis'. True to Nazi orthodoxy, which regarded everything opposed to Nazism as a Jewish–Communist conspiracy, he deemed the Yes campaign a submission to the influence of the Soviet Union.[21]

With Austria looking certain to vote for independence, Hitler faced the intolerable prospect of being rebuffed by his own homeland. He therefore took measures to derail the plebiscite and to install a puppet chancellor. The pliable right-wing politician (and secret Nazi) Arthur Seyss-Inquart was his choice. Seyss-Inquart was already Minister of the Interior, having been appointed as a concession to stave off German invasion earlier that year. Now Hitler planned to dial up the pressure. Otto Skorzeny and his comrades were ready to play their parts.

Friday 11 March 1938 was unbearably tense in Vienna. The government and the nationalist youth movement had campaigned hard all day, air-dropping leaflets and driving round in flag-draped trucks. But in the evening the atmosphere grew ugly; the Nazis came out on the streets and marched with flaming torches into Leopoldstadt, the Jewish district – with a terrifying menace. The German army was at the border, and an ultimatum was sent to Schuschnigg – to call off the plebiscite or face invasion. Nazi forces were already in de facto control of parts of the country; SA men occupied the Vienna Ringstrasse, and Kaltenbrunner's SS surrounded the Chancellery. About 10 pm a special group of 40 young SS troopers from 89 Standarte entered the building. Schuschnigg finally buckled before the threat of violence and resigned.

That same evening, Seyss-Inquart became chancellor, and the next day, at his invitation, German forces entered Austria.

Otto Skorzeny would later distance himself from the events of that Friday evening, claiming he had assembled at the gym with other members of the Deutschen Turnerbund (which of course was a Nazi front organisation), because of the dangerous situation outside. 'I had arrived and was just about to change,' Skorzeny disingenuously claimed, 'when the news of the resignation of Schuschnigg's government came over the radio. It took us completely by surprise.'[22]

Actually, Skorzeny and his comrades had already left the gym, clad in mountain coats and ski-pants, and were among the Nazis forming a ring around the Chancellery as Schuschnigg resigned. Just after midnight, Bruno Weiss, the local head of the Gymnastic Association, burst excitedly out of the Chancellery building with a 'special mission' for Skorzeny, on behalf of the new leader, Seyss-Inquart.[23]

A confrontation was brewing, he said, and Skorzeny was needed to forestall it. Head of state President Wilhelm Miklas, Austria's internationally respected figurehead, having reluctantly accepted Schuschnigg's resignation and appointed Seyss-Inquart, was returning by car from the Chancellery to the Presidential Palace in Reisnerstrasse. Miklas's safety could not be guaranteed. An unreliable contingent of SA men was reported to be moving to take control of the palace, while inside was a detachment of the president's Guards Battalion. Someone needed to intervene, and Skorzeny, being 'a man with a cool head and common sense' (as Weiss allegedly described him), and one of the few Viennese at the time with access to a car, was ideal. 'In the name of the new chancellor,' said Weiss, 'I instruct you personally to go to Reisnerstrasse and calmly but energetically intervene to avoid any incident.'[24] There was no time to lose:

> Luckily I was able to recruit a dozen comrades on the spot, who were loaded into two or three cars or jumped onto their motorcycles. We roared into the night, straight through the crowd, which cleared a path for us. We arrived at the front of the palace just as the president drove in. We stayed right behind him and I ordered that the large entrance gate be closed.[25]

As Skorzeny and his men entered the hall, the president and his entourage were about to go up the stairs. At that moment, Leutnant Friedrich Birsak of the Guards appeared at the first-floor balustrade with 20 guardsmen, and drew his pistol. Pandemonium broke out, the guards shouting, the presidential entourage crying out – finally, Frau Miklas appeared and added her screams to the din.

'Quiet!' Skorzeny yelled.

'Present arms!' ordered the Leutnant, and 20 rifles were aimed at the Nazi intruders.[26]

Skorzeny attempted to calm the situation; he arranged for Miklas to speak by phone to Seyss-Inquart, who confirmed that the young man was acting on his orders. Satisfied, the president asked Skorzeny to take command of the Guards detachment, while the SA kept order in the street outside. Skorzeny had saved the day; he even became friends with Leutnant Birsak.

At least, that was the way Skorzeny told it. Others, including President Miklas and Leutnant Birsak, remembered it quite differently. Miklas testified that, far from offering his good offices as an intermediary and preventing bloodshed, Skorzeny had actually arrested him – and he by no means felt secure in his custody.[27] Birsak maintained that it was only because of his own robust defence of Miklas that Skorzeny's men backed down from violence.[28]

In truth, Skorzeny's orders from Weiss probably originated not from Chancellor Seyss-Inquart but from Ernst Kaltenbrunner. Seyss-Inquart had no connection with the incident at the time; he was, he claimed, 'just a telephone girl' acting as an intermediary between Berlin and the outgoing Austrian administration.[29] Directing the action that evening was one of Kaltenbrunner's men, Odilo Globocnik, who had taken personal control of the Chancellery switchboard. Acting in the chancellor's name, Globocnik was coordinating the SS and SA seizures of police stations, barracks and government offices all over the country – including, naturally, the presidential palace. Globocnik's men also detained government officials felt to be unsympathetic to the Nazi cause – 'detaining' sometimes being a euphemism for murdering.

Miklas, who had compromised Nazi plans by refusing to buckle earlier in the evening, was almost certainly on the SA hit-list. Yet he wasn't killed. Skorzeny, notwithstanding his glossing over of his true mission that night, probably did play a role in calming things down. Kaltenbrunner would have realised that the murder of such a respected international statesman would have dire consequences for the public image of Anschluss – and by extension that of Hitler himself. It is clear from Kaltenbrunner's later warmth towards him (going well beyond their casual friendship) that Skorzeny was owed a debt of gratitude. Safeguarding Miklas's life may well have been the cause.

Whatever the details, Skorzeny had made his first small mark in the history books, and raised his stock with the SS elite.

* * *

Most Austrians, presented with a fait accompli, welcomed Anschluss. A minority – particularly the Jews – regarded it with dread. Anti-Semitic persecutions began right away – baiting in the streets; mob punishments; shops, businesses, and homes confiscated; expulsions from professions and from schools and colleges. This was only the beginning; worse was to follow.

Whether Otto Skorzeny took an active part in this is unknown. As a member of the local SS, it seems highly likely; although the SA tended to be more active in mob behaviour than the SS, Skorzeny would certainly have been involved in the systematic confiscations, looting, and repression of Jews.

That includes the direst single act of anti-Semitism in the months following Anschluss – the night of violence known as Kristallnacht, on 9–10 November 1938, when Jewish properties and synagogues throughout the

Third Reich were smashed and burned by squads of SA and SS. Jewish men were arrested in their thousands and deported to Dachau and Buchenwald concentration camps. Otto Skorzeny allegedly joined in the destruction of at least two of Vienna's synagogues that night, though he later denied it.[30] As an active and ambitious member of the SS, it would be extraordinary if he did not take part in Kristallnacht, which was no spontaneous outburst of mob violence but a planned and systematic assault on the Jewish population, carried out on the orders of Himmler via his deputy Reinhard Heydrich – who was by now head of the Gestapo (the state secret police).[31]

* * *

Sport had been Skorzeny's route into the Nazi Party; now it brought him into conflict with it. No sooner had Anschluss been implemented than the Nazis banned duelling. Skorzeny was furious, considering it a denial of manly self-expression. He made his views on the subject forcefully known.[32] But to no avail. He consoled himself by taking up motor racing. The SS motor section, to which he was attached as a Staffelhauptscharführer (master sergeant), supplied the cars. Skorzeny won three gold medals during the 1938 season, also excelling at motorcycle-and-sidecar racing.[33]

Sport even played cupid in his life; he met his second wife, Emmi Linhart, at a swimming pool. They married in March 1938.[34] He moved out of his apartment in Rothemühlgassesstrasse 59[35] (close to his scaffolding company in working-class Meidling) to a bigger one in Aichholzgassesstrasse 8. There they were to remain until, some time after the death of Skorzeny's father in April 1942, the couple would move to the family home at Peter-Jordan-Strasse 37, in the more salubrious Döbling district.[36] His only child, a daughter named Waltraut, was born in February 1940.

Skorzeny's views on women were patriarchal, meshing perfectly with the Nazi Party's doctrine of Kinder, Kirche, Küche*. Many years later, Waltraut summed up her father's attitude: 'Women were just an accessory to him, not really part of his vision. They were not important in his life. He had no empathy for them. And if they were ill, or weak, he had no interest in them.'[37] Waltraut was a disappointment to him – during Emmi's pregnancy, Skorzeny had not only believed that the child would be a boy, but decided on a name, Klaus-Dieter.[38] How unkind of providence to give him a girl.

He would see very little of Waltraut in the early years of her life for, by the time she was born, Skorzeny was at war.

---

*   Children, church, kitchen

2

Accidental Soldier

Skorzeny had signed up for military service the minute war broke out. His transition from Nazi sportsman and thug to SS warrior was not a straightforward one, proceeding by way of a stint in the Luftwaffe.[1]

There was very little of the conventional soldier about Otto Skorzeny. He was headstrong, disliked obeying orders and had an erratic tendency to improvise as he went along: not the sort of things likely to endear him to the military mind. When he volunteered for the Luftwaffe on 1 September 1939, it was the most sophisticated air force in the world, which resonated with his passionate interest in leading-edge technology; also, as the glamorous junior service its traditions were less hidebound. But although he had a small amount of flying experience,[2] the heroics of aerial combat were to elude Skorzeny. He was too big to be a fighter pilot, and at 31 too old for flight training. (He must have known this in advance, but probably thought he could bluff his way through.) Reluctantly, he spent the next five months in a Viennese communications depot – an experience he loathed.

Transfer to the Waffen-SS came about almost by accident, though his longstanding Allgemeine-SS membership smoothed the way. By 1940, thanks to increased mechanisation, the Waffen-SS was on the lookout for officers with a technical background – preferably ones who were already SS members. Stuck in a rut, Skorzeny volunteered in the hope of becoming a commissioned officer.[3] His age was a disadvantage, but he got through as the oldest of 12 (out of 20 applicants) who made the grade as engineer officer-cadets. On

1 February 1940 he began basic training in Hitler's personal SS regiment, the Leibstandarte-SS 'Adolf Hitler'.[4]

By 1940 the Waffen-SS was already growing into the elite national guards corps Hitler desired. It embodied new thinking about warfare. What mattered was mobility and the ability to improvise in the heat of battle. The basic unit of warfare was not the small section of military tradition, but the middle-size Kampfgruppe or versatile battle group. Out went the traditional infantryman's rifle and in came front-line weapons of much greater flexibility, primarily sub-machine guns, hand grenades and explosives. A new battledress, consisting of camouflage blouse and suit, came to replace the traditional field service uniform. Camaraderie and a warrior ethos were instilled in the troops, reminiscent of the spirit among the soldiers of Sparta. The ideal was a force of supple, adaptable, battle-ready athletes capable of covering 3 kilometres on foot in 20 minutes.

Traditional distinctions between ranks – a fetish in the Prussian military establishment – were minimised. Officers and NCOs were encouraged to share the same hardships as their men – and indeed to compete in the same training teams. All would-be SS officers had to serve for two years in the ranks before graduating to military academy. Ethical standards among recruits were extremely demanding; in barracks, all doors and cupboards were left unlocked, in the belief that trust fostered a sense of fellowship.

Strictly speaking, the Waffen-SS that Skorzeny had joined was a relatively new military institution[*] – the 'armed' as opposed to the political wing of the SS[†] – which had been incorporated shortly before war broke out. In practice, its roots were much older. Its origin is to be found in a lie, and a criminal act of extreme violence.

The lie was Adolf Hitler's, and the criminal act the event of 30 June 1934 known as the Night of the Long Knives. In eliminating the leadership of the increasingly troublesome SA, Hitler was also striking a Faustian pact with the Prussian-dominated military establishment: they would be allowed to retain the integrity of their traditions and responsibility for the external security of the country, at the price of Hitler having exclusive authority over its internal security apparatus. Except, it wasn't that simple. In disposing of, or at least emasculating, one private army, Hitler and Himmler circumspectly created the conditions for breeding another – that of the SS.

The SS could, in a tenuous way, trace their military traditions back to the storm-troopers of late World War I and the post-war Freikorps, but

---

[*] So new that nominally, but not organisationally, 'Waffen-SS' dates to March 1940.

[†] Allgemeine-SS or General-SS

their practical purpose was as a police force and bodyguard dedicated to the protection of various party Gauleiters*, of which Hitler was the most important. Only when Hitler came to power as Reich Chancellor did the bodyguard role take on an explicitly military dimension with the creation, on 17 March 1933, of what came to be known as Leibstandarte-SS 'Adolf Hitler'. It originally consisted of 120 men selected from Hitler's former bodyguard in Munich, but was soon upgraded to several companies. And it was commanded by his former chauffeur, bodyguard and redoubtable fellow World War I veteran, Sepp Dietrich. Dietrich was a natural warrior in the storm-trooper mould, but lacked the necessary sophistication to create a crack Guards regiment.

Ostensibly, these Third Reich Household Troops were ceremonial – concerned exclusively with protecting Hitler's person in the Chancellery. The Night of the Long Knives soon demonstrated they had a very different purpose and capability. The carefully elaborated programme of targeted assassinations – nearly 300 in all – that took place on the evening of 30 June and morning of 1 July 1934 must be credited to Himmler's rapidly rising adjutant Reinhard Heydrich – a man to whom the adjective 'sinister' barely does justice. But the lead part in the butchery was actually carried out by Dietrich and several companies of the Leibstandarte-SS 'Adolf Hitler'.

This ruthlessly executed purge was a milestone in two respects for the SS. On the one hand, the organisation had been allowed to decapitate and displace its principal rival, the SA. On the other, the event fueled in Hitler and Himmler a desire to create a more broadly based military force fanatically dedicated to National Socialist ideology (in other words, to themselves) that would form a 'fourth element' in the Wehrmacht.

Naturally, they had to be careful to keep the military establishment on side. So, in raising three new regiments of what were now known as SS-Verfügungstruppe (SS-VT), they adhered to the polite fiction that these were solely for the internal security of the regime; only in time of war would they be used for military purposes. What exactly these 'military purposes' were would be established later. In the meantime, the new units were to be restricted to light armaments, and were forbidden artillery, in order to avoid friction with the Reichswehr.

Most of the new recruits came from local SS Politische Bereitschaften (police units), which had been crudely forged into national units. Manifestly, they had neither the background nor training to deliver Himmler's secret

*   High-ranking Nazi Party official, usually head of a regional branch (Gau).

agenda – an elite national guards corps. That objective was only accomplished by attracting the services of two capable former professional soldiers, Paul Hausser and Felix Steiner.

Hausser was a Reichswehr general bored with retirement. Everything about him, other than his interest in forging Himmler's elite private army, was traditionalist: his personal bearing, his Prussian military family, his officer-cadet and general staff background, his ultra-conservative cultural values. Steiner was his diametric opposite: a Reichswehr officer of lesser breeding and rank but, much more importantly, a frustrated military reformer whose tactical brilliance would in time make him one of the great military innovators of World War II. At the risk of simplification, it could be said that Hausser provided the military discipline and Steiner the military culture so badly lacking in Dietrich's 'Asphalt Soldiers' – as the drill-perfect but combat-clueless Leibstandarte-SS 'Adolf Hitler' was disparagingly known by military professionals.

Steiner and Hausser convinced themselves that they were simply creating an elite military service. In reality, the Waffen-SS was always a much more complex, interleaved organisation. Its military ideals were never entirely divorced from its political origins. And its evolution was distorted, in equal measure, by what Steiner termed Himmler's 'sleazy romanticism'[5] and the Prussian military caste's unrelentingly hostile attitude towards a competitor. It lacked experienced officers with a proven aptitude for command. What looked like a meritocratic virtue – the career open to talent – was also a severe handicap. Fanatical belief compensated for the deficit in military sophistication; something very much to Himmler's liking. (Christianity, and 'soft', compassionate Christian ethics were verboten. Recruits found themselves under pressure to abandon the Church; by 1938 over half had done so.)

Recruitment, and the severe restrictions upon it imposed by the Wehrmacht, remained an issue until the eve of World War II. The SS-VT units were only able to evolve into a full-blown army thanks to a ruse devised by Himmler's éminence grise, SS-Brigadeführer Gottlob Berger. Berger was a flamboyant, controversial, out-and-out Nazi – later disowned by Waffen-SS apologists such as Hausser and Steiner who believed he had tainted the organisation's purist military ethos. They were right, he had; what they omitted to mention was that without Berger's outstanding administrative gifts, the Waffen-SS would never have gained sufficient scale to become the ultimate military backbone of the Third Reich.

Berger's solution to the recruitment ceiling was to tap sources exempt from service in the Wehrmacht. With Hitler's backing, he began to draft elements of the Ordnungspolizei (ORPO or civil police), and – much more damagingly for the reputation of the existing SS-VT units – concentration camp guards and their wartime reinforcements (known as Reinforced Totenkopfstandarten). To these were added a list of 50,000 men from the Allgemeine-SS.

Berger's stratagem cleverly solved the numbers problem. By merging these new draftees with the existing SS-VT regiments, he was able to create a force of three to four divisions, which was now formally renamed the Waffen-SS. Even in SS circles, the concentration camp guard units were regarded as the lowest of the low – ill-educated thugs in brown uniforms led by the notorious psychopath Theodor Eicke.

But a wider perspective is necessary. The Totenkopf concentration camp units represented no more than 6,500 new recruits in an army that had swelled from 18,500 at the outset of the Polish campaign in September 1939 to 100,000 by late spring the following year.[6]

More typical of the new Waffen-SS intake – so far as future officer material was concerned – were Skorzeny himself and his future adjutant, Karl Radl.[7] Both were drafted from the Allgemeine-SS, which they had served in a party police, intelligence or legal capacity.

Recruits were encouraged to believe that theirs was the only wholly reliable armed service in the Third Reich, and therefore the proper guardian of National Socialism – an attitude which fostered loathing for the conventional armed forces, particularly the army and its general staff officers. The feeling was reciprocated.

All basic training for the newly incorporated Waffen-SS was handled by the Wehrmacht's Infanterie-Regiment 9 at the Berlin-Lichterfelde barracks. This was where officer cadet Otto Skorzeny (holding, like all cadets, the initial rank of SS-Schütze or private) was posted in 1940. Aside from his age, Skorzeny was fairly typical of the officer cadet intake. His comrades in the Leibstandarte-SS 'Adolf Hitler' included doctors and chemists as well as other engineers – all middle-class SS careerists.[8]

Getting to the front was a long grind. Officer cadets did not graduate as officers right away; commissions had to be earned in service. After six weeks of basic training, and several more earning sergeant's rank in a technical induction course with the SS-Regiment 'Germania' (part of the SS-Division 'Reich'),[9] Skorzeny's reward was a behind-the-lines posting as a transport manager for the artillery regiment of the SS-Totenkopf-Division during the invasion of France.[10] Later, he was coy about the association, probably because of the division's reputation; formed in part from concentration camp guards, the Totenkopf division proved especially inclined to commit atrocities. However, Skorzeny saw none of that in France; all he glimpsed of the offensive was the returning formations of Luftwaffe warplanes and long columns of dust-covered prisoners of war.

Transferred back to the SS-Division 'Reich' as a technical sergeant,[11] Skorzeny found himself in Holland limbering up the tanks and armoured vehicles for an invasion of Britain that would never happen.

It was frustrating, and Skorzeny's natural tendency to insubordination soon got him into trouble. Always willing to take reckless shortcuts when conventional methods failed, he decided to resupply his trucks with new tyres stolen at gunpoint from a depot. It was one of several black marks on his record at the time, but not the most serious.

Several weeks after receiving a reprimand for this incident, Skorzeny and a fellow sergeant, Hans Jäger, were drinking schnapps in a Dutch bar when their attention was caught by a picture of German princeling Bernhard von Lieppe-Biesterfeld hanging on the wall. A controversial figure, with youthful affiliations to the Nazi Party and SS, he had later denounced Hitler and, after the fall of Holland, joined the London-based Dutch government in exile. Skorzeny, in his cups, told the Dutch café owner to take the portrait down. When he did not, Skorzeny threatened to shoot it down. Which he then did. 'That was a mistake,' admitted Jäger.[12] Skorzeny was brought before the general and 'given a hellish dressing down' for aggravating the newly conquered Dutch; he was confined to barracks for six weeks, and his promotion from sergeant to officer postponed.

In a more conventional army this would have halted his career. But the Waffen-SS was not a conventional army, and in March 1941 he finally received his commission as an SS-Untersturmführer (2nd lieutenant).[13] Aged 32, Otto Skorzeny was now poised for his first battlefront experience.

* * *

Hitler's timetable for invading the Soviet Union had been disrupted by an inconvenient coup d'état in Yugoslavia. The friendly neutral government of Prince Regent Paul was overthrown in March 1941 by a group of pro-British Serbian army officers. The German high command feared that Britain would be able to use Yugoslavia as a base to bomb Romania's oil fields, on which the Reich's war effort depended. They were also concerned that Italy, already bogged down in Albania in a war against Greece, would be routed. Operation *Barbarossa* would be impossible so long as part of its operational flank remained in enemy hands. On 6 April, Axis armies crossed the Yugoslav border on several sides, and the Luftwaffe bombed Belgrade. Among the invading forces was the SS-Division 'Reich', with SS-Untersturmführer Otto Skorzeny in its rear echelon.

The German victory over 30 Yugoslav divisions in just 11 days must have given Skorzeny a stunning (and misleading) impression of his nation's military prowess. It was lightning warfare at its most devastating.

Skorzeny's personal contribution was a minor role in the baggage train; cautiously approaching a Serbian-occupied village, his unit came under fire: 'a crowd of enemy soldiers came running towards us from behind. I told my men to hold their fire. When the nearest Serbian was about 80 metres away, I yelled out: "Stoi" (Halt). The men stopped, looked bewildered and turned round ... That settled it!'[14]

It was like a round-up after a turkey-shoot. The severely demoralised Yugoslav army showed little appetite for resistance. Skorzeny claimed he bagged 63 prisoners – including several officers – on this occasion, which may well be true. However, he also claimed that he was promoted to SS-Obersturmführer (lieutenant) as a result, which was not; promotion didn't come until over a year later.[15] What is significant about his first known contact with an enemy is his use of bluff and a 'no-fire' order to achieve his objective – a cool-headed move which would become Skorzeny's signature tactic.

For Hitler the stage was now set for *Barbarossa*. Two months later, Skorzeny and his comrades found themselves on a troop train moving through Poland. The eventual destination of the SS-Division 'Reich' was the western bank of the River Bug, which at that time was the border with the Soviet Union. None of them had any clue as to Hitler's real intentions, and the talk among the troops was of free passage through neutral Russia and Turkey, to attack the British Empire via the back door of the Middle East.[16]

This may account for why Skorzeny had a copy of T. E. Lawrence's *Seven Pillars of Wisdom* in his backpack. It is one of the very few books known to have influenced Skorzeny's intellectual formation. Whatever it was about Lawrence that attracted Skorzeny, it could not be the complex, tortured, self-loathing intellectual. The fact that Skorzeny called Lawrence 'the peculiar adventurer, archaeologist, secret agent and champion of Arab independence from the Turks'[17] suggests more of a *Boys' Own* romantic fascination.

Skorzeny's copy of *Seven Pillars of Wisdom* perished, like much else, in the course of the *Barbarossa* campaign. At first the invasion of the USSR was textbook Blitzkrieg. In just a few weeks the Germans penetrated deep into the interior, taking 300,000 Russian prisoners at Minsk, and a further 200,000 at

Smolensk. Then in late September the whole of the Russian southwestern front collapsed when German armoured forces completed the double envelopment of Kiev.

Skorzeny's unit, SS-Division 'Reich', was attached to Heeresgruppe Mitte*, whose objective was to seize Moscow before Christmas; Reich was the spearhead, and took extremely heavy casualties. By early December, German units were actually within a few kilometres of the Soviet capital, but a blurry sighting of the Kremlin through binoculars was as far as they ever got.

The whole character of the war was changing. The coldest winter of the century – with temperatures falling to minus 30°C – cracked engine blocks, reduced German armour to a crawl and grounded the Luftwaffe for days on end. Skorzeny, as an engineer, had to cope with endless technical problems. The Wehrmacht, now suffering crippling casualties for the first time in the war, was unprepared for a protracted campaign, whereas the Russians, camouflaged in their foxholes, proved masters of winter warfare. Stalin committed 18 divisions to a massive counter-attack. The German panzers – mostly under-armoured Mk IIs and IIIs – found themselves outclassed by what now emerged as the most versatile and indestructible tank of the war: Russia's T-34. By January 1942, Heeresgruppe Mitte had retreated up to 250 kilometres from Moscow. It was beginning to look like the rout of Napoleon's Grande Armée all over again.

Years later Skorzeny explained the situation:

It is like this. You go into Russia, win tremendous victories, advance hundreds of miles. Prisoners flow back, an endless river of humanity with one guard to five hundred of them. The fields and forests are a graveyard of captured tanks and vehicles left to rust.

When you retreat ... they all rise up to meet you ... Thousands of prisoners slip away into the forests. New leaders cross the line to them by night. Abandoned guns and tanks are secretly patched up. A host of special troops are dropped from planes skimming the snow ... And so there is a striking force where none was before.[18]

Skorzeny felt a grudging admiration for Russian stoicism and fortitude. His Nazi mentality rationalised it in terms of racial theory; having been led to expect the Russians to be 'just another sort, rather an inferior sort, of European', he and his comrades were shocked and bewildered to find that

* Army Group Centre

they were 'Orientals', a 'yellow swarm' with the martial ferocity of Genghis Khan's horde.[19] Forced onto the defensive, the Germans – conveniently forgetting that they had provoked the war in the first place with an act of extreme aggression – wrapped themselves in the mantle of defenders of Western Civilisation, battling to fence out a swarm of inferior beings.

Skorzeny had had an early taste of this new and brutal style of warfare. In mid-July 1941 his unit, II. /SS-Artillerie-Regiment, SS-Division 'Reich'*, took up position with the rest of the division near Yelnya, southeast of Smolensk, as part of a mobile armoured corps (which included the Wehrmacht's 10. Panzerdivision). The plan was to bypass the Russian forces under siege in Smolensk and create an assembly point for a rapid armoured assault on Moscow.

Instead, the German task force found itself overextended in a fragile salient, which now became the target for the first serious Russian counter-offensive of the war. By the beginning of August, the losses of SS-Division 'Reich' were so severe that 'we had to be taken out of the line to recuperate and make up our numbers', Skorzeny recalled.[20] But not before he had proved his courage by recovering a damaged vehicle under fire. For this he was awarded the Eisernes Kreuz 2. Klasse (EK II or Iron Cross Second Class).[21]

His tour of duty on the Eastern Front was cut short after six months. He suffered a chronic gall-bladder complaint, and when a shrapnel wound to the back of the head left him with recurring headaches he was withdrawn from the front altogether in January 1942. He was posted to Berlin, where he spent the following six months as an engineer officer and instructor with a reserve regiment at the self-same Lichterfelde barracks where he had begun his cadetship in 1940.[22]

* * *

And there he might well have remained for the duration of the war, a burnt-out case ingloriously serving out his time in a Berlin vehicle-repair depot.

In September 1942 Skorzeny's prospects momentarily brightened, when he finally received his promotion to SS-Obersturmführer and was transferred to the newly acquired tank battalion of the SS-Totenkopf-Division.[23] The division had returned to France for a complete rebuild and upgrade after experiencing near annihilation on the Eastern Front. By this stage of the war, the Waffen-SS was finally shedding its reputation as the Third Reich's military

---

*   II. SS-AR.Reich or the 2nd Battalion of the Artillery Regiment of the Reich

Cinderella starved of the best equipment by the Wehrmacht's high command. A token of this uprated status was the Totenkopf division's new armoured battalion, equipped with state-of-the-art Tiger I heavy tanks – and a new designation as the 3. SS-Panzergrenadierdivision 'Totenkopf'.

But this was small consolation to Skorzeny. The only action he personally witnessed was the occupation of Vichy France in November 1942. When the Totenkopf division returned to active service on the Eastern Front in February 1943, he did not accompany it. On the contrary, he was confined to hospital, where he was given a certificate excusing him from further front-line duties.[24] He then returned to the endless tedium of the repair depot. (According to one future colleague, Skorzeny had failed to pass his examination for company commander in 1942, denying him a front-line role.)[25]

'I felt like a shirker,' he recalled.[26] His behaviour deteriorated. During the summer of 1942 he had been accused of absence without leave, but was exonerated when investigators concluded that he was genuinely ill. The death of his father earlier that year may also have had a bearing on the situation. There was a further unruly incident, in the spring of 1943, which ended in Skorzeny being confined to barracks after misbehaving in a Paris bar.[27]

He was frustrated by the way the war was going. The Allies' declaration in January 1943 that they would accept nothing less than unconditional surrender from Germany, together with the resounding defeat at Stalingrad, steeled Skorzeny to a long slog requiring unconventional tactics and a high degree of improvisation. He felt convinced that if Germany were to regain the decisive military advantage of 1939–40, 'we must turn to daring methods and the tactic of surprise as we had in those years. We had to consider the entire nature of the war and discover and produce new weapons; weapons which were especially useful for specific purposes.'[28]

Stuck in a cul-de-sac, Skorzeny tried another tack. Hearing that an SS commando unit stationed within the Totenkopf division barracks was about to get a boost in its status and resources, he used his powerful contacts to find out more. His principal contact was Ernst Kaltenbrunner, who was now in overall charge of the Reich's security.

The inquiry bore fruit. In early April 1943, a mysterious order arrived, demanding Skorzeny's immediate presence at SS-Führungshauptamt, the headquarters of the Waffen-SS. Puzzled and intrigued, he answered the summons.

Headquarters was housed in a building on Prinz Albrecht Strasse. This street, located near Potsdamer Platz, was the nerve centre of the Third Reich's apparatus of power; here were the HQs of all the main branches of the SS: the Allgemeine-SS, the Waffen-SS, the Sicherheitsdienst (SD or intelligence), the

Gestapo, and the Reichssicherheitshauptamt (RSHA or the Reich Main Security Office).

At the Waffen-SS headquarters, SS-Obersturmführer Skorzeny was interviewed by chief of staff SS-Obergruppenführer Hans Jüttner. He was informed that a special training unit based in the old Totenkopf division barracks was being expanded into a fully fledged SS commando operation. At present it consisted of 100 men drawn from the multinational intakes of the Waffen-SS. It was named the SS-Sonderlehrgang 'Oranienburg' (SS Special Operations Training Unit 'Oranienburg'). An experienced Waffen-SS officer with a technical background was needed to run the unit. A promotion was involved. Would Skorzeny be interested in applying?

He would. With remarkable ease, he landed the job, and on 20 April 1943 he was appointed Leader of SS Special Forces[29] – an exciting and grand-sounding title which for some reason brought with it the rather modest rank of SS-Hauptsturmführer.

How had Otto Skorzeny, a man without any discernible qualification, landed such a position? The answer was rooted in old party friendships and a Machiavellian web of scheming, duplicity and backstabbing in the upper tiers of the Nazi regime.

3

Thugs in Field Grey

On 30 March 1943, Hitler summoned Himmler to a meeting at the Berghof, his mountain retreat in Bavaria. The purpose of the meeting was to discuss the future of military special operations.

Up to this point they had played only a minor role in the way Germany prosecuted its war. True, there had been isolated German successes: the SS-inspired Venlo incident in late 1939, which had rolled up Britain's spy network in Holland; masterly bluffs by the Brandenburgers as Hitler's armies rolled through northern Europe and the Soviet Union; and the Luftwaffe-devised raid on Eben-Emael in 1940. But these scarcely amounted to a blueprint for organised commando warfare.

Now, as the Third Reich found itself struggling on the defensive, the tactics of *Kleinkrieg* – commando raids, guerrilla warfare and special operations – assumed a new and urgent importance.

Somehow, the British – despite being on the losing side for most of the past three-and-a half years – had always done these things much better. Take the highly successful amphibious raids on the Lofoten Islands and Vågsøy during 1941; the epic combined operations assault on St Nazaire in March 1942 that put its dry dock out of use for the rest of the war; the daring assassination, planned with British assistance, of the Reich's most feared leader, Reinhard Heydrich, only two months later; to name but a few.

Why was Germany's performance in this area so much weaker? Hitler suspected treason. The solution he and Himmler decided upon at the Berghof was to vest greater responsibility for such operations in the SS.

Given its central status within the Nazi regime, it seems surprising that the SS was not handed this responsibility much earlier. The reason is to be found in the uneasy pact – sealed during the Night of the Long Knives on 30 June 1934 – that enabled Hitler to secure the cooperation of Germany's armed forces at the price of restricting the SS's military powers. Although it is true that certain clandestine operations had been carried out by a special SS unit commanded by Alfred Naujocks – notably the provocative destruction of a German radio station to create a casus belli for invading Poland – commando warfare came within the remit of the Wehrmacht, as the guardian of the Third Reich's external security.

In practice, the Prussian staff officers who dominated Oberkommando der Wehrmacht (OKW, the Wehrmacht high command) regarded clandestine operations as outside the orthodox code of warfare and doctrinally irrelevant. Imbued with Clausewitz, they believed the point of war was to bring the enemy to a decisive battle, winnable only through the concentration of overwhelming force. Special operations were viewed as a theatrical sideshow. In 1936, when the World War I guerrilla-war specialist Theodor von Hippel suggested that the Reichswehr* form an elite regiment skilled in foreign languages and sabotage, he received a curt rebuff. However, Admiral Wilhelm Canaris, head of the Abwehr (the German military intelligence service), had immediately seen the affinity with espionage and took Hippel on in the Abwehr's Section II, which specialised in training sabotage agents. Hippel's fledgling unit became the Bau- und Lehr-Kompanie (DK) z.b.V. 800, later known to history as the Brandenburg Regiment.† Technically, it was an army unit, but the command structure was convoluted, with Canaris reporting directly to OKW chief of staff Wilhelm Keitel.

The Brandenburgers were more or less synonymous with German special operations in the early Blitzkrieg stage of the war. Acting as small mobile field units behind the enemy's lines (and frequently disguised in enemy uniforms), they captured or blew up bridges and attacked enemy supply lines. At his interview at Waffen-SS HQ, Otto Skorzeny was told that Hitler was not satisfied with the Brandenburgers and wanted the RSHA to form a second unit to undertake such missions.[1] He had in mind undercover operations in

---

*   Predecessor to the Wehrmacht, the armed forces of the Weimar Republic.

†   Bau- und Lehr-Kompanie (DK) z.b.V. 800 was formed on 15 October 1939. By 1 June 1940 it had become Lehr-Regiment Brandenburg z.b.V. 800. 'Brandenburg' was a reference to its garrison at Brandenburg an der Havel.

occupied territories – which was beyond the military remit of the Brandenburgers.

In fact, Hitler's dissatisfaction centred not so much upon the Brandenburgers themselves as the people controlling them in the upper echelons of the Abwehr. Hitler suspected, rightly, that the Abwehr was playing a double game – outwardly advancing the Nazi war effort while secretly plotting his downfall. Assisted by a burgeoning SS dossier, he was beginning to conclude that Canaris was a traitor. And if Canaris were planning a putsch against the regime, which military units would he most likely rely upon in the first instance? The Brandenburgers, naturally.

Even Canaris's friends found his opaque and subtle personality an enigma. He had been appointed to head the Abwehr precisely because he seemed the sort of man who could build bridges with the Nazis while protecting the organisation's independence from the SS. Curiously, given their diametrically opposed political views, Canaris developed a close personal relationship with Reinhard Heydrich – a man described by his subordinate Walter Schellenberg as 'the hidden pivot around which the Nazi regime revolved'.[2] Heydrich had once served under Canaris in the navy, and the two men continued to enjoy a close affinity transcending customary service rivalries. Both were finely cultured men and there was nothing Heydrich liked better than a musical soirée chez Canaris, in which he accompanied the admiral's wife Erika, a concert pianist, on the violin. An agreeable alternative to such musical ensembles was an occasional croquet match. Behind this cloak of sophistication lurked a monstrous, manipulative personality, with (according to Schellenberg) 'an incredibly acute perception of the moral, human, professional and political weakness of others' and 'the ever watchful instincts of a predatory animal'. Schellenberg, in short, considered Heydrich 'the puppet master of the Third Reich'.[3]

In return for ceding key powers over internal matters, including counter-espionage, to the Gestapo, the Abwehr had been allowed free rein over all foreign intelligence matters. By 1937, Canaris had built an organisation with a staff of over 3,000 and tentacles extending into practically every country in Europe. There were, however, two ultimately fatal flaws in his pact with the Nazis. The first concerned the ambitions of Heydrich; the second, the character of Hitler.

Heydrich not only controlled the political police; he also had his own espionage organisation, the Sicherheitsdienst or SD, originally conceived as a means of spying on the party and its political enemies. Its appetite for expanding into every element of German life soon brought it into conflict with the Abwehr. It had assembled a considerable foreign intelligence service of its own – SD-Ausland. This and the SD's ideologically driven interference in military intelligence convinced Canaris he was dealing with a criminal organisation whose activities must be neutralised in every possible way.

By now the scales had fallen from Canaris's eyes about Hitler's behaviour as well. Like many powerful but politically agnostic collaborators with the Nazi regime, he became increasingly concerned that Hitler's brinksmanship was leading Germany into a European war. Accordingly, Canaris became more sympathetic to the anti-Hitler faction within the Abwehr headed by Oberstleutnant Hans Oster.[4] He was peripherally involved in two aborted military coups, in September 1938 and November 1939, which came close to deposing Hitler. The first, and more likely to succeed, was stalled by British prime minister Neville Chamberlain's wholly unexpected decision to yield to Hitler's demands over the Czech Sudetenland. The expected invasion of Czechoslovakia, which would have precipitated the coup, was called off at the last moment.[5]

After these two setbacks, Canaris resolutely stuck to the sidelines, while passively supporting the Oster faction. Hitler's string of foreign policy successes, followed by war, made it increasingly difficult to act against him without seeming unpatriotic.

At that time Hitler seemed blissfully unaware of any treachery. By 1943, however, the pile of circumstantial evidence implicating the Abwehr in conspiratorial activity against the regime had become difficult to ignore. Shortly before Hitler's March 1943 meeting with Himmler at the Berghof – so resonant for Skorzeny's future – the Gestapo had arrested Oster, who was now a Generalmajor (brigadier-general), and a fellow conspirator, on the technicality of suspected currency violation. A search brought incriminating files to light, damagingly hinting at the Abwehr's role in negotiating peace terms with British intelligence via the Vatican.[6]

Hitler began entertaining the idea of replacing the Abwehr with a more politically reliable intelligence service. He still felt compelled to camouflage his motives, on account of his delicate relationship with the Wehrmacht. But the order to relocate the Abwehr to Zossen – entailing a restructure that purged it of most existing department heads – was a clear presentiment of what, in slightly over a year's time, was to follow.

The Third Reich's up-and-coming spymaster – and Skorzeny's new boss – was SS-Oberführer[7] Walter Schellenberg, head of RSHA Amt VI, or

Department 6* – the redesignated name of SD-Ausland, the SS foreign political intelligence service. In late 1939 a reorganisation had brought the feuding Sicherheitspolizei and Sicherheitsdienst – the SS-controlled secret police and secret service – under a single roof, known as the Reichssicherheitshauptamt or RSHA. In all, there were seven sections within this new structure. To give the flavour, Amt V represented the Kripo (Criminal Police),[8] under the command of Arthur Nebe; Amt IV the Gestapo, under Heinrich Müller (also including Referat IV-B, the bureau headed by Adolf Eichmann that was immediately responsible for the extermination of Jews); while Amt VII, headed by Franz Six, concerned itself with research and propaganda, mainly of an anti-Semitic nature.

Originally at the helm of the RSHA was SS-Obergruppenführer Heydrich, the controller of both Sipo (Gestapo and Kripo) and the SD when they were still independent of each other. Inconveniently for the RSHA, Heydrich had got himself assassinated, on 27 May 1942, while performing another of his sinister roles – Acting Protector of Bohemia and Moravia.

The loss of Heydrich may have been a grave setback for the Reich, but indirectly it was the making of Skorzeny. Hitler and Himmler procrastinated over their choice of successor as head of the RSHA; admittedly their task was not easy. Their eventual appointee, in January 1943, was none other than Ernst Kaltenbrunner, Skorzeny's old university chum and SS patron, who – since Anschluss – had held the position of Höherer SS- und Polizeiführer (HSSPf)[†] in Vienna.

As an Austrian outsider catapulted into a position of power over the heads of more obviously qualified internal candidates because of Hitler's need for a reliable henchman, Kaltenbrunner was desperate for every ally he could find. Although just as ruthless as his predecessor, he was by comparison a bovine mediocrity, and a personally rebarbative one at that. Schellenberg, the most obviously endowed internal candidate (albeit rather young), could not abide Kaltenbrunner, and the feeling was mutual. Schellenberg called Kaltenbrunner 'a real lumberjack', physically coarse and with a character to match; 'I tried not to let our working relationship be affected by my personal feelings, but after only a short time this proved impossible. Perhaps he felt an equal antipathy towards me; anyway there was soon a complete breach between us.'[9]

Kaltenbrunner systematically undermined Schellenberg's authority, by blocking his hotline to Himmler (insisting that documents and reports of

---

*   Amt can be translated as 'division', 'department' or 'bureau'.
†   Higher SS and Police Leader

importance be routed through his own office) and introducing senior placemen who could counterbalance Schellenberg's authority within SD-Ausland itself. Skorzeny's appointment was one of several designed to bolster Kaltenbrunner's personal and professional insecurities. All were former associates dating back to his days in Austria. They were dubbed the 'Vienna Circle', and many were to play a part in Skorzeny's story.

* * *

The most senior member of Kaltenbrunner's Vienna Circle was Wilhelm Waneck, Gruppenleiter (section leader) of E desk at Amt VI, which dealt with southeast European affairs. A balding, bespectacled individual more skilled at bureaucratic infighting than subversion, Waneck – who had once held an administrative job at Dachau concentration camp – joined the SD in 1937. Like Skorzeny, he was an unruly colleague who – with Kaltenbrunner enthusiastically stirring in the background – made life difficult for Schellenberg.

A second significant member of the circle was Wilhelm Höttl, an early recruit to the Austrian SD. After Anschluss, he had been the Vienna bureau chief of Amt VI, specialising in intelligence collection and assessment in the southeast, Balkans and Italy. It was the quality of his spy network and, more specifically, the excellence of his signals intelligence that assured him direct access to Kaltenbrunner. By 1944, Höttl would become SD-Ausland's acting head of intelligence and counter-espionage in central and southeast Europe, working closely with Waneck, his immediate boss.

The third member of the gang was Werner Göttsch, whose SD-Ausland pedigree was long and murky. Though not an Austrian, Göttsch had for some time been based in Vienna. The most notorious aspect of his career was his leadership of a series of SD death-squad missions during the 1930s, culminating in the spectacular assassination of the Czech anti-Nazi radio broadcaster Rudolf Formis. By 1940, Göttsch had risen to be section chief of Amt VI-E, the position later taken on by Waneck. Göttsch's experience of covert operations made him a potential rival for Skorzeny, but he was let down by chronic tuberculosis.

In putting forward Skorzeny's name for the new post of Leader of SS Special Forces, Kaltenbrunner was hoping to purchase a fourth reliable ally as a counterweight to Schellenberg's leadership of Amt VI.

While all four individuals in the Vienna Circle were tied by personal loyalty to Kaltenbrunner, they didn't always act as a cohesive force. Göttsch soon found himself deployed in the less taxing environment of Amt VII (whose remit passed for 'research'), while the relationship between the Waneck/Höttl faction and Skorzeny later degenerated into jealous rivalry. But they retained a loyalty to Kaltenbrunner and the Nazi cause which lasted to the bitter end.

* * *

Shortly after his appointment, Skorzeny was drawn into an unexpectedly revealing tête-à-tête in which Kaltenbrunner described his difficulties in running the RSHA. During the interregnum between Heydrich's death and Kaltenbrunner's appointment, the seven departmental chiefs within the RSHA had grown used to a measure of independence, dealing with Himmler directly. Kaltenbrunner complained to Skorzeny that 'even today, I am often side-tracked and there is much that I can only find out afterwards. Your new chief Schellenberg, and the Gestapo chief Müller, are too fond of short circuits. Heydrich certainly knew his business, and built up his department in a cold, impersonal fashion, which we Ostmärkers* don't like.'[10]

Kaltenbrunner's confession underlined not only the snakepit of RSHA internal politics, but the huge influence that Schellenberg wielded behind the scenes – out of all proportion to his rank and status as a bureau chief.

In one sense only, Schellenberg was a typical SD product. As the frustrated and ambitious son of impoverished middle-class parents, service in the Allgemeine-SS seemed to offer him otherwise unavailable opportunities for rapid career advancement. Despite a difficult start in life, he had managed to acquire a degree in law. Soon thereafter he came to the attention of Heydrich, who admired his intellect, found his managerial nous useful, and exploited his moral pliability. Attached to Heydrich – with whom he had a bizarre love-hate relationship – Schellenberg rose rapidly in the embryonic SD, despite his youth, playing a decisive role in kidnapping two senior MI6 agents during the Venlo Incident in 1939. By late 1941, Heydrich had put him in charge of SD-Ausland (Amt VI). A slight, immaculately dressed man, of punctilious courtesy and feminine sensitivity, Schellenberg used his slippery charm to win the affections of Himmler, who became increasingly dependent upon him as a consigliere. Schellenberg enjoyed an outwardly easy relationship with his opposite number, Canaris – to the extent of exchanging minor intelligence tips on their regular morning rides together in the Tiergarten.

---

*   Fellow Austrians (as redefined after Anschluss).

'The fact that I could not help liking the Admiral made things more difficult for me,' Schellenberg wrote. 'He often said to me, "Schellenberg, always remember the goodness of animals. You see, my dachshund is discreet and will never betray me – I cannot say that of any human being."'[11] Certainly not of Schellenberg, who was ruthless in his quest to make Amt VI the Reich's paramount intelligence service. Later, following the July 1944 plot, he would be the man ordered to draw up Canaris's arrest warrant.

Skorzeny's first briefing from Schellenberg, on 20 April 1943, must have been quite an encounter: Skorzeny, the Herculean, irascible, nationalist zealot, clueless about espionage and its ways, who 'expressed his views aggressively',[12] and the supple, dapper, smooth-tongued spymaster behind his specially adapted desk that was in fact an office fortress, fitted with recording equipment, alarms and concealed machine guns, all operated at the push of a button.[13] Skorzeny was hugely impressed by the office, though rather less by Schellenberg himself.

Schellenberg's brief to Skorzeny was simple enough. First: to take charge of the schools which were being established to train agents of the new special operations unit. Second: to retrain the SS 'Oranienburg' unit into 'a sabotage and subversive organisation' which would be named SS-Jägerbataillon 502.[14]

Implementing these instructions was quite another matter, and not merely because they weren't written down ('All orders were verbal. Nothing on paper').[15] Skorzeny's job specification, as outlined by Schellenberg, did not live up to his expectations. Skorzeny had been told he would head a new department as Leader of SS Special Forces.[16] The job he was actually given was head of Amt VI-S, the 'S' standing for *Schulen* (spy schools) rather than *Sabotage* (as Skorzeny seems to have imagined).[17] In Schellenberg's view the new position was primarily an intelligence-based desk job. The training of a crack squad of SS commandos modelled on the Brandenburgers came a distant second in importance.

By now, Skorzeny knew quite a bit about the technical aspects of soldiering; he knew nothing of spycraft. Adding to his difficulties was the complexity of the reporting structure and the rivalries of his superiors within it – which made it nearly impossible to acquire the resources necessary to do his job. Inasmuch as he was training commando units, these were a part of the Waffen-SS, and therefore, in any military operation, he had to report to OKW. Kaltenbrunner took no interest in the commando units, and although financial support came from Schellenberg, he too had little to do with them. Thus, while Skorzeny consulted Schellenberg about some matters, on others he took orders directly from OKW and dealt with them without consulting his immediate chief.[18]

The new chief of Germany's special forces needed to be a consummate intriguer, playing his superiors off against one another. Skorzeny's trump card would prove to be the personal relationship he developed with Hitler, occasionally receiving from the Führer plenipotentiary powers. But that didn't come until later.

During the difficult early months his task was smoothed considerably by the friendship and support of SS-Obersturmführer Karl Radl, whom Skorzeny recruited as his 'adjutant' (despite Radl being only one rank below him). In Amt VI, Radl became known as 'Skorzeny's Nanny' because he was always defusing difficult situations.[19] Skorzeny and the round-faced, jovial Radl had known each other for years through Skorzeny's second wife, Emmi Linhart, with whom Radl was well acquainted.[20] They met again in April 1943 when Skorzeny bumped into Radl in a Berlin restaurant. He did not hesitate to sign up his old friend.[21]

Radl was well aware of his charismatic commander's flaws: he came to regard Skorzeny as gullible, over-enthusiastic, and a poor leader with a bad eye for detail. In reality, Radl was not quite the apple-cheeked, affable fellow he seemed. A dedicated Nazi, he had been a member of the Austrian SS since 1934.[22] After joining the Waffen-SS in July 1940, he was initially given leave to study law. However, in May 1941 he was assigned as 9. Armee's liaison officer with Sonderkommando 7a, one of the Einsatzgruppen tasked with exterminating political enemies behind the lines on the Eastern Front. In August 1941 he was present, along with his superior, SS-Obersturmbannführer Walter Blume, at the massacre of over 500 Jews at Wilejka in Poland*. Radl then returned to Berlin and his legal studies, which would have ended in him becoming an SD 'investigator', had he not run into Skorzeny.

According to Radl, Skorzeny was so unhappy with his new post that he had tried to wriggle out of it by returning to his former role as head technical adviser of artillery in 2. SS-Panzerdivision 'Das Reich'†, but his protest had been overruled.[23] Having Radl as his chief administrator must have made a nightmare job a lot more bearable. Certainly Radl's organisational skills should be credited with what small successes Amt VI-S enjoyed over the next few months in procuring extra resources. As a lawyer and practised operator in the ways of military bureaucracy, Radl was Skorzeny's Sancho Panza. While Skorzeny enthused over big ideas, Radl found practical ways of achieving them.

---

*   Now Vileyka, Belarus
†   Formerly known as the SS-Division 'Reich'

Skorzeny did not start entirely from scratch. He had, after all, inherited a specialist Waffen-SS unit known as SS-Sonderlehrgang 'Oranienburg', stationed at the Totenkopf division barracks in Berlin-Oranienburg, about 20 kilometres north of the capital. Commanded by a Dutch officer, SS-Hauptsturmführer Pieter van Vessem, it consisted of about a hundred men – mostly NCOs and about 30 privates – distinguished by their language skills, physical courage, and fanatical devotion to Nazism. The unit had been set up in 1942 to prepare for the invasion of the Republic of Ireland, as part of Operation *Fischadler* (*Osprey*). After the United States' entrance into the war, there had been much speculation in the German high command that the Allies would occupy neutral Eire, and the plan was to forestall them. SS-Sonderlehrgang 'Oranienburg' was essentially a training unit, whose primary task was to instruct Irish forces in modern weapons and leadership of small units on the ground, in close collaboration with the IRA. There were a surprising number of Irishmen in the Third Reich, at least two of whom – ex-Royal Irish Fusiliers privates James Brady and Frank Stringer – later joined Skorzeny's unit.[24]

Whether SS-Sonderlehrgang 'Oranienburg' was actually fit for special operations is open to doubt. Brandenburger Feldwebel Helmuth Clissman had assessed the unit's suitability for *Fischadler* and found it wanting. Morale was good, as was the unit's fighting ability, but blatant xenophobia and the SS military ethos of heavy-handed assault tactics made these men unlikely candidates for undercover operations.[25]

How to retrain the men recruited and trained for *Fischadler* was just one of the many problems sitting on Skorzeny's desk. Anyone less bullish might have despaired at the paucity of resources to carry out his ill-defined mission:

> I studied all the available reports on sabotage operations … I was amazed at what I read about the various enterprises of the English 'Commando Troops', which were under the command of Lord Louis Mountbatten. There was no limit to new features. The English 'Secret Service' was shrouded in mystery and hardly any publicity was given to it. Its activity in all parts of the world was a complete novelty to me.
>
> Simultaneously I studied the reports of the achievements of the German Brandenburg Division. It appeared that, in comparison with England, the resources at our disposal were greatly inferior, although remarkable results had been obtained on many occasions.[26]

In addition to van Vessem's SS-Sonderlehrgang 'Oranienburg', Skorzeny had been assigned a transport unit and part of another company, in all some

300 men; about 50 were Dutch or Flemish and there were a few ethnic Germans from Hungary. He obtained permission to beef them up to battalion status – about 500 men – initially with the new unit designation of SS-Sonderverband z.b.V. 'Friedenthal', renamed SS-Jägerbataillon 502 in August 1943.[27] The plan was to create a group of '500' series units – including a parachute battalion (which did not materialise until September 1943, and then not under Skorzeny's direct command).

Given the shortage of available personnel to fill the ranks (not helped by a direct prohibition on recruiting members of the Waffen-SS), Skorzeny and Radl were reduced to considering inmates of the SS penal camp in Chlum, Czechoslovakia. These were servicemen who had fallen foul of the draconian Waffen-SS code of discipline, usually for offences such as falling asleep on sentry duty or 'defeatist talk'. Most of these recruits proved unsuitable and had to be returned. After badgering Hans Jüttner, chief of staff at SS-Führungshauptamt (Waffen-SS HQ), Skorzeny and Radl were allowed to approach the Wehrmacht for recruits. But the Wehrmacht was experiencing severe recruitment problems of its own and was not well disposed towards the upstart SS organisation.

About a hundred new recruits of debatable military quality were dredged up from the Allgemeine-SS. Some were ex-SD, others recruited from the SS-Totenkopfverbände – concentration camp guards.[28] Few had had significant combat experience, and even when they had, they were rarely trained to fight in a cohesive unit. An exception was SS-Untersturmführer Otto Schwerdt, who had fought as an NCO in the SS-Totenkopf-Division and won the Eisernes Kreuz 1. Klasse (EK I or Iron Cross First Class). Similarly, SS-Untersturmführer Andreas Friedrich had fought with Skorzeny at the Yelnya bridgehead during August 1941, winning the EK I; and SS-Unterscharführer Hans Holzer, a machine-gunner with the Totenkopf division, was a decorated veteran.

Whatever its inadequacies as a commando unit, the new battalion managed, with Jüttner's help, to attract 50 recruits from the Luftwaffe and 150 from the army – including a number of disillusioned Brandenburgers. In time, this trickle would swell into a torrent.

The commando headquarters was at Friedenthal. Situated just north of Oranienburg, it comprised a large park surrounded by heath and woodland which had once served as a hunting reserve for Prussia's royal family. Early in 1943, a wooden barracks complex was hastily erected around it. Although bisected by the road between Oranienburg and Sachsenhausen, the camp was surrounded by a 4-metre-high alarmed fence patrolled by guards and dogs. To the north lay a riding circuit and an athletics field. To the south were the guards' and administrative personnel's quarters. Behind, bordered by a canal, were the officers' quarters and offices. Other features included ammunition dumps, a communications centre, garages and, in a special compound to the southwest of the camp, Amt VI-F – a department that dealt with special weapons, forged documents and sabotage equipment, to which access was strictly guarded. Skorzeny, ever passionate about military gadgetry, had a particular interest in this section, but found it incompetent and soon began to outsource his requirements.[29]

Originally attached to Amt VI-F was A-Schule West (Agent School West), based at a country house near The Hague in occupied Holland. This too was within Skorzeny's remit. Here some of the skills of sabotage were imparted, including sabotage methods, demolition, wireless transmission and weapons handling. The training was designed to be as varied and interesting as possible.[30] Alongside the course went more relaxing activities such as swimming, movies, sports and reading. At the end of each four- to six-week course, the 'students' – including Serbs, Italians, Arabs from the Italian–Arabian Legion, Frenchmen and Belgians – would be graded and found employment. The Serbs were considered the best material.[31] In charge of the school was the director of training, SS-Obersturmbannführer Knolle, whose superior rank was initially a source of friction with Skorzeny, who was only an SS-Hauptsturmführer at this stage despite being overall commanding officer.[32]

Skorzeny's first tour of inspection, in which he immersed himself in the A-Schule's techniques, was an eye-opener. In Holland, he discovered, 'we could work on a bigger scale than at home', and he learned about the activities of the British Special Operations Executive (SOE), parachuting agents on espionage and sabotage missions which were supplied from air-drops.[33] The intensity of SOE's operations was not matched by its competence. Skorzeny learned that 'half of these agents were caught soon after they landed, and almost three-quarters of the material dropped fell into German hands' – handy for his resource-starved organisation, whose 'difficult problem of securing enough of the necessary equipment was solved almost entirely by our opponents themselves'.[34]

He was also quick to learn lessons from the interrogations of captured agents; studying the reports highlighted 'what a lot of leeway we had to make up. I was particularly interested in the enemy's training and instruction methods. I asked our interrogators to devote special attention to that aspect … The English method of instruction proved a valuable method.'[35]

The ease with which captured agents were 'turned' by German counter-intelligence seriously influenced Skorzeny's thinking on the type and calibre of agent that his own organisation ought to recruit. He realised that only the most dedicated, idealistic volunteers could be entrusted with dangerous missions; 'If a man wants paying before he will risk his life, one cannot expect much force of character, though I admit that there were a few exceptions which proved the rule.'[36]

Britain was well ahead in the area of specialist weaponry. Skorzeny thought to play the British at their own game. He obliged a turned agent to make a request for a silenced pistol – apparently a single-action Welrod 7.65mm, standard issue to SOE agents from 1943.[37] (Silenced semi-automatic pistols were known in Germany, but their sliding action was far from silent.) Skorzeny also asked for a Sten gun silencer. His scheme to copy these weapons fell flat when presented to the military bureaucracy. It was felt that the stopping power and accuracy of the weapon were adversely affected by the Sten silencer.

No less frustrating than the quality of the recruits and resources at Skorzeny's disposal was the preparedness of his forces. He rapidly concluded they were not up to scratch.[38] His first reaction was to introduce 'the most comprehensive training possible to enable them to be used at any point and for any purpose'. All men must be proficient with mortars, light artillery and tank guns. Handling all kinds of general and specialised motor vehicles – even railway engines and boats – was also a requirement. Added to this were horse-riding, field sports and parachute jumping. There followed 'group training for special operations, languages and surveying courses and instruction on technical targets and tactics'.[39]

But how could he improve the group training programme if he did not know the nature of the missions he was expected to accomplish? Here was the defining problem of the SS commando unit at that time: no one wanted to take full responsibility for mapping out its mission. This probably helps explain why Skorzeny rather than a more obviously qualified candidate had been appointed in the first place.

Hitler's enthusiasm for improving SS competence in special operations did not yet extend to a willingness to undermine the Abwehr. Canaris's service might be seriously flawed and politically unreliable, but it was the only comprehensive foreign intelligence service the Reich had. Kaltenbrunner, having satisfied his own needs by appointing someone trustworthy and unlikely to rock the boat, was unhelpful: 'You are an SS leader, you are supposed to know how to organise and lead such a battalion,' he told Skorzeny during an early meeting.[40]

As for Himmler, he was full of fantastical ideas unbound by any sense of realism. A case in point was Operation *Ulm* – the operation that never was.

Initially a limited commando operation aimed at destroying a couple of power plants behind the Russian Front, it was transmogrified at Himmler's behest into all-out economic warfare on the Magnitogorsk blast-furnaces which lay behind the Urals, hundreds of miles beyond the front line. Skorzeny suspected Albert Speer, Hitler's armaments minister, of encouraging this. But the idea was a non-starter. There was no precise intelligence, the scale and complexity of such a raid was beyond the competence of Skorzeny's organisation (or anyone else's), and logistics would have been a big problem. The Germans had only two types of transport plane capable of flying such a distance: the ageing Fw 200 Condor and the newer Ju 290; both four-engined planes were in high demand and short supply.[41]

Despite the problems, no one was prepared to tell Himmler that *Ulm* was impossible. Skorzeny tried to (or so he claimed), but Radl stayed his hand, remarking that it would be very unwise to alienate the Reichsführer-SS, whose support was indispensable. Schellenberg's advice was typically cynical: 'The more fantastic and grotesque a project coming to you from "above" seems, with all the more enthusiasm must you take it up and find it brilliant. Then go on … as if you're working on it … until a new, even crazier plan comes and the previous one is forgotten. In this way you will earn the reputation of a man who shrinks from nothing and on whom they can depend.'[42] It would take Skorzeny 18 months to shelve *Ulm* definitively.[43]

The only active operation launched in this early period in mid-1943 was *Franz*, an attempt by Schellenberg to stir up rebellion against the British in Iran. It had begun in April, and when Skorzeny took up his post in June he was delegated the ongoing training and recruitment programme, under Schellenberg's direct orders. This was to be a unique situation – from July 1943 onwards, Skorzeny would take orders 'directly from the OKW or from Hitler personally'.[44]

Operation *Franz* involved sending military advisers and instructors to support the Qashqai, a nomadic Turkic tribe based in southern Iran, who had been in rebellion against the country's British overlords since 1941. Strategically the operation made a lot of sense – the 'Persian Corridor' was a vital supply line by air and rail into the USSR. Leaving nothing to chance, the British had deposed the Nazi-leaning ruler, Reza Shah Pahlavi, and replaced him with his young and pliable son, Mohammed Reza. Four British divisions occupied the south of the country, while the Soviet Union took over the north. The Qashqai uprising in support of the exiled Shah broke out in December 1942. Further unrest in February 1943 gave *Franz* its momentum. At the time, Germany's Eastern Front was not far away.

The scene looked set for a promising guerrilla war centred on the more exposed parts of the Iranian rail network – à la Lawrence. Practice, however, fell short of theory, for several reasons.

Operational planning was in the hands of Heinz Gräfe, not a military type, but a senior SD officer who had once run Amt VI-C (Russia and Japan section). Two Friedenthal officers and three NCOs, led by an Iranian trained at the A-Schule, were with great difficulty parachuted into Iran using a long-range Ju 290 supplied by a specialist Luftwaffe unit working for the Abwehr. Because of the short runway in the Crimea, much of the equipment – not to mention the military instructors who were to go with them – was jettisoned to reduce the plane's payload.

That was just the beginning of Franz's troubles. Mechanical problems with a second aircraft dashed any possibility of resupplying the commandos. Shortly afterwards British intelligence arrested a key German agent in Tehran, effectively terminating the whole operation. A single operative succeeded in escaping across the border to Turkey. One German officer committed suicide for fear of falling into Russian hands; the rest were eventually captured.[45]

* * *

The tally of Skorzeny's achievements in the first few months is hardly inspiring. Skorzeny was a big man, with big ideas, and a big mouth. He was lacking when it came to administrative detail and the subtle art of diplomacy. Luckily for him, he possessed a gift for befriending people with complementary skills, to whom he could delegate such responsibilities – men like Radl and, through him, Arnold 'Arno' Besekow.

SS-Hauptsturmführer Besekow was a former police detective. By 1943 he was working at Amt VI and, after a chance encounter with Radl in May, was persuaded to join the newly formed Department S.[46] Radl, as a lawyer, reckoned Besekow's police experience would make him the perfect candidate to run the spy network which the department had been mandated to build. Initially Besekow was sent to A-Schule, which he would end up running, as the resident expert on sabotage technique. But, right from the start, he also immersed himself in more practical matters. Besekow was the one who baited the trap in the Netherlands for incoming SOE parachutists. It was his turning of Dutch agents and his interrogation reports that provided Skorzeny with invaluable insight into British technique.[47] Besekow was appointed head of the fourth desk (Amt VI-S4), which would soon be amalgamated with S2 (Small Operations) – up to now the responsibility of the overloaded Radl. Besekow's enlarged brief was to train and operate all spy networks, with special emphasis on the 'stay-behind' sabotage units (I-Netze), which were to create resistance to an Anglo-American invasion force in the event of a new front in Western Europe.

Besekow was a man of rugged, saturnine appearance, rounded off by a hoarse, rasping voice; but his manner was ebullient, open and garrulous. He was popular with his SS colleagues – who soon nicknamed him the 'Obergangster' on account of his underhand methods, which went unregulated (particularly by Skorzeny). A prodigiously hard worker, an experienced pair of hands and a keen, if cynical, connoisseur of human nature,[48] he should have been an asset to the new special operations department. But Besekow's professionalism would be severely compromised by personal vices he was incapable of curbing.

Besides Radl and Besekow there was Werner Hunke, dubbed 'Chinese' Hunke and 'Pingfu' on account of having spent his earlier childhood in Tientsin. Born in 1918, Hunke completed his education to university grade in Germany and became a committed Nazi in the process. He joined the Hitler Youth at 15; by June 1937 he was a member of the NSDAP; and in November of that year he signed up to the Allgemeine-SS. Like Skorzeny, Hunke was an engineer but he had had more solid front-line military experience – on the Finnish and Russian fronts, where he attained the rank of SS-Obersturmführer.[49] Hunke could be relied upon to handle competently the tedious role of recruitment and training of military personnel. In time Hunke, who joined Amt VI-S in September 1943, would be promoted to SS-Hauptsturmführer. He was appointed commanding officer of SS-Jägerbataillon 502 in July 1944, and eventually became Skorzeny's chief of operations, responsible for the intelligible transmission of Skorzeny's orders to all units.

All three – Radl, Besekow and Hunke – were incredibly loyal and would stay by Skorzeny's side to the end. Buttressed by their help, Skorzeny got busy with recruitment and tinkered with the training programme. He can certainly be credited with acquiring greatly improved barracks and training facilities at Friedenthal during this time. But the truth is, he had a lot of time on his hands – and the siren attractions of Berlin were never far away.

4

The Liberator of Mussolini

Winston Churchill was livid when informed that a small force of Luftwaffe paratroopers and SS commandos had, on 12 September 1943, freed Benito Mussolini from an apparently impregnable mountain fastness and flown him to safety in Germany. Churchill told the House of Commons: 'We had every reason to believe that Mussolini was being kept under a strong guard at a secure place ... Mussolini has himself been reported to have declared that he believed he was being delivered to the Allies. This was certainly the intention, and is what would have taken place but for circumstances entirely beyond our control.' Even Churchill had to confess that history had been made, that 'the stroke was one of great daring, and conducted with a heavy force. It certainly shows there are many possibilities of this kind open in modern war.'[1]

What Churchill must also have known, because it had been all over the German and international press for the past week, was that this highly embarrassing setback for Allied prestige had apparently been planned and led by a lowly captain, SS-Hauptsturmführer Skorzeny, who was now the toast of the Third Reich.

In truth, Skorzeny's new reputation owed as much to the Nazi regime's stalling war effort as it did to any individual acts of derring-do on his part. By the summer of 1943, Germany was well on its way to losing the war. Hitler and his closest associates were in denial about it, but to those who were more clear-headed and well-informed – such as Canaris and Schellenberg – it was increasingly apparent that the Third Reich's days were numbered. On the

Eastern Front, German forces were bogged down in a war of attrition they could not possibly win outright. Two-thirds of the Wehrmacht were now committed there. Things were little better elsewhere. Grossadmiral Dönitz had had to recall his fleet of North Atlantic U-boats after their losses became unacceptably high. At the end of July, the RAF mounted their first night-time saturation bombing raid over Hamburg, with the explicit aim of razing every building to the ground. In late August, the USAF followed this up with a massive daylight bombing raid on Berlin itself. The Luftwaffe was powerless to protect Germany's civilian population, who were now being made brutally aware of defeat's consequences.

Finally – and crucially for the career of Otto Skorzeny – there was the rapidly deteriorating situation of Italy, Germany's most important ally. By July 1943, an Anglo-American army group had pushed the Axis forces out of North Africa and invaded Sicily. A mainland invasion could not be far off.

On 25 July, the King of Italy, Victor Emmanuel III, seeking an accommodation with the Allies, stealthily deposed Hitler's friend and ideological accomplice, Benito Mussolini, and replaced him with Marshal Pietro Badoglio. Supposedly, the Duce had 'resigned' after being betrayed by a Fascist Grand Council, incensed at his inability to confront Hitler now the war was being lost. But his subsequent mysterious disappearance fuelled Hitler's suspicion that the Badoglio regime intended to sue for peace and that Mussolini was actually being held as a bargaining chip in a high-stakes poker game with Allied negotiators.

If a peace deal were struck, the strategic consequences for Germany would be almost unthinkable. The whole Italian peninsula might overnight become an Allied possession, making the Balkans, the back-door to the Eastern Front, vulnerable. Even the heartland of the Reich itself might be exposed. Mussolini's rescue and restoration as dictator was therefore paramount among Hitler's many pressing concerns that summer.

* * *

On Monday 26 July, Otto Skorzeny made a telephone call from the Hotel Eden in Berlin to his headquarters at Friedenthal. He was off-duty, dressed in civilian clothes and coming to the end of a long and inebriated lunch with an old friend, a professor from Vienna. Deciding to check with his office to see if anything was happening, Skorzeny got the surprise of his life.

His frantic secretary had been hunting high and low for him during the last two hours. He had been urgently summoned to the Führer's HQ near

Rastenburg, East Prussia. A special plane would be waiting for him at Tempelhof airport at 5 pm; he must be on it. No explanation was given.

Skorzeny ordered Karl Radl to meet him at the airport with a fresh uniform and some necessary personal effects. He had never been to the Wolfsschanze (Wolf's Lair) before, had no idea of its exact whereabouts, and still less what would be demanded of him. Once aloft in the Junkers Ju 52, an old warhorse of a plane whose main concession to comfort was a VIP bar, Skorzeny sought Dutch courage. 'I put my head through the pilot's door and asked whether I could help myself. Two glasses of brandy soothed my nerves and I could sit back and contemplate the landscape below.'[2] There wasn't much else to do: he was the sole passenger, and the journey was to take three hours.

After touching down at dusk, Skorzeny was driven the last few miles in a black Mercedes. It was almost dark when he passed through the outer security of the Wolf's Lair.

As far as he could make out, it was not a particularly impressive sight:

[The restricted inner zone] was surrounded by a barbed-wire fence and resembled a park well laid out with birch plantations. Winding roads were bordered with low birch trees. Some buildings and barracks, apparently sited without any regard to symmetry, now came into view. Grass and small trees were growing on the flat rooves. Some of the buildings and roads were covered with camouflage nets, here and there surmounted by real tree-tops, to look like a group of trees in the bare places.[3]

His destination was the oddly named Tea House, a wooden building whose left wing contained Generalfeldmarschall Keitel's dining room. When Skorzeny entered the other wing, 'I found myself in a large ante-room, furnished with comfortable chairs and several tables. The floor was covered with a plain Bouclé carpet.'[4]

He was greeted by SS-Hauptsturmführer Otto Günsche, Hitler's aide-de-camp, who attempted to introduce him to five other officers, mispronouncing his surname. This happened often, but on this occasion Skorzeny was particularly annoyed, and probably more than a little drunk. He corrected Günsche sharply: 'My name's not all that difficult; if you pronounce it Skor-tsay-ny in ordinary German it's quite easy.'[5]

Had Skorzeny been less abrasive, he might have learned the identities of the five other officers, who were his rivals in the selection that was about to happen. All he recalled was that he was the most junior on a shortlist of special forces types. One was a Waffen-SS Sturmbannführer; two were from the army, probably Brandenburgers, and the other two were Luftwaffe, probably Fallschirmjäger.[6]

Günsche, having left the room briefly, returned and announced: 'Gentlemen, I am about to take you into the Führer's presence.'

Skorzeny was stunned. He had only glimpsed Hitler twice before, and from afar – first at the 1936 Winter Olympics at Garmisch-Partenkirchen, then, in 1938, from some scaffolding with his workmen when Hitler made his triumphal entry into Vienna.[7] Now, as he followed Günsche, he 'trembled in every limb', fearing that 'I should probably commit some frightful gaffe, or make a fool of myself!'[8] (As if he hadn't already.)

Günsche ushered all six candidates into a nearby wooden building. 'In the soft indirect lighting I glanced at the wall and saw a small picture in an unpretentious silver frame. It was Dürer's *The Violet*. It is curious that this detail remains in my memory, whereas I have almost forgotten far more important things.'[9]

He recalled the momentous encounter in filmic detail. The officers entered a large room. 'The right wall had windows with plain, bright coloured curtains. In front of them was a massive table covered with maps. In the centre of the left wall was a fireplace and facing it a round table with four or five easy chairs.' The officers lined up, with Skorzeny, as the most junior, on the left. 'My eye fell on a writing table which was placed at an angle to the window. A number of coloured pencils, placed exactly parallel, were lying on it. So, it was here that the great decisions of the age are taken, I reflected.'[10]

A door opened and Adolf Hitler entered. He wore 'a simple, open-necked, field-grey uniform, which revealed the white shirt and black tie'. Skorzeny noted the EK I and wound ribbon.[11]

Günsche presented the officers in order of seniority. Each was asked to give a resumé of his career. While Hitler talked to the man at the far end, Skorzeny forced himself not to crane forward to stare. 'All I heard was the Führer's deep voice as he put his curt questions.' He was struck by the fact that Hitler, who purported to embody the Prussian ideal, could not conceal his 'soft Austrian accent'.[12]

The impression Skorzeny made on Hitler would be vital to his career. Personal rapport was the key, and part of this would lie in playing the fellow-Austrian card. At last, the Führer was before him, holding out his hand. 'I made a great effort not to bow too low … smart and slight. In five sentences I gave my birthplace, education, military career and present assignment. While I was speaking he looked me straight in the face, not taking his eyes off me for a second.'

Then Hitler stepped back and asked an apparently odd question: which of them knew Italy? Silence for a moment, until Skorzeny ventured that he had been there twice before the war and gone as far as Naples on his motorcycle. He was the only one of the candidates to have visited the country.[13] Hitler asked the officers a second question: 'What do you think of Italy?'

Sensing a trap, the others responded with formulaic answers regarding 'Germany's Axis partner'. Skorzeny tried something different. 'I am an Austrian,' he said. To any fellow Austrian, these words were pregnant with meaning; as one of the victors in World War I, Italy had annexed the alpine South Tyrol, with its 200,000 Austrian German speakers. Hitler had only been restrained from re-annexing it by his need for Mussolini's collaboration.

Hitler fixed him with an impenetrable stare and then said: 'The others may go. I want you to stay, Captain Skorzeny.' Skorzeny noted with great satisfaction that the Führer pronounced his name correctly.

What followed was a private conversation in which Hitler became a lot more animated. He began to explain that Mussolini's 'resignation' was only a feint by the Badoglio regime. Although they professed eternal fraternity with Germany, in reality the King and Badoglio were attempting to cut a deal with the Allies. Hitler spoke with emotion of his well-known friendship with Mussolini, and his gratitude to him. He must be rescued before it was too late, come what may; and Skorzeny was the man to be entrusted with that mission.

Hitler cautioned extreme secrecy: only five people were to know the details at this stage. They included General der Fallschirmtruppe (Luftwaffe lieutenant-general) Kurt Student, who had been ordered to fly to Rome as soon as possible with an elite force of paratroopers. For the duration of the operation, Skorzeny would consider himself under Student's orders. On no account was Skorzeny to confide anything about the mission to Generalfeldmarschall Albert Kesselring, commander of German forces in Italy, still less to the German ambassador in Rome, Hans von Mackensen.

Completely mesmerised by the snake-charmer, Skorzeny shook hands, turned to salute at the door and left. Hitler's blue-grey eyes, he said, never left him all the while. 'His words seemed so persuasive that, at the moment, I had not the slightest doubt about the success of the project.'[14]

* * *

The mission, known already as Operation *Eiche* (Oak), was only one element in Hitler's strategy for dealing with the Italian situation. He believed that Kesselring had been duped by the new regime's professions of loyalty to the

Axis. Hitler was convinced from the outset that Victor Emmanuel and Badoglio intended to betray him when it was politic to do so. He was right.

There were two relatively mature plans for dealing with a military and political emergency in Italy. Operation *Schwarz* (*Black*) involved full German military occupation of the Italian peninsula. Operation *Achse* dealt with the capture or destruction of the Italian fleet. Added to these were two missions devised by Hitler himself. *Eiche*, the rescue and reinstatement of Mussolini, was to be complemented by Operation *Student*, involving the capture of Rome by a force of paratroopers. Refinements included the abduction of Badoglio, the King and even the Pope. Only with difficulty was Hitler induced to drop these latter ideas.[15]

There was a risk that by overreacting the Germans might create the very situation they sought to forestall, forcing the Badoglio regime to come to terms with the Allies. And in the event of hostilities, German forces were too thinly deployed to take on the Italian armed forces. Also complicating the matter were the 70,000 German troops in Sicily, fighting alongside the Italians.

The political situation in Italy was evolving rapidly. After Mussolini's disappearance, his Fascist regime had collapsed almost overnight. Mussolini had to be found at all costs so that he could, at the very least, fulfil the figurehead role in a puppet regime that would sugar-coat the brutal fact of German military occupation.

While the Allies were clawing their way to victory in Sicily, with the prospect of an amphibious landing on the mainland only weeks away, Germany surreptitiously poured a whole army group (11 divisions) over the northern border of Italy; King Emmanuel and Badoglio continued to procrastinate, painfully aware that safely disengaging their forces from France and the Balkans would be no mean feat if war broke out with Germany.

Meanwhile, Skorzeny got down to business. Immediately after his meeting with the Führer, he was introduced to Kurt Student, who himself had arrived for a conference with Hitler only hours earlier. Student, a jovial, rotund 53-year-old, was Germany's foremost expert on airborne warfare. In May 1940 he had devised the famously successful raid on the Belgian fortress of Eben-Emael with a glider-force of only 70 paratroopers. Later, in May 1941, he orchestrated the extremely costly airborne assault on Crete.

Student warmed to Skorzeny as 'a young man' with 'plenty of bright ideas',[16] and listened sympathetically to the suggestion that he supplement his strike force with 50 of Skorzeny's SS commandos. These men were, wherever possible, to be fluent in Italian and assist in the intelligence and police work needed to track down the Duce. So as not to give the game away,

Skorzeny's men would, for the duration of the mission, discard their SS uniforms and assume those of paratroopers, whose appearance in the Rome area was thought less likely to arouse suspicion. Likewise, Skorzeny himself would pose as Student's adjutant.

The meeting was attended by Himmler, who took an obsessive interest in Operation *Eiche* from its outset. Skorzeny was unimpressed: 'I had only seen photographs of him until this meeting ... At first sight the most remarkable thing about Himmler's face was his old-fashioned eye-glasses. His far-from-impressive features betrayed nothing of the man's character. He gave us a friendly smile.'[17] Himmler spent much of the evening lecturing Skorzeny on the situation in Italy and bombarding him with a list of 'useful' contact names, which he could never be expected to remember. Himmler was clearly staking a claim to ownership of the mission on behalf of the SS.

By 11 pm, Student and Skorzeny had outlined their plan. At that point, the chain-smoking Skorzeny, desperate for a cigarette and needing to give Radl a list of preparatory orders, burst out of the no-smoking Tea House and found a phone. While he was waiting to be put through, he lit up. Himmler, entering the room, was furious at the sight of Skorzeny smoking. 'These eternal weeds, can't you do anything without a cigarette in your mouth? I can see that you're not at all the sort of man we need for this job!'[18] Alarmed, Skorzeny was rapidly assured by Günsche that Himmler was 'like that with everyone' and would soon 'get over it'. Which, apparently, he did.

Schellenberg and Himmler clearly scented a major intelligence coup in the offing, should SD-Ausland succeed in identifying Mussolini's whereabouts. Better still if Schellenberg's organisation could also claim credit for the actual rescue by having its own man, Skorzeny, embedded in the military operation.

Whether Skorzeny appreciated all of this at the time is doubtful. Most likely, Schellenberg and Himmler believed they had found a useful pawn and were delighted to have foisted him on Hitler. Only later did it become apparent that Skorzeny was a maverick, whose actions sometimes had dangerous and unpredictable consequences.

* * *

The following morning, 27 July, Student and Skorzeny flew to Rome in a Heinkel He 111 bomber. At the controls was Student's personal pilot, Hauptmann Heinrich Gerlach. Their ultimate destination was the picturesque town of Frascati, near Rome, where Kesselring had his headquarters. For the next six weeks, it would also be the nerve centre of Operation *Eiche*.

On 28 July, Radl and the rest of the SS team from Friedenthal arrived at the local airport, clad in tropical Luftwaffe garb. Ten intelligence agents, inserted at Schellenberg's behest, completed the unit of 50. They had no prior knowledge of their mission, and Radl was stunned when he received the full brief.

The *Eiche* commando force was required to interleave the rescue of Mussolini with contingency plans for kidnapping Badoglio and the Pope. Kesselring – who by now had tumbled to what was going on – became overtly hostile to the whole 'hare-brained' Mussolini project.[19] Complicating the situation further, there were almost no useful intelligence leads on Mussolini's whereabouts. He had last been seen speeding away in the back of an ambulance shortly after his audience with the King in Rome on the afternoon of 25 July. There had been no sightings since. A huge manhunt ensued.

Student's intelligence officer, Hauptmann Gerhard Langguth, was the only member of the intelligence team with military planning expertise, and his relationship with Skorzeny was difficult. Skorzeny could tap into sources across the Third Reich, from Himmler downwards. That was sometimes a mixed blessing. The superstitious Reichsführer assembled a group of psychics, astrologers and fortune tellers (some in concentration camps, having been blamed for Rudolf Hess's 1941 flight to Britain) in a Wannsee country house, where they were set to work tracking down Mussolini.[20]

Not all of Himmler's suggestions were so daft. He provided two useful contacts, one of which was to produce the breakthrough result. The first was SS-Obersturmbannführer Eugen Dollman, a middle-aged socialite boasting easy access to the upper echelons of Roman society. The second was Herbert Kappler, police attaché at the German embassy in Rome, whose job involved keeping tabs on the Italian police.[21] Dollman and Kappler were part of Hitler's 'inner ring' of five who were privy to the intimate details of the operation, the others being Skorzeny himself, Radl and Student.[22]

Kappler discovered that Mussolini had briefly been incarcerated at some carabinieri barracks not far from Kesselring's headquarters. From there, Kappler identified the island of Ponza off the Neapolitan coast as the next probable destination. However, Hitler discounted the information, choosing instead to believe a rumour from naval intelligence that Mussolini was on the island of Santo Stefano. Hitler proposed an amphibious snatch operation, but cancelled it at the last moment when contradictory information came to light. Rommel had apparently unimpeachable evidence that Mussolini was in the port of La Spezia in northwestern Italy. Meanwhile, the Abwehr were convinced he was on Elba.

As mission commander, Student had to spend much of August shuttling between Rome and the Wolfsschanze to attend high-level intelligence conferences to evaluate all these conflicting reports.

In fact, Mussolini was in none of these places.

Badoglio and the King had contemplated handing him straight to the Allies as a pre-armistice goodwill gesture, but realised it would precipitate massive German retaliation. Having got wind of the German rescue plan, Badoglio hit upon a two-pronged strategy for protecting his valuable hostage. He repeatedly moved Mussolini – now under the protective custody of the carabinieri – from one hideout to another, keeping one step ahead of the German rescue effort. At the same time he instructed the Italian military intelligence service, SIM,* to plant a trail of disinformation, playing on existing rumours such as the former dictator being locked up in a mental institution, or the suggestion that he had killed himself. On 8 August, still wearing the increasingly wrinkled blue suit in which he had been abducted nearly two weeks previously, Mussolini was transported by destroyer to a new hideaway on the small island of La Maddalena, between Sardinia and Corsica.

Student heard of this, but took little interest; there had been too many red herrings already, and he was preoccupied with the deteriorating situation in and around Rome. So he put Skorzeny on to it. This was to be Skorzeny's big break and he was determined not to fluff it. 'He threw himself into this new assignment with fanaticism and astounding energy,' said Student later. 'Soon he had results.'[23]

Skorzeny and Radl spent a lot of time in Rome in civilian or Luftwaffe dress, looking for leads. It was difficult, as they only spoke tourist Italian. They came across an Italian naval officer in a club one evening – suspiciously fluent in German and possibly a plant – who fed them the false rumour that a warship had just taken Mussolini to La Spezia.

Their luck changed thanks to the German naval liaison officer on La Maddalena, Fregattenkapitän Helmut Hunaeus. He reported that the Italian garrison on the island had recently been supplemented by a detachment of carabinieri, and new, stringent security measures were in place around the La Maddalena seaport area.

But how to follow up the lead without giving the game away? Skorzeny's ruse was to infiltrate an undercover agent – SS-Untersturmführer Robert Warger, a Skorzeny commando and fluent Italian speaker, who would pose as Hunaeus's interpreter.[24] He would cruise the bars and cafés of La Maddalena in the hope of gaining information from locals. Unfortunately, Warger was a

---

* Servizio de Informazione Militari

teetotaller, and only with difficulty was Skorzeny able to persuade him otherwise. An effort to limber Warger up for the job with ample quantities of cognac merely made him ill.

Warger's modus operandi was simple. On encountering anyone who claimed to know a scintilla of information on Mussolini's whereabouts, he would challenge him to a drunken wager on Mussolini actually being dead.

Meanwhile, Skorzeny persuaded Student to lend him an He 111 bomber for aerial reconnaissance of the island's defences. Flying at high altitude over the harbour, Skorzeny lay in the glazed nose, armed with a camera and maritime chart. 'I was engaged in admiring the wonderful colours of the water when the voice of the rear-gunner came through the microphone: "Warning! Two aircraft behind us. British fighters!" Our pilot swerved and I kept my finger on the button of the gun, ready to fire if they came within range.'[25]

The plane ditched in the sea, smashing the glass-fronted canopy. Skorzeny, clinging to the gun, was submerged in water. The pilot managed to drag him to the upper cabin and out of the escape hatch. The two other crew members also escaped and the four of them were able to launch the rescue dinghy before the plane sank. Eventually, they were picked up by an Italian anti-aircraft cutter (no questions asked, apparently) and returned to the mainland via a Waffen-SS base in Corsica. Skorzeny was the only injured party: a few days later he discovered that he had broken several ribs.[26]

By 23 August, Warger's ploy had been rewarded with a solid lead. 'A fruiterer … was the unconscious victim of his own love of a gamble,' recalled Skorzeny. Challenged by Warger to prove that Mussolini wasn't dead, the tradesman led Warger to the Villa Weber (where he made daily deliveries). There, sitting on the terrace of a house next to the villa, was the Duce himself.[27]

Back in Rome on 24 August, Skorzeny and Radl conferred with Student, who was convinced that they had found their man. Others were not. Canaris once more suggested Elba as a more probable location. (Given his involvement in the conspiracy against Hitler, it is likely that Canaris planted this false intelligence deliberately to sabotage the operation.) Student was forced to attend yet another top-level conference in the Wolfsschanze, this time with Skorzeny in tow.

The conference was held in the Tea Room, with virtually the whole Nazi top-brass present. In addition to Hitler himself, Himmler, Grossadmiral Dönitz, Reichsmarschall Hermann Göring, Foreign Minister von Ribbentrop, Generalfeldmarschall Keitel, and Generaloberst Jodl were present. Skorzeny was placed next to Jodl.[28]

Student outlined the case for La Maddalena, then left Skorzeny the daunting task of briefing the top team in detail. (Student was a poor, halting speaker, and must have recognised that Skorzeny could make a better presentation.) As he immodestly recounted, Skorzeny had no trouble in rising to the occasion. His presentation convinced Hitler to retract his orders for an operation on Elba. Skorzeny outlined a plan for La Maddalena, which was approved. A flotilla of speedboats and several Waffen-SS units stationed in Corsica were placed under his command.[29]

The plan, which Skorzeny later claimed was his own, had in fact been devised by Student in conjunction with the naval officers involved. Any part Skorzeny played in it was probably minor and advisory. However, Skorzeny was crucial in the operation on Elba being aborted.

After returning to La Maddalena on the eve of the raid to confer with Warger, he discovered that Mussolini had disappeared, and the house by the Villa Weber was closed and deserted.[30] The following morning, clad rather amateurishly as German sailors, the two of them took some dirty washing to a local washerwoman in the port, where they came across a member of the carabinieri. Warger resorted to his tactic of claiming the Duce was dead. No, not dead, said the policeman, because he had seen him that very morning; indeed, he himself was one of the men who escorted Mussolini to an ambulance seaplane that flew him out of the harbour.

The commander of Mussolini's security detail, General Giuseppe Gueli, had sprung his hostage from the jaws of the German trap just as it was about to snap shut. After about an hour's flight, the seaplane landed on Lake Bracciano, a few miles northwest of Rome, under cover of an air-raid warning – which meant there were almost no witnesses to its arrival. Mussolini was bundled into yet another waiting ambulance to take him – who knew where? The German manhunt was back to square one.

Nearly a week passed without any news other than confirmation of the flight to Lake Bracciano. Then came a breakthrough. At 10 pm on Sunday 5 September, Kappler wired Berlin the following message: 'Thanks to information obtained from a police source in the Gran Sasso area, we have discovered that the Duce is, in all probability, holed up in a hotel situated on that mountain. Have asked some of my men to investigate this lead. They will return to Rome by Tuesday afternoon.'[31]

Kappler had managed to intercept a message from Gueli to the chief of police in the Italian Ministry of the Interior, stating, 'Security precautions around the Gran Sasso complete.'[32]

Gran Sasso is part of a range that includes Mount Corno, the highest peak in the Apennines range. Perched on a plateau just below, at 2,000 metres above sea-level, was the Hotel Campo Imperatore, built just before the war, primarily as a ski resort. It was inaccessible by road. The only way in and out was a ten-minute cable car ride to the village of Assergi, 1,000 metres below.

Kappler confirmed the location two days later, after his deputy Erich Priebke, who had been sent to scout the area around Assergi, returned with the news that all the staff at the Hotel Campo Imperatore had just been dismissed, which surely hinted at some top-level security operation. Leutnant Leo Krutoff, Student's personal physician, was sent to check out the hotel, ostensibly as a possible convalescence site for wounded German troops. Krutoff knew nothing of the real purpose of his mission, but was able to gather some useful information on unusual troop movement in the area before being rebuffed by the Italian security detail at the lower cable-car station.[33]

The intelligence was heartening but hardly amounted to reliable groundwork for a military operation. To remedy this situation, Skorzeny, Radl and Langguth set off on an aerial reconnaissance flight on the morning of 8 September.

Conducted in extreme secrecy (not even the pilot knew what they were doing, having been given the impression they were photographing harbours in the Adriatic), the flight took a long detour and eventually crossed Gran Sasso at over 5,000 metres. Just before the approach, it became apparent that the specialist stereoscopic spy-camera had jammed. Precisely what happened next is unclear. Skorzeny later claimed that Langguth became thoroughly uncooperative during the flight.[34] Their argument may have been about the pointlessness of continuing the mission using a hand-held camera as a substitute for the proper thing; with the plane flying so high to avoid detection, Langguth would have known the results were likely to be poor. Skorzeny and Radl apparently went ahead anyway, each taking it in turns to wriggle halfway through a large hole they had punched in the aircraft's canopy to get shots at the required angle. Conditions were freezing, and they were clad in thin tropical uniforms.[35]

As the spy-plane was returning to its Frascati base, American bombers struck the town in an effort to destroy Kesselring's headquarters. The Luftwaffe photo laboratory was destroyed, so Langguth and Skorzeny had to use an amateur facility at nearby Pratica di Mare. Not surprisingly, the developed photos revealed little detail about the hotel and its immediate surroundings.[36] All the same, Skorzeny claimed to discern a gently sloping meadow on the north side of the hotel which might just make a landing spot.

Despite the patchy intelligence, at 9.46 pm on 8 September, the order to proceed with the operation arrived from Berlin. The mission was on.

∗ ∗ ∗

That same evening, the Americans finally lost patience with Italian prevarication and unilaterally declared the terms of surrender over Algiers radio. The full measure of Italy's diplomatic duplicity over the past few weeks was exposed to the world.

Militarily outnumbered two to one in the vicinity of Rome, the Germans were forced to act preemptively. Kesselring immediately moved the 3. Panzergrenadierdivision southwards and Student's 2. Fallschirmjägerdivision northwards in a pincer movement converging on the capital. There was stiff Italian resistance, and some of Student's paratroopers were badly mauled. Resistance only ceased on the morning of 11 September after Kesselring threatened to firebomb Rome. The King and Badoglio fled, leaving the Germans masters of the capital.

The pressure to rescue Mussolini was intensifying by the hour. With Italy's defection from the Axis now publicly known, there was no reason not to hand him over to the Allies at the earliest opportunity. He might even be executed to prevent him falling into German hands. In fact, Badoglio had ordered exactly that.[37] Hitler was breathing down Student's neck for a result, and the SS were now determined to cash in on their intelligence coup.

At about 3 pm on 11 September, Student instructed Major Harald Mors, temporary commander of the Fallschirmjäger Lehrbataillon, to begin drawing up a detailed operational plan for the raid on Gran Sasso. Student had scheduled the commencement of Operation *Eiche* for 7.30 am on the following day, so Mors had less than 17 hours to be battle-ready. He consulted with Langguth and Student's chief staff officer, Major Arnold von Roon. He was frank about the inadequate intelligence acquired by Skorzeny. Then again, it was better than nothing. Skorzeny, at this stage, was not involved in the discussion.

Militarily, there were only three options: parachute drop, glider landing and ground assault.

Ground assault would allow more troops and heavier weapons to be used. But there was no road up to Gran Sasso, so the assault force would have to seize the lower cable station and travel up to the hotel, losing the element of surprise. Just as worrying, the bulk of the Italian 24th Infantry Division 'Pinerolo' was located only 12 kilometres away in L'Aquila.

A parachute drop had never been tried at that altitude in mountainous terrain. The commandos might be badly scattered by unpredictable mountain winds and find it too difficult to concentrate their force in time. The planners almost immediately turned this option down.

A glider landing offered the element of surprise plus greater initial concentration of force. It was also exceedingly dangerous. The planners were inspired by the legendary Eben-Emael raid, but also acutely aware of the different circumstances. In 1940, Student had had months to orchestrate his glider assault; here he had hours. Then, the terrain was relatively well known; here it was not. A glider-borne assault had never before been attempted at such an altitude, in such mountainous conditions. Skorzeny's alleged landing spot near the hotel, even judged optimistically, would be much smaller than the landing zone at Eben-Emael.

Student and his staff eventually came up with a twin-pronged strategy, synchronised to give the Italians minimum time to react. A two-company (260 men) motorised ground force would assault the carabinieri positions at the cable car base while a smaller force of over a hundred elite paratroopers would be landed by 12 gliders as close as 20 metres from the hotel. Mors would be in overall tactical command of the two units, but the glider force would be led by his trusted subordinate, Oberleutnant Freiherr Georg von Berlepsch. Mors felt he would be in a better position to influence events, if the glider attack miscarried in some way, by leading from the ground.

The strength of the Italian security detail was unknown. Best guess, supplied by Langguth on the basis of the intelligence from Krutoff and others, was about 200, split evenly between the hotel and the vicinity of Assergi. Mors was therefore taking a considerable risk, given he was attacking a well-defended position. Two days earlier, his battalion had encountered fierce resistance attempting to disarm an Italian division to the south of Rome, which left 12 paratroopers dead. Mors had every reason to expect a serious firefight. Therefore, the glider force would be issued with a number of the very latest FG 42 assault rifles, developed especially for paratroopers and capable of suppressive ground-fire.

Once Mussolini was secured, he would be brought down to Assergi in the captured cable car, and thence to a nearby airfield (which would have to be seized by an additional force of paratroopers). Alternatively, he could be flown out from a field near the cable car base station in a Fieseler Storch short-takeoff-and-landing light aircraft. As a backup, a second Fieseler Storch, with Student's pilot Gerlach at the controls, would be circling overhead to effect an extremely hazardous landing near the hotel itself. Skorzeny later reported that the planners also considered the use of an experimental Fa 223 Drache helicopter, but couldn't obtain one.[38]

Student approved Mors' plan and ordered the DFS-230 gliders to be flown in by tow-plane from the south of France as soon as possible. The DFS-230 was a standard and very basic workhorse dating from the 1930s. However, modifications enabled it, in the right conditions and in the hands of a skilful pilot, to pull up within 20 to 30 metres of landing. It could carry nine men plus the pilot, giving a maximum size of 120 for Berlepsch's raiding force. Student, a World War I ace and one-time glider pilot himself, felt the biggest single threat to the mission was the unknown and untested wind currents around the landing zone.[39] For that reason, the mission was scheduled for early in the day, before the mountain air had heated up and created unpredictable thermals.

Skorzeny would later claim that he was responsible for planning the operation: 'Student approved of my plan after hearing my report.'[40] The idea of a glider-borne assault, he claimed, was the result of a discussion between him and Student, and the planning was then passed on to 'the experts in air landings'.[41] His version of events is flatly denied by nearly everyone else who was in a position to know.[42]

Probably, Skorzeny did discuss the broader tactics of the raid on that evening of 11 September. Given he was Student's 'adjutant' and, more importantly, Hitler's personally selected emissary, there was every reason to keep him up to date with the evolution of the plan. Moreover, as already noted, Student warmed to Skorzeny's enthusiasm. Many (including Langguth and Student's general staff) had, all along, been sceptical about the mission. Not so Skorzeny, who always saw the glass half full. The technical experts were, unlike Student, untroubled by the compelling political rationale behind the raid. Where that was concerned, he had an ally in Skorzeny, and may well have confided in him. Lastly, let's not forget gratitude: it was Skorzeny's organisation, the SS, which had provided the breakthrough intelligence lead, allowing the commando team to locate Mussolini in the first place.

Which is a long way from saying that Skorzeny devised the raid. He had once aspired to be a Luftwaffe pilot[43] and may well have been inside a glider, but to suggest that he had, in any sense, a comprehensive knowledge of airborne assault tactics borders on the absurd.

Mors, on the other hand, could hardly be more experienced in them. By the age of 32 he had already led airborne assault troops in the Low Countries and served on Student's staff during the Crete campaign; in 1942 he was fighting in the Soviet Union.

Not only was Skorzeny not the author of the Gran Sasso raid; originally he was to have played no direct part in it. He was assigned to lead a subsidiary mission: the simultaneous rescue of the rest of Mussolini's family from the fortress-like Rocca delle Caminate outside Rome (where they had been tracked down by Kappler's team). But such a secondary role did not conform to his notion of glory. Exploiting his personal rapport with Student, he wangled a place for himself in the glider-borne assault. He had set himself the objective of winning the Ritterkreuz, and the Gran Sasso mission seemed tailor-made to achieve this. Indeed, just before the raid, Kaltenbrunner wired him: 'Hearty good wishes on the Ritterkreuz.'[44]

While the final touches were being put to the battle plan, Skorzeny persuaded Student to allow a further 17 of his SS commandos to accompany him. The strict understanding was that Skorzeny and his team confine themselves to a police role, which did not involve participating in the assault itself: 'Skorzeny was to function as a police organ for the personal protection of the Duce,' Student recalled.[45]

In acceding to Skorzeny's request, Student may have been influenced by what he had seen of his fighting qualities over the previous few days. Skorzeny had volunteered himself and his commandos in the ad hoc operation to secure Rome, following which he was awarded the EK I and invited to propose three of his men for the Second Class award.[46]

According to Mors, Berlepsch was 'furious' at having to leave behind paratroopers to make way for Skorzeny and his men, who were mere 'passengers'.[47] Berlepsch's temper was not improved the following morning when he discovered that a further two of his elite paratroopers had been squeezed out to make way for a photographer and a war correspondent. The opportunistic Skorzeny was already hijacking leadership of the glider assault, and preparing for his starring role to be publicised (although he was careful not to leave Student with that impression). It helped that he outranked Berlepsch and was far better politically connected.

Skorzeny (or possibly Radl) also came up with the idea of taking along a high-ranking carabinieri officer, capable of sowing confusion among Mussolini's guards. The candidate they selected, probably on Kappler's recommendation, was General Fernando Soleti from the Ministry of the Interior, who was well acquainted with Mussolini's chief captor, General Gueli. Soleti's known lukewarmness towards Mussolini and his Fascist regime (he had taken part in the coup against him) only made the tactic more appealing. With Student's approval, Soleti was contacted, and he agreed to cooperate, little realising what it really entailed.

By now, not only the scheduling but the entire rationale of the operation was coming under severe pressure. Mors continually adjusted his plan, but mounting pressure from Berlin for a result, the imminence of an Allied landing and the possibility that Mussolini would again be spirited away made the timescale immovable. On the eve of the operation, there was an unsettling news report that Mussolini had arrived in North Africa as a prisoner.[48] Analysis of the distances involved suggested this was an impossibility. But it underlined the mission's urgency.

* * *

At 1.05 pm on 12 September, the airborne force took off from Pratica di Mare. Mors' motorised battalion had departed early in the morning to make its circuitous journey from Frascati to Assergi on time. The gliders had been an hour late arriving at the airfield, and numbered only ten, not 12. Meanwhile, Soleti had been playing up. Having believed that he was there to provide details about Mussolini's captors, when he discovered that he was to accompany the glider expedition, he refused. It was pointed out to him that he had no choice. From that moment he was kept under guard.

Before departure, Student gave the first full mission briefing to the glider pilots and the ten glider commanders (including Skorzeny and Berlepsch), plus Langguth.

It must have been disheartening to hear Student apologise for having to send them off late. And still more so to hear his sober estimate of 80 per cent losses from glider crashes and enemy fire. Nor can the glider pilots have been impressed by Skorzeny's blurry 4-inch-square reconnaissance photos – the sole visual guide to their prospective landing zone.

In a last dent to morale, the airbase was bombed shortly before take-off. Miraculously the gliders and tow planes were undamaged.

Berlepsch's plan put him and his most experienced paratroopers in the first three gliders. They would land first and overpower any initial resistance. Skorzeny and Radl were in the fourth and fifth gliders, accompanied by 16 lightly armed SS commandos. Their task was to secure the landing zone, guard any prisoners and provide a bodyguard for Mussolini until he could be flown to safety. The remaining gliders were filled with paratroopers whose job was to seize the cable car head and take on any resistance around the hotel. Langguth, flying in the lead tow-plane, would guide them to the landing zone. Crammed into glider 4, at the front of the bench which passed for seating, just in front of Skorzeny, was the hapless Soleti.

The plan lasted just 20 minutes into the highly uncomfortable one-hour flight. The aircraft were buffeted by strong headwinds, which played havoc with some of the SS men, who had helped themselves to hearty breakfasts. Crucially, the winds slowed the climb-rate, so that the aircraft struggled to gain sufficient height to get over the mountains. Langguth ordered his tow pilot to circle, climb, and reapproach the ridge. The first two tow-planes did likewise.* Unfortunately, there was no radio communication between the tow-planes, and the others didn't follow suit. Now Skorzeny's glider was in the lead, and remained there for the rest of the flight. (See map on page 12.)

Skorzeny's account of what came next is contradicted by that of his glider pilot, Leutnant Elimar Meyer. Skorzeny claimed that, as he was now the only one with any real idea of the Gran Sasso topography, he guided Meyer in visually, through a hole he slashed in the glider's fabric.

> It was just short of zero-hour when I recognized the valley of Aquila below us and also the leading vehicles of our own formation hastening along it … 'Helmets on!' I shouted as the hotel, our destination, came in sight and then: 'Slip the tow ropes'. My words were followed by a sudden silence, broken only by the sound of the wind rushing past. The pilot turned in a wide circle, searching the ground – as I was doing – for the flat meadow appointed as our landing-ground. But a further and ghastly surprise was in store for us. It was triangular all right, but so far from being flat, it was a steep, a very steep, hillside. It could even have been a ski-jump.[49]

Meyer denied being guided by Skorzeny ('absurd'). About the only thing in his account that concurs with Skorzeny's is the unpleasant surprise of seeing the landing zone:

> I pulled the release device with my left hand and saw the tow-rope disappear below, while the nose of the glider dropped towards the objective …
>
> Despite extending the air brakes, the strong updrafts from the mountaintop pushed against the aircraft and it was difficult to keep on the glide-path towards the target … It was only when we were about 150 metres from the hotel that suddenly, like ants, many people began to emerge from the exit. Already I could see details. The soldiers did not show a hostile attitude. They had rifles and submachine guns, but all just stopped and stared, obviously surprised by the unknown aircraft.[50]

Some of the Italians thought they were Allied gliders, which added to the surprise factor. Meyer looked in dismay at the landing zone – 'steep slopes

---

* Gliders and tow-planes flew in units of three, known as Kette. Skorzeny's glider was head of Kette 2.

that dropped off into an abyss' – and realised that the other gliders were far behind him.

> Therefore, I seized upon a quick resolution. I put the glider into a steep left circle, which pressed the passengers hard. I deployed the braking parachute as we approached the windy slope, heading straight towards the hotel. A jolt went through the glider when it first hit the hard, stony ground, tearing up the barbed wire under the skid like string. When the glider stopped, it stood only 40 metres from the hotel.[51]

At about 2.05 pm, SS-Untersturmführers Schwerdt and Warger tumbled out of the glider's hatch numbed, dazed and probably suffering from airsickness. Next out was Skorzeny (who left his sub-machine gun behind in the confusion), closely followed by a distraught Soleti shouting to the Italians, 'Don't shoot, don't shoot' as one of the SS commandos trained a pistol on him.[52] Only Meyer kept his wits about him, mounting his MG-34 machine gun above the glider's cockpit, in accordance with Fallschirmjäger procedure.

What followed was far from a textbook assault. With the plan upended, Skorzeny was forced to improvise. He had taken lessons from the British raid on Rommel's headquarters in Tunisia the previous year, which had ended in disaster for the raiders after indiscriminate shooting broke out. During the pre-operation briefing, Skorzeny had been very specific in requiring his men to hold their fire until instructed to do otherwise; he guessed that the success of the mission would depend on surprise, not combat.[53] This was good thinking, and the raiders stuck to it. In other respects, however, the raid began to resemble a farce.

With Schwerdt behind him, Skorzeny ran up the hill towards the eastern end of the hotel shouting '*mani in alto, mani in alto*' (hands up), which had the desired effect on the solitary sentry in their way.

German intelligence about the hotel layout, and Mussolini's likely location within it, was extremely thin. Opening the first door he came to, Skorzeny found an Italian wireless operator within. Kicking the chair away, Skorzeny smashed the radio. Alas, the room was a dead end, with no access to the hotel. Skirting the back of the building, Skorzeny and Schwerdt found the ground-floor windows boarded up and still no sign of an entrance. By now, they had been joined by a couple of their NCOs. Having reached the western end of the hotel, their progress was blocked by a 2-metre raised platform. Skorzeny climbed onto it, using SS-Rottenführer Himmel as a human step.

About this time, glider number 5 – containing Radl and the rest of the SS team – crash-landed about 90 metres in front of the hotel. The landing was so rough that the glider commander, Oberstürmführer Ulrich Menzel, broke his ankle and spent the rest of the operation crawling about on his hands and knees. Radl collected up the other bewildered participants. Glider 6 slid badly, coming to a rest between the hotel and the cable car head. It contained the two war correspondents and the first paratroopers, unharmed but only seven in number.

Meanwhile, Skorzeny rounded the west end of the hotel and at last found the main entrance. Even more gratifying, he spotted a familiar-looking bald figure peering down from a first-storey window – Benito Mussolini himself.

While the raiding force landed and found their bearings, Mussolini's guards were immersed in some buffoonery of their own. General Giuseppe Gueli was taking a siesta when the first glider arrived, despite having been alerted that morning to Mors' approaching ground force. At 1.30 pm he had received a message from the Rome police chief warning him of an imminent German attack. Having increased the cable head guard to 40 men and readied some mules for a mountain-path getaway, Gueli had convinced himself the attack wouldn't happen until the following morning, and gone back to sleep.

The Italian security detail numbered about 120, most stationed immediately in and around the hotel. Their efficiency was impeded by Badoglio's political decision to divide responsibility between the civil police (about 30 men commanded by Gueli) and a carabinieri unit (43 men headed by Lieutenant Alberto Faiola), plus a rag-bag of reinforcements, some from Italian army detachments that had escaped Rome. They were only lightly armed with carbines, some light machine guns and hand grenades. Gueli's police unit were not combat material, and no one had thought to take such elementary precautions as stationing snipers on the roof. Gueli had been informed that Hitler had ordered the execution of any Italian officer who resisted the Germans, and was apparently most concerned with saving his own neck. Lieutenant Faiola was different. As Badoglio's pointman, he had been ordered not to let Mussolini be taken alive.

According to Mussolini, 'It was exactly 2 pm and I was sitting by the open window with my arms folded when a glider landed a hundred yards from the building ... The alarm sounded ... Lieutenant Faiola burst into my room and threatened me: "Shut the window and don't move."'[54] When Mussolini looked out of the window again, he spotted a group of German soldiers below, with Skorzeny at their head. 'The carabinieri had already got their guns at the ready when I noticed an Italian officer among Skorzeny's group whom, on approaching nearer, I recognised as General Soleti, of the Metropolitan Police Corps.' Mussolini began shouting at his captors: 'Can't you see? There is an Italian general there. Don't fire!'[55] Almost miraculously, they obeyed.

Faiola was in a near impossible position, what with having to rush up to the second floor to roust Gueli out of bed and get him to agree a plan of action, put the guards on standby, ready the mules, and pull Mussolini away from the window. In the end, he seems to have contented himself with the last. Also playing on his mind was what Mussolini now told him: if he, Mussolini, was killed, the Germans would execute the entire Italian security force.

Having spotted his man, Skorzeny set about securing him. Two of his NCOs, SS-Unterscharführer Holzer and SS-Rottenführer Benz, were sent shinning up the lightning conductors to gain access to the room via the window. When that didn't work, Skorzeny and Schwerdt decided to rush the building from the front entrance. With the rest of the assault force – including Berlepsch – now landing, time was running out for Skorzeny to take the lead and steal all the glory.

According to Skorzeny, he and Schwerdt disarmed two machine guns and forced their way through a tide of carabinieri. In fact, the only obstacle was a mass of furniture piled up against the doors. Most of the guards, including the machine gunners, had taken one look at the German force arriving and disappeared into their hotel rooms. 'On the right was a staircase,' Skorzeny recalled (truthfully). 'I leaped up it, three steps at a time, turned left along the corridor and flung open a door on the right. It was a happy choice.' There was Mussolini, accompanied by Faiola and his deputy, Lieutenant Antichi. When Schwerdt caught up, he 'took the situation in at a glance and jostled the mightily surprised Italian officers out of the room and into the corridor. The door closed behind us.' Skorzeny grandiloquently announced, 'Duce, the Führer has sent me to set you free.' To which Mussolini replied, 'I knew my friend Adolf Hitler would not abandon me.'[56]

Meanwhile, Holzer and Benz were still hanging from the outside of the building. At that point, Berlepsch arrived and began to take command of the situation.

Within just 12 minutes of Skorzeny's glider landing, the first phase of the operation was completed. The Italians had surrendered without a fight, the prisoner had been released unharmed (still wearing his battered blue suit), and both cable car stations had been secured. The only shot fired had been by a paratrooper accidentally discharging his rifle on climbing out of his glider, and the only fatalities were two Italians killed by Mors' battalion in a skirmish at the lower cable car station. All the gliders had landed safely except number 8, which encountered violent winds on landing, sheered off the edge and broke a wing. Several paratroopers and the pilot were badly injured.

At 2.17 pm Berlepsch was able to radio Mors, now in possession of the valley below: 'Mission accomplished.' At 2.45 pm, the two met at the upper station. It was time to discuss the next phase: Mussolini's extraction.

Meanwhile, having secured the hostage, Skorzeny had begun fraternising with his Italian 'hosts' in the most cordial way imaginable; the officers were allowed to keep their sidearms, and Skorzeny distributed wine from the dining room to both his own men and the carabinieri. It was time to toast the Liberated One – and of course his Liberator. During this 40-minute interval, not once did Berlepsch go up to Room 201 to meet Skorzeny and Mussolini. He was seething with anger at being upstaged and having his orders insolently disregarded. Nonetheless, it was all smiles for the cameras. Mors had brought a movie cameraman from the Propaganda Kompanie, who filmed the weary Mussolini, unshaven and wearing an oversized dark coat, congratulating his liberators and shaking hands with his former captors. The two war correspondents took a seemingly endless round of snaps.

Any tensions so far were a mooncast-shadow compared with the furore that erupted next. The plan to extract Mussolini by cable car and road to L'Aquila air base was ruled out when Mors failed to establish radio contact with Student. That meant the three He 111s (two as decoys) could not be flown in. Plan B involved the two Fi-156 Fieseler Storchs, circling overhead in readiness. The first, flown by Oberfeldwebel Hundt, made a landing on some seemingly easy terrain near the lower cable car station, but badly damaged its undercarriage in the attempt, rendering it unfit for flight. That left the Storch piloted by Gerlach. At 2.50 pm, he made a perfect landing near the hotel, using a headwind and slight incline as natural braking, on a strip 35 metres long.

Gerlach's satisfaction was short-lived. Skorzeny told him there would be not one but two passengers taking off with him: Skorzeny himself was coming along to guarantee that Mussolini was brought safely into Hitler's presence.

This was definitely not part of the script. Student had acknowledged Skorzeny's role as Mussolini's escort under Plan A but, fatefully, hadn't made it clear how his role was to be fulfilled under Plan B. (One of the Storchs may have been originally designated as Skorzeny's transport.) Whatever happened, Skorzeny was not going to let his prize out of sight by taking the long, winding road back to Frascati while Mussolini flew on ahead.

Adding a passenger of Skorzeny's bulk to the Storch would test the little plane well beyond its normal operational capabilities. There wasn't even a seat for a second passenger, and Skorzeny would have to squeeze into the luggage compartment. It was an invitation to fatal disaster. Gerlach's colourful response to Skorzeny's suggestion can only be imagined. 'I had to take him aside for a short but tense discussion,' Skorzeny recalled. 'The strength of my arguments convinced him at last.' Whatever those arguments were, they certainly weren't the flimsy, self-serving ones he gave in his memoirs – that, if Gerlach went alone with the Duce and there was some mishap, 'all that was left for me was a bullet from my own revolver: Adolf Hitler would never forgive such an end to our venture.'[57] More likely, Skorzeny hinted at retribution from Himmler or the Führer if he were thwarted.

Presumably he also used the same arguments on Mors, who should have put a stop to Skorzeny's demented plan. Mors had his vulnerabilities, having once been caught badmouthing the Nazi regime; he was politically suspect and the Gestapo held a file on him. Or maybe he was simply glad to be rid of an increasingly tiresome colleague. Mors had done his duty in rescuing Mussolini; what happened next was, strictly speaking, none of his business.

Mussolini, who was an experienced pilot, wasn't enthusiastic about the getaway idea either. The apprehension on his face was captured in the news footage as Skorzeny helped him into his seat. But he was in no position to openly complain.

Gerlach got several paratroopers to hold the wings as he ran up the overloaded Storch's engine to near maximum. In normal conditions the plane needed 80 metres for take-off. Here the strip was barely 90 metres long and strewn with stones. The air was thin and at the end was a precipice. On Gerlach's word, the paratroopers let go of the wings, and the Storch lurched forward, wobbling across the uneven ground. 'But although our speed increased and we were rapidly approaching the end of the strip,' Skorzeny recalled, 'we failed to rise. I swayed about madly and we had hopped over many a boulder when a yawning gully appeared right in our path. I was just thinking that this really was the end when our bird suddenly rose into the air. I breathed a silent prayer of thanksgiving ... Veering left, we shot over the edge. I closed my eyes, held my breath and again awaited the inevitable end.'[58]

The plane plummeted into the abyss, Gerlach executing a deliberate nosedive to gain extra airspeed. He just managed to pull the Storch level in time. Seconds later, Radl and the others saw the plane climbing agonisingly slowly on the other side of the valley. Gerlach realised that the engine had starting malfunctioning after the strain of take-off.[59] He fought to keep the plane flying, but couldn't get it to climb higher than treetop level. He told his passengers he was flying low to avoid detection.

At 4.15 pm the Storch hobbled into Pratica di Mare, its port undercarriage having been damaged during take-off.[60] Another film crew was on hand to record the momentous landing and Mussolini's transfer to the waiting He 111.

* * *

It was after dark when the Heinkel touched down at Vienna. Then it was off to the Hotel Imperial. There, Skorzeny was reunited with his wife, Emmi, who had been invited at Himmler's suggestion. That night, Skorzeny received congratulations by telephone from Himmler, Göring and Keitel. To his surprise and delight, he and Emmi were visited in their room by the Vienna garrison's chief of staff, who, at Hitler's behest, bestowed on Skorzeny his Ritterkreuz.

As midnight struck, Skorzeny was telephoned by Hitler himself. He recalled the Führer's words: 'You have performed a military feat which will become part of history. You have given me back my friend Mussolini. I have awarded you the Ritterkreuz and promoted you to SS-Sturmbannführer. Heartiest congratulations.'[61]

The following morning, with Skorzeny still accompanying him, a refreshed Mussolini was reunited in Munich with his wife Donna Rachele and family, who had been sprung from house arrest at their country estate by the SS snatch squad originally assigned to Skorzeny.

Then it was off to the Wolfsschanze for an emotionally charged reunion with the Führer – with Skorzeny and Kaltenbrunner acting as Mussolini's personal escorts. In no way were the SS going to miss out milking every last drop of credit for 'their' coup de main. Equally keen to bask in the reflected glory was Hermann Göring: it was a God-given opportunity to restore the tarnished lustre of the Luftwaffe. Having hurried to the Wolfsschanze in a special train, he there and then conferred the Flugzeugführerabzeichen in Gold (Gold Medal of the Air Force) on the returning hero.[62]

The meeting of the two dictators was an anti-climax. Hitler may have had tears in his eyes when Mussolini stepped down from the plane, but what he unmistakably saw was a man tired of life, a dull-eyed, burnt-out case in a sombre suit, a former dictator now visibly unfit for purpose. Mussolini's only desire was to retreat to his country estate and play the retired philosopher-king – a gesture he felt would avert civil war in Italy. As far as Hitler was concerned, that was out of the question.

Germany had out-bluffed the Badoglio regime, which was now forced to take refuge in Brindisi. Although Kesselring's forces had penned the Allied invasion force into a couple of bridgeheads from which it would only emerge with the greatest difficulty, Hitler needed a political fig-leaf. A puppet regime headed by the Duce was what he had in mind. Within 11 days of being rescued, a reluctant Mussolini proclaimed the Italian Social Republic, based at Salò on Lake Garda. For the last 18 months of his life he lived in a gilded cage, monitored by SS guards. In a curious twist, his former captor Gueli became the RSI's head of security.

The extinction of Mussolini's hopes was the fulfilment of Otto Skorzeny's dreams. The Skorzeny myth soon began to take on a life of its own, backed by the powerful advocacy of Himmler, Kaltenbrunner, Schellenberg and Goebbels, whose weekly *Deutsche Wochenschau* newsreel featured the rescue prominently, with Skorzeny getting more screen time than anyone other than Mussolini himself. Skorzeny had sealed his future.

5

Special Ops and High-Value Targets

Determined to extract maximum leverage from Gran Sasso in their ongoing secret intelligence war with the Abwehr (which had performed lamentably in providing accurate information on Mussolini's whereabouts), the SS had been taking 'ownership' of the raid even before it happened, claiming that Skorzeny was to lead the mission.[1]

Goebbels, too, was desperate to exploit his advantage: lately, there had been so little other positive news to trumpet. 'There has hardly been a military event during the entire war that has so deeply stirred the emotions and evoked such human interest,' he confided to his diary. 'We are able to celebrate a first-class moral victory.'[2] It was propaganda on a plate. Skorzeny exactly fitted Goebbels' requirements for a hero. Six foot four and titanically built, with macho good looks and a powerful, well-timbred voice, he was the perfect Aryan specimen. The sabre scar added to his martial credibility. His relative obscurity made the legend easier to mould. Moreover, he was a member of the Waffen-SS – now becoming the regime's only reliable stay.

Hitler, having hand-picked Skorzeny for the mission, evidently believed he was responsible for its success. Could there be a more incontrovertible recommendation than that? The Reich urgently needed an uncomplicated Nietzschean superman. And it got one.

Resentment of Skorzeny's success in stealing the glory was necessarily muted, but bitterly felt. Long after the war, he would be regarded by many as a fraud who used his political connections to trade on other people's achievements and claim the credit for himself. Among Otto Skorzeny's natural gifts was a charismatic personality. He could turn on the husky radiance at a moment's notice. Even his critics acknowledged his persuasive powers: 'He was huge, robust, intelligent, but not intellectual,' recalled Arnold von Roon, a major on Student's staff. 'He was quite a charmer, too, and could be very persuasive.'[3]

One day after the Gran Sasso raid, the official German news agency issued a statement attributing the operation to the SS 'aided by members of the parachute troops'. Already Mors and his men had slipped into an ancillary role. They were beside themselves with anger when, on 14 September, at Goebbels behest, Skorzeny appeared on *Deutschlandsender* radio and announced himself as the man who had liberated Mussolini.[4] He even embellished his tale with a wholly fictitious gun battle.

Mors complained to Student, who complained to Göring, but Göring's stock had fallen after the abysmal failure of his Luftwaffe airbridge at Stalingrad earlier that year and his inability to protect Germany from Allied bombing. He quietly told Student to drop the issue. According to Roon, Student 'didn't want to get into a row with Göring ... So he never protested. He thought history would provide the truth.'[5] As a gesture, Göring sent a film crew out to Gran Sasso two weeks later. The SS commandos – who by now had returned to Germany – were excluded from the cast. Skorzeny noted in his memoirs: 'It was nice to hear that a Propaganda concern was on its way to Gran Sasso to make a belated film of the "actual attack". Unfortunately, I was not able to prevent these photographs appearing later in periodicals.'[6]

While Skorzeny and a number of his commandos were feted at the Berlin Sportpalast, Mors', Berlepsch's and Langguth's medals were awarded on a nondescript field in Italy. Mussolini presented all the key players with monogrammed gold watches. But while he personally awarded Skorzeny the Order of the Hundred Musketeers, he never even thanked Student.[7]

In fairness, without Skorzeny the Gran Sasso raid might never have taken place. He was at the heart of the intelligence-gathering mission. His methods were sometimes rather amateurish,[8] yet they delivered the result that mattered. And having had the luck to land first, he exploited the element of surprise to the full. His action was a heroic bluff: if the Italians had chosen to, they could have shot or taken hostage the entire SS team in the opening minutes. Skorzeny's order not to fire unless he specifically said so is, very likely, a critical reason why this did not happen. Had the operation gone fully to plan, with Berlepsch's paratroopers landing first, Fallschirmjäger doctrine was to fire first and ask questions later. The operation might well have succeeded, but at a higher cost to both sides, and with a lot less propaganda value as a result.

Almost by accident, Skorzeny had discovered a new truth about special operations; to the furtherance of purely military objectives he had added a political and public relations dimension. The lesson of Gran Sasso was that the successful capture or elimination of prominent individual targets, with minimum lethal force, can be worth a whole army. The ultimate non-team player had, in Operation *Eiche*, found his metier.

* * *

Gran Sasso whetted the appetite of Hitler and Himmler for further surgical operations. The same methods might be used not only to rescue but to eliminate high-value targets. Wavering allies could be brought to heel by kidnapping their heads of state. The more the Wehrmacht faltered, the more attractive such covert operations became. Soon, Skorzeny had on his desk proposals for the assassination of Churchill, Roosevelt and Stalin, and various other decapitation missions.

The SS paratroop unit which, a few months previously, had seemed such a pipe-dream, now took concrete form, the SS-Fallschirmjägerbataillon 500 becoming active in October 1943. It wasn't ideal – the thousand or so recruits were mostly SS delinquents from the prison at Chlum, and the unit came under the direct command of Waffen-SS headquarters rather than Skorzeny's. But at least the SS now had its own airborne capability.

Moreover, Skorzeny began to attract high-calibre military personnel of the type he had previously lacked. One was the iconic Brandenburger legend Oberleutnant Baron Adrian von Fölkersam, who joined in November 1943. He was an improbable-looking military hero – slightly built, callow-looking, and rather cerebral. Underneath, however, was a fierce Volksdeutsche* patriot.

Born in St Petersburg in 1914, Fölkersam came from a long line of German service aristocracy who had served the Czar. His grandfather was an admiral of the Russian fleet, and his great-grandfather a Russian general. His family, like

---

*   Ethnic Germans who were not a part of the Reich and therefore German citizens as such. The term Volksdeutsche is reputed to have been defined by Hitler himself, though the phenomenon of an ethnic German diaspora may be traced as far back as Catherine the Great (an ethnic German herself) and, remotely, to the Teutonic Knights during the Middle Ages.

most of the German Baltic gentry, had been traumatically affected by the Russian revolution, which left the young Adrian (or "Arik" as he was known to friends) with an abiding hatred of the Bolshevik regime. After studying economics at Vienna, Fölkersam returned to his family roots in Riga, Latvia, where he worked as a journalist for the *Rigasche Rundschau* – then the most influential newspaper in the Volksdeutsche world – where he made a name for himself as a politically committed and charismatic youth leader.[9]

On the outbreak of war he, like his younger brother Patrick, immediately joined the Brandenburgers (specifically, 2./Lehr-Regiment z.b.V. 800, of which most recruits were either German Balts or from the former German colonies).

By September 1942 Fölkersam had won the Ritterkreuz after leading a 'false flag' mission of breathtaking audacity that secured the vital Transcaucasus Maikop oilfields in advance of a panzer spearhead.

By November 1943 the division into which the Brandenburgers had been consolidated was no longer being used for special operations but to plug gaps in conventional forces, a sheer waste of their specialised skills. Fölkersam and ten other Brandenburgers had requested transfer to the SS commandos.

Despite some prejudice about the arrogance of the Junker class, Skorzeny 'took a great fancy to Fölkersam, both as a man and a soldier'. He 'felt sure that in a tight corner, I would certainly find him an experienced and valuable helper.'[10]

Fölkersam was a foil to many of Skorzeny's professional weaknesses. For a start, he had been trained as a general staff officer, so meticulous planning was second nature to him. Where Skorzeny was impetuous and always formulating grand ideas, Fölkersam was down-to-earth, considered and practical. There was a tussle with Canaris over the transfer from the Abwehr, but once on board, SS-Hauptsturmführer Fölkersam became Skorzeny's indispensable chief of staff. Just as Radl, Skorzeny's political deputy, was known in Amt VI as 'Skorzeny's Nanny', so the 'very sympathetic and modest' Fölkersam was nicknamed 'Skorzeny's Brain'.[11]

Recollections of Fölkersam, unlike those of Skorzeny, rarely depart from the reverential. Wolfgang Herfurth, whose job as a military clerk on the *Ia* headquarters staff brought him into regular contact with Fölkersam, remembers him as follows: 'He was the classic man of few words. He was able to see all the angles of a situation and could accurately distinguish the important from the unimportant. He was always sceptical of orders coming down from on high. Each order was analysed and tested to determine its feasibility. And he would then modify it without waiting for further approval.

He was very aware of the family traditions he represented. He was a self-conscious elitist and a devotee of the poetry of Stefan George* – which gave us something in common as human beings. He prepared all his commando missions with exacting role-plays and question-and-answer sessions that participants found far from easy. He put great emphasis on individual combat training and endurance tests. He was not an arrogant boss. He must have been very well respected.[12]

Hans-Dietrich Hossfelder, who had served with Fölkersam as a Brandenburger and later joined Skorzeny's commando unit, described Fölkersam as 'shy, very quiet and analytical to the final degree', whereas Skorzeny was 'very boisterous, always energetic and the life of any party and always the centre of attention. He had a massive ego but he was a damned good leader.'[13]

Hossfelder's admiration for Skorzeny was not an isolated opinion. Hans Post, who served later in SS-Jägerbataillon 502, was struck by Skorzeny's common touch. This extended to all-night drinking benders at Friedenthal: 'At the end, some time around 3 or 4 am, there were only five of us still compos mentis and upright, keeping Skorzeny company around the table. He seemed to be totally unaffected, shook our hands, climbed into his Porsche [sic] outside the door, and roared off to Berlin … He was … our pirate captain, rubbing his hands with glee and leading us into unheard of exploits.'[14]

* * *

Fölkersam's and Skorzeny's first mission together, in late November 1943, stemmed from Hitler's increasing paranoia about his allies.

Marshal Philippe Pétain had been reduced to figurehead status in the French Vichy regime, now under full German control. But like Mussolini, Pétain remained of enormous symbolic value in cementing German power. In late 1943, intelligence reports indicated that Pétain was preparing to defect to the Allies. It was believed that he was in league with General Charles de Gaulle, and that de Gaulle was planning to spring Pétain from his heavily guarded headquarters at the Hotel du Parc in the spa town of Vichy with a crack team of French and British paratroopers. Countermeasures were needed, and Skorzeny was to help implement them.

---

*   Stefan George (1868–1933), mystical and symbolist poet, anti-Nazi in orientation. Another great admirer of George's poetry was Oberst Claus Schenk Graf von Stauffenberg, Hitler's would-be assassin in July 1944.

After being drawn into inconclusive discussions in Paris with police chief SS-Brigadeführer Carl Oberg, and making an exasperated call to the Wolfsschanze, Skorzeny finally got his orders. Several police battalions – not under his control – were to mount a show of strength around Vichy. Ostensibly this was a traffic control exercise, a ruse which must have fooled no one. Skorzeny and Fölkersam, meanwhile, took up quarters in the centre of town with the aim of familiarising themselves (in mufti) with the layout of the Hotel du Parc and its environs.

Several Waffen-SS battalions, including Skorzeny's own, were put on standby outside the town. On receiving the order 'The Wolf Howls', Skorzeny and his units were to converge with the police battalions and form a ring of steel around Vichy to prevent anyone getting in or out. Skorzeny was tasked with personally securing and guarding Pétain. His orders were to spirit him to Paris (for which no worked-out plan was in place).

Skorzeny's worst fear was of a night attack. If a substantial force of two or three thousand enemy paratroopers landed around Vichy in the middle of the night, with Pétain's prior knowledge, 'they would surely be able to take him'.[15]

What no one apparently considered was the absurdity of the mooted Anglo-French operation. How exactly would the Allies extract their prize – and their raiding force – from the middle of securely held enemy territory? It would be all but impossible. In fact, the whole thing was a fantasy dreamt up by Hitler.

Luckily perhaps for Skorzeny, the Wolf never howled; the operation was abruptly cancelled on 2 December, and all units were recalled.

* * *

The Pétain affair underscores a view of Skorzeny as a 'rear area commando'[16] whose exploits deserve lesser consideration because they were essentially police operations carried out behind his own lines – a dirty-tricks operator in field-grey, to be contrasted with the Brandenburgers, who took suicidal risks behind enemy lines.

It is fairer to see Skorzeny as a pioneer, blending for the first time the military technique of special operations with explicit political objectives. The scope of his operations was limited by Germany's deteriorating military situation. By the time he emerged on the commando scene, frontiers were shrinking, resources were under increasing pressure, morale was slipping, and allies were readying themselves to defect. It is no accident that many of Skorzeny's missions had a defensive character to them. But his special forces did also carry out behind-the-lines operations.

One of the earliest was Operation *Weitsprung* (*Long Jump*), so named because it presented such a challenge to German intelligence. In mid-October 1943, the Germans learned of an impending summit of the Big Three – Stalin, Roosevelt and Churchill – to take place in Tehran about six weeks hence. The objective of *Weitsprung*, handed down directly from Hitler, was to liquidate all three leaders.

Right from the beginning, Skorzeny was downbeat about its prospect of success because of the difficulty of gathering good intelligence on the ground: 'Our contact man in Tehran, a captain of the Abwehr, passed me the information by radio via Istanbul: the yield was rather meagre.'[17] By Skorzeny's estimate, up to 200 top-quality troops would be required, plus aircraft and special vehicles, together with solid intelligence about the terrain and enemy security. 'I was able to learn almost nothing about this. Under such conditions of course there was not the least chance of success: the plan was impracticable.' He reported his concerns to Schellenberg and Hitler, and the Führer agreed. End of mission, or so Skorzeny would have us believe – and blame for its muddled conception neatly passed on to Schellenberg, who had been 'so enthusiastic about the idea'.[18]

However, according to Soviet NKVD* records, the operation went much further, and was only aborted after being compromised by Russian intelligence.

Legendary NKVD assassin Nikolai Kuznetsov regularly penetrated far behind enemy lines to eliminate high-level Nazi officials. His chosen method was to walk straight up to his victims, announce their death sentence, and then shoot them. Sometimes he obtained valuable intelligence in the process. During one of these operations, the blond, Aryan-looking Kuznetsov – posing as Oberleutnant Paul Siebert – discovered that Skorzeny was training an assassination squad near Vinnitsa in the Ukraine, and that their mission was to attack the Big Three conference.

The information came from a German intelligence officer, who unwittingly revealed to Kuznetsov that the mission was to kill Stalin and Churchill and kidnap Roosevelt, thereby turning the tide of the war.[19] NKVD headquarters stepped up security for the conference, putting intelligence officer Gevork Vartanyan's unit in charge. German influence was thought to be powerful in Tehran at the time, with Nazi agents impersonating German émigrés under the control of an effective field station run by Franz Mayer.[20]

According to the NKVD, Skorzeny's assassins were dropped by parachute near the town of Qom, 60 kilometres from Tehran. Vartanyan's team tracked

---

* Russian ministry of the interior, including the secret police.

them – armed to the teeth and travelling by camel – to a villa in Tehran which had been prepared for them by Mayer's people. The Russians monitored their radio traffic and learned that the Germans were preparing to fly in a second group of commandos, led in person by Skorzeny, who (the Russians believed) had previously visited Tehran to gather intelligence on the terrain.[21] All the members of the first team were arrested and turned. 'It was tempting to seize Skorzeny himself,' Vartanyan recalled, 'but the Big Three had already arrived in Tehran and we could not afford the risk.'[22] Instead, one of the Germans was coerced into sending a message that the mission had been a failure. Operation *Weitsprung* was aborted.

Or so said the NKVD's man on the ground. In fact, German intelligence capabilities in Iran were not strong, and Franz Mayer was, as it happened, hors de combat, having been arrested by the British earlier that year while masterminding Operation *Franz*. A different Soviet account had Tehran-based SD agents working with a separate task force of trained assassins, who were rapidly captured or killed.[23] British and American intelligence were never convinced by the NKVD's stories about *Weitsprung*. Stalin had every reason to scaremonger, in order to take firmer control of security measures (and the agenda) at the conference. Sir Kenneth Strong, a senior British wartime intelligence officer (quoted by Skorzeny) suspected that 'the Russians used this alleged plot as an excuse to move Roosevelt to a villa near the Soviet embassy in Tehran; and you can be sure that this villa was bristling with microphones.'[24]

* * *

Around the same time as the abortive Pétain and *Weitsprung* missions, Skorzeny embarked on an operation so clandestine and so dark in its purpose that he omitted it from his memoirs. Operation *Peter* was to come close to getting him indicted for war crimes.

Hitler had tried to turn Denmark into a model of collaboration, to showcase how humanely the Reich could run its occupied countries. But by early 1943, tired of Hitler's broken promises and depredations, the Danes were fielding an increasingly effective resistance movement – abetted by British intelligence and special forces. Hitler responded with a massive deployment of force – 50,000 troops badly needed on the Eastern Front – and a ferocious police crackdown, mostly on Danish Jews.

Still the acts of sabotage proliferated. By autumn 1943 the local security police chief, SS-Standartenführer Rudolf Mildner, had to admit the situation was out of control. Far from collaborating with him, the Danish police were actively supporting the resistance. Hitler decided on a change of strategy: fighting terror with terror, in the belief that the Danish people would compel their police force to take zero-tolerance countermeasures against the insurgents. He recommended a campaign against Danish cultural institutions, spiced up with targeted assassinations. Mildner complained to Himmler that he was unable to carry out such measures as his men were too few and had no training in sabotage. The solution was obvious: Skorzeny's commandos.[25]

Skorzeny and Karl Radl later tried to minimise their personal responsibility for the mission they were assigned by Himmler in December 1943. They implied that the selected personnel were drawn from an intake that preceded Skorzeny's arrival at Amt VI-S, namely SS-Sonderlehrgang 'Oranienburg'. Skorzeny also claimed he was absent from Friedenthal when the orders came in and denied actively participating: 'I did not give a single order, neither in the planning nor the preparation, nor the execution; and didn't even know beforehand anything about the planning or the execution.'[26] Radl later asserted that it was Fölkersam who selected the men from Amt VI-S and dispatched them to Copenhagen (a rather convenient excuse, since by that time Fölkersam was long dead).

According to Radl, the Sonderkommando Dänemark team comprised an officer and six NCOs from Amt VI-S, with Alfred Naujocks from Amt IV in charge.[27] He then compromised his testimony (to post-war Allied interrogators) by revealing, under pressure, some identities: 'Fölkersam's Sonderkommando Dänemark team comprised: U/Stuf Peter; O/Schrf Fritz Himmel; O/Schrf Ludwig Huf; U/Schrf Walther Gläsner, U/Schrf Hans Holzer; and U/Schrf Adolf Römer.'[28] If some of these names seem familiar, it is precisely because they were not from an intake preceding Skorzeny's arrival at Amt VI-S, but some of his recently recruited 'chums' on the Gran Sasso mission. It beggars belief that Skorzeny knew nothing about what was going on. The evidence that nails his complicity is that the operational leader of the group, 'Untersturmführer Peter Schäfer', was an alias of Otto Schwerdt, who had been Skorzeny's right-hand man throughout the Gran Sasso raid.[29]

The unit was supplied with false passports identifying them as commercial travellers. Amt VI-F equipped them with blackjacks and silenced pistols that fired British ammunition, to make it look as if the Danish resistance was responsible for any killings they perpetrated. The *Peter* group crossed the Danish border on 28 December. They were soon joined by Gestapo agent Jacob Karstensen, who was assigned to them as an interpreter.[30] Within days they were in action.

Their first victim was Christian Damm, a Danish journalist who had written an exposé of Danish concentration camp conditions which had been smuggled past the authorities to Britain. On 30 December, just as Damm was putting the latest edition of his underground newspaper to bed, three men burst into his office and attacked him. They were Schwerdt, Karstensen and SS-Unterscharführer Walther Gläsner. Schwerdt pulled his pistol, shot Damm twice and left him for dead.

Miraculously, Damm survived – unlike their next victim, Kaj Munk, a noted Danish poet, priest and member of the underground. Around 4 January 1944, Schwerdt, Karstensen and SS-Oberscharführer Anton Gföller (another Gran Sasso veteran) abducted Munk from his home, drove him to the middle of the countryside and shot him. When Schwerdt was positive Munk was dead, he pulled a sign out of his pocket and pinned it to the body. It read: 'Swine, you worked for Germany just the same.'[31]

The *Peter* group was active in Denmark for most of that year, carrying out terrorist actions against cultural institutions and national landmarks (including Tivoli, Odin's tower in Odense and Nordisk Film), as well as cinemas and theatres, newspapers, publishers and key industrial facilities (such as Tuborg, ØK and Bang & Olufsen). They also bombed public transport. From February to August 1944, regular reports were submitted to Amt IV and Amt VI, where they were read by Schellenberg, Skorzeny, Radl and Fölkersam. In July 1944 it was calculated that the number of 'Danish acts of terrorism' was six to eight times greater than Operation *Peter*'s. Not only was the operation failing in its own terms, it was also getting out of control.

Skorzeny wanted out, and he got Radl to draw up a memorandum for Amt IV to the effect that VI-S should be excluded from further operations. By September 1944 most, but not all, of the VI-S men had been returned to other duties.

One temporary exception was the group leader. Schwerdt was not relieved until 10 November. After the war, he was on Denmark's 'most wanted' list. During his subsequent trial, he freely admitted being commander of the Sonderkommando Dänemark. He stated that every one of his actions was vetted by the highest German authorities in Denmark, and that every person in the group (which included a number of Danes) understood and accepted that the mission was to spread terror, even if that meant killing innocent civilians.[32]

The Danish post-war authorities would dearly have loved to get their hands on Skorzeny and Radl as well. To this day, the extent of Skorzeny's culpability is an open question.[33]

* * *

On 12 February 1944 Hitler decreed that the Abwehr should be dissolved and its elements subsumed into the SD.[34] A triumphant moment, it might be thought, for Himmler, Kaltenbrunner, Schellenberg and Skorzeny himself. So it was, until the complex practicalities of integration became apparent. Not for many months would the problem begin to be resolved. The situation was aggravated by internal rivalries and enmities – principally between Schellenberg and Kaltenbrunner. In spring 1944 an incident involving Skorzeny turned a simmering feud into an open rift.

On the night of 27–28 April 1944, ace night-fighter pilot Wilhelm Johnen crash-landed his damaged Messerschmitt Me 110 G-4 at Zürich-Dubendorf in neutral Switzerland. Although Johnen and his crew were quickly repatriated, the plane was another matter. Under international law, the Swiss had the right to repair the Me 110 and put it back into service. The Germans could not allow that; on board was the latest interceptor radar equipment and a sophisticated upward-pointing gun installation (known as *Schräge Musik*) which had proved highly effective in bringing down Allied bombers. The plane had to be recovered or destroyed at all costs. The matter was so sensitive that it went all the way up to Hitler.

The first Schellenberg knew of this was when he was awoken by a telephone call in the early hours of the morning.[35] He was summoned without delay to a small inn near Wannsee, where a conference was being chaired by Skorzeny under orders from Hitler and Kaltenbrunner. Present were many high-ranking Luftwaffe officers, including the German air attaché from Bern. With some incredulity and even more dismay, Schellenberg discovered that the meeting was no more than a rubber-stamping procedure, orchestrated by Kaltenbrunner and Skorzeny, to justify a parachute raid the following day on the Swiss airfield, with the objective of destroying the plane.

Only with great difficulty did Schellenberg manage to dismantle this hamfisted plan – pointing out in no uncertain terms that it might cause an irretrievable breakdown in relations between the two countries.[36]

After several weeks of diplomatic negotiations the plane was destroyed in the presence of German witnesses, in return for the sale to Switzerland of 12 new Messerschmitt Me 109 fighters. Schellenberg may have saved the peace, but a thwarted and no doubt humiliated Skorzeny had been left fuming.[37] Skorzeny would hold a grudge against Schellenberg ever after. The following year Skorzeny was to manipulate his inside track with Kaltenbrunner to unseat Schellenberg.

* * *

By spring 1944 Hitler was facing a serious problem in the Balkans, the back door to the Eastern Front. The problem was Yugoslavian partisan leader Josip Broz Tito.

Hitler's petulant decision to invade Yugoslavia in April 1941 had turned out to be a grave strategic mistake. German occupation of the Balkans protected the rear of Operation *Barbarossa*, but at a huge cost. Hitler had ceded a certain amount of autonomy to ethnically defined client states – primarily Ante Pavelić's Ustaše Fascist government in Croatia and the regime of General Nedić in Serbia – while farming out garrison duties to Axis troops from Italy, Hungary and Bulgaria. The outcome was disastrous. The region had plunged into turmoil, stoked by the Ustaše's reign of terror. Festering resentment crystallised into savage guerrilla warfare, to which the mountainous and wooded terrain of Yugoslavia was perfectly suited.

By late 1943, Tito was in the ascendant, with a partisan army of close to 300,000 which was proving doggedly resistant to all German efforts to crush it. The know-how of a hardened professional soldier and the discipline of being a Communist Party leader gave Tito an edge in guerrilla warfare. A commanding personality and the pan-nationalist appeal of his cause enhanced his magnetism.

Successive German commanders had done all they could to stamp out Tito's activities by attacking his suspected hideouts. Yet no matter how many specialist units, armoured vehicles or bombers they deployed, Tito and his partisans always escaped to fight another day.

The situation became critical in autumn 1943. The Wehrmacht's difficulties in covering their retreat in the Ukraine were compounded by Italy pulling out of the war. Overnight, Germany found itself 14 divisions down in the Balkans. Tito managed to disarm ten of them. Worst of all, Churchill at this point gave his unequivocal backing to Tito, which meant the presence of a British military mission coordinating combined special operations, and an endless resupply of armaments. Hitler's nightmare was that the Allies might use the Dalmatian coastline to open another front.

Generalfeldmarschall Maximilian von Weichs – who controlled German forces in the region – swallowed his aristocratic distaste for espionage and began to invest in human intelligence. Instead of annihilating partisan forces, the Wehrmacht – with Hitler's active backing – would now concentrate on eliminating their command and control structure. No matter the cost, the Germans must kill or capture Tito.

Only with the aid of accurate intelligence could German special forces hope to pinpoint and eliminate their target. How were they going to achieve this?

The German commander on the ground, Generaloberst Lothar Rendulic, was a Croat who knew the terrain and the people intimately. He had at his disposal three principal intelligence sources. The first was Abwehr Frontaufklärungstruppe (FAT) 216, comprising agent handlers charged with cultivating relationships with local communities and inserting agents. They proved to be of little practical value in the forthcoming operation to hunt down Tito.

The second, distinctly more useful, source was a Brandenburg detachment commanded by Oberleutnant Hans Kirchner. Kirchner's forward reconnaissance team correctly identified Tito's whereabouts at Jajce, near Banja Luka, in November 1943. But Rendulic chose to ignore the lead. In February 1944 Kirchner's unit was beefed up and reorganised as Verband Wildschütz, under the command of Major Ernst Benesch. Using signals intercepts, they successfully tracked down Tito's headquarters to the small logging town of Drvar. However, Tito's precise whereabouts remained elusive.

The third source of intelligence was SD-Ausland, which was completely outside Rendulic's control and would very likely lead to Otto Skorzeny's unpopular* Amt VI-S unit being directly involved in Tito's capture.

Skorzeny was late on the scene (having until now been sidelined by Rendulic). He arrived in Belgrade in April 1944 to begin Operation *Rösselsprung* (*Knight's Move*) in cooperation with a reluctant army command.

Amt VI-S had a head start in tracking down Tito, having previously devised its own kidnap plan back in January, under the codename 'Theodor'. The operation, led by SS-Hauptsturmführer Rupert Mandl, a Balkans expert, involved close cooperation with 'Croat gangs', who were supplied with arms, money and wireless sets. Radl later claimed that there was no connection between *Theodor* and *Rösselsprung*. That may well have been wisdom after the event.[38]

Mandl's expert briefing and Hitler's blessing should have given Skorzeny a trump card in dealing with Rendulic, but once in Belgrade he became frustrated by the poor intelligence he was receiving from the Abwehr and SD. He decided to improvise, driving to Zagreb in order to set up his own intelligence service. It was a hazardous, typically Skorzeny, enterprise, the roads

> controlled by the partisans. We had in fact encountered a group of bearded partisans, their rifles under their arms. We also had our machine pistols

---

*   Unpopular with the Wehrmacht, following Skorzeny's behaviour at Gran Sasso.

on the floor of the car – invisible from outside, with the safety catches on 'fire'. It was immediately obvious to me that we had committed an act of carelessness that could have had disastrous consequences: 'Tito captures Skorzeny!', a lovely headline for the *Daily Mirror* in 1944.[39]

Insouciantly, Skorzeny and his Waffen-SS officers made the journey in a Mercedes – a sure giveaway of their German identity.[40]

The escapade served a useful purpose, however. He set up three intelligence nets staffed by his own officers working independently of each other, and then returned to Berlin. Before long, as in the lead-up to Gran Sasso, the impromptu intelligence network bore fruit. A deserter named Tetaric from Tito's I Proletarian Corps revealed that partisan forces – numbering about 6,000 – were hunkered down in the Drvar area. Tito's headquarters were located in a cave 20 metres up a cliff, about a kilometre to the north, guarded by a battalion of 350 men. (In fact this was an underestimate; partisan forces were at least double that number.)[41]

Skorzeny's initial plan was to infiltrate a small force, disguised as partisans and led by himself, into Tito's headquarters and make the snatch. Just how evolved the operational plan became is not known, because when Fölkersam was sent to liaise with Rendulic he was met with an icy rebuff, killing the Skorzeny plan stone dead. It seems that Rendulic and Generalfeldmarschall von Weichs were already fully committed to an operational plan of their own, which excluded Skorzeny and his commandos from any role.

After a bombing raid on the target area in Drvar, the set piece of the operation was to be an airborne assault involving 650 SS-Fallschirmjäger paratroopers (on their maiden outing), about half dropped by parachute and the rest coming in by glider. A second wave of 220 paratroopers was to be dropped hours later for mopping-up operations. In an echo of Gran Sasso, a Fieseler Storch would spirit the captured Tito away. Simultaneously, XV. Gebirgskorps was to converge on Drvar to relieve the triumphant paratroopers. The mission was executed on 25 May. In the event it was let down by faulty intelligence and poor communication. Ignorant of the cave, and believing that Tito's HQ was in Drvar itself, the paratroopers took up a position in the town cemetery.[42] Although they overran opposition in Drvar fairly rapidly, they had no effective alternative plan once they realised Tito wasn't there. Realising their mistake, they began a bloody slog up the hillside towards the cave. The paratroopers, lightly armed and with insufficient air cover, took heavy casualties and failed to capture Tito's HQ.

Their sacrifice and near-success were, in any case, immaterial because the bird had long flown. All the Germans got for their pains was Tito's new marshal's uniform, which had been waiting in Drvar for tailoring alterations, and three British journalists, one of whom later escaped. The retreat from the cave back to the cemetery, to await relief by German ground forces, was as bloody as the advance. The Fieseler Storch came in handy for shipping casualties from the battlefield. So heavy were the casualties that by the time German reinforcements reached Drvar, only 200 paratroopers remained in action.

Tito was now well on his way to freedom. On 3 June he was picked up by an Allied aircraft and by 6 June had safely ensconced himself on the island of Vis off the Dalmatian coast, where he re-established his headquarters. Drvar reverted to partisan control within a few weeks.

Rösselsprung went disastrously wrong, yet came within an ace of success. Skorzeny's information about Tito's whereabouts wasn't perfect – his was simply the best available. His organisation alone had identified the cave near Drvar as Tito's real headquarters, yet had failed for one reason or another to communicate it to Rendulic. By 25 May Tito had, in any case, relocated to another cave in the village of Bastasi, 5 kilometres west of Drvar, sleeping there overnight and commuting to the cave near Drvar by day. Partisan intelligence was well aware of SS-Fallschirmjägerbataillon 500 massing nearby, and the imminence of a German assault was further signalled by the presence of a spotter plane circling Drvar on 22 May. Hence Tito's decision to relocate his headquarters.

Even so, the partisans were strangely complacent. Tito's chief of staff, Arso Jovanovic, swore that an airborne assault was impossible only a day before it happened.[43] And Tito himself adopted the same cavalier attitude. On the night of 24 May he had been celebrating his 52nd birthday at the cave in Drvar and – presumably hungover – elected to stay the night there. So, by coincidence, Tito was in fact present in the cave near Drvar on the day of the operation. Had the Germans targeted the cave rather than the town, the outcome of *Rösselsprung* might have been very different.

But the fact is, inter-service rivalry fatally compromised the raid before it began. The army resented interference from the roving SS political intelligence service.[44] There could well have been a personal dimension to this resentment. When Fölkersam presented Skorzeny's plan to Rendulic, it may be that Rendulic feared his whole operation would be hijacked by the outsized hero of Gran Sasso. Skorzeny certainly thought so, claiming that Rendulic 'saw in me only an undesirable competitor', so that 'through the petty jealousy of an officer avid of laurels, a large-scale project – which, if successful, might have had a far-reaching effect – was doomed to

As a student Skorzeny proved an exceptional duellist. In Mensur, how you deal with pain is even more important than winning. He fought 14 combats, an usually high number, receiving his trademark injury during the tenth, in 1928. Skorzeny likened duelling to a kind of Spartan discipline, with lessons for warfare. (SZ Photo/Süddeutsche Zeitung Photo)

'Der Duce ist frei': Skorzeny moves centre stage as 'The Liberator of Mussolini'. To his right is Major Harald Mors, the man who actually planned the rescue operation. To the left of Mussolini is Otto Schwerdt, who later headed the Sonderdänemark death squad. Far right is Karl Radl, Skorzeny's 'adjutant'. (Bundesarchiv, Bild 101I-567-1503C-15, Fotograf: Toni Schneiders)

Mussolini aghast: A bulky Skorzeny, standing behind him in the getaway Fieseler Storch, has just announced that he is coming along for the ride. The Storch had been designed for only one passenger, and its pilot, Heinrich Gerlach, was already facing an extremely hazardous mountain-top take-off. (Roger Viollet/Getty)

Seen here on the right is Kurt Student, overall commander of Operation *Eiche*. The rescue of Mussolini was a tiresome, politically motivated distraction at a time when his main preoccupation was securing Rome against an Allied invasion. He was prepared to cede the initial legwork to Skorzeny and the SS, but not the ensuing glory. (Bundesarchiv, Bild 146-1979-128-26, Fotograf: o.Ang.)

The Lion of Gran Sasso. Skorzeny's meteoric rise to fame was partly a matter of luck, but the SS were determined to milk every last drop of acclaim. Skorzeny, at the Wolfsschanze with Hitler after receiving his Ritterkreuz, is accompanied by Ernst Kaltenbrunner, his patron and – as head of the RSHA – his ultimate boss. (NARA)

'The Liberator of Mussolini' is seen here posing with his inner circle of Gran Sasso 'chums'. From left to right: Skorzeny, Robert Warger, Bernhard Cieslewitz, Ulrich Mendl, Schwerdt and Radl. This photo was taken in autumn 1943, shortly after Skorzeny's Sonderverband had moved to Friedenthal. (Sammlung Megele/Süddeutsche Zeitung Photo)

RSHA high command. From second left to right: Arthur Nebe, head of the Kripo (in full profile); Reichsführer-SS Heinrich Himmler; Reinhard Heydrich, head of the RSHA; and Heinrich Müller, head of the Gestapo. The photo dates to November 1939. On the far left is Franz Huber, head of the Austrian Sipo. Nebe later joined the July Plot and for a time evaded arrest and execution. (ullstein bild via Getty)

Walter Schellenberg, head of the SS foreign intelligence service. Youthful, suave, intelligent and infinitely pliable in pursuit of his aims, Schellenberg was Skorzeny's immediate boss. They hated each other. (Bettmann/Getty)

Admiral Wilhelm Canaris, head of the Abwehr, Nazi Germany's biggest and best-resourced intelligence service. Skorzeny suspected Canaris of treachery, and he was not alone. When in 1944 Canaris came a cropper, Schellenberg scooped up the prize and began building a unified intelligence service under SS direction. (Popperfoto/Getty)

Ernst Kaltenbrunner, RSHA chief from 1943. Though no match for his predecessor Heydrich in intellect, he proved his equal in brutality and ruthlessness. Kaltenbrunner saw Skorzeny, whose career he had boosted, as a reliable placeman who would bolster his own position. In this he was wrong. (Mondadori Portfolio via Getty)

The Tehran Conference 1943. The aim of Operation *Weitsprung* was to abduct or kill the Big Three: Stalin, Roosevelt and Churchill. Skorzeny insisted the Germans never seriously planned any such ambitious undertaking, but the Russians continue to claim otherwise. (Bettmann/Getty)

Marshal Tito (Josip Broz), seen here (right) with staff and advisers at his headquarters near Drvar shortly before Operation *Rösselsprung* in May 1944. Skorzeny acquired intelligence that might, accidentally, have led to Tito's capture. But German inter-service rivalry ensured that Tito narrowly escaped imprisonment or death. (Keystone-France/Gamma-Rapho via Getty)

lamentable failure'.[45] 'An officer avid of laurels' – a little rich coming from Skorzeny.

More likely there were faults on both sides. Skorzeny doesn't seem to have passed the crucial intelligence derived from Tetaric to either the Brandenburger or FAT 216 sources. The operational commanders of both were, unlike himself, attached to the SS paratroopers for the duration of the operation, and evidently weren't aware of the Drvar cave.

In the last analysis, either Rendulic deliberately ignored what Skorzeny had to offer or Skorzeny, in a fit of pique because his services had been rejected, chose to withhold vital intelligence. There is no conclusive evidence either way.

Even though the operation miscarried, there was a hidden dividend for Skorzeny, who successfully distanced himself from the fiasco. Within a few months a completely rebuilt SS paratroop battalion would be his to command. And many more Brandenburgers, finally severed from the utterly discredited Abwehr, would transfer to his expanded special forces operation – among them, Major Benesch and Oberleutnant Kirchner. Later, they would be joined by Oberstleutnant Wilhelm Walther, commanding officer of the Brandenburg regiment that came to the relief of the beleaguered SS paratroopers in Drvar, who would become Skorzeny's last chief of staff.[46]

6

Miracle Weapons

Karl Radl came to regard Skorzeny – for all his dynamism – as an inadequate leader whose flaws became more evident over time.[1] Skorzeny could not abide administrative detail of any kind, rarely read reports properly and hardly ever compiled them himself. As a result, 'his gullibility and enthusiasm led him to believe every dressed-up report submitted by his ambitious inferiors' – including, presumably, Radl himself. Skorzeny was a leader who was increasingly out of touch with the real progress of missions and the true state of numbers deployed on the ground.

As a man who liked to lead from the front, he was frequently absent from Friedenthal on active missions and, according to Radl, 'Hitler and Himmler used him for all sorts of special missions at the expense of the agencies he was supposed to be organising.'

Things only began to go to pieces, however, in early 1944 when Skorzeny – with Hitler's enthusiastic backing – became the obsessive chief exponent of the concept of *Sonderkampf* – 'special warfare'.[2]

By now, he had come to the reluctant conclusion there would be no final victory unless Germany unleashed new weapons of mass terror. We have already seen how the engineer in Skorzeny was preoccupied with the enemy's perceived superiority in commando assault weapons. He may not have convinced the general staff of the merits of the British Sten gun silencer and the silenced one-shot assassin's pistol he had captured, but that did not mean he gave up experimenting on his own account.

One consequence of this was the relationship he struck up with SS-Sturmbannführer Dr Albert Widmann, Head of Section VD-2 (Chemistry and Biology) of the Kriminaltechnische Institut der Sicherheitspolizei (KTI)*. Widmann was a technocrat, careless of the ethical ramifications of his experiments, which included euthanasia techniques such as gas and explosives. As an employee of Amt V (Kripo) Widmann was frequently called upon to investigate acts of sabotage, and in this capacity had amassed considerable experience of enemy techniques.

Exploiting Widmann's connoisseurship and natural curiosity, Skorzeny persuaded him to participate, unofficially, in a number of Amt VI-S projects. These included back-engineering the British Welrod pistol, manufacturing parts for a silencer-equipped Sten, devising specialist hard plastic explosives that could be drilled, threaded and milled, and – most controversially – the development of aconite nitrate poison bullets.

Skorzeny's appetite for more sophisticated special weapons was whetted by contact with Prince Junio Valerio Borghese, who was equally renowned for his heroic exploits and hard-line Fascist beliefs. Originally a submarine captain, he had developed a pioneering naval commando unit, the Decima Flottiglia Mezzi d'Assalto (10th Assault Vehicle Flotilla or X-MAS). His frogmen were trained in the use of a variety of specialist underwater weapons, primarily mini-submarines. Borghese's best-known exploit had been the near destruction in December 1941 of two Royal Navy battleships anchored in Alexandria harbour, by means of 'human torpedoes'. When Italy went over to the Allies, Borghese and most of his unit defected to Mussolini's Social Republic, which meant they came directly under German orders for the first time. By November 1943, their operations had been wholly integrated into the German navy's Kommando der Kleinkampfverbände der Kriegsmarine (KdK or K-Verbände)†.

The KdK was the maritime and riverine counterpart to Skorzeny's commando forces on land. After the effective destruction of the navy's 'big guns' – its capital ships and U-boats – during the summer of 1943, the Kriegsmarine high command turned to targeted sabotage missions as a means of offsetting their loss. The man masterminding this *Kleinkrieg* strategy was Admiral Hellmuth Heye, a Ritterkreuz holder and former commander of the heavy cruiser the *Admiral Hipper*.

Skorzeny later professed admiration for Heye as 'a seaman in the best sense of the word and a first-class tactician'.[3] Yet they were improbable bedfellows.

---

*   Technical Institute for the Detection of Crime

†   Germany Navy special units, literally 'small combat units of the German Navy'

Heye came from just the sort of traditional Prussian background that Skorzeny despised. While Heye seems to have genuinely respected Skorzeny's relentless vitality and willingness to challenge conventional military thinking, his real reason for wanting to collaborate was more complex and cynical. On the one hand, he needed recruits for what were effectively suicide missions (*Totaleinsatz*), and insufficient volunteers were forthcoming from the navy. Skorzeny, he rightly felt, could help to supply this deficit with suitably motivated SS men. On the other, according to Radl, 'he wanted to use Skorzeny for procuring the necessary material for the KdK training schools', exploiting Skorzeny's much-vaunted hotline to Himmler and Hitler.[4]

Accordingly, the two began cooperating on an informal basis late in 1943, Skorzeny initially sending Heye up to 30 'volunteers' from SS-Jägerbataillon 502 for specialist navy training.[5]

By the time of Heye's formal appointment as commander of KdK on 20 April 1944, Skorzeny had been nominally accorded equal status in forging the new commando force.[6] In reality, Heye called most of the shots and was careful to conceal the SS recruitment programme from his fellow naval officers, out of respect for service sensitivities.

This proved no easy task once Himmler became involved. The Reichsführer insisted that Skorzeny restrict himself to recruiting probationary (convict) SS soldiers – for fear of depriving the Eastern Front of the Waffen-SS's finest. Skorzeny, knowing full well the row that would erupt were the truth to get out, agreed only with the greatest reluctance. The probationers had to participate in a rigorous screening course at the barracks of the 1. SS-Panzerdivision 'Leibstandarte-SS Adolf Hitler', at the end of which about 25 per cent (around 150 men) were selected. Only after a struggle did Skorzeny succeed in persuading Himmler to recruit more widely from the Wehrmacht. Thereafter, his trusted aide Werner Hunke was put in charge of the recruitment drive.

Initially, much of the training was conducted in Borghese's former bases in northern Italy at Valdagno, Venice, Lake Como and Spezia. As the war ground on, these were replaced by securer bases at Bad Tölz and the Dianabad in Vienna. By mid-1944, the attempt to combine the Italian and German naval commando operations had broken down, and some of Borghese's unit subsequently defected to the pro-Allied partisans. However, the German side of the scheme kept going, and Skorzeny and Borghese remained in contact.

Though they owed much to Borghese's innovations, German naval stealth-weapons soon developed a sophistication of their own. The Linsen exploding motor-boats, for example, could attain a maximum speed of over 60 kilometres per hour (remarkable for the time). They were constructed of wood, about 5.75 metres long and were ultra low-profile to avoid radar detection. They carried up to 400 kilograms of explosive packed in the stern, and suspended just outside the top of the bow was a wrap-around bar of sprung steel that, when compressed against the front of the boat, created a live circuit. This triggered a small charge in the bow that blew off the front of the boat. As it sank beneath its target, the delayed main charge went off, inflicting (it was anticipated) crippling damage on the hull of the enemy vessel. They were employed in a formation of three, each with its own pilot. Two boats loaded with explosive were preceded by a lead, crewed by a commander and two radio operators. On attacking, the three boats would rush towards their target at top speed. Less than a kilometre out, the pilots of the two explosive boats, having made last-minute adjustments to their course, would eject, leaving the radio controllers to guide the boats to their target. Mission accomplished, the attack commander would then return to pick up his jettisoned crew.

More effective were the manned torpedoes. The best-known and cheapest to construct was the Neger, a live projectile containing over 600 kilograms of high explosive fitted beneath the carcass of an upper torpedo containing the pilot. Having approached as near as possible to his target, the pilot released the lower torpedo, turned and 'with God's help' (as Skorzeny put it)[7] made his escape. The pilots coped with the cramped, claustrophobic conditions and long hours of solitude by being pumped up with a drug cocktail called DIX, the active ingredients of which included morphine and cocaine.[8]

The first Neger assault was carried out against Allied shipping off the Anzio bridgehead during March 1944. It was a disaster. No ships were sunk and many of the human torpedoes were lost. By June, the focus of operations had switched to northern France – the aim being to disrupt Allied shipping supporting the D-Day landings. An initial attack on 5–6 July, operating out of the Seine estuary and involving 26 Negers, managed to sink two minesweepers and irreparably damage the destroyer HMS *Trollope*. A second mission on the following night was more ill-starred: 21 Negers and all but two of their crews were lost, but a second minesweeper and a Polish cruiser[9] were destroyed nonetheless. The biggest single achievement was the sinking of the cruiser HMS *Durban*, the destroyer *Quorn*, and five other vessels by a mass attack of 58 human torpedoes, 16 control motorboats guiding 28 explosive boats, plus speed boats and low-flying aircraft.[10]

By the end of August, it was all but over for Germany's naval stealth weapons. The element of surprise having dissolved, the Allies came to recognise the deadly Neger jellyfish by their floating cupolas, and they were pounded on sight by ships' guns and aircraft, with horrific consequences for those inside. The Germans were obliged to use decoy cupolas as a diversion. More importantly, the Allies had also broken out of their D-Day beachhead, threatening the Normandy ports from which these short-range vessels operated. What could be recovered of the special weapons fleets was transported south to harry the Allies from northern Italy, with negligible results.

Skorzeny always insisted that these naval 'trip to heaven' operations fell well short of suicide missions.[11] It is hard to agree with him; in the year to April 1945, KdK mounted 12 major sorties using 264 human torpedoes, of which 162 were lost and 150 pilots killed.[12]

More successful was KdK's Kampfschwimmer (frogmen) formation, which played a heroic role in impeding the Allied advance out of the D-Day beachhead by blowing up bridges and destroying gun emplacements that had fallen into enemy hands. Of the frogmen's 24 missions during summer 1944, most were successful, with relatively few casualties.

Attached to the unit was Skorzeny's KdK pointman, SS-Untersturmführer Walter Schreiber. By October he was leader of the SS-Kampfschwimmergruppe section of Skorzeny's newly formed SS-Jagdeinsatz Donau unit.[13] As the Allied invasion force swept northwards through Holland to the Rhine, Schreiber led two near-suicidal frogman commando raids. His attempt to mine the bridge at Nijmegen in the wake of Operation *Market Garden* was described in Britain as 'one of the most daring operations of the war'.[14] The other was an attempt to destroy a bridge at Remagen on 17 March 1945, in a last-ditch effort to thwart the Americans crossing the Rhine.

Heye and Skorzeny's Faustian pact was eventually outed by accident, with inevitable consequences. According to Friedrich Böhme, appointed chief of Kommando Stab West in June 1944, who himself was not initially aware of the situation:

The presence of SS men among the fighting personnel of K-Verbände first came to light in June 1944 when Böhme accompanied a party of 8 men to Berlin to receive decorations. During the proceedings, Skorzeny appeared and admitted that four of the men were members of the SS.

Böhme was subsequently informed by Admiral Heye that an arrangement had been made between himself and Skorzeny in May 1944 whereby KdK would absorb SS men under sentence who would be willing to undertake suicidal actions [*Totaleinsatz*] on a voluntary basis as a form of probation.

The Flotilla in KdK-Stab Sued subsequently received a number of men ... without knowing their real origin.[15]

How many of these men were actually probationers as opposed to Waffen-SS volunteers is not known.[16] The fact is, the rumour got out and it was not appreciated. Kriegsmarine officers resented the slight to honourable navy traditions implied by the employment of such men, forcing Heye – who in any case had by now got what he wanted from Skorzeny[17] – to purge at least 55 SS men from six commando units at the end of November 1944.[18] Nevertheless, informal cooperation continued. At Remagen, Schreiber and his frogmen fought alongside the Kriegsmarine's 'Puma' group.

* * *

The disproportionate havoc created by KdK human torpedoes persuaded Skorzeny that there must be an aerial equivalent capable of inspiring still greater terror: a piloted version of the V-1 flying bomb.

Amt VI-S had a close if sometimes fractious relationship with the Luftwaffe special unit Kampfgeschwader 200 (KG 200), which undertook various difficult or experimental missions. Skorzeny's first contact had been in late summer 1943 with the unit's predecessor, Staffel Gartenfeld z.b.V., commanded by Major Karl-Edmund Gartenfeld, a skilful night-pilot who had dropped a number of Abwehr spies over England and Ireland.[19] His unit had flown in the parachutists for Operation *Franz* and been involved in *Zeppelin* and *Weitsprung*.

In February 1944 Gartenfeld's unit had been integrated with a 'special projects' unit pioneered by bomber ace Oberstleutnant Werner Baumbach, who had won a clutch of medals for sinking Allied shipping. The merged formation was KG 200. Baumbach had a track record in experimental aviation, such as the *Mistel* system – composite aircraft typically involving a Focke-Wulf FW 190 fighter piggybacking an unmanned Ju 88 bomber packed with a huge explosive charge. Also on the agenda were suicide bombs, remote-control bombs, special-purpose gliders and – of particular interest to Skorzeny – the concept of a piloted V-1.[20]

The V-1 was a potent weapon, but had weaknesses. Crucially, its accuracy could only be guaranteed to within a 10-mile radius of its target. Right from the beginning, the manufacturer Fieseler had considered a piloted version as an alternative. The suggestion was turned down by Air Ministry supremo Generalfeldmarschall Erhard Milch, who feared the demoralising impact of such suicide missions on the German public. Milch's view was shared by Göring, and initially by Hitler himself. Skorzeny heard that Hitler considered suicide weapons to be 'not in character for the white races and opposed to German mentality. We should not imitate the Japanese Kamikaze.'[21]

Nonetheless, in early 1944, Hitler, Göring and Milch changed their minds. As the Luftwaffe was increasingly outgunned and outclassed by Allied planes, the prospects for a piloted V-1 began to look much more attractive. It was cheap to build (about £300 per unit at today's prices), used little fuel, and seemed to offer a means of penetrating heavily defended slow-moving targets.

Meantime, the case for recruiting a cadre of 'volunteer' suicide pilots had been enthusiastically taken up by test pilot Hanna Reitsch and her colleague Hauptmann Heinrich Lange.

Hanna Reitsch was among the greatest test pilots who ever lived. A former Olympic gliding champion who had piloted virtually everything from fighters and bombers to the Me 163 Komet rocket plane, Reitsch had famously flown one of the world's earliest helicopters, the Fa 61, *indoors* at the 1938 Berlin Motor Show. She was a dedicated Nazi and devoted to Hitler, who called her his favourite pilot. Although a civilian, she held the honorary Luftwaffe rank of Flugkapitän (flight captain) and was the first woman to be awarded the EK I.[22] It was rumoured that she was Otto Skorzeny's girlfriend, a myth which she apparently encouraged.[23] In fact, they had never met before spring 1944. Reitsch admired Skorzeny from afar, believing him to be a fellow pilot and accepting the official story that he had performed the Gran Sasso mission virtually single-handedly, piloting the aircraft which had flown the Duce to safety himself.[24]

Reitsch personally persuaded Hitler to give his blessing to the suicide pilot scheme. In doing so, she was forced to shatter his illusions about the war-winning potential of Germany's new jet aircraft – Hitler 'was living in some remote and nebulous world of his own and the appalling implications of this discovery suddenly burst upon me'.[25]

Reitsch and Lange thereby laid the foundations for KG 200 Gruppe V, also known as the Leonidas Squadron (after the Spartan king who pitted his 300 warriors against Persia's army at Thermopylae). All volunteers signed a declaration: 'I hereby voluntarily apply to be enrolled in the suicide group as pilot of a human glider-bomb. I fully understand that employment in this capacity will entail my own death.'[26]

Rather than the V-1, the initial platform chosen was the experimental Me 328 rocket fighter. It soon proved a failure: vibration caused by the pulse-jet power unit made the plane impossible to handle. By April, it was back to square one, with Reitsch bitterly regretting that the team had no alternative plan.

Enter Otto Skorzeny, with exactly that.

> Unexpectedly, the help came. One day in April, 1944, Otto Skorzeny introduced himself to me over the telephone and said he was anxious to meet me ... Skorzeny, it appeared, had recently been told by Himmler about our project and had himself been concerned in the development of special weapons. He was already in contact with those in the Navy who saw in the use of one-man torpedoes and frogmen a chance of bringing about a last-minute change in the course of the war in Germany's favour. Quite independently of us, Skorzeny had also come on the idea of the piloted V1 and had been anxious to meet me in order to discuss it.[27]

He had got the idea from a visit to the V-1 development centre at Peenemünde. When asked whether a V-1 flown by a pilot would be feasible, an engineering officer told him it would.[28] Back in Berlin, Skorzeny convened a meeting at the Wannsee Institut (part of RSHA Amt VII) which included Robert Lusser, the designer of the V-1. All evening and much of the following early morning was spent poring over calculations. The technical answer was yes, a man with a parachute could be shoehorned into a V-1 with a reasonable chance of flying it competently.

Skorzeny's conversation with Hanna Reitsch soon revealed the problems she was experiencing. 'When he saw how the situation lay,' she recalled, 'Skorzeny set to work in characteristic fashion, sweeping aside all objections and obstacles with the same simple pretext, "Hitler had vested him with full powers and had expressly called for a daily progress report."'[29] This was very different from Reitsch's experience with Hitler (he had asked her to get on with it and not to bother him), and no doubt spiced up with Skorzeny's trademark self-aggrandisement.

Next came the political problem. Milch gave Skorzeny a friendly reception, but the bureaucrats at the Aviation Ministry were less forgiving. He could build a prototype, they said, but could only use the existing stock of V-1s, of which none was available.[30]

Skorzeny had already worked his way around this obstacle, and was ready with a retort. He was close to the family of Professor Ferdinand Porsche, the founder of Volkswagen and builder of the Tiger I tank. (Close enough, certainly, to have holidayed with them.[31] Their connection probably came about through Nazi-sponsored Grand Prix racing in the mid- to late 1930s, in which Porsche and his son were involved as designers of the Auto Union racing cars.) Porsche happened to have a job lot of 2,000 unmodified V-1s at the Volkswagen plant in Wolfsburg[*], which were going to be scrapped on account of faulty construction.[32] 'I can assure you that he would gladly let me have a dozen!' Skorzeny told the bureaucrats.[33]

Who could refuse him when, apparently, he was working on Hitler's direct orders?

A number of surplus V-1 airframes were shipped to the Heinkel factory near Friedenthal, where Skorzeny was loaned a work-space, three engineers and five mechanics on an indefinite basis.

The first test models appeared within ten days.[34] The manned version of the flying bomb was dubbed the Fi 103R 'Reichenberg'. There were a number of variants: the R-I was a glider, the R-II a double-cockpit version, the R-III a single-seater with pulse jet fitted, and the R-IV was the fully operational model fitted with a warhead and without a ventral landing ski. The aircraft was launched aerially from under the wing of an He 111 bomber. It was envisaged that the pilot of the released projectile would steer towards the target, then, moments before impact, release the canopy and bail out with a parachute. In practice, the Fi 103R-IV was going to be a death-trap. Jettisoning the canopy would interfere with the pulse-jet air intake – making the rocket bomb almost impossible to handle. The survival rate was reckoned at less than 1 per cent – a fact well known to the pilots.[35] Nevertheless, the possibility of cheating death – however slim – gave those in authority a fig-leaf when accused of sanctioning suicide missions.

On a warm, summery day in September 1944, Otto Skorzeny and Hanna Reitsch observed the first test flight together at Rechlin–Lärz experimental station. Reitsch described it:

> Fascinated, we followed the Heinkel as it took off with its burden and climbed higher and higher. Then the moment came when we saw the test-pilot detach his plane from the bomber and drop away in the V-1 like some small, swift bird.
>
> The pilot flew in tight turns until, on a dead-straight course, he began to lose height, gliding at an ever steeper angle towards the earth. It did not take us long to realize that this behaviour of the machine was in no way intended by the pilot. The machine disappeared from sight and shortly

[*]   At that time known as Stadt des Kdf-Wagens bei Fallersleben

after we heard an explosion in the distance and saw a column of black smoke rising in the summer air.[36]

Astonishingly, the pilot was alive, although severely injured. The trials proved so hazardous that they almost caused the Reichenberg programme to abort. Milch, according to Skorzeny, halted the tests, pending an inquiry. That would likely have taken months, effectively terminating the Fi 103R programme. Reitsch told Skorzeny that the two KG 200 test pilots had no experience of jet propulsion, and had failed to appreciate the high stall-speed of the aircraft. She, having flown Me 163s, knew exactly what was involved. Why not let her pilot the next test flight?

Skorzeny was reluctant. The needless death of Hitler's favourite aviatrix would have dire consequences for his own career. But her wilfulness matched his own. Eventually he caved in – agreeing to dupe the station commander into releasing an He 111 for a further test flight.[37]

'I do not think I was ever in such a fluster as next day when Hanna was closing the cockpit and the airscrews began to turn,' he recalled. 'The start and release of the V1 were perfect and the handling of the machine and its beautiful circles soon showed what an amazing pilot this girl was.' Watching her come in to land, 'I sweated inside and out. There was a cloud of dust on the tarmac and when we rushed up a smiling Hanna greeted us from the cockpit. "Nothing wrong with it at all!" was her verdict.'[38]

In subsequent test flights, both Reitsch and her colleague Heinz Kensche had close scrapes with death. But her point had been made, and 175 Reichenberg V-1s were built. There was no lack of volunteers from the Luftwaffe to fly them – according to Skorzeny several hundred, of whom 60 were selected for training.

Yet despite Reitsch's and Skorzeny's efforts, no operational flights were ever made. The decisive moment for such weapons had already passed. Delays in development meant the Reichenberg was only ready to fly long after the Allies had landed in Normandy. Reitsch was scornful about 'the total failure on the part of higher authority to appreciate that the Suicide Group was no stunt, but a collection of brave, clear-headed and intelligent Germans who seriously believed … that by sacrificing their own lives they might save many times that number of their fellow-countrymen and ensure some kind of future for their children.'[39]

Furthermore, there was a growing aviation fuel crisis which, by the second half of 1944, was jeopardising all such experimental projects. The 500 cubic metres of aviation fuel Skorzeny had been promised at the beginning of summer 1944 was never forthcoming, which meant the number of pilots who could be trained was increasingly restricted. The Fi 103R was very fuel-efficient – it could even run on paraffin – but the He 111 launch aircraft was not.[40]

Everything was against the Reichenberg. When Milch was ousted after a plot to depose Göring backfired, Skorzeny became dependent upon the patronage of Albert Speer, head of armaments and war production, who was no fan of the Reichenberg project. As early as July 1944, Speer had written to Hitler deprecating the waste of unleashing such a unit on the Allied invasion force; suicide missions would be better deployed against Soviet power stations.[41] In November, Werner Baumbach, as commander of KG 200, shelved the Reichenberg project in favour of his own *Mistel* programme. The appointment at this time of a liaison officer between KG 200 and Amt VI meant Skorzeny was, in effect, frozen out of the chain of command.[42]

7

The Stauffenberg Plot – July 1944

It had been a scorchingly hot July day in Berlin and the young officer running alongside Skorzeny's railway carriage was visibly gasping for breath.

The overnight train was en route for Vienna. Skorzeny and Radl were going to review a new elite frogmen unit being put through its paces at the Dianabad, preparing for its first mission – to capture Tito in his island headquarters at Vis.[1]

Skorzeny recognised the young officer as one of Jüttner's staff at Waffen-SS HQ who had been acting as liaison to Schellenberg. He rolled down the compartment window, and the officer, catching his breath, told him that he was to report back to the Amt VI offices in Berkärstrasse immediately. A military coup was being staged in Berlin.

Earlier that afternoon, Skorzeny had heard from Fölkersam about an assassination attempt against the Führer at the Wolfsschanze. But Skorzeny and Radl had spent the rest of the afternoon drinking in a hotel while they waited for their train and had heard no further news.[2] It hadn't occurred to them that the assassination attempt was only the first act of a coup.

Skorzeny jumped out of the compartment; Radl passed his bags through the window and travelled on alone.

The situation at Berkärstrasse was chaotic. Skorzeny regarded with martial disdain the panicky officials in their smart Hugo Boss uniforms running amok with machine pistols. The normally suave Schellenberg, who for once had been wrong-footed by events, was 'green in the face. A pistol lay on his desk. "Just let them come," he said, "I know how to defend myself! They won't get me that easily."[3] He asked Skorzeny for a bodyguard detachment from one of the SS-Jägerbataillon 502 companies stationed at Friedenthal. Skorzeny contacted Fölkersam and told him to come to Berlin, bringing his acting adjutant SS-Untersturmführer Gerhard Ostafel and 1. Kompanie, led by SS-Hauptsturmführer Werner Hunke.[4]

Schellenberg had ample reason to be fearful; his agitated behaviour was not, as Skorzeny naively assumed, a case of blue funk. The events unfolding on Thursday 20 July 1944 were tumultuous and chaotic. The wires had been sparking with news and rumours ever since Oberst Claus Schenk Graf (Count) von Stauffenberg had detonated a bomb in Hitler's briefing room at the Wolfsschanze. Now a group of Wehrmacht rebels were attempting to seize control of the Third Reich from their power base within the Allgemeines Heeresamt (General Army Office) at Bendlerstrasse.

For years the German anti-Hitler resistance movement had struggled with self-doubt, conspiratorial ineptitude and sheer bad luck. But now, in Claus von Stauffenberg, it had finally found a man with not only personal access to Hitler, but the necessary willpower to kill him. As an assassin, however, Stauffenberg had one conspicuous flaw. He had lost his right hand and the third and fourth fingers of his left hand, and wore a patch over his left eye after being badly wounded in a strafing attack while serving in North Africa during April 1943. He was not, then, a man ideally suited to firing a service pistol,[5] or indeed to priming a bomb.

The conspirators' plan was, in its essentials, a masterly one, tapping into the Germans' propensity for obeying orders. Operation *Walküre* (*Valkyrie*) neatly turned a contingency plan for containing a national emergency into an action plan for overthrowing the Nazi state. After Hitler's death the conspirators would broadcast an announcement: 'The Führer Adolf Hitler is dead! A treacherous group of party leaders has attempted to exploit the situation by attacking our embattled soldiers from the rear in order to seize power for themselves!' Using this pretext, the new 'Reich government' would declare martial law – permitting the Ersatzheer (Reserve Army), under the conspirators' control, to seize all government ministries, Nazi party offices, radio stations and concentration camps. Party bosses would be arrested and SS units disarmed – their leaders shot if they refused to obey. The plan was focused on Berlin, but its roll-out took in the rest of the Reich. The conspirators hoped that initial success would win over sceptical Wehrmacht generals in the West, who would then be persuaded to open the gates to the Anglo-American invasion force.

The entire conspiratorial stratagem depended on two vital premises: Hitler's actual liquidation; and all the officers and soldiers who were ciphers in the *Walküre* plan obliviously carrying out their orders.

Had Stauffenberg exploded both of the two bombs he had at his disposal, Hitler and the other 23 occupants of the room would certainly have died.[6] But he did not. And when, having made his excuses and left the building, the single bomb duly exploded at 12.40 pm, Stauffenberg inferred from the force of the explosion and a body on a stretcher bearing Hitler's cloak, that he was dead. Without waiting to check, he sped back to Berlin by air.

The second of the conspirators' many mistakes that day happened not long afterwards. After Stauffenberg's departure from the Wolfsschanze, one of his accomplices attempted to warn his opposite number at the Bendlerblock*, Generaloberst Fritz Thiele, that Hitler was still alive. Extraordinarily, Thiele was so emotionally overcome by the information that he failed to inform Generaloberst Friedrich Olbricht – chief of the Allgemeines Heeresamt and the only man who could trigger *Walküre*. Instead, Thiele went out for a two-hour walk, during which he met with his friend Schellenberg at Berkärstrasse. No wonder Schellenberg looked nervous when Skorzeny turned up; clearly he knew a good deal more than he was letting on.[7]

Olbricht was left drumming his fingers and only learned later that the 'initial spark' of the coup had been a damp squib. Categorical confirmation was excruciatingly elusive. Should he go ahead with the coup or not? He could not authorise it without the agreement of the commander of the Ersatzheer, Generaloberst Friedrich Fromm, whose attitude to the plotters was ambiguous. Although opposed to Hitler, Fromm was above all a shrewd and ruthless careerist, and it was extremely unlikely he would sign the *Walküre* implementation order without certain proof of Hitler's death – in other words, assurance that he was on the winning side. In the circumstances, Fromm would have to be displaced from his command, an act which in itself could prematurely expose the plotters' motives and risk the coup's outcome.

Olbricht vacillated until just before 4 pm: the moment when Stauffenberg alighted at Rangsdorf airport and his adjutant phoned to assure the Bendlerblock plotters that Hitler was definitely dead. Even now, just as

---

* Military headquarters complex fronting Bendlerstrasse (now Stauffenbergstrasse) in the Tiergarten district of Berlin. Originally an HQ for the Imperial German Navy, under the Nazis Bendlerblock was comprehensively expanded to include various OKW and OKH commands, among them the Allgemeines Heeresamt, which occupied the original main building.

Olbricht had feared, Fromm refused to go along with the plotters. Instead, he phoned the chief of OKW, Generalfeldmarschall Keitel, and received the directly contradictory information that Hitler was alive, having suffered only minor injuries. Stauffenberg, now returned to Bendlerblock, stoutly maintained that Keitel was lying; Fromm was unmoved. At this point Olbricht and his accomplices acted: Fromm was locked away and *Walküre* finally activated. It was shortly after 4.30 pm.

By now Himmler, still at the Wolfsschanze, had finally come to grips with events. The Gestapo had for some time been aware of the German resistance movement and its inchoate plotting, but not of Stauffenberg's role. Such was Himmler's admiration for Stauffenberg that he had personally recommended his services to Hitler.[8] Only late in the afternoon did it become apparent that Stauffenberg must be the perpetrator of the assassination attempt – too late to have him arrested on touchdown at Rangsdorf.

The ineptitude of the supposedly all-seeing, all-powerful SS in protecting the Nazi state from its enemies was remarkable. Although Heinrich Müller, the Gestapo chief, had long been anticipating just such a situation and Kaltenbrunner could, by now, be in no doubt that something was going on at Bendlerstrasse, RSHA HQ remained curiously inert for many hours. No Waffen-SS units – such as the Leibstandarte division companies stationed at Lichterfelde, or Skorzeny's motorised battalion only a little further afield – were initially summoned. In fact, the only SS-controlled units to be seen on the streets of Berlin as *Walküre* picked up momentum were those of the Kripo.[9] And that was because their commander, Arthur Nebe, was up to his neck in the plot.

It was at this time that the fate of Germany came to rest in the hands of one man. Not Otto Skorzeny, whatever he might have subsequently tried to claim, but Wehrmacht Major Otto-Ernst Remer, the highly decorated, hard-bitten veteran commander of the elite Wachbataillon Grossdeutschland (Guard Battalion), the only fully mobilised military force in Berlin.

Remer was ordered by the Berlin military commandant, Generalleutnant Paul von Hase (a plotter), to seal off radio stations and move on buildings in the government quarter of the city. His most important assignment was to seize the Propaganda Ministry and its key occupant, Josef Goebbels. A dedicated Nazi, Remer became suspicious of his orders almost the moment he received them, but began implementing them anyway. Eventually he became convinced he was being set up, and made a personal visit to Goebbels at about 7 pm. When he entered with his pistol ready, prepared to arrest him, Remer was eagerly greeted by Goebbels, who asked for a full briefing on the situation and informed him that Hitler was still alive: 'The assassination failed! You've been tricked.'[10]

Remer spoke to Hitler on the telephone, and 'involuntarily snapped to attention' at the sound of the Führer's voice.[11] He was promoted on the spot to colonel, and invested with plenary powers to bring the revolt to an end. The military cordon surrounding the government quarter was immediately dismantled and Remer set about blocking access to and from the Bendlerblock. By now, the radio was broadcasting the news of Hitler's survival.

While all this was going on, Skorzeny was on a tour of inspection of the government quarter. Having dismissed Schellenberg's fears as hysteria, and the putative plot as 'a comic opera revolt',[12] he had left Fölkersam at Berkärstrasse to await the arrival of his motorised company and set off with Ostafel to discover what was going on. He had no orders at this stage beyond securing the Amt VI headquarters building.[13] The fact-finding mission was his own initiative.

What he encountered was more disturbing than he had earlier imagined. A senior panzer officer of his acquaintance, Generalmajor Ernst Bolbrinker, had summoned a number of tanks from the Wünsdorf Panzerschule, 55 kilometres outside Berlin, and deployed them around the Fehrbelliner Square area. Bolbrinker was confused by the orders emanating from Bendlerblock. The impression he had gained, no doubt deliberately encouraged by the plotters, was that the Waffen-SS was behind the putsch. When Skorzeny encountered him, Bolbrinker was about to send out an armed patrol to the Lichterfelde barracks. The high probability of an armed clash – and even civil war, as the Waffen-SS units stationed there responded to unprovoked aggression – loomed large in Skorzeny's mind.[14]

Accompanied by two of Bolbrinker's officers, Skorzeny then 'raced' by car to the barracks in an attempt to defuse the situation.[15] He may even have played a pacificatory role in what followed, but doubt is cast on his account by his claim to have met SS-Standartenführer Wilhelm Mohnke, who subsequently became commander of the 1. SS-Panzerdivision 'Leibstandarte-SS Adolf Hitler'. In fact, Mohnke was in Normandy at that time, commanding a regiment of the 12. SS-Panzerdivision 'Hitlerjugend'.[16] Whoever the commander actually was on that day, he seems to have already been alerted to the false nature of *Walküre* by Goebbels.[17]

Skorzeny's next port of call was newly promoted Generaloberst Student's XI. Fliegerkorps HQ in Wannsee. No one there knew anything, and no orders had been received. About 9.30 pm, Skorzeny visited Student's home in Lichterfelde, where he was met with a scene of incongruous domestic bliss. Student 'was on the garden terrace, wearing casual clothes and sitting beneath a half-darkened lamp, in front of him a mountain of files. His wife sat nearby, busy with her knitting. The General welcomed us warmly.'[18] Apparently Student had forgiven Skorzeny his former behaviour. He was dumbfounded by the news of a plot.

It was only now that Skorzeny himself began to be put into the loop. While he was at Student's home, a call came through from Hermann Göring confirming the plot and identifying Stauffenberg as its ringleader. Returning 'at top speed' to Berkärstrasse, where Fölkersam had by now rendezvoused with the motorised company, Skorzeny received his first direct order from FHQ* – probably at Göring's behest.[19] He was to proceed with his entire force to Bendlerstrasse to support Remer's Grossdeutschland battalion. Shooting had apparently broken out there.

It was nearly midnight when Skorzeny, in a Kübelwagen† with Fölkersam, led a column of 'about twenty vehicles' through the streets. At the Tiergarten–Bendlerstrasse intersection, they were met by two cars, one of which had come from the Bendlerblock. Both stopped. Skorzeny waited a moment, then got out to investigate. From the first car, Ernst Kaltenbrunner emerged, and in the other was Generaloberst Fromm, commander of the Ersatzheer. Skorzeny overheard Fromm say to Kaltenbrunner, 'I'm tired and am going home. I can be reached there at any time.' What Skorzeny didn't hear was that the coup was over, and Fromm had played a key role in its last act.

As Fromm was leaving, Albert Speer arrived in his Lancia sports car, accompanied by Remer. 'An SS officer signalled me to stop,' Speer recalled. 'Almost unrecognisable in the darkness under the trees stood Kaltenbrunner … and Skorzeny, the man who had liberated Mussolini, surrounded by numerous subordinates. These dark figures looked like phantoms and behaved as such. When we greeted them, no one clicked his heels … Everything seemed muted; even the conversation was conducted in lowered voices, as at a funeral.'[20] Speer 'rather expected Kaltenbrunner and Skorzeny would execrate the army, which they had always regarded as their rival, or at any rate gloat over its moral defeat'. To his surprise they did neither, Kaltenbrunner telling Speer that the SS would not 'suppress the rebellion or carry out punishments' because SS intervention would stir up trouble with the army.

Saying goodnight to Kaltenbrunner and Skorzeny, Speer spoke to Fromm, who told him, 'The putsch is finished … General Olbricht and my chief of staff, Colonel Stauffenberg, are no longer living.'[21]

---

*   Führerhauptquartiere or Führer headquarters

†   VW-manufactured all-purpose military vehicle – though, unlike a jeep, lacking 4-wheel drive.

How had Fromm escaped, and what exactly had he done beforehand? About 11 pm, a number of middle-ranking general staff officers, uneasily aware they had become accomplices in a failing coup, armed themselves with machine pistols and burst into Olbricht's office, demanding to know what had happened to their commander, Fromm. The unfortunate appearance of Stauffenberg there created a scuffle as the counter-putschists made a grab for him. He clumsily fired off a shot in self-defence but received a bullet in his upper left arm as he made his escape. It was not long before Fromm was sprung from confinement in the apartment upstairs. Wasting no time and now backed by a retinue of followers, Fromm marched into the map-room and placed, at pistol-point, the six main conspirators under arrest, with the immortal words: 'So, gentlemen, now it's my turn to do to you what you did to me this afternoon.'[22]

Only, Fromm went much further. One of the conspirators, former chief of general staff Generaloberst Ludwig Beck – and putative president of the new German republic – chose to commit suicide on the spot.[23] But that left several others who presented Fromm with a pressing problem: they were eyewitnesses to his own perfidy – or at any rate, to his foreknowledge of a plot which he had failed to communicate to anyone else. Such conduct would hardly play well with Himmler, who was now known to be on his way from the Wolfsschanze.[24] Fromm, hearing that a unit of the watch battalion had just arrived in the courtyard outside, acted swiftly. He 'convened' a court-martial, presided over exclusively by himself, in which all the eyewitnesses – Stauffenberg, his adjutant Werner von Häften, Olbricht and Olbricht's chief of staff Oberst Mertz von Quirnheim – were summarily condemned to death by firing squad.[25]

The four were led downstairs – Stauffenberg still bleeding – into the courtyard where a number of parked military lorries, their headlights blazing in the pitch darkness of the blackout, lit up the place of execution. Each man was positioned in turn before a small pile of sand, and shot by a firing squad of ten NCOs. Later, Beck's crumpled body was dragged down the stairs and dumped under a tarpaulin with the other four. It was shortly after midnight. Fromm immediately dispatched a teleprinter message to FHQ: 'Attempted putsch by disloyal generals violently suppressed. All leaders shot.'[26] Thereafter, descending to the courtyard himself, he jumped onto the tailboard of one of the lorries and delivered a rousing loyalist speech which ended with three 'Sieg Heils', which were enthusiastically applauded by the surrounding soldiers.

Then Fromm got into his staff car and started to drive off – only to encounter Speer's Lancia and Skorzeny's Kübelwagen coming the other way.

Remer, who knew Fromm but was at this stage unaware of his true role in the day's events, suggested he should make his way immediately to Goebbels' residence where he could be updated on the unfolding political situation.[27] And that is exactly what Fromm, keen to get his point of view across before anyone else's account muddied the water, did. He was to be unlucky. When Remer got back to his temporary command post at Goebbels' home around 1 am, he was surprised to find Himmler had arrived, and that Fromm was under arrest.

In the meantime, Remer had come to an agreement with Skorzeny and the SS. Remer would concern himself with external security, while Skorzeny and his unit were to occupy the interior of the Bendlerblock until further notice. This occasion was Skorzeny's first encounter with Remer, who was to become a long-term friend.

Skorzeny was familiar with the Bendlerblock and its personnel as he had often visited it on official business. He was acquainted with Stauffenberg, and had bumped into him at Rangsdorf airport, near Berlin, only nine days earlier. Skorzeny had been on his way to France, and Stauffenberg was about to fly to the Wolfsschanze to brief Hitler about troop requirements on the Western Front. They conversed for a few minutes; Skorzeny recalled finding Stauffenberg 'very calm and friendly'.[28] He knew two of the counter-putschists better – Oberstleutnants Karl Pridun (who had winged Stauffenberg prior to his capture) and Franz Herber, from whom Skorzeny got his first detailed account of what had happened.

With the three most senior Berlin-based army officers eliminated, there was a power vacuum. When Skorzeny, even at this late stage, was unable to establish contact with OKW, it became apparent that Skorzeny himself – surely the Reich's most unsuitable bureaucrat and general staff officer – would have to step into the breach. The priority was to countermand the plotters' orders.

Skorzeny and four of his officers occupied Olbricht's and Stauffenberg's offices on the second floor. Sitting down at Stauffenberg's desk, Skorzeny rummaged through the drawers. In one he found 'the real Valkyrie plan' along with two dice and a board game. The game was a parody of Heeresgruppe Süd's* progress on the Eastern Front. 'The declarations in the various boxes were so cynical and mean that I was quite shaken.'[29]

In its small way, the board game summed up all of Skorzeny's suspicion and contempt for these treasonous Prussian aristocrats in their red-striped

---

* Army Group South

trousers, plotting while the Wehrmacht was 'fighting on three fronts against the strongest armies in the world'.[30] Fölkersam, Hunke and Ostafel, who were with him, shared his disgust. But he was precluded from meting out any drumhead justice. His orders were quite specific: no more shootings. A live prisoner who could be tortured into giving away his accomplices was infinitely more valuable to the Gestapo than a dead one.

Skorzeny contented himself with parading the other principal plotters at Bendlerstrasse – Fritz-Dietlof Graf von der Schulenburg, Ulrich-Wilhelm Graf Schwerin von Schwanenfeld, Peter Graf Yorck von Wartenburg, Stauffenberg's brother Berthold, Oberstleutnant Robert Bernardis, the Protestant theologian Eugen Gerstenmaier and a few others – who until now had been held captive in Stauffenberg's and Mertz's offices. Without a word, he approached in turn each of the captured officers, ripped off their medals and decorations and dropped them into an upturned steel helmet lying on the floor behind him. Then he forced them to listen to Hitler's national radio broadcast – which finally made the airwaves at 1 am – during which the enraged dictator promised swift and brutal retribution to all those who had plotted to displace him.

Years later, Skorzeny allowed himself a more measured view of Stauffenberg: 'I may say that I have the greatest respect for any man who is prepared to give his life for his convictions. In that respect there is no difference between the battlefield and the concentration camp. No normal human being wants to lose his life, but a moment may come for all of us in which we have to choose between our existence and what we believe in.'[31]

At the time, however, he felt disgust, which soon gave way to mounting anxiety about the avalanche of general staff orders piling up on Stauffenberg's unoccupied desk. Only at 3 am did Skorzeny manage to get through to OKW and speak to Generaloberst Alfred Jodl, who himself had been wounded by the bomb blast. His instructions were not what Skorzeny wanted to hear. He was to be master of the Reich's military papermill until relieved. He was kept at the grindstone for 30 hours, occasionally dozing in the armchair and living on coffee provided by Stauffenberg's secretary.

* * *

Skorzeny's exhausting vigil at Bendlerstrasse ended on the morning of 22 July, with the arrival of Fromm's replacement as Ersatzheer commander – none other than the Reichsführer-SS himself. He was accompanied by Skorzeny's patron at Waffen-SS Führungshauptamt, SS-Obergruppenführer Hans Jüttner. Only

Hitler seems to have believed Himmler was competent to perform his new role. Skorzeny noted drily: 'In truth, Jüttner bore the entire responsibility, for Himmler was incapable of understanding military problems.'[32]

Himmler, abetted by Müller and Kaltenbrunner, had by now instigated one of the most savage manhunts in history. In the months that followed *Walküre*, over 7,000 suspects were arrested and more than 5,000 met their deaths.[33] Some committed suicide; others chose to endure the unspeakable tortures of the Gestapo – finger spikes, the Spanish Boot and the rack among them. The discovery of compromising documents in the homes of suspects led to a widescale purge. Property was expropriated, and wives and children were either incarcerated or left homeless.

This wave of terror was accompanied by a series of show-trials. Inevitable conviction led to a cruel death. In accordance with Hitler's direct order – 'I want them to be hanged, strung up like butchered cattle' – the condemned were hanged by the thinnest of hemp nooses from butcher's hooks attached to a girder. The whole scene was floodlit and intimately recorded on camera for the delectation of Hitler and his cronies. A handful of high-ranking individuals were spared execution and instead sent secretly to concentration camps, where they were later to become bargaining chips in an SS scheme to negotiate peace terms with the Allies.

Otto Skorzeny and his commandos were only minimally involved in the manhunt and subsequent persecution – with one notable exception.

Having returned to Friedenthal, on 23 July, Skorzeny was phoned by Schellenberg, who told him that he had just been informed by Himmler and Heinrich Müller that Admiral Wilhelm Canaris, former head of the now defunct Abwehr, was 'deeply involved in the conspiracy'. They had instructed Schellenberg to have him arrested as a test of his loyalty (of which Müller, for one, was highly suspicious).

In fact, Canaris had only marginal personal involvement in the conspiracy. When Stauffenberg telephoned to tell him Hitler was dead, Canaris reportedly replied: 'Mein Gott! Who did it? The Russians?'[34] (Admittedly, it was always difficult to tell when Canaris was being ironic.) But the circumstantial evidence implicating him was overwhelming. Some of his closest Abwehr associates were in the thick of the plot. Oberst von Loringhoven, for example, head of Abwehr Section II, had provided Stauffenberg's detonator charge. Loringhoven's subsequent suicide led to the Gestapo discovering documents incriminating Canaris in other treasonable activities.

'I find myself in an uncomfortable situation,' Schellenberg told Skorzeny. Hitler wanted Canaris's arrest to be handled 'with a certain degree of respect'.

Schellenberg asked Skorzeny for a Jägerbataillon detachment as escort, as he expected resistance.[35] Skorzeny, who read this as another example of Schellenberg's weak spine, made a sarcastic quip about being savaged by Canaris's dachshunds and promised that Fölkersam would lead a detail to the admiral's house to arrest him. Skorzeny had not a scintilla of doubt about Canaris's guilt. He recalled how 'the good admiral' had 'wanted to send us to a small island near Elba to look for the Duce, who was certainly on Santa [sic] Maddalena'.[36]

Schellenberg's discomfort about arresting Canaris stemmed for the most part from a reluctance to damage the tricky takeover of Abwehr operations by SD-Ausland – a process ongoing since Canaris's dismissal in February that year. It was a case of a snake trying to swallow an elephant. Now dubbed the Militärisches Amt (Mil Amt or Military Intelligence Department) the Abwehr was vastly larger than the organisation absorbing it, and employed up to 16,000 people compared with SD-Ausland's 1,000 or so.[37] In garnering the Abwehr's superior resources, Schellenberg had got what he had long coveted, but had also acquired a mammoth managerial headache. He had to rely upon a large pool of intelligence officers who had served under Canaris. Actively being seen to persecute their former commander would devastate morale in an already severely damaged organisation. Personality also played a part. While Schellenberg had relentlessly intrigued to gain control of Canaris's department, he liked and admired Canaris as a man. He had had to be coerced by Müller (making great play with Schellenberg's purported closeness to the conspirator Thiele) into arresting him, under threat of 'consequences' from Kaltenbrunner, who hated Schellenberg and would take any opportunity to bring him down.[38]

Schellenberg was careful to select Fölkersam to escort the prisoner, seeing him as a more delicate pair of hands than Skorzeny and – as a former Brandenburger – someone who could be relied on to treat the admiral with respect. It was a doubly tricky situation for Schellenberg, who had by now developed a deep loathing and distrust of Skorzeny, perceiving him as very much Kaltenbrunner's man. (He later referred to Skorzeny as a 'swine'.[39])

The arrest went without incident. Fölkersam discreetly waited in the hallway of the admiral's Berlin-Schlachtensee home, while Schellenberg went in alone and offered Canaris the honourable way out with a service pistol. Canaris declined, placing his faith – wrongly, as it would ultimately turn out – in Himmler's intervention.[40]

For now, Skorzeny remained aloof from the intrigue brewing around Schellenberg, Kaltenbrunner and Himmler, in which Kaltenbrunner sought to discredit Schellenberg for his failure to detect the plot and his closeness to Canaris. Skorzeny was biding his time. His long-term objective was to wrest control of all military matters from Schellenberg, relations with whom had reached an all-time low since the so-called 'night-fighter incident' in April.* Skorzeny would not be satisfied until he could unseat Schellenberg and take over his role.

* * *

July 1944 was the month when the destruction of the Third Reich became assured. The Allied break-out from Normandy, the collapse of the Wehrmacht in the West, the colossal disaster in the East that was Operation *Bagration* – resulting in the destruction of 30 irreplaceable German divisions and a gaping hole hundreds of kilometres wide in the front – were counterpointed by the failure of the military putsch at home. The one organisation to benefit from these disasters was the SS, which now tightened its grip on power.

Himmler, by becoming head of the Ersatzheer – for which, as Skorzeny and others were quick to point out, he was personally inadequate – once and for all extended his power-base out of state security and into military affairs. He was now in charge of armaments, army discipline, prisoners of war, reserve personnel and training. Almost two million men on military service were directly under his control.

More specifically, the Waffen-SS gained access to resources it had been denied. Himmler's appointment was a godsend for those capable Waffen-SS administrators, Gottlob 'God Almighty' Berger and Hans Jüttner, who were now able to streamline the entire organisational structure of the army. These reforms would profoundly affect Skorzeny, enabling him to radically expand his special forces, but at the cost of complex negotiations and intrigues in which he would not get all he wanted.

The fusion of the Abwehr and SD-Ausland had proved extremely problematic. Kaltenbrunner and Müller demanded rapid integration of Espionage (Abwehr I) and Sabotage (Abwehr II, which included responsibility for the Brandenburgers) into Amt VI; most of Counter-espionage (Abwehr III), on the other hand, was to be incorporated into Amt IV (that is, the Gestapo). Schellenberg, favouring a more hands-off approach, had advocated a new department, Mil Amt, which left the structure of the former Abwehr unchanged to the extent that it could work side by side with Amt VI within the broader framework of the RSHA.

The failed coup of 20 July necessarily speeded up integration of the two intelligence services at the top level, by removing from the scene those senior Abwehr figures who had been conspirators. Schellenberg was formally put in

*   See page 92.

charge of both agencies by a direct order of Kaltenbrunner. Further down the hierarchy, however, many issues remained to be resolved. Some never would be.

Skorzeny's responsibilities at Amt VI-S were a case in point. He sought to integrate the sabotage operations he had inherited from the Abwehr – which came to be known as Mil Amt D – with his own. But how was the scope of these sabotage operations to be defined? Should they include the Division Brandenburg, which technically reported through Abwehr II? Should they also include the extensive network of military reconnaissance agents (Frontaufklärung), which worked in close coordination with the intelligence officers of army units on the front? Skorzeny thought the answer to both these questions was 'Yes'. In this way not only would he serve the interests of operational efficiency, but he would also expand his power-base. He could then make a good case for jettisoning, once and for all, the political and personal shackles of Schellenberg by creating a specifically military unit, reporting not to Amt VI but to Jüttner at Waffen-SS HQ.[41]

Unsurprisingly, Schellenberg was having none of this. But nor, as it turned out, was the Wehrmacht high command, which was to resist with a series of adroit, bureaucratic manoeuvres Skorzeny's attempts to gain full control over Frontaufklärung sabotage units.

These units were part of an organisation hugely important to the prosecution of the war. Each German army normally had one Frontaufklärungskommando II (FAK II, corresponding to Abwehr II, typically with a complement of 40), whose dedicated purpose was sabotage operations behind enemy lines. At the next level of command, each of the army's three corps had one unit apiece of Frontaufklärungstruppen II (FAT II, typically 15 to 30 men). Most operations – comprising up to five agents – were initiated at the FAT level, and typically involved disrupting the flow of enemy supplies. By 1944, a sizeable number of agent operations were being aimed at consolidating 'stay-behind' resistance groups as the German army retreated. Mirroring the II system were FAK and FAT I, and FAK and FAT III units, which handled intelligence and counter-espionage respectively.

The staff and agents of the Frontaufklärung organisation were the eyes and ears of military tactical intelligence behind the enemy's front line – all the more so once the Luftwaffe began to lose air supremacy, and with it the ability to supply comprehensive aerial photography. How Frontaufklärung personnel were selected, trained and deployed was therefore of vital concern to the Wehrmacht, particularly on the Eastern Front. The last thing OKW wanted was Skorzeny pulling its strings from his 'rear-area' command post.

What it *did* relinquish control of – very much to Skorzeny's advantage – were those parts of the former Division Brandenburg it judged no longer relevant to the Wehrmacht's prosecution of the war. Already, in June 1944 the Wehrmachtführungsstab had spun off the special forces (z.b.V.) elements of the division, prior to turning the bulk of it into a conventional panzer division. The germ idea was to convert those Brandenburgers trained in special ops and conversant with foreign languages into so-called Streif Korps, which were to be attached to army corps for the execution of covert military missions. After complicated negotiations, Skorzeny was allowed to use these Streif Korps as the nuclei of four Territorialen Jagdverbände, known as Jagdverband Ost, Südost, Südwest and Nordwest. These were special battalions drawn from political and nationalist groups in the countries where they were to operate, but with a larger, purely German component that was never supposed to be less than 2:1.[42] In fact, the figure was often below that ratio, as German manpower was by now becoming a serious problem.

These regional units were part of a package of reforms activated by Jüttner at the end of September 1944, by dint of which Skorzeny could recruit a further 800 Brandenburg volunteers.[43] He actually recruited 1,200, but this figure was reduced to 900 after 300 were eliminated as unfit. Simultaneously, the motorised unit SS-Jägerbataillon 502 was dissolved and its personnel absorbed into a new unit, the three-company-strong Jagdverband Mitte (i.e. 'central', to complement the four regional units). Additionally, Skorzeny was given overall command, for the first time, of the SS parachute battalion – now reconstituted as SS-Fallschirmjägerbataillon 600 and commanded by SS-Hauptsturmführer Siegfried Milius. Like SS-Jägerbataillon 502 before them – but unlike the territorial Jagdverbände – both these units were almost exclusively made up of Germans.

Radl, more reliable than Skorzeny in these matters, estimated that Jagdverband Mitte – the core component of Skorzeny's expanded special forces – numbered only 400 men, and that 60 per cent were drawn from the army, with the Waffen-SS, Staffel Gartenfeld z.b.V. (predecessor of KG 200) and a tiny element from the Kriegsmarine making up the rest. By contrast he estimated the strength of the reconstituted parachute battalion at 500, with 40 per cent drawn from Gartenfeld's unit and the rest accounted for by army and Waffen-SS volunteers in equal numbers.[44] Long gone, even in Himmler's mind, was the idea of a suicidal penal force of SS men seeking glorious redemption in death.

The Territorialen units comprised companies known as Jagdeinsätze, which were organised according to nationality. German personnel within them – largely former Brandenburgers – were expected to speak the native languages of their respective units. Staff and liaison issues were dealt with centrally through Skorzeny's HQ at Friedenthal, but recruitment was carried out locally. Radl reckoned Südost – drawn from reconstituted Streif Korps in Croatia, Slovakia and Romania – was the biggest with about 800 men. Next came Ost – covering Russia, the Baltic republics and Poland and based in Hohensalza near Posen – with about 300 men; then Südwest – covering France and Italy – with 130 men. There was also an embryonic Nordwest, covering Belgium, the Netherlands and Denmark, which recruited a maximum of 70 personnel. Skorzeny's estimates of all these numbers were up to three times higher, but may have represented paper-strength – or simply been a product of his imagination.[45]

Skorzeny and Fölkersam, who had been working on plans for these new units since at least June 1944, were painfully aware of the need to avoid the mistakes of the past. The last thing they wanted was a repeat of the Brandenburg saga, where irreplaceable specialists had ended up being sacrificed as cannon-fodder in conventional combat formations. They vowed, therefore, to keep the organisation of the Jagdverbände as independent as possible by avoiding the traditional regimental system.[46]

Jüttner's September 1944 military reforms represented the organisational apogee of Skorzeny's special forces. They mirrored on a smaller scale Himmler's full-tilt incursion into the military sphere. Skorzeny's SS commando services, having absorbed the Brandenburgers, now encompassed the vast majority of German military special operations.

Yet Skorzeny's triumph was more apparent than real. His consolidation of power did not include the integration of Frontaufklärung II intelligence operations. More importantly, it came too late in the war to matter very much. By mid-1944, German special operations were permanently on the back foot. Instead of being able to capitalise on his gains, Skorzeny was constantly having to improvise with what little he could get as the war entered its final – and most destructive – phase.

8

The Scherhorn Affair

If the Gran Sasso mission marked Otto Skorzeny's zenith, the Scherhorn affair in late 1944 was perhaps his nadir.

In later years, Skorzeny would portray Operation *Scherhorn* as an epic and noble bid to rescue a 'Lost Legion' of German soldiers cut off behind the Russian lines. It was many years before he realised he had been duped – and even then, he failed to appreciate just how thorough the deception had been. The operation demonstrated the rank inadequacy of the newly 'unified' German intelligence system: organisational weakness, poor coordination and, above all, extraordinary gullibility stemming from a culture of arrogant racial superiority.

Events began to unfold in August 1944. Heeresgruppe Mitte had lost over half a million men in the Red Army's massive *Bagration* offensive. On 19 August, FAK 103, attached to what remained of Heeresgruppe Mitte, received a message from a Soviet spy ring called Flamingo, which was working for the Germans. The operator's codename was 'Aleksandr'. The Germans believed him to be a captain in a specialist signals detachment of the Red Army. His message said that his unit was stationed at Berezino, near Minsk. He had information, extracted from a captured German corporal, that there was 'a large German unit' cut off and hiding in the forest of Berezino.[1] The leader of this group was Oberstleutnant Heinrich Scherhorn. He intended to lead his 2,500 men back to German lines, but was hampered by a substantial number of wounded soldiers and inadequate supplies and ammunition.

Aleksandr added that he didn't know exactly where the stranded unit was located, but if the German commanders wished it, he would be able to get in touch with Scherhorn through his agents in Berezino.

Of course the Germans wished it, but they were also suspicious. It was entirely conceivable that German units would be left stranded after the rout of Heeresgruppe Mitte. But how could a mere corporal know so much about the Scherhorn group? And who, in any case, was Scherhorn?

Head of Heeresgruppe Mitte intelligence (Ic) Oberst Hans-Heinrich Worgitzky suspected a Russian intelligence deception aimed at diverting German resources. Even if Scherhorn existed, the Russians might be using his captured papers to simulate his existence. Worgitzky therefore asked Flamingo (via FAK 103) for Scherhorn's exact position, in order to drop supplies and permit radio operators to establish direct contact with the group. On 6 September Flamingo reported back that Aleksandr had established direct contact with the lost unit, which was short of ammunition, food, medicine and general supplies, but still determined to fight its way back to the German lines. Flamingo gave a detailed description of the group's position, 50 kilometres northwest of Berezino, as well as the exact location for an air-drop and the signals that could be used to alert a rescue mission if necessary.

Worgitzky's doubts were silenced by the intervention of a more senior intelligence figure, Oberst Reinhard Gehlen, head of Fremde Heere Ost (FHO or Foreign Intelligence East). Gehlen later became a legendary Cold War spymaster whose path would more than once cross that of Skorzeny. Operation *Scherhorn* was the occasion on which they first collaborated and probably first met.

FHO was indisputably the most successful German intelligence organ of World War II. Gehlen had won the respect of the German General Staff and raised the status of intelligence to a skill of almost mythical prescience. Gifted with remarkable analytical and organisational talents, Gehlen was far from a typical intelligence officer. He had no interest in foreign languages[2] and, in his earlier career as a Reichswehr officer, had studiously avoided the intelligence career path, knowing how low in esteem it was held by the Prussian officer caste that dominated the German General Staff (into which he was inducted as a Major in the OKH Operations Department during 1936).

Gehlen's rapid career advancement arose out of his attachment to the rising star of Generaloberst Franz Halder, who became indebted to Gehlen for the valuable and meticulous planning work he had carried out on critical aspects of Operation *Barbarossa*. When Halder, as Army chief of staff, had to clear up the mess left by the Germans' unexpected rout at the gates of Moscow, one of his key priorities was the improvement of intelligence. Gehlen was a shoo-in as the new head of FHO on account of his organisational skills.

The quality of German intelligence was, however, severely circumscribed. There was no equivalent of Britain's Bletchley Park decryption system. Consequently, intelligence officers were dependent upon circumstantial information gleaned from aerial photography, field signals interception, analysis of Soviet media and whatever could be derived from behind-enemy-lines reconnaissance by the FAK and FAT units. These intelligence deficiencies mattered more and more as the tide of war turned. Since 1942, Gehlen had routinely cooperated with Schellenberg in Operation *Zeppelin*, which trained Soviet prisoners of war as saboteurs and sent them back behind the Russian lines (despite Gehlen's dislike of the SS and distrust of the ambitious Schellenberg).

In mid-1944, FHO cooperation with *Zeppelin*'s HQ (Amt VI CZ) was stepped up to embrace all possible information on anti-Soviet partisan and nationalist groups active in the Russian rear. Information was collated and channelled through a new RSHA-sponsored department, Forschungsdienst Ost (Research Service East), whose remit included 'Sabotage of communications ... propaganda by leaflet, blowing up of bridges and railway installations, ambushes of small Red Army units ... looting, derailment.'[3]

This was where the connection with Skorzeny and his Jagdverbände came in; and how Gehlen and Skorzeny came to collaborate on the nascent Operation *Scherhorn*. For, by the beginning of September, doubts about Scherhorn's existence had been resolved by the discovery that an Oberstleutnant Heinrich Scherhorn, commander of Landesschützen-Regiment 36 of the 221. Sicherungsdivision – a unit involved in anti-partisan activities, attached to 4. Armee – had indeed gone missing in June.

This was doubly interesting information. First, Scherhorn's father was known personally to Hitler and had been a significant contributor to Nazi Party funds during the 1930s. That made his safe recovery an important political objective. Second, the Kampfgruppe of over 2,000 men he was leading included a unit highly experienced in partisan warfare. Of course, the essential objective was to rescue them but it soon occurred to Gehlen and Skorzeny that, if linked with anti-Soviet partisan forces behind the lines, the Scherhorn group could do considerable damage to the Red Army on the way back.

The rescue and behind-the-lines operations would be a test mission for Skorzeny's Jagdverband Ost. The unit had been supplemented by Balts, Russians and Poles, and Skorzeny was, at that very moment, forging it into a behind-the-lines force. Once Jodl at OKW had given the go-ahead for the mission and Hitler was in the loop, there was no going back.

Initially the operation was named *Freischütz* (*Marksman*) – an allusion to an opera whose hero, Max, is a forester. This was a sly reference to the Berezino forest where the lost troops were stranded, and to 'Max', an alternative codename for the spy Aleksandr who had supplied information about their whereabouts. Most likely the name was dreamt up by Fölkersam, Skorzeny's chief of staff, who took a keen personal interest in this operation.[4] The name was later discarded in favour of the more literal-minded Operation *Scherhorn*.

The operation went ahead in mid-September. The first objective was to establish direct radio contact with Scherhorn, cutting out the need for Flamingo's cumbersome mediation. To do that, commando units needed to reach him.

On 15 September KG 200 dropped a FAK 103 agent and his radio operator near the derelict town of Sanetevo, a mission which ended in radio silence.[5] Then, on 20 September, just as the Germans were about to give up, Heeresgruppe Mitte received (via Flamingo) a detailed message from Scherhorn himself. It confirmed the safe arrival of the two agents but remained vague about why they had failed to contact their handlers. Suspicions were raised by Scherhorn naming as senior officers individuals who were known to be in Soviet captivity.[6]

On 7 October the Germans inserted a second, carefully selected, FAK 103 radio operator, without having warned Scherhorn in advance. The operator soon confirmed he had arrived safely. To add belt and braces, on the night of 9 October, KG 200 dropped two four-man units from SS Jagdverband Ost in the Berezino zone. They were disguised as members of a German prisoner of war work battalion escorted by Russian-uniformed NCOs.[7]

The results were mixed. One group, under the command of an NCO identified only as 'SS-Oberscharführer P',[8] established radio contact with base after a 'difficult landing' and encountering 'enemy machine-gun fire', but nothing more was heard of it for a month. However, in due course a second group, under SS-Oberjunker Schiffer,[9] reported making successful contact with the Scherhorn group. And on 4 November Heeresgruppe Mitte received a message, with the correct radio code, to the effect that the missing unit had arrived on site.[10]

Now that they were assured of their man, his Kampfgruppe of 2,500 and its exact location, the Germans could begin the complex task of extraction.

Frequent supply drops by KG 200 transport planes began to take place, and conversations with Scherhorn and the SS radio operators in the field became everyday occurences. The problem, as Scherhorn soon pointed out, was that many of his men were too weak to retreat unassisted to the German lines some 300 miles away. Indeed, 850 of them were wounded. Two doctors were parachuted in, one of whom was badly injured on landing and subsequently died. It was decided that Scherhorn's men should build an airstrip so that they could be extracted by KG 200. A junior Luftwaffe officer, Jeschke Wild, was sent out to advise.

Progress was slow, held up by poor weather and the need to work at night for security reasons. Signs of enemy activity in the area further hampered the work. On 26 November, Scherhorn reported that Russian planes were bombing the forest nearby.[11] It could only be a matter of time before his Kampfgruppe was discovered. Under pressure, the German high command agreed to a change of plan. Scherhorn and his men would have to exfiltrate themselves after all. The Kampfgruppe split itself into two parties. The sick and the wounded, travelling in requisitioned farm carts, were to make their way slowly to the Reich's ever-receding border. A faster, more battle-ready unit under the command of Scherhorn and Schiffer would simultaneously head north towards the icy plateau at Nrocz Lake on the borders of Lithuania, where it was hoped an airlift would be possible.[12]

As a morale-booster, at Christmas the Führer and the German high command sent personal messages of congratulation.[13]

Progress was painfully slow. Skorzeny tracked the two groups' movements through radio reports: 'Both groups were forced to fight, then disappeared, changed the direction of their march, hid by day and moved by night.' Supply drops by KG 200 were sent in at night, targeted on arranged grid squares. 'The groups marched constantly, taking every security measure, through swamps and forest, but scarcely made more than 4 to 5 kilometres per day. We followed this daily progress with concern, but we soon had the terrible feeling that our poor comrades would never return to Germany. We struggled to suppress these thoughts: such men deserved to stay alive.'[14] This desperate situation dragged on month after month, as the Red Army grew stronger and German resources diminished; 'we did our best to ease their misery and scrape up the fuel necessary for the supply flights. Soon there was only one flight per week. Then catastrophe struck us all. KG 200's fuel supplies dried up. Although we tried everything, the supply drops had to be stopped.'[15]

During these last few months, Hitler mooted an emergency rescue plan, in which Skorzeny himself would be sent in with his commandos.[16] But it was too late. The German war effort was collapsing, and there was no more fuel to be had for such operations. By this time Skorzeny's attention was focused on other, more pressing, operations. The Scherhorn group had to content itself with Hitler's personal message on 23 March, promoting Scherhorn to Oberst (colonel) and awarding him the Ritterkreuz.[17]

In April 1945, Schiffer radioed that his group had reached the frozen rendezvous. Unable to send the promised airlift, the German radio operators could only listen passively to his last message, which Skorzeny described as 'heart-rending'. Schiffer requested fuel to power the generators used to charge their radio batteries, and added: 'I just want to stay in touch with you ... hear your voices.' After that, all contact ceased.[18] Neither Scherhorn nor any of his men – nor any of Skorzeny's commando groups – were ever seen in the Third Reich again.

Later, Skorzeny was racked by doubts about Operation *Scherhorn*: 'I spent many a sleepless night thinking about it ... I wondered whether the Russians were having a game with us all the time. Of course we had taken precautions against the possibility. Every wireless operator was given a special keyword, which he must use to show that he could speak freely.' Nonetheless, he had doubts. 'I had a wholesale respect for the skill of the Russians and their allies. Perhaps the puzzle will be solved one day.'[19]

The puzzle was solved, and Skorzeny proved absolutely justified in his doubts. The whole 'Scherhorn' affair was a deception on a massive scale intricately planned and executed, on Stalin's direct orders, by the Soviet intelligence service.

Aleksandr, otherwise known as 'Max' to the Germans, who had provided the original intelligence about the Scherhorn group, was in reality Aleksandr Petrovich Demianov, known as 'Heine' to the Russians, who had been working for Soviet counter-intelligence since 1929. The son of a Czarist officer killed in the Great War and nephew of the head of counter-intelligence for the White Army, Demianov had the perfect aristocratic credentials for ingratiating himself in Russian emigré society, and thus the Abwehr; they recruited him as 'Agent Max' shortly before *Barbarossa*.

After the German invasion, Demianov joined the Soviet cavalry, but his ultimate boss was Lieutenant-General Pavel Sudoplatov of the NKVD (the man who oversaw the thwarting of Skorzeny's Iran operation in late 1943). Sudoplatov's department set up a fake pro-German underground organisation called Prestoll ('Throne'), which offered to collaborate with German forces in return for 'appropriate roles' in the German regime once it had conquered the Soviet Union. Throne's ultimate purpose was to infiltrate German intelligence and the occupation government.[20] Demianov was a Throne operative.[21] With him established as a double agent, the scene was set for an ambitious deception.

Demianov's whole family seems to have been complicit in the scheme, in particular his wife Tatiana – an NKVD agent ostensibly working for the

Russian film studio Mosfilm – and her father, whose Moscow apartment became a safe-house for Throne – a Venus fly-trap for Abwehr couriers who either mysteriously disappeared or were turned by the NKVD. More importantly, it was the nerve-centre of Operation *Monastery*, which 'created major defeats for the Abwehr', according to Sudoplatov; 'the German high command made fatal mistakes because it relied too much on the Abwehr's efforts to penetrate the Soviet high command.' Max was trusted by the Germans because his information 'always contained elements of truth ... Max, as a source of information, although impressive, was taken too much on faith.'[22] Gehlen was certainly taken in, even years later, by the spurious authority of Max.[23]

Just before Operation *Bagration* in summer 1944, Sudoplatov and other key NKGB[24] counter-intelligence personnel were summoned by Stalin: 'We were directed to create the impression that German units, already surrounded by the Red Army in Byelorussia, still had the ability to hamper Soviet communications and supply lines. Stalin's intention was to trick the Germans into expending their resources in supporting and trying to break through to besieged forces.'[25]

The Russians called it Operation *Berezino*. Although Sudoplatov was in overall charge, Colonel Mikhail Maklyarsky did most of the planning, assisted by Leonid Eitingon (an experienced assassin who had organised the murder of Leon Trotsky in 1940), Yakov Serebryansky and Willie Fischer,[26] who acted as Demianov's controller during the operation.

Painstaking preparation went into baiting the trap through *Funkspiel* (radio deception), conjuring into existence Scherhorn's stranded Kampfgruppe. Scherhorn himself was real, and had indeed been in command of Landesschützen-Regiment 36. But his force was almost annihilated in intensive fighting during the opening round of *Bagration*. He and 200 other survivors had surrendered on or around 9 July 1944. In captivity, he was vulnerable to Soviet manipulation.

The Russians had selected Scherhorn with care, as someone whose profile was not so high that his whereabouts could be easily checked, but who would nevertheless have some resonance with the upper echelons of the Nazi Party. According to Russian sources, Scherhorn agreed to cooperate because he had become disillusioned with Hitler and was desperate to see his family again.[27] Important too was the fact that his unit had conducted anti-partisan activities and the threat of a death sentence hung over him. He apparently displayed scepticism about the Russian bluff actually working, pointing out to his captors that every German commander knew that the area around Minsk was swarming with partisans, and the idea that a sizeable Kampfgruppe could go undetected for weeks, let alone months, was frankly ludicrous.[28]

Initially, the deception was restricted to Scherhorn himself and a few other German prisoners of war who had been turned. Once the German high command had been given the physical coordinates of 'Camp Scherhorn' (in reality, a former partisan camp near the River Berezina), the pressure was on to make the illusion work.

No effort was spared in creating the force that would meet Skorzeny's SS commandos in their Red Army disguises. Sixteen senior Soviet counter-intelligence officers, including Sudoplatov's top Special Tasks team, were dispatched to the area, together with a number of prisoners of war, pro-Soviet Germans and NKGB troops posing as Germans in battered uniforms. The campsite was ringed by special patrols to detain unwanted intruders, and several anti-aircraft batteries were placed under cover in the near vicinity.[29] Scherhorn himself was kept in a hut on site.

When Skorzeny's Group Schiller finally turned up, they were greeted in a friendly way and one of the radio operators was taken to the hut, where he actually spoke to Scherhorn – who was aware all the while that NKGB machine pistols were pointed at him from behind its blanketed windows.[30] Having verified Scherhorn's authenticity to Heeresgruppe Mitte, the SS commando left the hut, and was immediately captured. He was given an unappetising choice: cooperate or die. He handed over his radio passwords and agreed to play along.

He was not the first German commando to be turned. The first, FAK 103-sponsored, radio operator had surrendered to the Russians on touchdown, handing them his invaluable codebook, transmission schedule and safe-arrival instructions. One of the SS radio operators, a certain Vedenin, contacted Soviet counter-intelligence to inform them of his arrival, unbeknown to the rest of his unit. As Soviet motorcycles sped to intercept the commando unit, Vedenin shot his three comrades and then surrendered.[31]

Most of the radio messages transmitted from Scherhorn's camp to Heeresgruppe Mitte were devised by NKVD officers Fischer and Maklyarsky. The deception played out until almost the very end of the war.

Scherhorn himself was one of the very few Germans who survived to tell the tale. Sudoplatov kept him under house arrest in Moscow, and at one time, in late 1945, toyed with the idea of using him to turn Grossadmiral Raeder, former head of the Kriegsmarine. But the two were judged incompatible and Scherhorn found himself repatriated to East Germany in 1949.[32] All but two of the radiomen who cooperated with the Soviet bluff were shot in late 1945.[33]

Operation *Berezino* had been a stunning success. The diversion and wastage of Germany's diminishing military resources was substantial. From September 1944 to May 1945, the Germans made 67 air sorties and parachuted in 25 German personnel, who were arrested and turned by the NKGB; in addition, the Russians seized 13 radio sets, countless drops of weapons, food, ammunition, uniforms and medicine, plus ten million rubles in cash.[34]

The Scherhorn affair is a monument to the arrogant credulity of the German intelligence machine, epitomised in the person of Gehlen, who overruled Worgitzky's sounder judgement that the whole thing was probably a fake. Gehlen seems to have allowed his intellectual conceit to get the better of his usually sound judgement. Sublime in his sense of racial superiority, he simply could not conceive of the Russians being capable of carrying out such an intricate deception. He was not alone in his arrogance, which was endemic among the Nazi hierarchy.[35]

In fact, compared with the espionage system baked into the Bolshevik police state, the Nazis' spy apparatus – whether because of its inferior size and organisation, its prejudices, its lowly status within the regime, or simply its relative lack of practice – was rather amateurish. Gehlen was a model of efficiency and insight compared with other contemporary German spymasters – but he was the one-eyed man in the kingdom of the blind.

As for Skorzeny, he allowed himself to be played for a mug.[36] His agenda was slightly different from Gehlen's. As time went on and it became apparent the Scherhorn group would not succeed in making it back to Germany, Skorzeny's concern was to turn it into a kind of makeshift anti-Soviet partisan force. The Russians deliberately fed this absurd fantasy with stories of Scherhorn successfully attacking a Soviet column, destroying over 100 vehicles and acquiring 70 tons of foodstuff.[37] The arch-manipulator was completely out-manipulated.

For all its dazzling technical success, however, Operation *Berezino* leaves questions unanswered. Why were so many Soviet intelligence assets and so much planning poured into the degradation of what by then had become marginal German resources? Stalin's orders, of course, had to be obeyed. But what was the greater strategic objective that the Russians hoped to achieve? On the face of it, Operation *Berezino* does not compare with Demianov's earlier and successful attempt to dupe Gehlen into believing that the main Soviet offensive of winter 1942 would come through the Rzhev salient, instead of around Stalingrad. It may be that the Soviets hoped *Berezino* might yield greater results or spawn further similar operations. Or it may have been valued as a proof-of-concept operation, foreseeing that deception could have a key role in post-war rivalry between the USSR and the West.

Arguably, the biggest single prize of Operation *Berezino* would have been the massive propaganda coup of capturing or killing 'Hitler's Commando' himself, Otto Skorzeny.[38] Near the end, that had seemed on the cards, with Hitler giving his endorsement to Skorzeny flying in to rescue *Scherhorn's* stragglers as they neared the end of their epic fictitious journey to the East Prussian border. It was a twist typical of Skorzeny's strange career that his life should be saved by the unexpected collapse of German resistance in April 1945.

9

The SS Changes Tack

In late 1944, Skorzeny was at the height of his power and influence. The Jüttner reforms had given the Leader of German Commandos unprecedented military and logistical resources. What had previously been three companies, a couple of spy schools and a headquarters staff based in Friedenthal was morphed into a brigade-strength force of over 2,000, with regional establishments across the Reich.

With German defeat looming, Hitler increasingly focused on two equally desperate stratagems for turning the tide. Either the British and Americans would be persuaded, by means of one last decisive counter-offensive in the West, to see the error of their ways and make common cause against the Bolshevik menace, or Germany would succeed in producing definitive miracle weapons.

In this climate, unconventional military tactics – psychological warfare, guerrilla fighting, collaboration with partisan armies, stay-behind spy networks and sabotage units – anything in short to slow up the Allied advance – began to assume a more central role in Nazi thinking. All these things came directly within Skorzeny's remit. But he was hamstrung. He could never iron out the ideological contradictions in his leaders' thinking or suppress the internal factionalism he'd inherited from the reorganisation. And with the Reich dwindling, he found it impossible to requisition the resources he needed. Skorzeny suffered two further disadvantages. He was forever being distracted from his core responsibilities by Hitler's demands. And being a man of action rather than an administrator, he lacked the temperamental discipline to bring focus to his responsibilities.

* * *

On 16 September 1944, Himmler issued an order to RSHA chief Kaltenbrunner to institute a new SS programme to recruit Nazi political and guerrilla 'resistance' movements in former occupied territories which had been lost to the Allies.[1] The task fell to Skorzeny, and the extent of his mandate was clarified in an OKH directive of 12 November: 'Resistance groups composed of Ukrainian nationalists; groups of the Polish national resistance movement ... Russian anti-Soviet resistance groups to be found as deep into Russia as the Caucasus and consisting of opponents of the system, refugees etc; other anti-Soviet resistance groups composed of non-Russian elements (prisoners of war, deportees, criminals).'[2]

The huge area of responsibility was in itself a challenge. The loyalty of the resistance groups was doubtful, and frequently pointed in contradictory directions. Nowhere were such tensions more apparent than in the deteriorating situation on the Eastern Front. Skorzeny was expected to link up with partisan organisations – primarily the Ukrayins'ka Povstans'ka Armiya (UPA or Ukrainian Insurgent Army), the Polish Armija Krajowa (AK or Home Army) and the Lietuvos Laisvės Armija (LLA or Lithuanian Freedom Army) – which were fundamentally *anti-Nazi* resistance forces. It is particularly hard to credit the AK being willing to collaborate after the Nazis' atrocities in Poland. And yet collaborate the AK did, on the grounds that they and the Nazis shared a hostility to Soviet occupation.

Skorzeny established just such an ambivalent relationship with the leader of the UPA, Stepan Bandera, who had been a prisoner in Sachsenhausen concentration camp since early 1942. Originally an anti-Nazi splinter from the Axis-aligned Orhanizatsiya Ukrayins'kykh Natsionalistiv (OUN or Organisation of Ukrainian Nationalists), the UPA was perfect material for what the German intelligence community termed a 'Green' resistance movement (distinct from White anti-Bolshevik reactionaries or Red pro-Bolshevik partisans). It had strong nationalist roots that could be depended upon to oppose Soviet reconquest. Ukrainian affinity to the Catholic Church – as against Russian orthodoxy or official state atheism – also helped. Most of the UPA commanders – including Bandera himself – were the sons of Uniate Catholic priests.[3]

As the Ukraine fell to Soviet re-conquest during summer 1944, Stepan Bandera was released by the SS and sent back to his homeland, on the understanding that he would collaborate. This laid the foundation for what became Operation *Sonnenblume* (*Sunflower*).[4] As in Belarus and the Scherhorn affair, so in the Ukraine: a multitude of small to medium-size German units had been left stranded by the Soviet advance. Many of these ended up with the UPA, some forcibly, some voluntarily. In autumn of that year, Skorzeny 'decided to form a commando unit, whose mission it would be to find Bandera and negotiate with him'.[5] The plan was to forge the stranded soldiers into small units, which would try to reach the German lines. The UPA would be given weapons and medical supplies, and airstrips would be improvised to fly out the wounded.

The man chosen to lead the *Sonnenblume* commando unit was a Wehrmacht officer with great experience in such operations. 'Hauptmann Kirn' was the nom de guerre of Dietrich F. Witzel, former Brandenburger, Abwehr II operator and larger-than-life character who was a protegé of Gunter d'Alquen, a Waffen-SS psychological warfare expert. Kirn had performed conspicuously well in d'Alquen's pioneering psych operation, *Skorpion Ost* – designed to lure Red Army soldiers to the German side. Skorzeny selected neither Hauptmann Kirn nor his men: he merely took responsibility for the mission. Kirn's appointment was personally approved by Himmler,[6] and came about because d'Alquen had Himmler's ear.

Kirn was provided with a team of a dozen Skorzeny commandos, plus around 20 'proven anti-Stalinist Russians' from Jagdverband Ost. These 'well-trained, determined volunteers ... were provided with Russian uniforms, boots, tobacco and false papers. With their shaved heads and two-week beards they looked like real Russian soldiers.'[7]

Sonnenblume was launched in October 1944, the initial aim being to replace the sporadic and rather unsatisfactory UPA radio and courier liaison with a direct link comprising Kirn and his commandos. *Sonnenblume* was managed through a complex command structure that did not augur well for its outcome. Kirn was formally appointed by Skorzeny as commanding officer of FAK 202, the front-line unit with immediate responsibility for the mission, but day-to-day management was mediated through the cumbersome device of Mil Amt D* with which Amt VI-S felt it unwise to tamper.

Nevertheless, within weeks of crossing the German lines with only seven men, Kirn had established contact not only with Bandera but with officers commanding a number of stranded German units. He acquired invaluable intelligence on the situation behind the Soviet lines, created reliable logistic and

*   See page 138.

radio communication links with the UPA and helped to set up guerrilla training camps employing a number of the stranded German officers and NCOs. By the beginning of November, Kirn and most of his original team were on their way back, mission accomplished. His efforts would later be rewarded with the Ritterkreuz.

Kirn's achievement can be measured by Stalin's order of 18 December 1944, creating five new NKGB divisions, each numbering 5,000 men, to suppress the insurrections that had sprung up behind his lines. These were not exclusively concerned with suppressing the UPA, but UPA insurgents were certainly some of Stalin's most troublesome customers. Kirn accomplished much in mapping the remnants of German troop formations and providing training assistance to the UPA. He even persuaded the UPA to attack Soviet prisoner of war camps and liberate their inmates.

He was much less successful in fulfilling one of Skorzeny's prime mission objectives: the repatriation of German soldiers to the Reich. German and UPA war aims fundamentally diverged. The Germans wanted the UPA to concentrate on ambushing military command posts and transport columns, but the partisans were more interested in advancing their political aims by attacking the apparatus of the Stalinist state. The Germans never held a whip-hand over UPA commanders: they could cajole and plead, but bullying and intimidation were no longer possible.

Sonnenblume illustrated a wider truth about the folly of sponsoring nationalist resistance groups. Since the 1930s, Bandera and his intelligence chief had kept open a channel of communication to the British SIS*, and Britain and the USA now seemed a better bulwark against the Soviet Union than the beaten Germans. There were also internecine conflicts between nationalist groups themselves, often with a barbarity that gave even the Germans pause – such as the UPA's ethnic cleansing of Poles in the Western Ukraine.

After *Sonnenblume*, Kirn and FAK 202 continued to act as the principal liaison with the UPA from a fixed base in Cracow – until forced back into Silesia towards the end of the war. By March 1945, however, all contact had been lost, owing to the inability of KG 200 to commandeer the fuel for supply and parachutist drops.

The legacy of Skorzeny's ambitious scheme lived on long after the war ended. Thousands of German stragglers remained behind, and the UPA continued to be sponsored by Britain and America. Some of the agents they covertly dropped over the Ukraine as late as 1947 had been members

---

* Secret Intelligence Service, also known as MI6

of the SS-Freiwilligen-Division 'Galizien'', which had been active in the Ukraine at the time of *Sonnenblume*.[8] Bandera's insurrection became sufficiently serious for Stalin's boss in the Ukraine, Nikita Khrushchev, to bring in top NKVD general and Skorzeny nemesis Pavel Sudoplatov to suppress it.

* * *

Whatever its shortcomings, *Sonnenblume* was a paragon of efficiency compared with most other resistance and subversive activities 'orchestrated' by Skorzeny in the dying months of the war – *Scherhorn* being the conspicuous example. Others were even more inchoate, clumsily improvised, less well resourced and – as often as not – overtaken by events.

The organisational problems started at the top with Skorzeny's merely nominal command of the forces at his disposal. The (predominantly civilian) stay-behind groups, or I-Netze, were supposedly under Schellenberg's direct supervision,[9] and were therefore mediated through his section chiefs – men not necessarily disposed to take orders from Skorzeny's S section. Similarly, most military agents engaged in sabotage operations were handled via the FAK II units, under de facto control of the Wehrmacht, with Gehlen pulling the strings. The very last thing FHO wanted or needed (as Gehlen saw it) was SS thugs meddling with their delicate attempts to build bridges with 'Green' nationalist groups.

Pivotal in obstructing Amt VI-S efforts to absorb FAK/FAT operations was Major Fritz Naumann, head of Mil Amt D (the rump of Abwehr II), and technically Skorzeny's deputy chief. Naumann also served as deputy to Oberst Hugo von Süsskind-Schwendi, the man in charge of a special Wehrmacht agency set up specifically to thwart Skorzeny's designs. The relationship between Skorzeny and Naumann was, at best, frosty. Radl, who had to act as liaison between them, found cooperation minimal, although Naumann did write regular reports for Skorzeny and make his presence felt at Friedenthal and Berkärstrasse from time to time. Skorzeny, it seems, never returned the compliment by visiting Mil Amt D headquarters. He did, however, meddle in several Mil Amt D appointments. In December 1944, Naumann applied for a transfer, allowing Skorzeny to impose his own candidate, the sinister bemonocled lawyer Dr Roland Loos – another Kaltenbrunner protegé.

---

*   At the time of *Sonnenblume* the division was briefly dubbed 14. Waffen-Grenadier-Division der SS (ukrainisch Nr 1).

Almost immediately, the Wehrmacht moved to ringfence all FAK operations within the new department of Mil Amt F, under the command of Oberst Georg Buntrock. Buntrock may have been a more enthusiastic Nazi, but like Naumann and Süsskind-Schwendi he had scant respect for Skorzeny's scheming. The new compromise agreement with OKW was brokered by Schellenberg, who was not displeased to see Skorzeny curbed.[10]

Even within Skorzeny's own organisation there were tensions that seriously undermined its efficiency, such as the smouldering feud between two Amt VI-S Balkan experts, SS-Obersturmbannführer Ernst Benesch and SS-Hauptsturmführer Rupert Mandl. Benesch was the commander of the largest Jagdverbände unit, Südost. As a Brandenburger he had taken part in the attempt to capture Tito at Drvar. Mandl hailed from Amt VI-E, but also served as Balkans liaison officer for Amt VI-S. In December 1944 their lack of communication led to Benesch entrusting a group of his Serb Chetniks to Ustaše paramilitary leader Colonel Luburić, a Croatian nationalist psychopathically hostile to all Serbs; he had the party arrested and shot 40 of them. Had Benesch consulted Mandl – an expert on Croatian politics – he would have discovered that Luburić was not to be trusted with the protection of Serbs. All hope of setting up a stay-behind operation in Yugoslavia was extinguished because of this incident.[11]

Incompetent in a very different way was one of Skorzeny's senior henchmen – SS-Hauptsturmführer Arno Besekow, a criminologist and expert in sabotage, who had been director of the A-Schule in The Hague. Besekow was a ruddy, thick-set, superficially affable man, popular with his colleagues; he enjoyed a cigar – and liked a drink even better. He was also a womaniser and a hopelessly indiscreet one at that. While Besekow was trying to persuade his glamorous Belgian mistress, Rosita Casier, to run his Brussels-based stay-behind network 'Henriette', and apprising her in pillow talk of Friedenthal's secrets, Casier was simultaneously spilling the beans to British intelligence. Or so Friedenthal came to suspect. For her own safety, Besekow packed her off first to Austria, then to San Remo in Italy, where she spent the remaining days of the war in hiding.[12]

Of similar clay was SS-Sturmbannführer 'Dr' Manfred Pechau, who for a while was Besekow's successor at the A-Schule. Pechau, a violent Nazi racist, was a protégé of Besekow; they had first met when engaged in murderous police activities around Riga during the early stages of *Barbarossa*. Later, they formed part of Skorzeny's SS detail conducting the search for Mussolini.

Pechau cut an athletic figure but one whose glass eye gave him a chilling air. This menacing demeanour was frequently belied by lapses into drunkenness. On one occasion, while still director of the A-Schule, Pechau became so disorderly that he was shot by one of his sentries – and spent the next few weeks recuperating in hospital. Despite his manifest unsuitability, during September 1944 Pechau was tasked with creating a stay-behind network of agents to operate in the Baltic. In all, he managed to recruit and train about 30, who were formed into Jagdeinsatz Balticum, loosely associated with Jagdverband Ost. It became a microcosm of all that was most wrong with Skorzeny's undercover operations. Pechau was unfit for his task, and Jagdeinsatz Balticum was riddled with political difficulties.

Skorzeny, who was smart enough to realise that minority nationalities would not fight for Germany without rights of self-determination, had consulted with Reichsminister for the Occupied Eastern Territories Alfred Rosenberg, and successfully laid the groundwork for limited Baltic independence, only to find his concessions immediately revoked by the newly appointed Nazi commissioner for the Baltic, Erich Koch. This most diehard and intransigent of Nazis had already left a trail of destruction behind in the Ukraine, where he had been civil overlord for much of the past four years. He now intended to adopt exactly the same brutal and unswerving policy in the Baltic republics. This, said Skorzeny later, with uncharacteristic understatement, 'caused great resentment'.[13] Jagdeinsatz Balticum was in any case doomed by mounting problems on the Eastern Front. Swept up into hastily improvised local missions in early 1945, none of Pechau's agents ever returned to Friedenthal.

∗ ∗ ∗

Not every undercover operation was marred by ideology or ineptitude. Nor did Skorzeny attract only flawed mediocrities, unsavoury mavericks and racist bigots. He brought in outstanding talent – Adrian von Fölkersam and Wilhelm Walther, for instance. And while Skorzeny may have fallen down on the detail of leadership, his charismatic personality as a figurehead of the organisation and his can-do attitude were major attractions. Moreover, the organisation he and Radl built was capable of creating its own stars. Or, at any rate, one of them.

Walter Girg liked to think of his recruitment into the Waffen-SS as almost an accident, having joined up because 'I could not provide for myself'.[14] Like all Waffen-SS men, Girg had to rise from the ranks. Having served in France, the Balkans and the USSR (in the same Reich division as Skorzeny), he was selected for officer training in 1943; after graduating, he became an instructor.

With the Eastern Front deteriorating, Girg volunteered for special operations. He came up with an idea for 'assembling groups of German volunteers and members of our allied armies who would execute long-range intelligence missions and thus enable the German High Command to be on its guard against Russian surprise attacks and give it time to retreat'.[15] His transfer as a platoon commander to SS-Jägerbataillon 502 came in August 1944. Under Skorzeny's direction Girg underwent a crash course in intelligence work and sabotage. On 26 August he received the briefing for his first mission.

It was a top secret *Reichsauftrag* (Reich mission) from Jodl at OKW, and was personally handed to Girg by Skorzeny – such was his confidence in the new recruit.

Three days earlier, Germany's ally Romania, facing imminent defeat, had changed sides. A community of about 250,000 Romanian Volksdeutsche in West Romania now faced being overrun by the Soviet invaders. The Wehrmacht's 6. Armee (rebuilt after Stalingrad) was unable to cover an orderly evacuation because it too had been taken by surprise and completely cut off. Scrambling for a strategy, Himmler appointed the brutal SS-Obergruppenführer Artur Phleps as plenipotentiary and trouble-shooter. His orders were to rally resistance among the Volksdeutsche, coordinate military assistance with Hungary, and do whatever he could to relieve the retreating 6. Armee.

This was the backdrop to Operation *Landfried*, Skorzeny's cobbled-together response to the growing crisis. Walter Girg's mission brief was to take six KG 200 aircraft and 55 men from SS-Jägerbataillon 502 and land in the area of Temesberg*. 'I had plenty of extra weapons and was to distribute them among the civilian population, to organise them and thus establish a defensive line between Temesberg and Kronstadt†. This was supposed to halt the advance of the Russians and Romanians until German troops would relieve me.'[16]

The operation looked doomed from the beginning. Preparation was sloppy and the equipment Girg was given faulty. Arriving in Vienna by train, he received further briefing from the local Amt VI section chief, Skorzeny's rival SS-Obersturmbannführer Wilhelm Waneck. While the aircraft were on standby at Vienna aerodrome, Girg spent a day at Waneck's office sifting through intelligence reports on the fast-changing military situation. He soon discovered that a landing at Temesberg was no longer possible, as the city had already fallen into enemy hands.

---

*   Timişoara
†   Braşov

Improvising quickly, Girg flew to Neuburg* in Hungary, taking with him an extra 40 Romanian Volksdeutsche volunteers, and then made his way by truck to a village on the German-held Romanian border, where he rendezvoused with Phleps, who acceded to Girg's hastily devised alternative plan.

Girg now divided his force into three units – one of which he personally commanded – to conduct long-range reconnaissance work behind the Russian lines and, if possible, slow the Soviet advance by sabotaging the Carpathian mountain passes. All units were equipped with light paratrooper uniforms which deliberately resembled Allied tailoring; they also carried locally adapted civilian clothes. They took only three days' rations, intending to live off the land, and carried British Sten guns hidden in rucksacks, pistols, hand grenades and ample supplies of the innovative plastic explosive Nipolit. On 31 August, the three units stole across the Hungarian border unobserved.

Two of the units acquired valuable tactical information and reported minimal losses, blowing up a number of bridges, destroying the water mains at Kronstadt, rescuing 200 German soldiers and gaining valuable intelligence that prevented the encirclement of a German army corps. Serving in one unit was James Brady, formerly of the Royal Irish Fusiliers, who had joined 2. Kompanie SS-Jägerbataillon 502 only that summer: 'We were in Romania for about three weeks, during which time I helped to blow up two river bridges and one railway bridge.'[17] Girg's own unit had more mixed fortunes. Ambushed at night by the Russians, his men escaped after heavy fighting, and proceeded to make a detailed report on the progress of the Russian 6th Army. Disguised as civilians, they stumbled into a Romanian army depot. 'As we were weaker than they, we tried to talk it over with them. We asserted that we were Romanian stragglers who had left our German units.'[18] The Romanians weren't convinced, and Girg and his men were forced to the ground and beaten. 'Soon the Russians arrived and we were condemned to death immediately. We had to stand against a small tree and 20 Russians in front of us were ordered to execute us.' Girg managed to escape while the Russians were distracted, although his men were shot. He was wounded in the head and foot, but reached German lines and delivered his report.[19]

Girg reckoned total losses at about 40 per cent of his force. But the timely information he brought back about massing Russian armoured units was enough to prevent the encirclement of significant German forces. Enough, certainly, to earn Girg the Ritterkreuz – personally awarded by Skorzeny once Girg was out of hospital – and his promotion to SS-Obersturmführer.

*   Abaúj

But however epic and courageous Girg's exploits, Operation *Landfried* achieved little of lasting value. Phleps, acting on the intelligence he was given by Girg and others, was able to shepherd some German units back through the lines, but he failed to evacuate the Volksdeutsche population. *Landfried's* achievements weighed little in the balance of the 18 divisions (including 6. Armee) annihilated by the Red Army. Critically, Germany lost access to the Romanian oilfields at Ploesti, on which its ability to wage mechanised warfare largely depended.

The message sent out to the Reich's remaining allies was clear. Finland disengaged from the Axis in September, while Bulgaria switched sides and declared war on Germany. German occupation of Greece and Yugoslavia became untenable. Meanwhile, the Reich's Slovakian client state had imploded into civil war. Germany's only defensive bulwark was its remaining ally, Hungary; and that under duress – its own departure from the Axis having been forestalled in March 1944 by German occupation.

After convalescence, Girg was required (as a former panzer commander) to form a tank company of captured T-34 Russian tanks (designated as 3. Kompanie Jagdverband Mitte). The Panzerkompanie, its German personnel equipped with authentic Russian uniforms, weapons and papers, planned to make a first foray into enemy-occupied Hungary during December 1944, but Girg could amass neither enough trained personnel nor tanks to be ready in time.[20] He did, however, mount a successful long-distance reconnaissance and sabotage mission in East Prussia, which by mid-January 1945 was overrun by Soviet forces. Girg and his 54 men[21] – a number of them Russian nationals – got as far as Danzig but were there persuaded by the embattled commander of 2. Armee to redirect their mission – without Skorzeny's knowledge or consent – to enemy-held territory in Silesia and Poland, where German forces were still thought to be holding out.[22] Wearing Russian uniforms, the SS commandos filtered through Soviet lines on 1 February. For the next six weeks, Girg – with characteristic panache – spread mayhem in enemy ranks. Travelling over 1,000 kilometres, he commandeered Russian trucks and armoured vehicles, skirmished with the Red Army and Polish militia, shot up NKGB troops and demolished bridges, telephone lines, railway signal installations and munition dumps.

However, the reconnaissance element of the mission was aborted when Girg lost his radio operator, his sole R/T set and the lorry carrying them to the icy waters of the Vistula. He could no longer contact Friedenthal. Making their way northwards, the remaining 35 members of the commando unit reached the besieged coastal garrison of Kolberg on 15 March,[23] only to be arrested by the commander, who threatened to have them shot as suspected Seydlitz agents (German prisoners of war coerced into fighting for the Soviets). Girg had no form of identification other than his Ritterkreuz, which he wore beneath a neckerchief.[24] With the radio operator dead, it was impossible to produce the wavelength and code word that would have established the unit's bona fides.

Salvation came when Girg was recognised by an officer. He and his men were freed, and immediately joined in the defence of the fortified position, 'continuing the engagement until the enemy cleared the area'.[25] Only hours before the city surrendered, Girg was allowed to make his exit by sea.

The significance of Girg's mission, and the intelligence he was able to bring back, were such that he was given a silver Nahkampfspange (Close Combat Clasp), awarded for 25 hand-to-hand combats with the enemy, and promoted to SS-Hauptsturmführer. He was also personally awarded the oak leaves to his Ritterkreuz by Adolf Hitler.

∗ ∗ ∗

All these special operations, dissimilar though they were in scope, tactical importance, resources, and calibre of personnel, had one thing in common: the autonomy with which they were run. They were typical of Skorzeny's leadership style.

A high degree of delegation to the commander on the spot is an inescapable element of undercover operations. Any leader in Skorzeny's place would have faced a formidable, and perhaps impossible, task in bringing coherence to the tangled skein of operations and their organising departments. But Skorzeny's idea of leadership was to play to his strengths and wholly ignore his weaknesses. He thought it enough to lead from the front through charismatic forcefulness, and disdainfully delegated the tedious parts of his job, at which he was inept – the administrative detail, training and military planning, the secretive, dissimulative business of setting up stay-behind networks. Occasionally, as with Radl and Fölkersam, his subordinates were competent; often – step forward Besekow and Pechau – they were not. The ability to delegate is an important quality in leaders; in Skorzeny's case, it became an irresponsible vice.[26]

These were not the only side-effects of his dysfunctional leadership. Skorzeny's zealous intervention on 20 July 1944 had earned him the undying hatred of the military caste, especially general staff officers. Herein lay the reason for the roadblocks put in his way when attempting to exert executive control over the Frontaufklärung system. Werner Ohletz, the Luftwaffe's liaison officer to the RSHA, called Skorzeny 'the most hated man in the whole of Mil Amt'; he 'hated army officers and declared at every opportunity that for him there was no such thing as an officer's code of honour; it was only a cloak for cowardice in the face of the enemy'. The July coup made him 'mad with rage' and 'he would have seized and closely interrogated' the entire Abwehr if Schellenberg hadn't stopped him. Ohletz claimed that Randel-Semper, chief of operations with KG 200, 'knew Skorzeny thoroughly – and detested him, as did all who knew him and were not merely his yes-men', and that Skorzeny did 'nothing but hound people whom he suspected of being connected with the July 20th affair'. Skorzeny was 'a complete megalomaniac and drew up the most fantastic projects. There existed no law for him; he did and permitted what he pleased.'[27]

Harsh words, probably coloured by personal enmity, but not without justification. Skorzeny was a vindictive enemy, as may be judged from his dealings with the leader of one of his late-war commando operations in Slovakia, Major Erwein Graf von Thun-Hohenstein.

Thun was an uncompromising eccentric whose admiration for Adolf Hitler was far from uncritical. He came from a long line of Tyrolean noblemen. After service in World War I, he took part in the abortive Kapp putsch which attempted to overthrow the Weimar Republic. Serving in the Brandenburg Regiment, Thun proved a gifted commander of renegade troops – mostly Russians and Ukrainians – and affectionately called his volunteers *Thunfische* (a pun on the German word for tuna fish). His swashbuckling style was admired by his troops, but not so much by his superiors in the Abwehr, who found his unbridled behaviour and increasing fondness for drink difficult to deal with.

Skorzeny first crossed paths with Thun in late summer 1944, shortly after taking executive control of Mil Amt D. Only weeks before, Thun had been assigned to a new counter-insurgency role in Slovakia in which the RSHA was to take a sinister hand. The Germans had been surprised by the scale of the anti-Nazi rebellion in August, involving the defection of part of the pro-Axis Slovak national army. They needed to flush out resistance before setting in place their own measures for a guerrilla war against the Red Army. The chosen instrument for this repression was a new Sonderkommando unit known as 'Edelweiss', made up of Caucasian (Muslim) separatists and Cossacks, plus Slovak auxiliaries who had nailed their colours to the Nazi mast. They were officered by Germans from FAT 218, led by Thun and operationally controlled through Mil Amt D.

Proving that he had lost none of his panache, Thun led his men into battle kitted out in a gentleman hunter's loden coat, knee-breeches and sturdy stick. On one occasion, he donned the uniform of a Soviet major and – exploiting his excellent Russian and gift for subterfuge – surprised the pro-Soviet partisans in their own camp. Although only fully activated in late September 1944, Edelweiss carried out over 50 anti-partisan search-and-destroy operations, killing 300 and capturing over 600. On 26 December 1944, Thun's men captured an Allied mission of 12 American OSS (Office of Strategic Services) and three British SOE officers who were acting as a liaison unit to the Slovak partisans deep in the lower Tatras, at Polomka. The exploit merited a personal telegram from Himmler to Thun.

Skorzeny later took care to draw a veil over his connection with Edelweiss, because of what happened next. Although the Allied agents were wearing uniforms, they were handed over to the Gestapo as spies, and imprisoned at Mauthausen concentration camp. On 23 January 1945, on Kaltenbrunner's direct order, they were executed. The same month, heavily armed Edelweiss troops led by Thun surged into the mountain hamlet of Ostry Grun after hearing reports of guerrilla activity in the area. They captured 62 people, mostly women and children. Some hours later, a motorised detachment of Waffen-SS troops pulled up and executed the villagers with machine pistols. The Edelweiss and SS units moved on to another village, Klak, where a further 84 civilians were rounded up and massacred. The following month, an Edelweiss patrol flushed out 18 Jews in the valley of Ksina. They were summarily shot, apparently on Thun's order. Atrocities like this jarred with the clean-cut, man-of-action image of himself that Skorzeny later cultivated. But of his being zealously active behind the scenes there can be no doubt.

Skorzeny detested Thun for his aristocratic bearing, but even more for his suspected disloyalty to Hitler. When Thun was recommended for a Ritterkreuz, Skorzeny blocked the recommendation on the grounds that Thun had, in 1937, married a woman who was half-Jewish.[28] The allegation was groundless: it was Thun's brother who had married someone of partly Jewish ancestry. But Thun never did get his Ritterkreuz. In May 1945 he was captured by the Russians and tried by military tribunal. Thun was sentenced to death and shot in the neck – his last words reputedly being: 'Tell Stalin to kiss my arse.'

Thun was not the only victim of Skorzeny's vengeful behaviour. In the very last days of the war, he had the despised head of Mil Amt F, Georg Buntrock, tried as a traitor.[29] The real motive for his summary trial was probably the elimination of a rival source of intelligence who might compete with Skorzeny – post-war – for the Allies' favour. Certainly Reinhard Gehlen and Adolf Heusinger (a former army chief of staff) suspected Skorzeny of similar liquidation plans for themselves.[30]

Skorzeny's feuds and personal rivalries were magnified by the poisonous culture of Amt VI. The wider context was Skorzeny's membership of the Vienna Circle – the group of Kaltenbrunner friends, supporters and protegés installed in Amt VI. Aside from being relentlessly hostile towards Schellenberg, all were wedded to the romantic notion that the power of Austria could be restored to some of its former imperial glory through association with the Third Reich. They later developed the equally delusional idea of building an independent post-war 'democratic' Austrian republic backed by the Western Allies that would serve as a bulwark against the Soviet Union.[31]

The crackpot Free Austria scheme helps to explain Kaltenbrunner's obsessive interest in the day-to-day running of Amt VI's E desk, which specialised in Balkan affairs.[32] Skorzeny liked to treat the Balkans as his special playground for guerrilla warfare training and weapons testing; not unreasonably so, as the place, though nominally under German occupation, was in a state of civil war from late 1943 onwards. With typical impetuosity, in April 1944 he set up a second A-Schule, very deliberately siting it at a tourist hotel in the Fruska Gora mountain range on the front line between Croatia and Serbia. The idea was that the 'students' – mostly Italians, Serbs, Russians and Hungarians – would gain immediate combat experience from the incessant partisan activity in the area. And so it proved, Skorzeny famously observing that the cadets and local guerrilla bands ended up sharing the same doctor, who was obliged to divide his time between them.[33] In September, the advancing Red Army brought these guerrilla games to an end and forced Skorzeny to abandon the school.

Skorzeny would never be master of his own Balkan backyard. Wilhelm Waneck, head of Amt VI E and another Kaltenbrunner appointee, was intensely jealous of his fame and influence. Under the pretext of 'streamlining' operations between the SD and Skorzeny's Jagdverband Südost, and with Kaltenbrunner in the background pulling strings, Waneck was forever interfering in the planning of operations taking place within what he clearly considered his personal appanage.

Another member of the circle was the former head of Amt VI-E, SD death-squad leader and Heydrich accolyte Werner Göttsch. So rated by Kaltenbrunner was Göttsch that in July 1943 he had been selected alongside Skorzeny as one of two SS candidates to rescue Mussolini. He'd had to drop out due to chronic tuberculosis, leaving Skorzeny the uncontested choice.[34] Despite being reassigned to light, ideological duties (which seemed to comprise the pursuit of occult literature and his Jewish mistress, Ursula Hegewald, in Vienna), Göttsch continued to play an active conspiratorial role in Amt VI affairs.

The final significant member of the Kaltenbrunner-sponsored coterie was Waneck's deputy, Wilhelm Höttl. In the Heydrich era he had been accused of ideological unsoundness (possibly to do with 'unseemly' relations with Jews and devout Catholics), and committed for trial in an SS court. The charges were eventually dropped. His rehabilitation rapidly followed the appointment of Kaltenbrunner.

Kaltenbrunner's protegés were committed Nazis, but in their own view they were 'moderates' who wanted a federal system to emerge from the post-war Reich that would allow Vienna, and indeed Austria-Hungary, to prosper as a regional powerbase.[35]

Despite Kaltenbrunner's faith in him, only in one respect – their shared hostility towards Schellenberg – did Skorzeny fully live up to his expectations. He was a loose cannon, incapable of obeying anyone's orders for very long. More problematic still was the astonishing personal rapport that Skorzeny quickly forged with Hitler and his immediate associates. It made Skorzeny ungovernable and incapable of being trusted.

The rest of the Vienna Circle was equally wary in its dealings with him. Höttl restricted all contact with Amt VI-S to a functional minimum, preferring to rely on his own sources of intelligence.[36] Höttl's verdict on Skorzeny echoes that of Ohletz: he 'developed into an unpleasant type in the last stages of the war … His pretensions to greatness had increased enormously as a result of his apparent triumphs. He became obsessed with a boundless ambition and felt himself destined to scale the heights of fame to their very peak.'[37]

In short, Amt VI-S in late 1944 was in a state of dynamic chaos. Burdened by the task of absorbing elements of an organisation much bigger than itself, increasingly starved of basic resources, it was led by a man whose success had gone to his head. Skorzeny was neither in control, nor controllable. His contempt for administrative detail had left him isolated from everyday reality; his megalomaniac delusion, tactlessness and arrogance made many of the departmental heads on whom he depended reluctant to deal with him; and his bosses were wary of intervening on account of his special relationship with the Führer.

Worst of all, perhaps – Skorzeny was rarely there to take charge. His demonic energy had been misdirected towards that elusive 'miracle' weapon which would turn the war around. To cap it all, in September 1944, the Führer devised a further special mission that could only be carried out by his favourite commando. Personally.

10

Operation *Panzerfaust*

Budapest, October 1944

On 10 September 1944, Skorzeny received an order from Generaloberst Jodl to attend a situation briefing at the Wolfsschanze.

Russian troops were now only 120 kilometers away from Hitler's HQ, and the embattled dictator had taken the precaution of installing himself in a newly created Führerbunker – a 7-metre-thick steel and concrete bomb shelter, devoid of daylight or natural air, whose walls exuded a steamy miasma of wet cement.

Jodl, number two to Keitel, was head of operations at OKW and also the man charged with primary military responsibility for the Balkans. The fact that he had signed the order must have given Skorzeny a strong hint as to where his next executive mission would be focused. The evening conference, which took place in a big hall about 50 metres away from the bunker, was one of two 'appreciations of the military situation' that occured daily.

It was an eye-opener for Skorzeny, who had to introduce himself because so many senior officers had been replaced by new people since the July plot. 'We all stood. A stool was provided for Hitler: the coloured pencils, a magnifying glass and his glasses lay on the map table.' When Hitler entered, 'I was shocked when I saw him up close. I scarcely recognised him. This was not the man I remembered from the previous autumn: he walked bent and dragged one leg behind him. His left hand trembled so badly that he sometimes had to hold it with his right. His voice sounded veiled and brittle. He greeted a few generals. When he spied me he had a few kind words. Then he said, "Skorzeny stay for everything that concerns the Balkans."'[1]

The rumour, emanating from his physicians, was that Hitler was in the grip of a degenerative motor-neurone disease – almost certainly Parkinson's. Then again, only seven weeks previously he had been blown up, had both his eardrums punctured and received injuries to his head, legs, one arm and his back. Skorzeny was inclined to dismiss the Parkinson's rumours, noting Hitler's phenomenal residual drive and near-perfect memory for complex battlefield dispositions. One other thing he could not fail to notice, at first hand, were Hitler's fits of uncontrollable fury: 'He flung his pencils down on the map table and some of them fell on the floor. He railed against Jodl, OKH and the Luftwaffe. No one stirrred or said a word and I myself shrank back behind the others.' Skorzeny was equally disturbed by the way Hitler would suddenly recover and return to dealing with technical matters as if nothing had happened.[2]

After three days of this, the specifics of Skorzeny's new mission emerged. He was asked to stay behind after the evening conference. Present also were Keitel, Jodl, Ribbentrop and Himmler. No ordinary mission, then.

Hitler pointed out that, though stabilised, the front in Hungary had to be maintained 'at all costs'. Over a million German troops were now caught in a salient and must be protected from encirclement and collapse. 'We have received secret reports,' Hitler said, 'that the head of the Hungarian state, Admiral Horthy, is attempting to get in touch with our enemies with a view to a separate peace. It would mean the loss of our armies. He is approaching both the Western powers and the Russians ... You, Skorzeny, must be prepared to seize the Citadel of Budapest by force, if he betrays his alliance with us.'[3]

Jodl outlined the military units to be committed to this potential coup de main. The core element would comprise: a reinforced company of Jagdverband Mitte, numbering about 250; a reinforced company of the reconstituted SS parachute battalion (now SS-Fallschirmjägerbataillon 600, under the command of Milius), also numbering 250; two companies of KG 200 paratroopers equipped with gliders; and about 700 officer-cadets drawn from the military academy at Wiener-Neustadt in Austria. The key staff officers were to be: Fölkersam (chief of staff), Radl and SS-Untersturmführer Ostafel (adjutants), Hunke (operations chief), and Milius himself. The composition was exclusively Aryan – no suggestion of using Jagdverband Südost, the locally based commando force, on a mission of this political sensitivity.

To whom Skorzeny should report on the spot was left vague. His sole guidance seems to have been a personal written order given to him by Hitler at the end of his briefing on a sheet of ornate 'state paper': 'SS-Sturmbannführer Skorzeny is carrying out a personal and highly confidential order of the highest importance. I order all political and military authorities everywhere to give him all the help he needs and comply with all his wishes.'[4] At the bottom was a very shaky, but unmistakable, signature. Skorzeny was 'more than amazed at the possibilities' offered by this document.[5] In reality, despite being Hitler's personally appointed military agent, Skorzeny was never an isolated actor in the complex events unfolding in Hungary.

Miklós Horthy, Hungary's ruler, was – as Skorzeny observed – an admiral without a fleet and a regent without a king or queen. He was a career naval officer in the one branch of the Austro-Hungarian armed services that had performed well during World War I, and emerged a hero and a unifying national figure in the bloody aftermath. Although officially regent to the exiled king, Horthy was more in the mould of a Cromwellian 'Protector'. He ruled through a crown council that vested him with the power to appoint and dismiss parliaments and prime ministers, and – critically for the events about to take place – gave him exclusive command of the armed forces.

No one could accuse Horthy of being an ardent Nazi. According to Höttl, Hitler profoundly distrusted Horthy, regarding him as 'a fossilised old Austrian admiral, completely in the hands of his Anglophile and Jewish entourage and imbued with a strong aversion to National Socialism and the person of its Führer'.[6] Where Horthy and Hitler did agree was on foreign policy; both had a violent antipathy towards Versailles and its ancillary treaties, Hungary having lost two-thirds of its historic kingdom to Romania, Yugoslavia and Czechoslovakia. Likewise, Horthy – together with most of his countrymen – shared a visceral distrust of the Soviet Union. Hitler had inveigled Horthy into Axis alignment, redrawing the map of Hungary and restoring its lost territory. Hungary duly became a co-belligerent in the great crusade against Bolshevism. But all three of the armies Horthy committed to the Eastern Front suffered heavy casualties, and one was almost annihilated (84 per cent casualties) in the aftermath of Stalingrad.

With the outcome of the war looking bleak, Horthy tried to back out of the Axis, via a deal with the Western Allies. Secret negotiations were opened between Horthy's cabinet and an OSS colonel, Florimond Duke, through the offices of Hungary's security chief, Major-General István Ujszaszi.

The Germans, with their own agents planted in the Hungarian intelligence service, knew all about these negotiations, and decided to act preemptively. In March 1944, Operation *Margarethe* – the military occupation of Hungary – was set in train. Horthy was summoned by Hitler, allegedly to sort out the fate of four beleaguered Hungarian divisions.[7] The conference was a hoax devised to delay Horthy's return to Hungary. As his train trundled back across the frontier, the Regent found he was no longer in full control of his own country. It had just been occupied by three German panzer divisions.

Although reduced to figurehead status and saddled with a pro-German prime minister (General Döme Sztójay), crucially Horthy remained commander of the armed forces, and could summarily withdraw from the war. Doing so would force the Germans to stretch a front line already at breaking point while also precipitating a civil war in Hungary. Horthy had given an undertaking to drop any peace overtures to the Allies, but Hitler added belt and braces by sending in a Reich plenipotentiary, SS-Brigadeführer Edmund Veesenmayer, to superintend the administration. Technically, Veesenmayer reported to Ribbentrop at the Foreign Ministry. In reality, he was involved in a complex power-play with Himmler's special representative in Hungary, Höherer SS- und Polizeiführer Otto Winkelmann. Supposedly subordinate to Veesenmayer, Winkelmann was able to outmanoeuvre his nominal boss by appeals to Kaltenbrunner and Himmler, from whom he actually took his orders. Very soon, Hungary was crawling with Gestapo men (under Adolf Eichmann) making up for lost time in applying the Final Solution to a country that had escaped it.

Meanwhile, Horthy had retired to the Royal Palace perched on the southern tip of the Burgberg in Budapest, surrounded with personal bodyguards. His uneasy stand-off with the German authorities might have continued but for a dramatic development on the international front.

On 23 August – to the Germans' total surprise – the pro-Nazi Romanian dictator Ion Antonescu was toppled in a coup and replaced by a Soviet-aligned government which immediately declared war on the Reich. The military catastrophe facing Heeresgruppe Südukraine was immense. Not only had a gaping hole appeared in its front line due to the withdrawal of Romanian divisions; it was also denied the means of strategic retreat through the Carpathian mountain passes held by hostile Romanian forces.

Clearly the Kingdom of Hungary was about to become a Soviet battleground. There was no alternative, so far as Horthy and his advisers were concerned, but to seek an armistice with the Russians if the country was to be spared total devastation.[8] Now came the challenge of disengaging from the

Axis without giving Hitler time to implement effective counter-measures. There followed a desperate cat-and-mouse game. Horthy dismissed his pro-German coalition government and appointed a new and more tightly controlled military administration. He plotted with the secret service chief Ujszaszi and the commandant of the Budapest garrison to arm the resistance and seize Budapest's vital bridges, stations, roads and factories as part of a coup de main against the German garrison;[9] then he secretly dispatched his gendarmerie chief to Moscow to negotiate. By 11 October, Horthy had before him an armistice agreement that required only a date and his signature.

The Germans were ahead of him. Intelligence about the Moscow mission had trickled through to Höttl's SD-Ausland unit in Budapest, which operated from the offices of Winkelmann and his deputy, the commandant of the security police and SD, Hans-Ulrich Geschke.[10] Höttl had little trouble in penetrating the Hungarian secret service. Having got incriminatory evidence against Horthy, the Germans hesitated over what to do about it. SD-Ausland thought Horthy should be retained as head of state, but shackled by a generalissimo in German pay.[11] Hitler, however, had lost patience. Horthy had to go. His replacement was to be Ferenc Szálasi, head of the Fascist Arrow Cross Party. All that now mattered was the most efficient means of removing the Regent.

Hitler's preferred method in such cases was to throw every available resource at the problem, and let commanders on the ground sort out the tactics. Skorzeny was merely one of a number of alpha males – including Veesenmayer, Winkelmann, Geschke and Höttl – vying for control of Operation *Panzerfaust*, as the Horthy putsch was codenamed. To bolster Veesenmayer's grip on the political agenda, Hitler seconded to him Rudolph Rahn, who had shown marked diplomatic skill in Italy.

Commanding Waffen-SS forces in Budapest was SS-Obergruppenführer Karl Pfeffer-Wildenbruch – at his disposal, an 8,000-strong unit of the newly activated Hungarian Volksdeutsche 22. SS-Freiwilligen-Kavallerie-Division 'Maria Theresia' which was easily capable of throwing a ring around the Burgberg. Also sent as advisers were SS-Obergruppenführer Erich von dem Bach-Zelewski, freshly returned from crushing the Warsaw Uprising, and General der Panzertruppen Walther Wenck, the youngest general in the Germany army.

According to Skorzeny, Bach-Zelewski came to Budapest equipped with the self-same 650mm howitzer, nicknamed 'Thor', with which he had recently reduced the capital city of Poland, and before that Sevastopol in the Ukraine, to rubble: 'He was a sort of bespectacled scarecrow and didn't impress me in any way, although many officers were impressed by him. He suggested "finishing off the Burgberg without a lot of fuss", destroying the royal palace with "Thor" and with it, the entire garrison. I don't believe I'm injuring the memory of poor Bach-Zelewski when I say he wanted to identify himself with his howitzer.'[12]

Not much, he isn't. This is unadulterated literary score-settling. Bach-Zelewski denied ever bringing the howitzer with him, still less planning to use it.[13] He may well have been a vicious buffoon, but he was also an acknowledged expert on siege warfare and the crushing of uprisings. The fact is his brutal humourlessness seems to have rubbed Skorzeny up the wrong way. The two were to meet again on the Oder Front, in the closing stages of the war; it was not an encounter to Skorzeny's advantage. Literary licence aside, the aim of Skorzeny's caricature is to contrast the superiority of his rapier with Bach-Zelewski's sledgehammer. It was lucky for Budapest – at least in the short term – that Skorzeny won the tactical argument.

Having received his orders from Hitler, Skorzeny began to assemble his commando force in Vienna. By the beginning of October it had been deployed to the suburbs of Budapest.

Skorzeny donned a sharp business suit and a false identity as 'Dr Wolff' – allegedly the representative of a Cologne-based company spending a few days' holiday in the Hungarian capital, as the guest of wealthy Hungarian industrialist (and Waffen-SS officer) Karoly Ney, who was in the service of Winkelmann. Armed with a Baedeker guide, he spied out the land. What he found was not encouraging. The glider-based assault favoured by OKW was completely inappropriate. The only viable landing place was the Vérmezö, or 'Blood Field', beneath the Burgberg, which 'would have earned its name all over again' as the Hungarians 'would have shot us down like rabbits from the walls of the fortress'.[14]

Even a surprise attack from troops already on the ground would face formidable opposition. Skorzeny's intelligence revealed that the Burgberg was guarded by 3,000 troops, with mortars and heavy machine guns deployed behind the Vienna Gate. 'At the other end of the hill, among the palace's terraced gardens above the Danube, were five solid positions with bunkers and machine-gun nests; tanks had been positioned in front of the citadel; behind it in the courtyard were six anti-tank weapons.'[15] Skorzeny believed that the palace was guarded by a regiment, while the adjacent government buildings were defended by two battalions. Horthy described his force as consisting of a regiment of guardsmen, none of whom had access to heavy weaponry, still less a tank.[16] Whatever the case, the Burgberg was still a formidable fortification for any task force to assault. No wonder Skorzeny looked favourably upon a more psychologically subtle means of achieving regime change.

Winkelmann, with the assistance of Höttl, had devised just such a plan. They would kidnap both Bakay – the commander of the Budapest garrison – and Horthy's 37-year-old son, Miklós Junior (known as Nikki). Bakay's abduction would, he hoped, forestall any insurrection; while Nikki's would force Horthy to accede to German demands.[17] On 10 October Bakay was apprehended without incident in thick fog outside the Budapest Ritz. But seizing Nikki – a mission labelled Operation *Mickey Maus*[18] – proved riskier and the prize more elusive.

The SD were well aware that the militantly anti-Nazi Horthy Jr was personally brokering a deal with the Russians, lately via Tito. If they came to a formal agreement, then Tito could be expected to intercede favourably on Hungary's behalf with Stalin. Nikki Horthy's contact, via secret service chief Ujszaszi, was the frontier control officer at Gyékényes. Little did Nikki know that he was a double-agent, relaying Horthy's plans to the Germans.

An attempt by the SD to entrap and abduct Nikki at a meeting with a bogus 'Titoist' envoy failed when Nikki caught sight of a grim-looking and suspicious character who nearly gave the game away. According to Höttl,[19] this was none other than Geschke's deputy, Kriminalkommissar Gerhard Clages – the Gestapo man in charge of the snatch.

Surprisingly, Nikki agreed to a second meeting on Sunday 15 October. Skorzeny was called in to add armed support. This time Nikki specified the time and place: 10 am at the offices of an industrialist (and friend of his father) named Bornemisza at Eskü-Tér on the Pest side of the river. Just in case, Nikki brought with him an escort – two Guards officers according to Nikki; a substantial force according to Höttl and Skorzeny.[20]

Gestapo agents took up position in the room above Bornemisza's office, with a view to making a quick arrest on a given signal. Skorzeny, meanwhile, deployed a detail of about 30 commandos under Fölkersam's command, in covered trucks. Skorzeny himself – still posing as Dr Wolff – drew up in the square about 10 am, just after Nikki had arrived. Skorzeny parked his Mercedes right outside the office, bonnet facing Nikki's car, in which a chauffeur was waiting. Behind it was parked a Kübelwagen with two Hungarian Guards officers inside. 'Dr Wolff' got out and began fiddling under the bonnet, feigning engine trouble.

The Gestapo men struck first. Nikki and Bornemisza had only just sat down to their meeting with the fake Titoist envoy when the door was smashed open and Nikki knocked unconscious. He came to with a sack over his head; he and Bornemisza were dragged to a police truck parked outside, wrapped in blankets, and driven at high speed to the airport.[21] At the same time, a firefight broke out in front of the building. The Hungarian Guards officers attempted to enter the building but were denied access; Horthy's car was blown up by a grenade; and one of the Guards officers was shot dead, but not before he had mortally wounded Kriminalkommissar Clages in an exchange of fire. The chauffeur escaped and was able to tip off Horthy Senior.[22]

In his subsequent account of *Mickey Maus*, Skorzeny invented a whole company of Honvéd* guardsmen whom he managed to hold off in an unequal battle before being rescued from behind his bullet-riddled Mercedes by Fölkersam. Not exactly. According to Winkelmann, Skorzeny did singlehandedly deal with a Guards company, but it was posted under the Danube Bridge, not outside the office: 'When the first shots rang out,' Winkelmann reported, 'the leader of this company came rushing out to see what was going on. Skorzeny, in civilian clothes, ran up to him and shouted: "There's shooting going on. Back! Back!" The officer instantly turned around and took his men back to the bridge and safety.'[23]

Skorzeny reached the airport in time to shepherd his hostage past Hungarian officials and onto a waiting plane. Bornemisza was released afterwards, but Horthy Junior spent the rest of the war in Mauthausen concentration camp in Austria.

While *Mickey Maus* was in full swing, the Germans arrested a number of other Hungarian generals suspected of being party to an anti-German coup. But if they thought these stage-managed abductions would persuade the Regent to go quietly, they were wrong. Later that same morning, an emollient Veesenmayer visited the embattled Regent and was met with a tidal wave of rage and grief over the seizure of his son. When Veesenmayer pleaded ignorance about the abduction, Horthy hurled some spent German cartridge cases – freshly collected from Eskü Tér – onto the desk in front of him, screaming 'And what is that?' After Hungarian reinforcements finally arrived and cordoned off the square, an inspection of virtually everyone's papers therein had revealed them to be members of the Gestapo.[24]

Horthy, far from caving in, determined to bring forward the armistice he had informally agreed with the Soviet Union. At 2 pm he announced on the radio that the armistice had just been signed. Shortly afterwards, General Béla Miklós, Horthy's intermediary, defected to the Russians. What Horthy

---

*   Royal Hungarian Army

did *not* do was tip off his remaining co-conspirators about his intentions. He also failed to order the armed forces to resist should they be attacked by the Germans. Those who were already wavering in their support now felt more inclined to collaborate with the Germans.

Winkelmann quickly took control of the situation. Waffen-SS troops commanded by Pfeffer-Wildenbruch seized strategic points throughout Budapest, supported by 40 Tiger tanks. The Budapest garrison, leaderless, went over to the Germans. Radio Budapest was occupied and a new Nazi regime proclaimed.

That left the inconvenient presence of an angry old man on a near impregnable hill who doggedly refused to rescind the cease-fire; and still less to abdicate in favour of Ferenc Szálasi. Veesenmayer's entreaties, reinforced by Hitler's special envoy Rudolf Rahn, were unavailing. Both envoys were trapped in the German embassy within the citadel as the Burgberg went into total military lock-down and Horthy prepared for a last-ditch stand against the Germans.

From the seizure of Nikki to military takeover, 15 October had been an eventful day. At midnight Skorzeny held a military conference before deploying his forces for the final assault at 6 the next morning. The last touches to the plan (devised in detail by Fölkersam) were overseen by Wenck and a sulky SS-Obergruppenführer Erich von dem Bach-Zelewski, for whom Skorzeny had by now conceived a visceral dislike.

There were to be three simultaneous diversionary attacks and one main thrust, from different points of the compass. In the south, a battalion of Wiener-Neustadt cadets would blow up the iron fence around the castle park, enter the gardens and pin down any defending Hungarian forces. The cadets would be cannon-fodder, engaging heavily entrenched machine-gun posts. Meantime, a platoon of Jagdverband Mitte, under the command of Hunke and reinforced by two Tiger II tanks, would force an entry on the western side. Skorzeny had a map detailing the underground passages leading from the Danube quayside to the War Ministry, deep inside the citadel – probably supplied by Hitler himself. The tunnels were to be stormed by a platoon of the SS-Fallschirmjägerbataillon 600, who would have to blast their way through several steel doors guarding the royal treasure vault to reach their destination.

The main commando force – commanded by Skorzeny himself and comprising two motorised companies of Mitte, four Tiger II tanks and a number of remote-controlled Goliath tracked mines – were to spearhead a frontal assault through the north-facing Vienna Gate (where all four roads within the citadel converged), leading directly to the Royal Palace.

Accompanying Skorzeny were Fölkersam, Ostafel and five Gran Sasso-veteran NCOs.

At 3 am, with still no sign of capitulation from inside the Burgberg, Skorzeny had all his officers fall in on the Blood Field to give them their final instructions. Not a shot was to be fired unless there was major resistance; weapons were to be carried with safety catches on, and stowed out of sight. At 5:59 am, with the first light of dawn, Skorzeny raised his arm to signal the advance. The long cavalcade of trucks and tanks – their engines and caterpillar tracks creating a tremendous din in the still morning air – began to lurch up the hill. Skorzeny and most of his key team – armed with Sturmgewehr 44 assault rifles, grenades and the brand-new Panzerfaust anti-tank weapon that lent its name to the operation – were dangerously exposed in the command truck leading the column, with the tanks and Goliaths just behind.

Having taken a sharp right turn into the Vienna Gate they were relieved to find it open, guarded by only 'a few astonished Hungarian soldiers'; Skorzeny 'saluted them cordially'.[25] Passing the barracks, the German force carried on. With still nearly a kilometre to go before reaching the Royal Palace, the convoy speeded up, Skorzeny's half of the column swerving to the right past the German embassy, the other half following a parallel road. As they passed the War Ministry on the left they heard two loud explosions: the SS-Fallschirmjäger unit blasting its way through the tunnels.

As Skorzeny's force ground to a halt in the courtyard before the palace, they found the gateway had been barricaded.* Suspecting a trap, Skorzeny pulled his truck aside and had the tank behind him break down the barrier, revealing six anti-tank guns ranged against them.[26]

Skorzeny and his men 'leaped over the debris of the barricade and burst through the shattered gate. A colonel of the Guard got out his revolver to stop us, but Fölkersam knocked it out of his hand. On our right was what appeared to be the main entrance, and we took it at the run, almost colliding with a Honvéd officer, whom I ordered to lead us straight to the commandant. He immediately complied and at his side we rushed up the broad staircase.'[27]

On the first floor the Honvéd officer led them to an anteroom, where a soldier was firing a machine gun into the courtyard. 'Holzer, a short, stocky NCO, clasped the gun in his arms and flung it out of the window.' Skorzeny passed through into the next room, where he was met by Major-General

---

*   According to Skorzeny, it was barricaded with building blocks. Other sources claim they were merely wooden barricades.

Károly Lázár, commander of the Guards. Skorzeny instructed him to surrender the citadel. 'If you don't, you will be responsible for any bloodshed.'[28]

It's a recurring scene in the Skorzeny legend, from President Miklas in Vienna to Mussolini at Gran Sasso: Skorzeny, with epic disregard for his personal safety, seizes the keys to the castle, with scarcely a shot fired.

He must have wondered at the casual way in which Lázár acceded to his request to surrender. In fact, the keys to the whole kingdom had already been handed over. A deal had been done at about 4 am, brokered by Veesenmayer and Winkelmann while Skorzeny was mustering his troops. At this very moment, Horthy was in the office of the local Waffen-SS commander, awaiting his fate. In return for his personal safety, and that of his family, plus guarantees sparing Hungary from civil war, Horthy had agreed to revoke the Soviet armistice agreement, declare a cease-fire within the castle walls and stand down. No wonder Skorzeny's surgical strike had been greeted with nothing but mute surprise.

Skorzeny had not been alerted to the development because Winkelmann had his doubts about Horthy's motives for caving in, ascribing them to a 'cur-like concern for his own skin' rather than for his country; and he also suspected a trick.[29] Therefore, the military operation still had to go ahead. It was mitigated by a unilateral cease-fire on the Hungarian side. Whether the cease-fire was due to Horthy's ineptness in spelling out what his Guards should do in the event of a German attack, a result of a direct order to lay down arms, or of informal talks between German and Hungarian staff officers the previous day (with which Skorzeny would have been familiar),[30] is not known.

There were pockets where the message did not get through. A Guards unit commanded by Andreas Kállay, son of the former prime minister, shot dead four Germans. Elsewhere, a street-lighter turning off the gas lamps accidentally detonated a mine, the explosion causing an exchange of fire between Hungarians and Germans.[31] In all, the Germans suffered 16 casualties – four of them dead; and the Hungarians 18, three of them dead.[32]

The Hungarian putsch, the last of its kind during the Nazi era, was a complex operation involving a large cast of actors. Skorzeny provided the coup de grâce, but was not primarily responsible for the coup de main. He was not the organiser of *Mickey Maus*, although the abduction succeeded because of his intervention. He was probably not the primary tactician behind *Panzerfaust*. That was more likely Winkelmann or Bach-Zelewski.[33] Nonetheless, Skorzeny's unmistakable leadership style stands out. It was slightly old-fashioned, chivalrous almost, a replay of one-to-one 'Mensur' swordsmanship in an era of mechanised warfare – daring his enemy, through a conspicuous display of personal gallantry, to strike first; yet sublimely certain that the other side would not succeed.

Horthy – beaten and demoralised – signed the document swearing in Szálasi as prime minister. A smooth succession of political power was secured, without further outbreaks of violence. One further humiliation lay in store for the old man. Returning to the palace to retrieve some belongings, Horthy 'had been prepared to find a search had been made, but the disorder of the scene mocked my wildest imaginings'. Skorzeny's troops 'had made themselves comfortable on the damask-upholstered furniture. Cupboards and drawers had been broken open … and these barbarians had helped themselves to everything that seemed to them of value, from my wife's jewellery to the servants' savings.'[34]

∗ ∗ ∗

For all its panache, *Panzerfaust* achieved little. Having displaced Horthy, Hitler proceeded to turn Hungary into a geographical sandbag capable of absorbing the impact of the Russian juggernaut while safeguarding the Reich's remaining oilfield production. It did little good. Hungary without Horthy was a busted flush. The army, severely demoralised by the coup, fought on to the end under German control, but many senior officers showed the utmost reluctance to serve Szálasi. By Christmas Eve 1944, the Russians had Budapest surrounded and began strangling the Germans' lifeline. It took two months of bloody urban warfare to sever it.

It was at this point that Skorzeny's commandos were dragged back into the Budapest imbroglio. Joachim Rumohr, the 34-year-old commander of one of the SS divisions defending the city, happened to be Skorzeny's friend and former commanding officer in the II. SS-AR.Reich. Rumohr appealed for help in breaking the Russian stranglehold. Although Skorzeny was then at the other end of the Reich, fighting the Americans in Belgium, he volunteered the services of his specialist frogmen unit, SS-Jagdeinsatz Donau, based in Vienna.

In Operation *Forelle* (*Trout*), an eight-man task force attempted to sail a small armed vessel, the *Walter*, through the Russian blockade to offload 600 tons of food and ammunition. The operation, under the command of SS-Obersturmführer Stanzig and SS-Untersturmführer Wouters, set sail down the Danube on 31 December 1944, but two days later ran aground on a sandbank 20 kilometres short of Budapest. Stanzig transferred some of the goods onto a small cargo ship that managed to run the blockade. Radio contact was maintained with the *Walter* for only five days. A week later a Jagdverband Südost patrol reported the ship had been abandoned. Although looted by the locals, it had not been seized by the Soviets. Nothing more was heard of the crew.[35]

On 11 January 1945, a major relief force that included the Totenkopf, Wiking* and Das Reich SS panzer divisions came close to achieving breakout for the city's defence. But, at the last moment, Hitler switched the focus of the attack. From then on, the shrinking garrison of 70,000[36] – confined to an area 1 kilometre square around the Burgberg – was doomed. Only 700 SS men made it back to German lines. Rumohr was not among them. Badly wounded, he committed suicide rather than face humiliation and death at the hands of the Russians. Budapest was Stalingrad all over again. More than 80 per cent of the city's buildings were damaged or destroyed, including the Royal Palace, and about 40,000 citizens perished. And all for what, exactly?

---

*   5. SS-Panzerdivision 'Wiking'

11

Everything on One Card

Operation Greif

On 22 October 1944, six days after the conclusion of Operation *Panzerfaust*, Skorzeny returned to the Wolfsschanze to report to Hitler on the outcome of the operation.

Back in the hastily erected Führerbunker, he was treated to a one-to-one briefing: 'Hitler gave me his usual friendly reception and seemed in better form than on the previous occasion. Coming forward with outstretched hands, he burst out: "Well done, Skorzeny. I've promoted you to SS-Obersturmbannführer [lieutenant-colonel] with effect from 16th October, and awarded you the German Cross in Gold*."'[1]

This medal had been introduced in November 1941; ranking higher than an EK I and below the Ritterkreuz, it was awarded for repeated acts of bravery in combat.

The Führer listened with polite, even amused, interest to Skorzeny's anecdotes about bundling Nikki Horthy into a carpet. As Skorzeny was about to leave, Hitler held him back. There and then, he confided to

---

*   Deutsches Kreuz in Gold

Skorzeny 'in every detail' the plan for the forthcoming Ardennes counter-offensive.[2]

'I will very likely entrust you,' said Hitler, 'with the most important mission in your career as a soldier.' Skorzeny and his commandos were to occupy 'one or another of the Meuse bridges between Liège and Namur' and operate behind enemy lines 'in English or American uniforms'. Hitler had heard that American troops had employed the same type of deception at Aachen. Skorzeny's disguised commandos were to 'misdirect enemy troops and spread confusion' behind the lines. 'I know that you have only a little time to organise such a large operation of this kind,' Hitler concluded. 'But I also know that you will do your best. Generaloberst Jodl will answer your detailed questions.'[3]

Up to this time almost no one besides Hitler, Keitel, Jodl and a few essential planners knew anything about the prospective Ardennes counter-offensive, codenamed Operation *Wacht am Rhein* (Watch on the Rhine). Even the commanders on the ground who would lead the offensive were excluded. Generalleutnant Siegfried Westphal – chief of staff of Oberbefehlshaber West, the highest military authority in the West – and General der Infanterie Hans Krebs, chief of staff to Heeresgruppe B, had only been apprised of it a few hours before Skorzeny.

This confidential interview with Skorzeny illustrates a number of important points: the esteem in which he was held by Hitler; how critical Skorzeny's mission was perceived to be to the overall success of the offensive; and the absolute control that Hitler intended to exercise over the campaign, down to minute operational details.

Hitler himself had dreamt up the idea of a counter-offensive as early as August, an intuitive response to the loss of initiative since D-Day. The provisional date was November (later pushed back to December), when the Allied air forces were likely to be grounded due to poor flying conditions.[4] After their catastrophic setback at Arnhem the Western Allies had stalled short of the Rhine and were vulnerable to a counter-offensive. With the Allied line weak in the middle, Hitler correctly guessed that the British 21st Army Group would next focus on opening the Scheldt estuary, while the Americans would attempt to penetrate the Westwall at Aachen, creating a breakthrough into the Ruhr heartland. If the Germans could destroy a third to a half of the Western Allies' divisions, Hitler believed it would irreversibly alter the momentum of the war. Huge amounts of enemy matériel, fuel and supplies could be eliminated or captured, and the enemy massively demoralised. Hitler could then transfer his forces to the East, in order to repel an expected Soviet winter offensive. Even limited success in the West could buy the Reich six to eight weeks' respite. A crushing victory would bring the Allies to the negotiating table.

Germany could nowhere near match Allied strength. Hitler reckoned on 30 divisions doing the trick, spearheaded by a panzer army. Crucial to success was the element of surprise. Poor weather conditions, particularly low cloud and fog, would cloak the panzer columns. Protecting them would be a force of 1,500 Luftwaffe fighters, among them Me 262As – the world's first fully operational jet fighter. Adding to the surprise, Hitler selected the 130-kilometre strip of the Ardennes between Monschau (south of Aachen) and Ecternach (on the Luxembourg border) for the breakthrough, where only four sub-standard American divisions held the line. The terrain was densely forested, especially in the Eifel area on the German side of the border; this would provide excellent cover for massing German forces. Shock troops would force the breakthrough, allowing the tank units to advance rapidly towards Antwerp. First stop was the Meuse bridges, to be secured after two days. Protecting the flanks of the two-army panzer thrust would be two further armies, north and south. Antwerp having been retaken, the British 21st Army Group, the US 9th Army and most of the US 1st Army would be cut off from their own supply line, creating the conditions for a new Dunkirk.

However brilliant the surface concept of Hitler's campaign, most of its underlying assumptions were rotten. His increasing isolation, his paranoid distrust of the military establishment, and his obsessive micro-management left him out of touch with reality. His comparison of numbers failed to consider the degraded state of the German forces. Heeresgruppe B had suffered irreplaceable losses in men, armour and artillery, leaving them outnumbered nearly ten to one by Allied armour. The position in the air was, if anything, worse.[5] Germany was also increasingly short of resources, due to lost territory and Allied bombing. Non-stop fighting had exhausted most of the surviving troops; many were psychologically maimed. Generalleutnant Westphal pointed out, on hearing that Hitler planned to send Hitler Youth aged 15 to 16 into battle: 'The majority of the boys wouldn't be able physically to withstand the major agonies of war.'[6] One could hardly pick a location more inimical to a rapid armoured breakthrough. The topography that shielded a build-up of forces spelled deep trouble for tanks and armoured vehicles once they advanced – hilly, thickly wooded, riven by steep river valleys. There would be rain, fog, and heavy snow. The road system simply compounded the physical difficulties facing the attacking German armies. The Ardennes was thinly populated, for the most part in villages of no more than 4,000 inhabitants. These villages usually featured narrow, winding, streets through which traffic must pass in a single direction. To avoid bottlenecks, it was therefore absolutely vital that Hitler's panzer armies seize early control of road-junctions for the relatively few *routes nationales* passing through the major population centres of Malmédy, St Vith, St Hubert, Bastogne and Neufchâtel.

Gerd von Rundstedt, overall commander in the West, protested vigorously to Hitler about 'this stupid offensive', although he stopped short of resigning.[7] Walter Model, head of Heeresgruppe B, who would lead the offensive, thought the strategic objective of Antwerp vastly too ambitious and favoured a limited counter-offensive to relieve pressure around Aachen. Even Jodl confessed that *Wacht am Rhein* was a 'gamble', but concluded: 'We must not shrink from staking everything on one card.'[8]

In no serious way, however, was Hitler prepared to modify his game plan or relax his grip on planning. He was building his hopes for a successful outcome like a card house – each set of assumptions resting precariously on those beneath. At the apex was Speed, and its fragile supporting card, Surprise. The plan, once implemented, had no tolerance for delay: the panzer spearhead must cross the Meuse bridges within four days and capture the Allied supply dumps at Liège, or risk running out of fuel long before it reached Antwerp.

Maximising the crucial element of surprise was Hitler's joker in the pack: Skorzeny, a relentless optimist as addicted to gambling as his master. Hitler had hardly exaggerated when he referred to Skorzeny's camouflage operation – codenamed Operation *Greif* – as the most important mission of his career. Two days ahead of the panzers, Skorzeny must take his mechanised force, with its leading units disguised as Americans, across the inimical Hohe Venn (High Fens) and capture those Meuse bridges intact, before the enemy had an opportunity to react. His mission would be pivotal to the success of the panzer divisions, and therefore to that of the whole counter-offensive.

* * *

Skorzeny's biggest initial concern was that he had very little time to develop such a sophisticated operation. He reminded Hitler that the raid on Eben-Emael in 1940 had taken six months to plan,[9] while he was expected to hone a battle-ready force, complete with fluent foreign language skills, in less than eight weeks. But there was no way around it; he was committed.

Despite Hitler's emphasis on *Greif*'s importance, the military gave Skorzeny very little practical help. This was likely due to suspicion among the general staff about deception operations in general and about Skorzeny and his SS commandos in particular. Such prejudice was engrained in the Prussian officer class, and where Skorzeny was concerned, it had been given a visceral twist by his 'unfriendly' role in the events of 20 July. More materially, the general staff of HQ West were having to cope with an immense shortfall in resources.

There were also doubts in military circles about the legality of Skorzeny's camouflage operation. Article 23(f) of the 1907 Hague Convention stated that forces 'may only use enemy uniforms to infiltrate enemy territory without combat and to approach the target objects. If they become involved in combat they must clearly show their true identity before opening fire.' More ambiguously, and worryingly, it went on to point out: 'If they are captured members of such commandos are only to be treated as spies when they have been carrying out reconnaissance in the enemy uniforms. If they have, additionally ... opened fire then they are guilty of war crimes.'[10]

A sudden lawyerly regard for the articles of war in the sixth year of the most brutal conflict the world had ever known might seem rather odd coming from senior officers who had shown little compunction in flouting them whenever it served their purpose. False flag operations, involving firing on the enemy while wearing their uniform, had been a commonplace on the Eastern Front on both sides. Fölkersam, for example, had legendarily disguised himself as an NKVD major in an operation to seize Russian oil facilities at Maikop in 1942. The Germans seemed to have one set of rules for the Asiatic hordes, from whom they could expect little quarter if captured, and quite another for the Western Allies. On the other hand, while the war was generally fought in a more 'civilised' manner in the West, it was there that the camouflage operation had actually been pioneered, by the Brandenburgers in 1940, during the seizure of the Gennep Bridge on the Meuse.

The Western Allies had drawn similar conclusions about the irrelevance of Article 23(f) to modern warfare, but were more discreet about breaking the rules. Skorzeny was aware of the admired but unsuccessful 1941 Rommel Raid (Operation *Flipper*), during which British commandos opened fire while wearing German uniforms. He had also heard claims of an American operation during the siege of Aachen, shortly before Operation *Greif* was scheduled to take place, when (according to Skorzeny) 'the Americans infiltrated several detachments of Rangers into the city dressed as German soldiers, with falsified papers and German weapons'. These 'phoney Germans' attacked German positions 'and destroyed them'.[11]

Although Hitler used the Americans' alleged deception as a justification for his own, he forbade Skorzeny to cross the front line in person during the operation: 'In no circumstances must you let yourself be taken prisoner!'[12]

Skorzeny would be a valuable trophy to the Allies. Capture would lead to a high-profile court-martial and quite possibly execution by firing squad.

So serious was this matter and so unclear the potential consequences that Skorzeny was persuaded to take legal advice from a jurist on the OKW staff. Skorzeny's senior officer during the planning stage, Siegfried Westphal, chief of general staff at Oberbefehlshaber West, believed the proposed action was criminal, and told Skorzeny so to his face, with predictable consequences. They met aboard a train from the Wolfsschanze to Berlin; Skorzeny, 'a casual acquaintance from the Italian campaign', told Westphal about his mission and declared that Oberbefehlshaber West must supply him with American uniforms taken from prisoners of war. 'I told him that he couldn't count on us to do this. To take away any item of clothing worn by prisoners-of-war, particularly in the cold time of the year, was indecent and violated international law. Besides, it might cause serious repercussions in the treatment of our own prisoners-of-war. Shortly afterwards I heard that Skorzeny had reported to Hitler that I was "sabotaging the planned offensive".'[13]

The explosive implications of this enmity soon became apparent. Shortly afterwards, Jodl notified Skorzeny that there would be a call for suitable English-speaking personnel and captured equipment. On 27 October, Westphal openly posted to all units an explicit order relating to this extremely sensitive operation:

> The Führer has ordered the formation of a special unit of about two battalions for employment on reconnaissance and special tasks on the Western Front.
>
> The personnel ... must fulfill the following requirements:
> a) Physically A-1, suitable for special tasks, mentally keen, strong personality
> b) Fully trained in single combat
> c) Able to speak English, also with American dialect
> Particularly important: Knowledge of military technical terms.
> ... Volunteers ... are to be sent immediately to Friedenthal near Oranienburg to Skorzeny HQ to be checked over for their suitability ...
> Army Group B, Army Group G, Army Supreme HQ West, Luftwaffe HQ West and General HQ XXX are to pass on the contents of this order in a suitable manner to their subordinate troops and posts (with the exception of strongholds, the Channel Islands and voluntary units).[14]

The extraordinary stupidity of posting an order directly contravening the strict secrecy enjoined by Hitler has to be savoured. About the only thing the order did not mention was the timing and location of the proposed offensive. Allied intelligence could be relied upon to pick up the message.

Skorzeny was beside himself with anger. 'It could be assumed that many of the divisions issued copies to their regiments and battalions, bearing the legend "Secret Commando Operations". No wonder I had a fit ... I learned after the war that the American Secret Service knew about it within eight days.'[15] More astonishing still was that 'the Americans did not draw any inferences or apparently take any precautionary measures.'[16] An Ultra intercept at Bletchley Park picked up the Lorenz-coded order and MI6 passed it on to the relevant Allied military authorities. But, thanks to an ineptitude matching the Wehrmacht's, the American General Staff failed to grasp its importance, interpreting it as an isolated operation and failing to perceive that it was part of a major offensive.[17]

Believing that the operation's cover was blown, Skorzeny attempted to shut it down. Despite having been briefed personally by Hitler, he now found himself obstructed by 'official channels'. Initially, he had to go through SS-Obergruppenführer Fegelein*, who admitted that the whole thing was 'incredible and incomprehensible, but for that very reason the Führer must know nothing about it'. The mission could not be halted. Skorzeny tried again with Himmler, who commented, 'It's idiotic, but it has been done.'[18] The Führer was apparently blissfully unaware that the secrecy of his special operation might be utterly compromised. Given the deep scepticism of Westphal, Rundstedt and Model about *Greif*, it is not impossible that the security breach was a deliberate attempt to have it aborted. If so, the stratagem failed.

As if this were not trouble enough, the order's call for 'a special unit of about two battalions' would be nowhere near robust enough for the operation's purpose. The order of battle for *Wacht am Rhein* theoretically comprised nearly 300,000 men. In the south was the 7. Armee-Oberkommando, relatively small and lacking a heavily armoured formation; its tactical purpose was to protect the left flank of the advance. In the centre was the 5. Panzer Armee, itself not fully armoured and intended to play a supporting role. In the north, on a 30-kilometre front below Monschau, was the newly formed 6. Panzer Armee commanded by Josef 'Sepp' Dietrich, one of Hitler's most trusted and toughest SS generals. A mixed SS and

*   Himmler's liaison officer to Hitler

Wehrmacht formation, 6. Panzer Armee was the steam hammer of the offensive. It contained little *but* armour and included the most elite and battle-hardened troops of the Waffen-SS – the 1. SS-Panzerdivision 'Leibstandarte-SS Adolf Hitler', the 3. SS-Panzerdivision 'Totenkopf' and the 12. SS-Panzerdivision 'Hitlerjugend'. Its specific objective was to barrel across the Meuse bridges secured by Skorzeny within four days, and to take Antwerp within seven.

According to Hitler's original plan the Wehrmacht's 15. Armee was supposed to protect the right flank of the 6. Panzer Armee's main thrust. In the event, 15. Armee was a phantom force, too tied up in operations around Aachen to be of practical assistance during the offensive. This was to have a significant negative impact on the whole campaign.

Given his assignment to take the Meuse bridges at Engis, Amay and Huy quickly and hold them until the armoured spearhead could catch up, it made sense for Skorzeny to equip himself with a fully mechanised cross-country formation that could speed directly over the Hohe Venn the minute the front line was pierced. That meant mechanised infantry and reconnaissance units, as well as a considerable body of lighter tanks, were an absolute requirement. The miserly 'two battalions' of volunteers specified by the Wehrmacht would simply not suffice to hold three bridges.

The disguised *Greif* force also had to be capable of fraternising with retreating American forces as they passed by. That required close attention to authenticity in American accent, uniform and military equipment.

Despite a lack of cooperation, Skorzeny and Fölkersam set about trying to build this larger, more muscular force – which became known as Panzerbrigade 150. Even if all the military planning conditions were fulfilled, the bar to success would still be very high. In practice, compromise was the name of the game from the very beginning: 'Even the term *Panzerbrigade* was a bluff,' Skorzeny recalled. He was told 'it was out of the question for us to have enough captured American or British tanks for one section, let alone for a whole regiment.'[19]

Nevertheless, the following request was accepted by Jodl on 26 October:

2 tank companies with 10 Sherman tanks each;

3 reconnaissance companies with 10 American scout cars each;

3 motorised infantry battalions using American trucks, with two rifle companies and one heavy machine-gun company each;

1 light anti-aircraft company;

2 anti-tank companies;

1 mortar section;

1 signals company;

1 Panzerbrigade and 3 battalion headquarters;

1 Kommandokompanie; and

auxiliary services to be kept to a minimum to save manpower.

Total troop strength: 3,300 men.[20]

The Wehrmacht's appeal for volunteers was, to say the least, disappointing. The idea of all 3,300 members of Panzerbrigade 150 being fluent English speakers was, it soon became apparent, just a pipe-dream. Skorzeny's hopes were dashed when he saw the first English-speaking volunteers arriving at Friedenthal. Men with 'perfect English and some knowledge of American English' numbered just ten. There were some who spoke perfect, but not American, English, plus 120 to 150 with 'intermediate language proficiency' and about 200 'with a small amount of school English'.

The better English speakers tended to be former merchant seamen, who were improbable commando material. Some had volunteered under the false impression that they would be employed as 'interpreters'. One man, Gefreiter Otto Struller – later captured and shot – was in civilian life a professional ballet dancer. Keitel tried to help by leaning on Kaltenbrunner to produce linguists who had assisted English-speaking sportsmen and guests during the 1936 Olympics in Berlin (presumably SD men). In this way a further 162 candidates were found, although not all managed to turn up in time.[21] Culturally and linguistically speaking, some of the rough edges could be smoothed by sending the most appropriate candidates to American prisoner-of-war camps, where they would master the finer points of contemporary slang, but also observe at close quarters the more relaxed, gum-chewing, mannerisms of the typical 'Ami'.

Most candidates were wholly unsuitable. 'I was literally forced to establish a silent brigade after assigning 120 of the best men to the Kommandokompanie Panzerbrigade 150. The brigade soldiers would have to join the retreating American columns, pretending to be grieving in silence.'[22]

By the end of November it was clear voluntary recruitment was simply not going to work. Skorzeny was forced to turn to the Ersatzheer for help. He was soon in receipt of two Luftwaffe paratroop battalions, a Panzerkompanie and signals company. He dug deeper into his own resources by supplying two reinforced companies from Jagdverband Mitte and his SS-Fallschirmjägerbataillon 600 – both recently returned from service in Budapest. The final make-up of the unit was, approximately: 360 men from

Mitte; 380 SS paratroopers; up to 800 KG 200 parachutists; 240 men from two Panther tank companies; 520 panzergrenadiers; 200 men from two anti-tank companies; and 100 from a signals company. In all, this was under 3,000 men – eventually reduced to about 2,500 because non-combat elements remained behind when the unit was committed to the front line.[23]

The addition of Skorzeny's own forces and the Luftwaffe units was supposed to give Panzerbrigade 150 some infantry backbone. But while these units had combat experience, they were specialists with little conventional infantry training.

The men were sent to Grafenwöhr, a rambling training complex in East Bavaria. Under conditions of the utmost secrecy they underwent intensive training in an effort to forge tactical coherence and esprit de corps. The Südlager, where all the preparation took place, was sealed and ringed by SS guards with orders to shoot anyone who tried to leave without permission. Mail was rigorously censored. Even those who acquired an exeat were obliged to sign a deposition committing them to total secrecy about the mission, on pain of death. An NCO in 4. /Panzer-Regiment 11 recalled that one man who managed to post some uncensored mail was shot.[24]

The equipment situation was even worse. Despite repeated requests, Skorzeny found himself painfully short of the captured enemy vehicles which were a basic constituent of his camouflage operation. Captured equipment was hard to come by. Germany had been involved in few offensive operations lately, and whenever tanks, jeeps and trucks were acquired they tended to be put into front-line service straightaway by the units that had captured them. Westphal was persuaded to hand over some rather damaged but highly prized jeeps, captured at Arnhem, and a raid on a weapons depot at Stettin resulted in a haul of serviceable Sherman and Cromwell tanks, as well as some weapons.[25]

Skorzeny realised that he would never get the number of American tanks and vehicles required. He received '10 English and American scout cars from the captured stock. We might have been worried as to what use to make of the English specimens, if they had not solved the problem by breaking down on the training ground ... In the final result we had perhaps 15 genuine American trucks available and we had to make good the deficiency with German Fords.'[26] Four American scout cars were supplemented with German ones painted US olive green; ditto the German Fords. Despite Skorzeny's complaints about the Shermans, one of his two tank units – 4. /Panzer-Regiment 11 – ended up acquiring four mechanically reliable models,[27] and there may have been more. All the same, the numbers were insufficient.

Skorzeny pulled some strings with his old chum Generalmajor Ernst Bolbrinker, the Chef des Stabs der Inspektion der Panzertruppen* in Berlin, who found him five Panthers.[28] These underwent some ingenious modifications back at Grafenwöhr to disguise them. The cupola was removed from the top of the turret and sheet-metal was added to the turret and muzzle-brake (at the end of the barrel) so the Panthers resembled M10 tank destroyers – close cousins of the M4 Sherman. But, as Skorzeny realised, this deception was likely to work only at night, from a distance, or when practised on inexperienced enemy troops.[29]

As for American weapons, Skorzeny had only half the required number of rifles, and no American anti-tank or mortar ammunition. A consignment of ammunition delivered to Grafenwöhr blew up due to poor stowage aboard the train. German weapons would have to do for most of his men, with only the Kommandokompanie carrying American arms.[30]

To complete the catalogue of woes, there was a dearth of authentic enemy uniforms. A delivery of 'miscellaneous articles' including bits and pieces of British kit was followed by a consignment of useless overcoats. American field jackets taken from prisoners of war were, it turned out, marked with a distinctive prisoner of war triangle. Skorzeny noted that 'It was an eloquent comment on the way the business was handled that the commander of the brigade – myself – got nothing but an American army pullover in my size.'[31] Most members of the unit, clad in whatever genuine items of American uniform they could lay their hands on, would end up being confined to covered trucks during daylight hours, for fear of giving the game away.

Skorzeny's order of battle was necessarily simple. Panzerbrigade 150 would be divided into three combat units, Kampfgruppen X, Y and Z, whose staging areas just behind 6. Panzer Armee's breakthrough units corresponded directly with their geographical destinations: from north to south. Kampfgruppe X, stationed behind 12. SS-Panzerdivision 'Hitlerjugend', would make for Engis, while Y and Z, further south in the assault zone of 1. SS-Panzerdivision 'Leibstandarte-SS Adolf Hitler', would make for Amay and Huy respectively. The idea was that the Skorzeny Kampfgruppen would race directly towards their objectives once initial breakthrough had been achieved.

Skorzeny himself, overstretched by various operational commitments across the Reich, was forced to delegate the formation phase of *Greif* at Grafenwöhr to a deputy, SS-Obersturmbannführer Willi Hardieck. Alongside him were Oberstleutnant Hermann Wulf and Hauptmann Walter Scherf.

---

*　Chief of Staff of the Panzer Troops Inspectorate

Wulf and Scherf were to command X and Y respectively; Hardieck – once the attack began – would hand brigade command to Skorzeny and take over Z in the field. 'Hardieck was a splendid officer,' Skorzeny recalled, 'but had never led this sort of operation before.' The same was true of Wulf and Scherf, 'but the enthusiasm with which they entered into their new duties made me certain that somehow, everything would be all right. I did not forget that I myself had no previous experience of leading an attack in borrowed plumage.'[32]

Uniquely, in fact, there was someone who knew all about 'borrowed plumage', who spoke excellent English, and who was at the very heart of the operation: Adrian von Fölkersam. Wulf and Scherf, moreover, were highly decorated veterans, both holding the Ritterkreuz; Scherf also had the Deutsches Kreuz in Gold. An abnormally high number of Panzerbrigade 150 recruits were Ritterkreuz men.[33] Hardieck was the oddity. There is reason to believe he was rather less 'splendid' than Skorzeny esteemed him. Besides criticising his limited front-line experience (briefly commanding 12. SS-Panzer-Regiment in October 1944), Scherf thought him 'rather egocentric … We heard he had come from an SS-Führerschule and had been responsible for political assignments.'[34] Hardieck's self-importance probably stemmed from knowing that he was one of only three people (the others being Skorzeny and Fölkersam) who were intimately aware of what *Greif*, and the camouflage commando operation associated with it (known as *Aktion 2* by the general staff), were actually about. Even Scherf and Wulf were kept in the dark until early December, a fortnight before the start of the offensive. Hardieck, on the other hand, not only knew the real status of the plan, he was also in overall charge of training and camp security at Grafenwöhr. Hardieck controlled preparations to the last detail, whereas Skorzeny, on his own admission, only visited the training camp once (on 20 November – the day the train laden with American ammunition blew up).[35]

One thing Hardieck could not control was the burgeoning rumours about the mission's ultimate objective. The fact that Skorzeny would be taking command in person at some point led to a belief that some Gran Sasso-like operation was in the offing. 'Hardieck took the strongest possible measures against rumour-mongering,' Skorzeny recalled, 'but in vain. Security was seriously imperilled.' One rumour was that the brigade was 'to rush straight across France to liberate the beleaguered garrison of Brest'. There were 'dozens of stories' going around, 'and each had their advocates, who were not to be shaken in their belief.'[36]

Powerless to suppress the rumours, Skorzeny, Fölkersam and Hardieck decided to make a virtue of necessity by manipulating them into an instrument of psychological warfare. They allowed the rumours to multiply while making a show of suppressing them. Thus, if leaks occurred, 'enemy Intelligence would simply not know what to make of the medley of lurid and conflicting information which reached their ears.'[37]

The three of them can have little realised that they had hit upon the one outstandingly successful element of the whole campaign. Quite how the rumour about capturing General Eisenhower came about remains a mystery. The only account of its origin is from Skorzeny himself. An officer in the Kommandokompanie came to him claiming to know the 'truth' about the mission, which was to go straight to Paris by various routes, assemble at the Café de la Paix, and then, wearing American uniforms, seize or assassinate Eisenhower at his headquarters in the Hotel de Trianon in Versailles. The officer, who spoke good French and knew Paris well, begged to be assigned to the mission.[38] Given Skorzeny's association with operations targeting prominent figures, it was inevitable that someone would dream up this imaginary mission. The stroke of brilliance was in exploiting it as a deception measure, which Skorzeny anticipated would sow panic in the enemy camp.

(It is not impossible that the Eisenhower scheme was more than a rumour, and was actually considered for implementation. Skorzeny later had good reason to be evasive about it, and to deny he ever truly planned to target Eisenhower. However, it seems improbable that he could have engineered a mission so complex given his many other responsibilities.)

The chief instrument for propagating rumours was to be the Kommandokompanie Panzerbrigade 150, set up in parallel to but not as part of *Greif*. It would be made up of advance parties wearing American uniforms and riding in jeeps. 'I'm afraid I had to be prepared that one or two of these jeep teams was likely to be captured right at the start of the offensive,' Skorzeny recalled. 'We didn't even have time to give them detailed instructions on how they should react if they were interrogated by enemy intelligence officers. As the knowledge of these teams was based only on rumours and they knew nothing about the real aim of the operation I didn't feel there was any danger concerning our main objective. On the contrary: the multitude of rumours was bound to lead the enemy up the wrong track.'[39]

Breathtakingly cynical though the rumour ploy may have been in exploiting the lives of the men in Kommandokompanie Panzerbrigade 150 – who would be shot as spies after interrogation – this was not the unit's only or indeed main role.

Special training was given to the Kommandokompanie in 'causing alarm, confusion and despondency in the enemy ranks', in which none of the volunteers had any training or experience. 'In the few weeks at our disposal we could hardly hope to teach them their jobs properly.' They were aware that their mission could result in their being executed as spies, but 'were clearly animated by the most glowing patriotism'.[40] Because it was impossible to predict how the operation would play out, the planners had to rely on the men's initiative. They would act primarily as a forward reconnaissance force. Additionally they were to spread alarm, by means of scare stories about the German advance, misdirecting enemy troops by altering signposts, and cutting telephone lines, as well as blowing up ammunition dumps.[41]

The two prime organisers of the Kommandokompanie were Korvettenkapitän Philipp Freiherr von Behr, a grizzled naval veteran, and Oberleutnant Lothar Stielau, the French-speaker who had hoped to join the Eisenhower mission. Behr was in overall command, responsible for testing the language competence of the volunteers and also the maintenance of secrecy within the camp, but he involved himself in their training. He reported directly to Hardieck, who he claimed 'gave me an ampoule of poison. I believe each member of the commando crew was given one … in order to poison ourselves in case we were captured … I do believe Hardieck also gave me some poisoned bullets.'[42] Stielau was to be leader of the pick of the crop in what became 'Einheit Stielau', the Stielau Unit. The less linguistically gifted group two was entrusted to Oberleutnant zur See Studik, and the one beneath that put in the hands of Oberleutnant Schmidthuber. The rest, now group four, were turned into a reserve.

There were a few seven-man teams in trucks, but the basic Kommandokompanie unit consisted of three- or four-man jeep teams each specialised in reconnaissance, radio/signals communication or engineer/demolition work.[43] By Skorzeny's reckoning, there were no more than 160 commandos in total, comprising about 39 teams. Twenty-four were reconnaissance, eight were radio teams and seven were engineers. Skorzeny personally controlled up to ten teams behind the lines by radio, one of which was Behr's,[44] but he seems to have had an additional reserve pool for short-term reconnaissance assignments. Finally, about four teams each were attached to the Kampfgruppen X, Y and Z.[45] Figures are imprecise because of the improvisation that took place.

Overall, the training and preparation for *Greif* and its subordinate Kommandokompanie operation was inadequate. Panzerbrigade 150 was neither of brigade strength nor in any meaningful sense a panzer formation – indeed, Kampfgruppe X had no tanks at all. No less critically, Panzerbrigade 150 had no artillery support, since it was designed for speed rather than offensive action. Attempts to turn the unit into a plausible English-speaking force were hamstrung, with too few English speakers to allow for more than one per jeep, which might lead to the rest of the team jeopardising the mission if challenged by suspicious Americans.

Nevertheless, during the night of 4 December – after further delays in the scheduling of *Wacht am Rhein* – Skorzeny and Fölkersam's seriously under-prepared force began entraining for barracks at Cologne-Wahn, just behind the campaign staging-areas in the Eifel.

* * *

In the meantime, Besekow, acting on Schellenberg's orders, had been working indefatigably to tilt the balance in the forthcoming offensive with covert operations involving the stay-behind spy network 'Jeanne'. The plan was to blow up key sections of the fuel pipelines that ran from Boulogne and Le Havre, on which the American forces depended. Good agents were scarce, however, as it was no longer easy to find Frenchmen prepared to serve the Germans.[46]

The Allied pipelines had been traced in late September by Operation *Charlie*, led by Ludwig Nebel, otherwise known as SS-Untersturmführer Neuman, alias 'Leo', a Swiss-German who was one of Skorzeny's earlier recruits. Nebel worked with a team of two, infiltrated across the front line with a brief to link up with 'Jeanne'. Contact was established and a pipeline identified, but the mission was fatally compromised when Nebel was captured and turned. He became double-agent 'Ostrich'; in late December, he was to be found sitting in the Café de La Paix, under careful OSS supervision, in the expectation of spotting Skorzeny and his commandos as they assembled prior to assassinating Eisenhower.[47] If nothing else, at least the rumour-mill had worked.

Further pressure from above to create diversionary pre-offensive activity resulted in Operations *Toto* and *Schlange*, neither garlanded with great success. The aim of *Toto* – carried out in early December by Amt VI-S/4 and Jagdverband Südwest – was to blow up the pipeline to Patton's army and attack fuel dumps near the front lines. One fuel dump in the Alsace area was destroyed. *Schlange* was directed at the pipeline running east from Le Havre. Nothing more was heard of it, or its personnel.[48]

Hastily devised covert operations behind the lines were hardly Skorzeny's main concern at this time. *Wacht am Rhein* had been deferred to 1 December, then the 9th and finally the 16th, as matériel and weather problems took their toll on the planners. Skorzeny attended no fewer than three of Hitler's daily situation conferences, now held on the first floor of the battered Reich Chancellery in Berlin (the Wolfsschanze having been finally abandoned). All civility was stripped away as the generals fought tooth-and-claw over fast-depleting resources. Heinz

Guderian, recalled Skorzeny, 'grudged every tank battalion which was taken away from his hard-fighting eastern front for the new operation in the west'.[49]

At one of these conferences Skorzeny witnessed the terrifying spectacle of a Führer-tantrum, triggered by Göring. The meeting was held in 'the Führer's room', which was so small that only the most senior staff were admitted, and had to stand shoulder-to-shoulder. 'Captain Fölkersam was with me as usual, and we had agreed that this time I should speak with no uncertain voice about the failure to supply us with air photographs of the three bridges.'[50] Göring happened to be present, and had just broken the distressing news that the huge force of jet fighters blithely promised by Hitler for *Wacht am Rhein* would number 250 at most. Hitler, in a state of ecstasy at the prospect of his big offensive, or perhaps pumped up by the cocktail of drugs that he now ingested daily, seemed to brush the information aside as inconsequential. But when Skorzeny raised the issue of aerial reconnaissance of his bridges, promised by Göring a week earlier but still not delivered, 'Hitler rose in fury and reproached the Reichsmarschall in the most violent terms. I was in a most painful position, as a Lieutenant-Colonel is not usually present when a Reichsmarschall is being "carpeted".'[51] After protesting overwhelming Allied air supremacy, Göring promised to supply a jet-fighter equipped with a reconnaissance camera.

The results of the aerial sorties conducted between Maastricht and Givet on 3 December brought unexpected good news.[52] Although pictures of the bridge at Engis were missing, the photographs revealed the anti-aircraft gun positions on both other bridges. Skorzeny 'almost jumped for joy when I observed that there were no signs of any special preparations for defence of the river crossings. No unpleasant surprises need be anticipated.'[53] Allied intelligence was blissfully unaware that an offensive was imminent.

On his third situation briefing a few days later, he was accompanied by Radl, who had been complaining that Skorzeny 'always' took Fölkersam to these briefings with Hitler.[54] Skorzeny was asked to stop by at Göring's office in the heavily bombed left wing of the Reich Chancellery building. Göring – affability itself to both of them – disclosed that Skorzeny's was not to be the only special mission contributing to the element of surprise. A Fallschirmjäger operation, codenamed *Stösser*, had been planned, in which a parachute battalion would be dropped at Mont Rigi in the Eifel, in order to seize an important crossroads and block Allied reinforcements from the north. Skorzeny was to coordinate with *Stösser*'s leader, Friedrich von der Heydte, in order to prevent the camouflage jeep teams running into 'friendly fire' from the *Stösser* force.[55]

Stösser had been added to the Operation Order of Heeresgruppe B less than a week before Z-Day,[56] apparently due to Model's (very reasonable) fear that 15. Armee would be unable to block American reinforcements from the north, so blunting the progress of the armoured spearhead. The skimpy preparation for *Stösser* made *Greif* seem a paragon of military planning. All that can be said is that its military objectives were relatively straightforward, and it was led by one of the outstanding special forces commanders of World War II: Friedrich August Freiherr von der Heydte. Whereas Skorzeny had had a total of eight weeks to prepare his operation, Heydte got precisely five days. Even then he was misled, being told that his force was expected to operate behind Russian lines. To torque up the pressure one more notch, he would be leading the first, and only, major night-drop in the Luftwaffe's history. He lacked intelligence on enemy troops; was given inexperienced pilots, sub-standard weaponry and poor radio communications equipment; and fewer than 150 of the 800-strong Kampfgruppe were veterans.[57]

Skorzeny knew Heydte from Italy, where he had played a conspicuous role in disarming Italian forces in Rome, in which Skorzeny and his commandos had lent a hand.[58] That being so, Skorzeny would have been wise to follow Göring's advice and seek out Heydte to exchange notes on the forthcoming operation.

Yet he simply ignored Göring's advice.[59] Heydte, on belatedly learning of Skorzeny's involvement, immediately requested, and was granted, a cordon sanitaire between the two operations. The ostensible reason was the avoidance of friendly fire. The suspicion lingers that he was also motivated by distaste for the SS in general, and for legally dubious camouflage operations and Skorzeny's high-handedness in particular.[60]

Sepp Dietrich, who had overall responsibility for both *Greif* and *Stösser*, probably agreed with Heydte on the latter points. He later described Skorzeny as 'a shady character, always in with Himmler on any dirty work', and considered him an inexplicably decorated coward.[61] Dietrich nevertheless declined Heydte's request for carrier pigeons as a back-up communication channel: 'I am not running a zoo,' he is reputed to have snapped.[62] It was a decision both parties were to regret.

12

Operation *Greif*

Mission and Aftermath

Saturday, 16 December 1944, 5.19 am. Darkness still untouched by the smear of dawn. Snow and ice on the ground. Dankness in the air, fog clinging to the Nordeifel forest concealing the German lines. Near silence reigned, apart from the persistent drip-drip of water condensing in the branches and the subdued click and bustle of equipment being checked for the very last time.

In a farmhouse in the village of Schmidtheim, 5 kilometres from the Belgian border, on the southeast edge of the Eifel, Otto Skorzeny had set up his command post. He was elated by the weather. The forecast had been spot on; overcast skies and fog meant no Allied ground attack aircraft to deal with.

His three combat groups were lying well camouflaged in the forest next to the two panzer divisions of the I. SS-Panzerkorps, waiting for 'zero hour'. Along the 130-kilometre front, nearly a quarter of a million German soldiers, airmen and sailors were poised to contest the course of history, as the Third Reich stiffened its overextended sinews for a last, decisive, battle. Silence.

At 5.20 am, the air was rent by the deafening thunder of artillery and swoosh of *Nebelwerfer* rockets laying down a devastating barrage along much of the front, lighting up the pre-dawn dark.[1] All the careful preparation – the decoy Luftwaffe flights to mask the noise of panzer engines, the artillery drawn by horses with hooves muffled by straw, the convoys at night without headlights – had paid off. The Americans, unable, or unwilling, to believe that Hitler could still be capable of launching an offensive, were taken utterly by surprise by the massive bombardment.

At 5.30 am the thunder of the barrage was joined by the roaring of engines as the panzer formations and infantry battalions began their advance. At 5.35 am, the eastern clouds began to glow as anti-aircraft searchlights, placed especially for the purpose, created a false dawn to light the troops' way.[2] While the vast military traffic moved, Skorzeny's Kampfgruppen bided their time. Their role would begin the moment the initial hole had been punched in the enemy lines; then they would cut through to the enemy's rear and race ahead to their objectives. They waited … and waited … and waited.

The enemy front line was not proving as easy to break through as anticipated. On the main road to the assault zone near Skorzeny's command post, there was chaos, traffic snarled and immobile. Hours passed, and by midday he was fuming – literally, chain-smoking.

Oberbefehlshaber West had correctly assessed the weakness of the two inexperienced and thinly spread US divisions in front of I. SS-Panzerkorps. But foolishly the Germans had dismissed as insignificant the additional presence of the US 2nd Infantry Division, east of a critical road junction at Malmédy. The 2nd, having recently taken a mauling in the Saar area, was wrongly assumed to be debilitated; in fact, it was wholly prepared for combat, and had been about to take part in an attack.[3]

Furthermore, the opening barrage was less effective than anticipated. The artillery was ranged too far, and although it temporarily pinned the Americans down and disrupted their communications, no serious damage was done. When the infantry advance began, it met stiff resistance. The low quality of most of the Volksgrenadier divisions negated their numerical superiority. Poor light, sodden ground, sinuous forest paths, minefields and abatis laid by the Germans themselves when retreating earlier in the year, all contributed to painfully slow progress. Within hours, the stalled advance had created a bottleneck stretching back kilometres, with wheeled vehicles and tanks immobilised on narrow roads made impassable by mud.

Skorzeny attempted to drive ahead to Losheim to find out for himself what was going on, but was forced to do a 10-kilometre detour on foot, such was the congestion. Had the element of surprise so essential to *Greif*'s success already been squandered? The three infantry divisions comprising LXVII Armeekorps, to the right and front of the armoured divisions, were making such heavy weather on the way to Elsenborn that it was clear by midday that the 6. Panzerarmee would be unable to achieve its first-day objectives.

In the afternoon, the 12. SS-Panzerdivision 'Hitlerjugend' was brought in ahead of schedule to assist the breakthrough, but failed to clear two of the five routes on which rapid access to the Meuse depended. (See map on page 13.)

Only towards the end of the day did the bottleneck begin to unblock. Skorzeny's Kampfgruppe X (Wulf's command) was still locked in behind the severely hampered 12. SS-Panzerdivision 'Hitlerjugend', but Z (Hardieck) and Y (Scherf) were on the move. Skorzeny had sent Fölkersam ahead to sort out some radio communication problems he was having with the three commanders. X and Y confirmed that Fölkersam had successfully liaised with them, but the message from Z was highly disturbing. Hardieck had been killed when his car hit a mine during a reconnaissance trip. This was a double setback. Hardieck was the one field commander fully immersed in the *Greif* mission. Skorzeny had to appoint Fölkersam in Hardieck's place, thereby losing the only man on his headquarters staff with the organisational ability to make orders work smoothly. Fölkersam probably didn't mind; he loathed being Skorzeny's chief of staff and later asked to be relieved. [4]

That evening, Skorzeny reported back to divisional headquarters at Schmidtheim. He would give *Greif* another 24 hours. Everything depended upon 1. SS-Panzerdivision 'Leibstandarte-SS Adolf Hitler' – specifically Kampfgruppe Peiper, the elite armoured unit commanded by 29-year-old SS-Obersturmbannführer Joachim Peiper, achieving a breakthrough the following day.

Skorzeny's confidence in Peiper was not misplaced. His Kampfgruppe was equipped with a significant number of Tiger IIs – the ultimate German heavy tank. They had an armour carapace so thick (180 mm in places) that no Allied tank could pierce it, unless lucky enough to strike from the rear; and the chances were they would already have outgunned their opponent from over 2.5 kilometres before contact could be made. But lugging that mass came at a heavy cost: the Maybach engine, developing nearly 700 horsepower, consumed petrol at the rate of half a mile per gallon.[5] Without rapid resupply, the panzer force would soon run out of fuel. Peiper was just the kind of resourceful, relentlessly aggressive commander to take that risk. Kampfgruppe Peiper set off shortly after midnight to exploit a breakthrough achieved by paratroopers at Lanzerath. By 1 pm on 17 December, Peiper had taken the village of Ligneuville*, only 6 kilometres south of Malmédy.

---

*   Engelsdorf

There the atrocities began. Shortly before reaching Ligneuville, Peiper encountered a column of Americans cutting across its westwards trajectory at the Baugnez crossroads. They were lightly armed members of B-Battery, 285th Field Artillery Observation Battalion, and offered no serious resistance before surrendering. They were passed towards the rear while Peiper pushed on. Soon 84 of them were dead, machine-gunned at close-range by Waffen-SS soldiers. Who gave the order to kill them, and why, has never satisfactorily been explained. Many would later allege that Peiper was responsible. And although neither Skorzeny nor any of his units were recorded as being anywhere near the scene of the massacre at the time, the incident would return to haunt him.

By dusk, Peiper had reached the outskirts of Stavelot, having covered an extraordinary 25 kilometres in one day; Engis, the nearest Meuse bridge, was only 75 kilometres farther, and from now on the topography would be more hospitable. Peiper halted outside Stavelot, thinking it was more heavily defended than it actually was, to await the infantry before engaging in messy street-to-street fighting.

His achievement that day had been remarkable but brittle. With the paratrooper assault force as infantry support – some actually perched on the tanks – Peiper had forced a long but narrow corridor into the enemy lines. The rest of I. SS-Panzerkorps was strung out behind in a 30 kilometre-long snarl-up. To the north, the 277. Volksgrenadierdivision and the 12. SS-Panzerdivision 'Hitlerjugend' were making glacially slow progress against the Americans and were nowhere near seizing the strategically critical Elsenborn Heights.

Skorzeny's morale during this second day had been boosted by the achievements of his Kommandokompanie. At least eight, possibly ten, jeep units with up to four men in each had exploited the chaos reigning at the front line – either by breaking away from behind Peiper's panzers during an engagement, or by going cross-country via the rough, muddy tracks – to penetrate deep behind enemy lines.

One of the team leaders, Feldwebel Heinz Rohde (alias American Sergeant Morris Woodahl), recalled his first moments of contact with the enemy. Having advanced behind the panzers into 'no man's land', he and the rest of the team discarded their German uniforms; they couldn't stop, so they had to change on the move: 'For the driver this was a real feat of acrobatics ... Our jeep jumped around like a young deer, and while the driver kicked frantically at the accelerator pedal, the co-driver tried to steer the vehicle around the obstacles with desperate wrenches of the wheel.'[6] They came up against American defences almost immediately, encountering a unit placing an anti-tank gun. 'How relieved we were to find that apart from being splattered with mud nothing else hit us.' An American sergeant tried to halt the jeep, but Rohde ignored him and raced on. A few minutes later, they ran into a military policeman. 'An *Ami* as tall as a tree was standing there. The white stripes on his helmet, with the MP legend, left no doubt as to his genuineness. With a motorcycle carelessly thrown down beside him, he pulled us on to a side road and the artillery fire falling on the main road ahead convinced us that his efforts were directed towards protecting us from it.'[7] Their imposture still undetected, Rohde and his team sped on.

Skorzeny's jeep teams were now roaming over 100 kilometres beyond their starting point – as far west as Amay on the further side of the Meuse, Engis and Liège, and as far north as Tongres and the area around Verviers and Monte Rigi.[8] They acted on their own initiative with only rudimentary briefing beforehand. Radio communication was patchy, so Skorzeny had little idea what was going on. 'Of the nine teams originally dispatched, probably somewhere between six and eight had really got behind the enemy lines,' he later believed. Even after the event he couldn't be sure about the reports he received. 'One can well understand that some of these young soldiers were too ashamed to admit that when faced with their real trial – the penetration of enemy-held territory – their courage and resolution failed them.'[9]

In fact, the Kommandokompanie teams had a devastating psychological impact on the Americans out of all proportion to their numbers. Some of the most effective participants were those who paid with their lives.

The team made up of Oberfähnrich Günther Billing, Obergefreiter Wilhelm Schmidt and Unteroffizier Manfred Parnass was one of these. All three men were intelligence personnel: Billing from the navy, Parnass from army intelligence and Schmidt from the Luftwaffe. They had orders to reconnoitre the Meuse area in the vicinity of Namur. They made rapid progress through American lines, thanks to Kampfgruppe Peiper, and reached the bridge over the Amblève at Aywaille, about halfway to the Meuse. There the jeep was halted at a roadblock and its team arrested after failing to produce the requisite password. A search of the jeep revealed wads of counterfeit money, grenades, a German pistol and paybooks disclosing their true identities. The three men were tried by a US military court and executed by firing squad, but not before they had spilled a remarkable story about the nature of their mission. Much of what they said corroborated a document found on a captured German officer on the first day of the offensive, giving an outline of *Greif* – although not its ultimate purpose – and revealing a code for identifying the camouflaged Kommandokompanie operatives when they returned to German lines.[10]

This information precipitated 'spy-hysteria' in American ranks. General Omar Bradley, in command of 12th Army Group, commented that 'half a million GIs were ... playing cat and mouse with each other every time they met'. Bradley himself was stopped at every roadblock and asked to prove his nationality, 'the first time by identifying Springfield as the capital of Massachusetts (my questioner held out for Chicago); the second time by locating the football guard between the centre and tackle on a line of scrimmage; the third time by naming the spouse of a blonde called Betty Grable'.[11]

All this was trivial compared with the pantomime that unfolded next. On the night of 19 December, Staff Sergeant Hansen of the US military police stopped a jeep on the main road over the Albert Canal outside Liège. It was a routine check, and Hansen's suspicions were apparently not aroused by the four occupants, one of whom was a captain.* It was the papers that gave them away: they were a bit too new and shiny, and the captain a tad too fastidious in opening his paybook at exactly the right page. Americans just weren't that polite. A thorough search followed, uncovering explosives, detonators, hand grenades, two machine guns and a signal pistol, plus German fatigues and rations.

The four arrested soldiers – Leutnant zur See Günther Schilz, Leutnant William Wiesenfeld, Feldwebel Manfred Bronny and Stabsgefreiter Hans Reich – were duly tried and shot. Two, Wiesenfeld and Bronny, had been born in America; their mastery of dialect must have been near perfect. Schilz, disguised as Corporal John Weller but in fact the team leader, revealed under interrogation that they were part of a sabotage group, tasked with erecting roadblocks and causing confusion around the Liège area. A preliminary report on Schilz's interrogation confirmed the earlier rumours:

> The leader of a German group, who specializes in the kidnapping and assassinating of higher personages, passed through our lines one or two days ago together with ... his men with the mission of killing General EISENHOWER. His name is SKORZENY ... SKORZENY and his men will be wearing American uniforms and have American identification papers, weapons etc ... One of their rendezvous points is said to be the Cafe de la PAIS [*sic*] in PARIS where German stay behind agents and collaborators will meet to furnish all the necessary information regarding

---

*   It was highly unusual for Americans to travel four-up in a jeep, something the *Greif* planners overlooked.

General EISENHOWER's whereabouts, security guard etc. These men are completely ruthless and are prepared to sacrifice their lives in order to carry out their mission.[12]

In Paris the next day, Kay Summersby, Eisenhower's driver and personal assistant, witnessed the pandemonium caused at Supreme Headquarters Allied Expeditionary Force (SHAEF) by the spectre of The Most Dangerous Man in Europe:

Security officers immediately turned headquarters compound into a virtual fortress. Barbed wire appeared. Several tanks moved in. The normal guard was doubled, trebled, quadrupled. The pass system became a strict matter of life and death, instead of the old formality. The sound of a car exhaust was enough to halt work in every office, to start a flurry of telephone calls to our office, to inquire if the Boss were all right. The atmosphere was worse than that of a combat headquarters up at the front, where everyone knew how to take such a situation in their stride ...

The staff insisted he move in from the von Rundstedt house, which was comparatively isolated from the Trianon. They pointed to the lonely, wooded stretches along the road ...

Finally only after his closest associates begged, as personal friends rather than staff officers ... he reluctantly moved into the compound ...

With General Ike thus ensconced ... security then ordered Ruth Briggs and me to follow suit ... None of us was permitted outside the area. Security explained to Ruth and me that we knew too much about top-level affairs to risk our safety. They even asked General Eisenhower not to walk outside the office, for fear a sniper might have slipped through the toe-to-toe guard ...

This new, personal tension, coupled with the flood of bad news and rumors from the Ardennes, left most of headquarters frankly apprehensive and depressed. Ike, the one solely responsible for the success or failure of our counter-attack ... had to smother his own feelings and act as the eternal optimist, the confident bucker-upper.[13]

A lookalike decoy, Lieutenant-Colonel Baldwin B. Smith, travelled back and forth every morning and evening in Eisenhower's car, to selflessly take the bullet should Skorzeny's men strike.[14]

The Americans would long hold a grudge against Skorzeny for running rings around their top brass.

Skorzeny's psychological warfare tactic even gained grudging traction with the German General Staff. On 22 December, General Westphal issued an order for 'further jeeps … to be sent out to increase disorder among the enemy', and on 29 December, Heeresgruppe B – in assessing the overall validity of special operations during the campaign – concluded that 'small commando teams were successful'.[15]

But psychological impact was only one – secondary – element of Einheit Stielau's mission. Its tactical success on the ground is harder to gauge.

The team that reached Huy – led by Hauptmann Fritz Bussinger – was said to have diverted an American tank column by means of false information. In fact, elements of the 84th Infantry Division did go missing at this time, but it was due to the commander finding his way blocked by advancing Germans and taking a wide detour without notifying his headquarters.[16] However, en route to the German lines, Bussinger's team did tear up 'a newly laid telephone cable and removed signposts for the use of various American supply units'. Skorzeny and Rohde independently confirm reports that teams were laying mines and blocking roads, destroying ammunition dumps and causing panic among American troops.[17] On 17 December, a whole regiment of the American 1st Infantry Division was led astray at the Monte Rigi crossroads, a scene witnessed by Sergeant Keoghan of the 291st Combat Engineer Battalion:

> The MPs were just getting the traffic unsnarled. I talked to one and he told me … some jokers had thought it would be funny to change all the road signs. When the MPs caught onto it and got down to the crossroads, the whole regiment had been sent down the wrong road … He said that when they got [there] two of the men were still directing the outfit down the wrong road. When they saw the MPs coming, they hauled out so fast that one of them couldn't get into the jeep. He was standing on the front bumper hanging onto the wire-cutter. And they went down the road as fast as the jeep would go.[18]

On 16 and 17 December, Korvettenkapitän von Behr, an 'elderly naval captain' (Skorzeny's words) who led a team in Kampfgruppe Z, found himself acting as a glorified errand boy for Scherf, Skorzeny and Fölkersam. His original orders (a vague instruction to defend the bridge at Huy) had apparently died with Hardieck.[19] While carrying out liaison duties with Peiper's forward units on 17 December, Behr, who was in German uniform, made a momentous wrong turn in the country lanes around Thirimont and accidentally alighted at Malmédy, which was only lightly occupied by the

Americans. He made a quick U-turn and raced back to Ligneuville, 'So we got off with nothing worse than a fright,' he remarked. Skorzeny was intrigued that 'no special defence measures had been taken in the town'.[20] Behr's intelligence report was to have significant consequences.

The human cost of the Kommandokompanie activities was high. Although Skorzeny calculated that a mere eight men out of 150 (of whom only about 44 were active behind American lines) were lost over a two-week period,[21] Heinz Rohde gave a more chilling account, reporting that when the surviving teams regrouped at Schloss Vallerode, north of St Vith, Behr found that he only had enough men left for three teams. Two-thirds had been lost. Rohde blamed 'the hurried and consequently inadequate training in Grafenwöhr'.[22]

The Americans made inflated claims about the number of disguised Germans they captured, indiscriminately counting any German found wearing an item of captured uniform – the American field-jacket being an especially prized piece of kit at this late stage of the war.[23] Even so, the most conservative estimate points to at least 15 being executed by firing squad.[24] Additionally, Oberleutnant Schmidthuber was killed during the siege of Malmédy on 20 December. At least a third of Einheit Stielau perished. When in 1950 Skorzeny published his own triumphalist version of events, Rohde spoke out publicly about 'how lightly you sent us out to almost certain death'.[25]

At the time of the operation, Rohde and his surviving companions must have had little idea of the panic they had sown within the enemy's ranks. The mood was downbeat when they returned to base: 'We openly spoke about the failure of our operation.'[26] *Greif*, the operation they had been trained to support, was doomed by circumstances beyond anyone's control.

Nobody had been able to keep up with Peiper, least of all the combat units of Panzerbrigade 150. Stronger than expected resistance around Elsenborn meant that the Americans, far from fleeing in panic, continued to control two of the five march routes (A and B) that were essential to the Germans' tactical development. Worse, they were soon to retake Büllingen on the alternative main route to Malmédy (C). (See map on page 13.) Further south, Manteuffel's 5. Panzerarmee was also running into trouble around St Vith and Bastogne. This funnelling effect onto the remaining main roads had left the nearest Panzerbrigade 150 unit, Scherf's Kampfgruppe Y, stranded 10 kilometres behind Peiper's armoured spearhead. Peiper later expressed frustration at the lack of backup he received from Skorzeny: the *Greif* force, he said, 'might just as well have stayed at home, because they were never near the head of the column where they had planned to be'.[27]

It's true that communication between the two units was not a model of efficiency. Skorzeny's staff of three was inadequate, and so was the intermittent radio transmission. He had to rely upon Kommandokompanie teams, and these could hardly be expected to relay orders and information instantaneously. Ultimately, however, Skorzeny's problem was gridlock; even with the best information, his Kampfgruppen could not have reached the front in time to capitalise on the developing situation.

Late in the evening of 17 December Skorzeny was forced to face up to the reality of his situation at a 'council-of-war' presided over by Sepp Dietrich at Panzerkorps headquarters in Manderfeld. Skorzeny accepted that the concept of racing to the Meuse, with the Americans in panicked retreat, 'had to be abandoned'. Without that 'panic flight', *Greif* could not succeed. And with enemy reserves moving in, there was no chance of the Meuse being reached anytime soon. 'After ripe consideration, I reported to Army Headquarters my suggestion to renounce our original intentions, and received its approval.'[28] *Greif* was aborted.

Skorzeny stood down most of the Kommandokompanie teams. With few exceptions, they were confined to the pedestrian role of carrying out tactical reconnaissance for conventional units. Operations were scaled down, and the teams henceforth wore only German uniforms.[29]

* * *

The Ardennes offensive was to drag on for another month, and despite some local successes, the campaign objective of capturing the Meuse bridges, let alone Antwerp, would become as quaint and fantastical as the name of the aborted special operation devised to catapult the German army there.

Skorzeny ordered his Kampfgruppen to bivouac overnight where they were, and put himself and his troops at the disposal of SS-Oberführer Wilhelm Mohnke, commander of 1.SS-Panzerdivision 'Leibstandarte-SS Adolf Hitler', in whose zone of operations they were deployed. Mohnke had become overextended. On the one hand, he needed to protect Kampfgruppe Peiper from being cut off. On the other, thanks to the serious underperformance of 12. SS-Panzerdivision 'Hitlerjugend' and accompanying Volksgrenadier units, this task had been made infinitely more difficult by the exposure of his northern flank.

The Americans, having recovered from their initial surprise, were forming an effective defensive line. Particularly critical for both sides was Malmédy, the nexus of major roads north–south and east–west. If the Americans could secure the town, they would be able to channel reserves from the north towards Stavelot, putting serious pressure on the rear of Kampfgruppe Peiper, which was probing northwestwards for an alternative breakout point, the Americans having blown up the bridges on his intended route to the Meuse. If the Germans could take the heights north of Malmédy, they might well outflank the Americans' positions around Elsenborn, so unblocking I. SS-Panzerkorps' northern flank.

Operation *Stösser*, whose mission was precisely to block American reinforcements reaching Malmédy from the north, had been an almost unmitigated disaster. The drop had been delayed for 24 hours owing to transport difficulties. High winds and inexperienced pilots, plus the difficulties of a night-time operation, ensured that the majority of the 800-strong force[30] never made it to the drop-zone. Heydte, by now suffering from a fractured arm, managed to assemble 300 men, but they had lost most of their heavier weaponry, ammunition, food and radio equipment. Although Heydte carried out valuable reconnaissance, he was incapable of conveying the information gleaned to 12. SS-Panzerdivision 'Hitlerjugend', the nearest mobile force. After several days of pointless skirmishing, he decided to abandon the mission and exfiltrate towards the German lines. Days later, on reaching Monschau – which was supposed to have been taken by 12. SS-Panzerdivision 'Hitlerjugend' – he found it still occupied by Americans. Exhausted and ill, he briefly went into hiding before surrendering to the Americans on 24 December. So ended *Stösser*, and with it Heydte's illustrious military career.

The only unit in the area now capable of mounting a diversionary attack on Malmédy was the redundant *Greif* force. Hauptmann Scherf had been assembling Kampfgruppe Y at Ligneuville, about 8 kilometres south of Malmédy, since 18 December. Wulf's tankless Kampfgruppe X was still hopelessly isolated behind 12. SS-Panzerdivision 'Hitlerjugend'. That left Fölkersam's Kampfgruppe Z. This, too, had been loitering near the start-line – held up by the traffic jam. Nevertheless, Skorzeny was prepared to pay a time penalty of two days to muster Z at Ligneuville in order to assemble a sufficient force.

That Mohnke and Skorzeny could seriously entertain such a plan of action is a measure of both men's desperation. The exposure of the Germans' northern flank had provided the Americans with an opportunity to thrust southwards from Malmédy. 'I was asked whether I could avert that menace by an attack on that town,' recalled Skorzeny. 'Artillery support being out of the question, we decided to make a surprise attack from two sides of Malmédy, at dawn on the 21st. Our objective would be the heights on the north of the town, where we could establish a position and be prepared to beat off counter-attacks.'[31]

Mohnke was apparently prepared to do almost anything – including sacrifice a force wholly unsuitable for the task – in order to pull Peiper's irons out of the fire. Skorzeny's ability to organise a surprise attack ought to have been based on extensive reconnaissance of the enemy's position. Instead, he apparently relied upon a single report by Behr – dating back to the 17th – describing Malmédy as lightly held by the Americans. He therefore surmised that the attack could succeed without artillery.[32]

Since Behr's report, the situation in Malmédy had radically altered.[33] Responding to the threat of Peiper's advance, General Courtney Hodges had ordered a scratch taskforce – made up of one combat battalion (the so-called 'Norwegians') and another of engineers (823rd Tank Destroyers) – under the command of Lieutenant-Colonel Hansen to seal all exits to the town and take up defensive positions on the hills to the south, dominating the arterial road junctions and railway line. Though small, Hansen's force was well equipped with tank destroyers and anti-tank guns. At the same time, Hodges sent in a whole reserve division – the 30th Infantry, under Major-General Hobbs, equipped with tanks, tank destroyers, engineers, artillery and anti-aircraft batteries – to link up with Hansen and reinforce the line between Malmédy and Waimes*, 9 kilometres to the east.

In fact, the Americans were deploying against a phantom enemy. Although Peiper had looked as if he were threatening Malmédy, he had invested Stavelot instead.

By the time Skorzeny had both his combat units in position for a 'surprise' attack on Malmédy, American engineers had laid mines and built barriers in terrain that naturally favoured the defenders. Supporting dug-in tank destroyers and anti-tank batteries were six artillery battalions north of Malmédy. Furthermore, a prisoner had been brought in who warned of a fresh attack being prepared on the town. The Americans were on high alert.

Skorzeny had set up his field headquarters in a villa a little way out of Ligneuville on the road to Bellevaux, selected because it was on the reverse side of a slope – safe from American shells. If only he had given his plan of attack the same careful consideration. Skorzeny would later gloss over this less-than-illustrious moment in his career.

It was a simple pincer movement: Fölkersam was to attack from the southwest and Scherf from the southeast. Scherf, who was far more experienced in these matters, was distinctly unimpressed by the plan. His own knowledge of the situation led him to believe that Behr's report on Malmédy 'couldn't be

*   Weismes

correct', but although he gave his opinion, 'the operational order for Kampfgruppe Y still stated that Malmédy was enemy-free'.[34]

It was decided by Skorzeny and the SS HQ staff that Malmédy and the Stavelot road would be taken by night, so that the supply column could reach Peiper the next day. 'I protested against this,' recalled Scherf,

> but nobody was prepared to listen to my misgivings. I was understandably uneasy about carrying out an operation at night against positions already occupied by American infantry and artillery, who had already been able to adjust their fire. The 'gentlemen' just didn't seem to understand that we wouldn't be able to even find our targets in the dark.[35]
>
> Skorzeny ordered: 'During the night Kampfgruppe Y thrust forwards across the Baugnez crossroads towards Malmédy, occupy and secure the northern and western town exits and establish a connection to Kampfgruppe Z, who drive forward via Bellevaux-Falize. The Warche bridges have to be secured so that the supply column, which it is hoped will arrive on the following day, will be able to reach Stavelot.' Kampfgruppe Z, led by SS-Hauptsturmführer von Fölkersam, were already on their way but probably wouldn't be deployable until the following day.

Faced with questions about the many holes in his plan, Skorzeny 'brushed them aside by saying: "We will have to decide each individual case as it arises as we go along!"'[36]

Skorzeny's scheduling seems to have been primarily driven by the need to be seen to be doing something dramatic to relieve Peiper. Logically, he should have synchronised the pincer movement to achieve maximum surprise. But Fölkersam's unit was slow to consolidate at its Ligneuville muster point. Instead of waiting for the rest of Z to turn up some time early the next morning, Skorzeny assigned its three already-arrived Shermans to Kampfgruppe Y and instructed Scherf to commence his assault at 8 pm on the 20th, when it was pitch black.

Scherf's attack soon ran into difficulty in the deep snow, darkness and against the well-prepared American positions. It was a hybrid regular and undercover operation; Scherf's unit – in German uniform – was accompanied by at least one Einheit Stielau team in full American kit,[37] whose primary task was probably to bluff the column's way past the American sentries. One 'American' half-track, advancing towards a US roadblock, hit a mine and lost its two front wheels. Two GIs manning the roadblock recalled hearing German soldiers calling out in English, 'Hey we're American soldiers, don't shoot.' But they did all the same, and managed to knock out a 'tank destroyer' (in fact one of the borrowed Shermans) coming up behind.[38]

Scherf's force had little room to manoeuvre, with a gully on one side of the road and an embankment on the other. Then artillery shells began to rain down. After several hours of engagement, having lost nearly half his men, and with 11 vehicles knocked out, Scherf decided to withdraw. His temper was not improved when he rang Skorzeny and found he was asleep. 'The only comment he had to make to my report was: "Let's wait until tomorrow. Maybe the fuel supply columns won't make it!"'[39]

Worse was to follow. Scherf claimed to have been present, in the early hours of the following morning of 21 December, when Skorzeny – despite all the foregoing – ordered Fölkersam to advance via Bellevaux, and clear the Malmédy–Stavelot road.[40] The fact that Scherf had been beaten back should surely have made it obvious that Skorzeny's battle plan was impossible. Aside from the strength of American opposition, how could Fölkersam execute a pincer movement when one claw – Scherf's – had been snapped off? 'Skorzeny and I were screaming at each other,' Scherf recalled. 'He – a Waffen-SS man – wanted to tell an experienced army panzer man how things were done! ... Everyone knows that there was a lot of tension between the army and the Waffen-SS after the assassination attempt on Hitler. There were often differences of opinion about "troop leadership". I was sure that the mission would be a flop and it was.'[41]

And yet Fölkersam – despite the aggravated difficulties of his task – agreed to go ahead with it. According to one of Fölkersam's panzer platoon commanders, Leutnant Mandt, Skorzeny still thought that only a small American force was holding Malmédy, and told Fölkersam this when issuing his orders. Evidently, Fölkersam believed him. Nonetheless, as Mandt later pointed out: 'We had already suffered badly under their artillery in Ligneuville. We also reckoned that the Americans would have set up positions in the paper mill and on the Warche bridge itself' as a precaution against a German push towards Stavelot.[42] Mandt was correct. The Americans, aware of the strategic significance of the bridge on the main Stavelot road, had mined it, heavily fortified the paper mill, and taken up defensive positions on the railway viaduct overlooking both.

However, Fölkersam 'was sure ... that the American defenders were too weak to withstand our attack if it was started skilfully and we had the element of surprise on our side'.[43] His plan was to send a combat patrol of SS grenadiers and paratroopers on foot, before light, across the Warche and round the valley edge, skirting the enemy's defensive position and enabling a

Despite his flaws, Claus von Stauffenberg was the only man with the resolution to kill Hitler. After the 20 July 1944 coup failed, Skorzeny was brought in to organise security at the plotters' Bendlerblock headquarters in Berlin. He occupied the executed Stauffenberg's former office. (ullstein bild via Getty)

As commander of the Berlin garrison, Otto-Ernst Remer was a key, but unwitting, player in the July Plot. Goebbels convinced him Hitler was still alive and he promptly put his orders into reverse, foiling the plot. Hitler immediately promoted Remer from Major to Oberst. He finished the war as a Generalmajor. (Keystone Features/Hulton Archive/Getty)

The Wolfsschanze, later that afternoon, 20 July 1944. Miraculously, Hitler was left almost unscathed by the exploding bomb, but many of his associates were not. On the right is a wounded Alfred Jodl, OKW chief of operation staff. To Hitler's right is Martin Bormann, Reichsleiter and personal secretary to the Führer. (Keystone/Hulton Archive/Getty)

Hanna Reitsch, EK I holder and arguably the Reich's greatest test pilot. Reitsch first met Skorzeny when they collaborated on the manned V-1 project in 1944. The Reichenberg was in effect a suicide weapon, and on several occasions Reitsch almost lost her life when, against Hitler's orders, she test-piloted it. (Paul Popper/Popperfoto/Getty)

Skorzeny and one of Remer's officers at the Bendlerblock. In the aftermath of the coup, Skorzeny was responsible for internal security at the Ersatzheer headquarters, while Remer took charge outside. It was the beginning of a friendship that encompassed post-war German politics, and later, gun-running in North Africa. (Bundesarchiv, Bild 146-1972-109-18A, Fotograf: o.Ang.)

Reinhard Gehlen as chief of FHO. He later headed West Germany's intelligence service, the BND. In 1944 Skorzeny and Gehlen collaborated on the ill-fated Operation *Scherhorn*. Although Gehlen distrusted Skorzeny, he was at pains to prevent him falling into the hands of the Russians after the war ended. (Bundesarchiv, B 206 Bild-GN13-08-24, Fotograf: o.Ang.)

Miklós Horthy, Regent of the Kingdom of Hungary. In October 1944, Horthy was about to do a deal with the Russians. Skorzeny was part of Hitler's team of enforcers sent to stop him, and led a coup de main against Horthy's Budapest fortress. Hungary's armed forces remained loyal to Hitler until the end of the war. (Keystone-France/Gamma-Keystone via Getty)

By 1943, Hans Jüttner was the chief of SS-Führungshauptamt and the most powerful man in the Waffen-SS bureaucracy. In the aftermath of the July Plot, his power-base was enhanced: he became commander of the Ersatzheer. His support was critical in Skorzeny's tireless campaign to build up and better equip his commando force. (Bundesarchiv, Bild 183-J28010, Fotograf: o.Ang.)

SS-Obergruppenführer Erich von dem Bach-Zelewski was a siege expert who had reduced Warsaw with great brutality. During Operation *Panzerfaust* he and Skorzeny disagreed over how to seize the Burgberg, though Skorzeny's tactics won out. Later, Bach-Zelewski became Skorzeny's Korps commander on the Oder – with predictable results. (Bundesarchiv, Bild 183-S73507, Fotograf: Unger)

Otto Winkelmann (far right, with then head of Orpo Kurt Daleuge in 1940) was head of SS operations in Hungary from March 1944. He, rather than plenipotentiary Edmund Veesenmayer, SS-Obergruppenführer Karl Pfeffer-Wildenbruch, Bach-Zelewski or Skorzeny himself, was the ultimate engineer of Horthy's downfall. (Bundesarchiv, Bild 121-0393, Fotograf: o.Ang.)

16 October 1944, after the coup. Skorzeny leaves the Burgberg citadel, accompanied by his deputy commander, Adrian von Fölkersam (centre), and his adjutant, Gerhard Ostafel. Ostafel was killed and Fölkersam reported missing in action during the defence of Hohensalza in Poland on 21 January 1945. (Bundesarchiv, Bild 101I-680-8283A-30A, Fotograf: Faupel)

Paying the price of deception: One of Skorzeny's jeep Kommandokompanie is shot after being caught in American uniform behind enemy lines. Captured members of the team told the Americans that Skorzeny's real mission was to assassinate the supreme Allied commander, Eisenhower. The rumour caused havoc behind American lines. (Chronicle/Alamy Stock Photo)

Wilhelm Walther, Skorzeny's last chief of staff. A former Brandenburg Oberstleutnant with a distinguished service record in Holland, the Soviet Union, Croatia and Romania (where he was badly wounded), Walther should have been an asset. However, he had scant respect for Skorzeny as an officer. (Gordon Williamson)

Sepp Dietrich (left), Hitler's former chauffeur and hitman. In autumn 1944, Dietrich was commander of 6. Panzerarmee, the key component of Hitler's plan to drive a wedge between the Allies in Operation *Wacht am Rhein*. It was to him that Skorzeny reported as commanding officer of Panzerbrigade 150. (Bundesarchiv, Bild 183-J28625, Fotograf: Roeder)

A 'Panther' Mk V German tank disguised as an American M10 tank destroyer; note the platework on the turret to enhance the deception. This was one of five tanks used in Fölkersam's Warche Brück/Malmédy assault on 21 December 1944. After the attack failed, the tank retreated to the command post at Café du Rocher de Falize, seen here with the tank's barrel reversed into it. (NARA)

Skorzeny with his para commander, Siegfried Milius, at the Schwedt bridgehead east of the Oder, February 1945. Skorzeny expected Schwedt to be pivotal in a counter-offensive against the Red Army, but the attack was a damp squib. Afterwards, he couldn't wait to get back to Berlin. Obligingly, Himmler dismissed him. (Bundesarchiv, Bild 183-R81453, Fotograf: o.Ang.)

surprise attack on the paper mill's exposed flank. 'It was a very smart move,' said an American officer, 'because if we blew the bridge we would have trapped many of our own men on the wrong side of the Warche.'[44]

To reach the mill required crossing a swampy water meadow with little cover other than darkness and fog. Masked by the sound of the river, the advance force had got within about 500 metres of the mill when there was a blinding flash of light illuminating the whole field, followed by machine-gun and rifle fire. Someone had stumbled upon one of the many trip wires attached to flares which had been laid across the field in anticipation of just such an attack.

Fölkersam's infantry force was pinned down, well short of their target and unable to advance or take aim against their enemy in the dark. Casualties began to mount, aggravated by incessant artillery bombardment. Many of the American shells had been fitted, for the first time in action, with so-called proximity fuses – which caused the charge to explode slightly above the ground, widening the fragmentation effect.

Fölkersam, who had established his command post less than 800 metres away, at the Café du Rocher de Falize on the junction of the Falize–Malmédy and Warche bridge roads, now faced an unpleasant tactical dilemma. His force could not retreat, so it had to be supported. Once further paratrooper reinforcements failed to alleviate the situation, Fölkersam knew he had no alternative but to commit his armour. This consisted of an already depleted Panzerkompanie of four Panther 'M-10' lookalikes and a genuine Sherman, his other three Shermans having been loaned to Scherf.

Lack of numbers was not the only problem. The tanks, with no night-sight capability, were effectively useless before daybreak. Even then, heavy fog hung in the river valley. The tank attack did not get under way until after 8 am. Fölkersam split the tank force into two, each supported by paratroopers – with a view to the two groups attacking the Malmédy road in parallel. The first unit, with three tanks, was to make a frontal attack on the bridge and paper mill. (See map on page 14.)

'We saw how the paratroopers were working their way forward between the trees and bushes on the hillside,' recalled one of the tank gunners. They received the order: 'Frontal attack!' and 'we rolled slowly forwards and drove first through a small orchard. The terrain fell fairly steeply and the track into the valley curved to the left as we approached the paper mill and the houses in front of it, where we could see muzzle flashes.' Progress was painfully slow, taking half an hour to advance 100 metres. 'It was now lighter and we could see the railroad line which ran to the right of the road and the viaduct.

Meanwhile we were under full fire from the American artillery. They caused such a hell of a noise that we couldn't make out any other battle noises.'[45]

The other tank unit had set off northeast along the Falize–Malmédy road with their two tanks and about 30 paratroopers to secure the railway tunnel further up the road. Within minutes of reaching the tunnel, the lead tank hit a mine – illuminating the early morning gloom with a vivid blaze of orange flame and acrid black smoke.

Within a few hours four of Fölkersam's five tanks had been knocked out by mines and bazookas, and the fifth forced to retreat to the Café du Rocher de Falize. Very soon the road to the Warche bridge was strewn with dead and wounded paratroopers, grenadiers and tank crew. The German infantry penetrated the American line near the paper mill and tried to place machine-gun crews at the base of the railway embankment, but at about 10.30 that morning the fog lifted, and the Americans were able to engage in a turkey-shoot.

A renewed attempt by Fölkersam to attack the paper mill soon failed. Not one to admit defeat easily, he would not give the order to retreat without Skorzeny's say-so. By early afternoon his command post was being pounded by American artillery barrages, leaving Fölkersam and his small staff, their radio smashed, no choice but to decamp to a fall-back position on the ridge east of Falize, where the Germans set up the thinnest of defensive perimeters against an attack which, fortuitously, never happened. By this time, Fölkersam had received a superficial shrapnel wound in the buttocks, making it painful to sit down. This was nothing compared to the ordeal he had put his men through in the execution of a poorly thought-out attack. The bigger blame, however, attaches to Skorzeny for consigning so many of his men to a needless death through his irresponsible reconnaissance blunder.

In a later assessment of casualties, Skorzeny reckoned Panzerbrigade 150 dead and wounded to be 20 per cent of the total force,[46] or about 400. This estimate is probably conservative, and the losses were not evenly distributed across the three Kampfgruppen. Wulf's saw no action, while Scherf's lost over 70 men on the night of 20–21 December. Casualties within Kampfgruppe Fölkersam on 21 December must therefore have been very high indeed. The attack on Malmédy was a self-manufactured military fiasco.

Some responsibility may be attributed to a misguided Waffen-SS belief that sustaining heavy casualties without buckling was a substitute for having a sound tactical plan. But most blame must be placed on the assault's two senior commanders, who had proved incompetent. Skilled though they were in the tactics of deception and skirmishing, neither had experience of commanding infantry troops in a set-piece battle.

On the evening of 21 December Skorzeny was hit by artillery shrapnel while attempting to make contact with 1. SS-Panzerdivision 'Leibstandarte-SS Adolf Hitler' headquarters. He received a slight leg wound and more serious damage to his face: at one point he thought he might lose the sight of his right eye. Typically, he attempted to carry on as if nothing had happened, pestering Panzerdivision headquarters for extra artillery cover. But it was perfectly evident he was no longer up to the job – 'It is extraordinary how a wound in the eye can handicap a man. I found it quite hard to find my way about.'[47] Confined to his farmhouse command post, he let Wulf take over.

Panzerbrigade 150's mission had effectively finished. For the next week the broken and virtually armourless force carried out the only duties it could – as sentries on a security perimeter around Bellevaux and the Baugnez crossroads, while the action moved elsewhere, to the southwest.

Kampfgruppe Peiper, cut off irredeemably, had finally given up. The narrow lanes in which they were jammed made the panzers sitting ducks in American air attacks, now favoured by clearer skies. Deprived of infantry support, fuel and food, on 23 December Peiper and his men were forced to abandon their few remaining tanks and fight their way back to the German lines on foot.

On three successive days during Christmas, Malmédy came under a renewed attack more lethal than anything Skorzeny's combat units had inflicted. In an extraordinary display of sustained incompetence, US bombers managed to kill over 200 civilians and a substantial number of their own forces in the mistaken belief that Malmédy was actually under German control.[48]

On 26 December, command of the now wholly redundant Panzerbrigade 150 passed officially to Oberstleutnant Wulf, who was ordered to disband the unit at the Cologne-Wahn training ground. By the beginning of January all non-SS elements – with the exception of a few Kommandokompanie jeep teams – had been reassigned to their parent units. Curiously, in view of Panzerbrigade 150's lacklustre performance, a number of volunteers – including officers – chose to stay on with Skorzeny's Jagdverbände.

On New Year's Eve, Skorzeny was summoned to Hitler's temporary campaign headquarters at Ziegenhain. The whole experience was slightly surreal. The bandaged 'hero' was expecting a tirade, but the mood at FHQ was inexplicably upbeat. Hitler, all solicitude over Skorzeny's suppurating head-wound, immediately referred him to his chief surgeon, Dr Ludwig Stumpfegger, whose infra-red treatment and antibiotic injections may well have saved Skorzeny's sight.

That afternoon, Skorzeny had what he describes as his 'last long talk with the Führer', who was euphoric about his plans for 'a great offensive in the southeast'. To Skorzeny, Hitler's mood was 'very puzzling and I wondered whether he was deceiving himself or was under the influence of Professor Morrell's injections. Dr Morrell had been able to acquire almost unlimited power over him.'[49] Morrell was Hitler's favourite physician; his nickname was 'Der Reichsspritzenmeister', on account of his drug-laced injections.

Having turned down an invitation to see in the new year at FHQ, Skorzeny – cheered by the news that he and all four Panzerbrigade 150 Kampfgruppen leaders were to be awarded the Ehrenblattspange (Honour Roll Clasp) – rejoined his brigade. He claimed to hear the bells of Cologne pealing in the distance as he left.[50] Hitler's delusional behaviour must have been infectious. Either that or Skorzeny's hearing was uncommonly acute. Cologne is over 170 kilometres from Ziegenhain.

Towards the end of January 1945, just after Wulf had wrapped up demobilisation of Panzerbrigade 150 at Grafenwöhr, he received an urgent order to reverse the process: 'Renewed assembly of Panzerbrigade 150 and transport to Schwedt an der Oder for a new mission.'[51] The Russians had launched a huge new offensive on the Vistula front in Poland. Everyone and everything was required to stem their advance.

Panzerbrigade 150 – having already been consigned to history – could not take part. Otto Skorzeny, on the other hand, would be playing a leading role.

13

Implosion

The Schwedt Bridgehead

In January 1945, Skorzeny lost the man he regarded as his finest and most loyal comrade. The last anyone saw of Adrian von Fölkersam was his near lifeless body being transported in the back of an artillery tractor. His unit, Jagdverband Ost, had made an initially successful break-out from its forlorn defence of Hohensalza* in Warthegau, western Poland. Within two days, what remained of a battalion-strength force was annihilated by the Russians. Neither the tractor, nor Fölkersam, was ever seen again. They had been swept up in a military disaster that dwarfed the aftermath of *Bagration* the year before. A synchronised offensive was overpowering the comparatively puny German forces standing in the Red Army's way.

It wasn't as if Hitler had not been warned of the military and political catastrophes facing him. He simply refused to take them seriously.

The warnings had originated with Reinhard Gehlen, head of Fremde Heere Ost. On Christmas Eve 1944, a week before Skorzeny arrived at Ziegenhain, Hitler had received a visit from Guderian, army chief of staff

---

*   Inowrocław

and the man tasked with propping up the Eastern Front. Accompanying him was Gehlen's military analysis, which suggested that the Red Army on the Vistula enjoyed a superiority of 11:1 in infantry, 7:1 in tanks and 20:1 in artillery and aviation. Gehlen also forecast that the Russian attack was timed for 12 January.[1]

Guderian's predictions of doom were scoffed at by Hitler's sycophants, including Himmler. Not content with controlling all the repressive apparatus of the state, Himmler now imagined himself a great military leader, having recently been appointed to the position of army group commander on the upper Rhine, a role which clashed with that of Rundstedt. (Himmler apparently didn't realise that this appointment was engineered by Hitler's powerful gatekeeper Martin Bormann – Reichsleiter and Chief of the Party Chancellery – to winkle him out of Berlin and away from the centre of political intrigue.)

The Soviet Vistula–Oder offensive opened up exactly as Gehlen and Guderian had predicted, right down to the date. German defences crumbled with terrifying rapidity. Warsaw was abandoned and Heeresgruppe A routed within a matter of days. The Germans attempted to create 'breakwaters' in fortified cities such as Bromberg, Thorn, Posen and Breslau* to stem the Red tide.

South of Bromberg, in a tongue of land between the Rivers Vistula and Warthe† (both at this point flowing east–west) was the ancient trading and garrison city of Hohensalza – headquarters of one of Skorzeny's most numerous Volksdeutsche units, Jagdverband Ost.

Fölkersam, exasperated with staff work, had requested the command immediately after the disbandment of Panzerbrigade 150 in early January. Skorzeny consented with the greatest reluctance,[2] signing the papers promoting Fölkersam to SS-Sturmbannführer. He arrived to take command in Hohensalza on 18 January. On the same day, the Soviet 8th Guards Army, six days into the offensive, stormed the besieged city of Lodz, 200 kilometres to the southeast.

The elite Panzergrenadierdivision 'Brandenburg', on its way to relieve Lodz, exposed and outnumbered, had to retreat rapidly. Fölkersam was tasked with providing what cover he could for the Brandenburg's retreat, by mustering the defences of Hohensalza – mostly its gendarmerie and shattered remnants of the German 9. Armee. Fölkersam hated the Soviet regime which had destroyed

---

*   Bydgoszcz, Toruń, Poznań and Wrocław
†   Warta

the wealth and position of his family. Moreover, his wife and young daughter were, like thousands of others, resettled Baltic Volksdeutsche, living not 120 kilometres to the southwest in Posen. By 20 January Hohensalza was completely cut off, with Soviet armour raining fire on the garrison's sole tank.

Skorzeny had been unable to alleviate the situation beyond sending a few trucks laden with supplies. Reinforcements were out of the question. Fölkersam retreated to an artillery barracks near the city centre, from where he radioed Friedenthal that the situation was 'untenable' and that he was organising a breakout. During the fierce street-fighting that followed Fölkersam was wounded in the head – mortally, according to Skorzeny.[3]

In fact, the tractor and its wounded passenger were almost certainly captured by the Russians. According to information supplied by his colleague Wolfgang Herfurth many years later, Fölkersam was taken to Moscow and there exhaustively interrogated. He seems to have survived Russian captivity until at least 1949.[4]

At all events, no more than ten Germans made it out, most of them officers. Among those who died was Skorzeny's former adjutant, Ostafel.[5]

One last service Skorzeny performed for Fölkersam was the rescue of his wife and daughter. He sent one of his senior medical team, Hellmut Slama – a decorated veteran of Panzerbrigade 150 – to Posen. Fölkersam's family were extricated, and lived out the rest of the war in Austria.[6]

'Fölkersam was my best comrade and my most loyal friend,'[7] Skorzeny later wrote, in one of his rare moments of earnest appreciation. Intense, introverted and methodical, Fölkersam had been the perfect foil to a charismatic braggart impatient of the fine detail of staff work.

The loss in expertise was made good with the appointment of Wilhelm Walther, an immensely experienced Oberstleutnant in the Panzergrenadierdivision 'Brandenburg'. Unfortunately for Skorzeny, Walther had been badly wounded in Romania the previous autumn and remained hospitalised until the end of February.

Like Skorzeny, Walther had been a noted student swordsman; they shared a technical background, and had both worked in the construction industry during the 1930s. There, however, the similarity ended. Every inch the professional soldier, Walther was frankly contemptuous of a man who had risen through political preferment and had never even attended officer-training school. 'As far as I'm concerned,' Walther said of Skorzeny later, 'he wasn't officer material. He may have been a lieutenant-colonel like me, but I never saw him as an officer.'[8] No doubt Walther kept these thoughts to himself at the time, but they disbarred the kind of personal chemistry that had existed between Skorzeny and Fölkersam.

* * *

On 30 January, Skorzeny was in his office at Friedenthal when, at around 5 pm, he received an urgent telephone call from Himmler. He and all the forces he could muster were to proceed immediately to the town of Schwedt in Brandenburg, 95 kilometres northeast of Berlin, and there establish a bridgehead on the eastern bank of the Oder in preparation for a counter-offensive.[9]

On the way, the hastily prepared Kampfgruppe was to take time out to relieve Bad Freienwalde, a small spa town 50 kilometres south of Schwedt (and worryingly close to Berlin) that had already fallen into the hands of the Red Army.

Skorzeny and his staff struggled to make sense of these orders. They were contradictory, preposterous even. If the Russians had already breached the Oder, how could a small scratch force of commandos repel them? And what was the point of then creating a bridgehead further downstream on the opposite side of the river if they were already facing encirclement on the nearside?

The orders were symptomatic of the chaos now enveloping German Heeresgruppe Mitte and Heeresgruppe A; and the muddled military response of the man charged with sorting it out: the Reichsführer-SS. Since 24 January, Himmler had been commander-in-chief of the cobbled-together Heeresgruppe Weichsel* – to the utter dismay of Guderian, who was, as OKH chief of staff, the man with overall responsibility for the Eastern Front. In Hitler's view, the troop formations in headlong retreat from the Soviets needed the smack of authority imposed upon them; that task was consistent with the Reichsführer's role as the Third Reich's First Policeman. Hitler told Goebbels that Himmler was the right man for this role and expressed himself 'extremely pleased' with his work,[10] utterly blind to Himmler's proven incompetence as a military strategist. Martin Bormann, Kaltenbrunner and Fegelein enthusiastically supported Himmler's appointment, foreseeing political advantage for themselves in his failure and humiliation.

Himmler's operations chief, Oberst Hans-Georg Eismann, his sole professional general staff officer, was shocked at the lack of preparation. His staff arrangements were completely inadequate; he had one out-of-date map, and a single telephone aboard his special headquarters train (the one he had used to contact Skorzeny) was his only means of communicating with the outside world, let alone the two armies under his command.[11]

---

*   Army Group Vistula

Himmler had no grasp of the enormity of the task before him, and had no hope of assessing it operationally. 'He stared, mesmerised, at the vast gap he had to close,' Eismann noted; blind to the vulnerability of 2. Armee's flank, 'For him there seemed to be nothing but "attack".'[12] He was incapable of seeing beyond the tactical clichés of Hitler, and became furious when challenged about them. His single contribution to 'strategy' was a reign of terror behind the lines to snuff out the least hint of 'defeatism' with summary execution. His order to Skorzeny to recapture Freienwalde en route to Schwedt demonstrated complete ignorance of the Russians' whereabouts, as Skorzeny soon ascertained through enquiries at FHQ.

In fact, during the night of 30 January, a vanguard force from the 1st Belorussian Front had crossed the frozen Oder just north of Küstrin*, 70 kilometres due east of Berlin. The following day, a Soviet tank brigade managed to establish a second bridgehead south of Küstrin. The most the Germans, utterly wrong-footed, could do was to send a few Focke Wulf FW 190s to bomb and strafe the Russians the following morning as they dug in.[13]

Skorzeny and his senior officers, wholly unaware of these breaking developments to the southeast, spent the night of 30–31 January frantically assembling their Schwedt task force.

This makeshift unit would eventually swell to 15,000 men, the bulk made up of transitory armoured and Luftwaffe brigades. Kampfgruppe Schwedt would be the biggest field force Skorzeny would ever command – giving him the acting status of an SS-Brigadeführer (divisional commander), although he was never promoted to that rank. For the moment, however, all he could count on were: Jagdverband Mitte (four companies, about 700 men), commanded by SS-Hauptsturmführer Karl Fucker; the SS-Fallschirmjägerbataillon 600 under SS-Hauptsturmführer Siegfried Milius (also four companies, about 700 men); and two companies of the understrength Jagdverband Nordwest, under SS-Hauptsturmführer Heinrich Hoyer (a Skorzeny trusty) which comprised 90 men, the majority Norwegians, Dutch, Danes, Belgians and French.[14]

The availability of these men was dictated by their proximity. Handily, the whole of Milius's para battalion was back in its barracks at nearby Neustrelitz, recuperating and refitting after heavy losses during the Ardennes offensive. Nordwest was the only territorial commando unit not actively engaged at the time – its theatre of operations being the still unoccupied areas of Holland and Norway; and it, too, was based at the Neustrelitz Kampfschule. Finally,

*   Kostrzyn

there was a reserve company of light tanks and armoured vehicles commanded by the now promoted SS-Hauptsturmführer Otto Schwerdt.

Attached to Mitte, and of a tactical significance out of all proportion to its size, was a 44-strong detachment of snipers under the command of SS-Obersturmführer Odo Willscher. They were one of those occasional Skorzeny whims that paid off. The Wehrmacht had little valued the skill of marksmanship until it learned the hard way from the Russians – whose snipers were past-masters at picking off German officers from up to 400 metres away. Willscher was one of a small number of Germans skilled in the art. Only in autumn 1944 when he left the Brandenburgers for Skorzeny's Jagdverbände was he actively encouraged to develop his sharpshooting tactics. Willscher's snipers, who worked in units of two attached to other formations, were to prove versatile at countering the Russians' overwhelming superiority in tanks and artillery during the forthcoming conflict.[15]

Numerous non-SS volunteers from Panzerbrigade 150 also joined the expedition, including a number of the former Kommandokompanie,[16] among them Korvettenkapitän Philipp Freiherr von Behr.

Unprepared to condescend to detailed planning, Skorzeny selected his trusted collaborator Hunke as operations chief. His job was to make sense of Skorzeny's orders and pass them on to the different units. With Fölkersam believed dead and Walther still in a sanatorium at Jugenheim, Hunke soon found he was obliged to combine this taxing role with acting chief of staff.

Schwedt was about 95 kilometres from Friedenthal; badgered by Himmler, Skorzeny sent ahead two paratroop patrols at about 3 am on 31 January, only 33 hours after receiving his initial orders, while the main force of around 2,000 men battled against icy roads and -10°C temperatures to arrive later that morning. With them came a monitoring service, a supply company and two signals platoons. Friedenthal was stripped of all but a skeleton staff and its sabotage specialists. Radl remained behind with a unit of Romanian Volksdeutesche Waffen-SS guards.[17]

When Skorzeny arrived in Schwedt, a picturesque garrison town on the northwest fringe of the Oder marshes, there was no sign of any Russians, and almost nothing to repel them should they inconveniently turn up. There were no fixed fortifications and no artillery. The only trained forces standing in the path of over two million advancing Russians were, it soon transpired, three battalions of aged reservists and a battalion of pioneers, with an amputee colonel doped up on morphine in overall command.[18] Projecting southeast of the town into the designated east-bank salient was a bridge complex nearly a kilometre long spanning the Oder Canal, the river itself and the band of marshes and water meadows that lay between them. The whole had frozen solid, offering the Russians a seamless causeway capable of bearing tanks.

Clearly bluff and a great deal of luck were required if Skorzeny was to fortify the Schwedt enclave in time. He lacked neither. Having relieved the colonel of his 500 men, he roped in the major commanding the pioneer battalion. Skorzeny knew little about positional warfare and still less about creating fixed defences, but the major did. He helped Skorzeny establish a bridgehead on the east bank of the Oder:

> ... with an outer semicircle with a radius of about 8 kilometres running from the Oder to a small tributary, the Rörike. Rifle pits and strongpoints were dug on this frontline by a labour service regiment from Stettin and the male population of Schwedt. A second line of fortifications was laid down within this semicircle, with strongpoints, machine-gun nests, communications trenches and small hedgehog positions. The third ring was laid down around the east end of the Oder bridge in a radius of about one kilometre.

This was intended to protect both Schwedt and Skorzeny's command post at Niederkränig* on the east bank of the river.[19] These sophisticated defence works – not the normal metier of commandos and paratroopers – were completed within four days of Skorzeny's arrival. Meanwhile the commander of the pioneer unit took charge of blowing up the ice on the Oder.

On the very first day, having established his command post at Niederkränig, Skorzeny set off by car to Königsberg in der Neumark†, 12 kilometres southeast of Niederkränig, to appraise the situation. No Russians, but a flood of refugees; among them, stragglers from dismembered German units were pouring down the road in their thousands. He ordered the Königsberg mayor to round them up and send them directly to the barracks at Schwedt, where they were fed and re-equipped. Skorzeny reasoned that these were experienced soldiers who could inject more fighting mettle into Schwedt's sub-standard battalions. To ensure his orders were carried out, and to provide early warning in case of a Russian incursion, he left a screening force of paratroopers at settlements beyond the bridgehead perimeter.

At the same time, Skorzeny began to tackle, with his customary energy and drive, the deficiency of artillery and heavy weapons. Rapidly tiring of the broken

---

*   Krajnik Dolny
†   Chojna

promises and obstructive behaviour from Heeresgruppe Weichsel headquarters, he put his supply chief SS-Hauptsturmführer Georg Reinhold Gerhard onto the problem. Gerhard was the one outstandingly competent officer in Amt VI-F (weapons procurement), an expert on sabotage matériel, responsible for procurement of all kinds of unconventional weapons, including the experimental plastic explosive Nipolit. At an arms dump near Frankfurt an der Oder he laid hands on a supply of MG 42 machine guns and ammunition, and requisitioned 15 anti-tank guns abandoned in an arms factory south of Schwedt.

A personal telephone call to Göring gained Skorzeny two Luftwaffe flak battalions. Ingeniously, Skorzeny had six of their guns mounted on some commandeered trucks and used them as 'flying batteries', racing up and down a 20-kilometre strip within the bridgehead to create the illusion that his firepower was far greater than it actually was. He also mounted a flak battalion on three refloated Oder barges, randomising their position to create the maximum amount of confusion among the enemy. It was all smoke and mirrors, but helped to create credible cover while the bridgehead defensive works were being built.

By 3 February, Skorzeny's battle plan was assuming its final shape. On the north and south perimeters of the bridgehead were stationed two of the reserve battalions (reinforced with a number of Luftwaffe paratroops), to act as an alarm bell in the event of a sudden Russian incursion. To provide backbone, Skorzeny's elite Mitte units were stationed in the central sector, behind the second defensive line, with Nordwest to their left. Further forward, but still in the centre, was much of the SS-Fallschirmjägerbataillon 600. Skorzeny rightly suspected that any serious Russian attack would come down the main road from Königsberg.

The completed bridgehead resembled a spearhead, with the baseline of the blade lying on the Oder and its tip projecting about a kilometre beyond the village of Grabow on the main road. The axis ran southeast towards Königsberg, about 5 kilometres beyond the defensive perimeter. (See map on page 15.)

Skorzeny garrisoned Königsberg with two Volkssturm* units, one led by the local mayor and composed mainly of farmers (about 250 in all), the second largely made up of Hamburg dockers (about 550) who were well armed and, apparently, more highly motivated than the locals.[20] Skorzeny hardly expected serious combat potential from either unit. He therefore

---

*   National militia of those too young or too old for military service, set up by the
     Nazi Party in the closing stages of the war.

stationed paratrooper 3. Kompanie, under the command of Joachim 'Macki' Marcus, east of the town to instil backbone in the cannon-fodder.[21]

The difficulty in early February lay not in engaging the enemy but in locating where he was; and then in second-guessing his intentions. The German high command could hardly know it at the time, but a fierce debate on that latter topic was raging in the highest reaches of the Stavka, the Soviet General Staff. Having unexpectedly seized hundreds of kilometres of territory in the first few weeks of the offensive, should the Red Army continue on a roll straight to Berlin while German forces were still too stunned to put up a meaningful defence, or consolidate its massive gains and dig in against a counter-offensive before tackling Berlin? The second was the course of action Stalin chose.[22]

Skorzeny sent out reconnaissance parties – mostly paratroopers – to all points northeast and southeast of the bridgehead. The pattern of Soviet troop movements in the first week of February gradually became apparent. On 5 February, a patrol near the village of Altenkirchen*, about 25 kilometres south of the bridgehead, detected Russian T-34 tanks and trucks on the main road to Zehden†. The patrol leader 'got the impression that the Russians were trying to cross the Oder River by Zehden … Against our bridgehead, they only seemed to be employing light forces. A definite offensive against Schwedt with assembly areas could not be found. Probably they were located near Zehden.'[23]

In other words, the Russians were using Schwedt as a feint, diverting colossal German resources into defending a bridgehead they did not intend to storm.

Skorzeny's attention had, by this time, been distracted by developments to the east. Russian skirmishers from the 2nd Guards Tank Army were prowling in the area of Bad Schönfliess‡, a small watering hole less than 15 kilometres due east of Königsberg.[24]

Skorzeny's interest in this development was partly tactical, partly political. Such importance was attached to the Schwedt bridgehead that a hotline had been set up to the Reich Chancellery,[25] which gave Skorzeny a convenient means of bypassing the bureaucratic incompetence of Heeresgruppe Weichsel. But it also made him a cat's-paw in Berlin's political intrigues. He had received a mysterious order to retrieve some vital 'state documents' left behind in a forest east of Bad Schönfliess during the retreat. Closer scrutiny revealed these

---

*   Łukowice
†   Cedynia
‡   Trzcińsko-Zdrój

were in fact compromising party documents and that Bormann was pulling Skorzeny's strings.[26] Having little option but to obey orders, on 4 February Skorzeny launched an elite reconnaissance mission to Bad Schönfliess, consisting of Hunke, four Gran Sasso sidekicks and Skorzeny himself, accompanied by his German Shepherd, Lux.

Leaving their two staff cars some way out of the town, 'we told our drivers to follow us later. Not a sound came from the first houses and we soon reached the medieval gateway ... Two civilians were lying dead close by. At length a man peered out from a window and then sidled out of his house, apparently unable to believe that he was seeing German troops.'[27] He revealed that Russian troops were in the town, and were bringing in troops and supplies by train. A three-man patrol to the station spotted over 30 tanks parked in the yard and noted enemy formations to the south and east of the town. Clearly, an attack on Königsberg was imminent. Skorzeny and his party quietly withdrew, taking with them two refugee mothers and their children. This was the sole occasion, in two years as head of Germany's SS commandos, when Skorzeny went behind enemy lines.

Returning to his command post, Skorzeny, who loathed party officials as much as he loathed the general staff, took great satisfaction in telling Bormann that it was impossible to retrieve his papers because they were already in the hands of the Russians. And, in any case, he and his men had far more important things to do than run party errands.

Only hours later, the Red Army attacked Königsberg. The odds were overwhelmingly stacked against the Germans, the Russians throwing in over 40 tanks and several infantry battalions. The German defence was a shambles. Although Marcus's paratroopers knocked out a few Russian tanks, their position was compromised when the Volkssturm broke and their leader – the mayor, Kurt Flöter – fled. Marcus, out of ammunition, was forced to retreat to Grabow, abandoning Königsberg to the Russians in the early hours of 5 February.

Skorzeny, a vigorous adherent of Himmler's 'not one step back' doctrine, reacted with Führer-like rage. Marcus was threatened with court-martial for dereliction of duty, death by firing-squad being the penalty. Milius, Marcus's commander, apparently got him off, but only with difficulty.[28] Skorzeny zealously punished the least sniff of defeatism with summary execution. In Schwedt, he was responsible for a kangaroo court that resulted in the deaths of at least ten civilians; he also tried seven of his men for desertion and sentenced four to death.

By far the most high-profile victim was Flöter, the mayor. Charged with desertion, he was left to hang from an apple tree in the main square of

Schwedt with an admonitory placard round his neck. The execution plunged Skorzeny into even deeper water with Bormann, since Flöter was a Kreisleiter, the highest-ranking local official of the Nazi Party. Party officials could only be tried by party courts, in which an *Alter Kämpfer** like Flöter would probably have got off. Skorzeny was well aware of this, having consulted his legal expert, SS-Sturmbannführer Pinder, beforehand. A former SS magistrate, Pinder had a reputation for uncompromising brutality.[29] In Schwedt he acted as Skorzeny's instrument of terror, his main purpose being to cow the local population. In the case of Flöter, he had uncharacteristically counselled caution, but Skorzeny chose to proceed regardless, casting himself as the champion of military integrity over party-political corruption.

Skorzeny clearly derived satisfaction from settling a score with Bormann, who 'fumed and foamed' when he found out. The day before Flöter's execution Bormann sent a high-ranking emissary to intercede. Emil Stürtz was not only the Gauleiter but the Reich Defence Commissar for the Brandenburg region. Skorzeny was not to be bullied: he remained adamant that Flöter had been found guilty under martial law. Skorzeny never heard another word on the subject from Berlin.[30]

This wasn't the only irritant. A few days previously, on 4 February, Skorzeny had learnt that Kampfgruppe Schwedt – the hastily cobbled-together force from Friedenthal and Neustrelitz – had officially been redesignated a division which, together with Kampfgruppe Klossek and a naval unit – 1. Marine-Infanterie-Division – posted further south along the Oder, would now form part of the newly created Oderkorps, commanded by Generalleutnant Günther Krappe, a battle-hardened professional soldier.[31] For Skorzeny this meant the insertion of a new bureaucratic layer in the already muddled command structure of Heeresgruppe Weichsel, making direct communication with Himmler near impossible. His sense of grievance was compounded by Krappe's dismissive attitude to Kampfgruppe Skorzeny: he visited the Schwedt headquarters just once.

After the loss of Königsberg, Skorzeny managed to stem the Soviet advance at Grabow, but only after heavy losses and at the cost of surrendering all other outposts beyond the bridgehead perimeter. The sole exception was Nipperwiese†, a small fishing village on the east bank of the Oder, 7 kilometres north of the command post at Niederkränig. A ring of Soviet steel now began

---

*   'Old Fighter': one of those who joined the NSDAP before the Reichstag elections of September 1930.

†   Ognica

pressing at all points of the bridgehead. The fragility of the German defence there was underlined by the incursion of an infantry patrol with two T-34 tanks, which managed, on the morning of 5 February, to penetrate from the direction of Nipperwiese to within a couple of hundred metres of the Oder bridge before being routed by a scratch force of Panzerfaust-toting paratroopers and Willscher snipers.

At this point, Skorzeny – possibly due to orders from Korps headquarters – harboured the unrealistic idea of recapturing Königsberg, which possessed two vital communications assets: a station on the north–south Stettin–Küstrin railway line, and an abandoned Luftwaffe airfield.[32] At very least, high command would wish to deny these assets to the Russians; but their recapture and consolidation within an expanded bridgehead would also be vital in the forthcoming counter-offensive that was still an article of faith at Heeresgruppe Weichsel headquarters. Less understandable is how Skorzeny was supposed to achieve these objectives, with so few troops, little or no artillery, no tanks and no air cover.

In the short term, his priority was to eject the Soviets from the bridgehead: they had seized the village of Hanseberg* on the southeast perimeter, and were massing for another attack on Grabow. Despite a huge force of armour, the Russians were at a local disadvantage.[33] The terrain around the bridgehead was thickly wooded and hilly, and the water meadows were now flooded by an early thaw. If they were to cross the Oder, the best route for Russian armour was along the main road to Schwedt – on which Grabow was the key forward defensive position.

They initially took Grabow, but Skorzeny was able to mount a limited counter-offensive, recapturing it on 6 February after a fierce action involving all four companies of the SS paratroopers, who suffered heavy casualties. Skorzeny himself played an active combat role for the first time since Rome.[34] He was able to summon more power the following morning with the deployment of the temporarily available Sturmgeschützbrigade 210, a substantial armoured force equipped with brand-new StuG IV assault guns recovered from a factory, their camouflage paint not yet applied.

Skorzeny had been pleading with Himmler for armour since the beginning of the month, believing that Korps command was deliberately starving his forces of the weaponry it needed to make a success of the bridgehead. Matters came to a head when, faced with a major Russian irruption, Skorzeny was forced to abandon Nipperwiese. Judging the Grabow axis more important, he

---

*   Krzymów

left a light screen of Luftwaffe troops bolstered by SS paratroopers in and around the village, and laid minefields in the surrounding area. Korps headquarters did not approve. Nipperwiese guarded a system of dykes across the Oder marshes which could support Russian artillery and armour – an Achilles' heel in the defence of the bridgehead as a whole, and an essential link with Gruppe Denecke holding the Oder line immediately to the north.[35] On 8 February, just as Skorzeny was about to set off for Grabow, Korps demanded to know whether the officer commanding at Nipperwiese had been court-martialled or shot. Skorzeny, in a fit of pique, wired back abruptly that he had not, and would not be.

Early that afternoon, Skorzeny was outside Grabow when an order came through to present himself at Heeresgruppe HQ at 4 pm. 'My immediate reaction was that Korps, who did not like me, had probably repeated my ill-chosen words verbatim to Army Group. I was in trouble again.'[36] Skorzeny refused to tear himself away from the fighting until the German position had been re-established. As a result he arrived at headquarters four hours late, in a battle-stained uniform.

The staff officers 'treated me as if I were a disgraced criminal, and Himmler's ADC told me that … the Reichsführer was in a rage over my belated appearance'. Indeed, Himmler was initially more incensed by Skorzeny's lateness than he was by the loss of Nipperwiese. Skorzeny's behaviour during the encounter was not exactly calculated to conciliate; during the long wait in Himmler's anteroom, he had fuelled himself with some of the Reichsführer's cognac. In the explosive exchange that followed Himmler stomped around the room and, according to Skorzeny's account, threatened him with court-martial and demotion. In fact, by this stage of the war, Skorzeny's status as a Reich hero made him invulnerable to criticism. He waited for Himmler to simmer down before pointing out that the position at Nipperwiese was impossible to hold and that he himself had ordered his men to retire to the bridgehead. Having mollified Himmler, Skorzeny stuck the knife into Korps command, pointing out that he'd had 'a whole lot of silly orders … but nothing at all in the way of supplies'.[37] Himmler, perhaps taken aback by the ferocity of Skorzeny's riposte, ended the encounter by placing an avuncular hand on his shoulder and inviting him to dinner.

And yet this reconciliation with Himmler did nothing to improve relations with Skorzeny's immediate superiors.[38] On 10 February, Krappe was relieved of the command of Oderkorps and replaced by the very last person Skorzeny would wish to take orders from – his old antagonist from Operation *Panzerfaust*, SS-Obergruppenführer Erich von dem Bach-Zelewski. Skorzeny called him an out-of-his-depth 'police general' who had borne a grudge against Skorzeny ever since Budapest and was now more interested in settling old scores than winning the war against the Russians.[39] Bach-Zelewski made Skorzeny's life a misery and was no more sympathetic to his desperate need for supplies and reinforcements than his predecessor.[40] He dropped in unannounced at Schwedt Castle HQ, casually chatting to staff officers and tippling their cognac while Skorzeny himself was out in the field.[41] Skorzeny, probably rightly, suspected Bach-Zelewski of undermining his position with Himmler by obstructing the arrival of critical ordnance and issuing a mass of impossibly contradictory orders.

There was, however, one influential Nazi prepared to offer Skorzeny help. On the morning of 7 February, a 17-year-old paratrooper in the counter-attack on Hanseberg was clinging for dear life to a welded handle on the armoured exterior of one of the StuG IVs as it sped towards the battlefield. 'At a fork in the road, there is a short stop. There's a car with a pennant, and a group of officers seems to be holding an important briefing. We take little notice of it, until one of us picks out the stout form of the Reichsmarschall. He's here? On the front line?'[42] Hermann Göring was indeed there. The florid comic opera warrior had for once dispensed with his glittering medal collection in favour of a plain grey air force uniform, more befitting a tour of inspection.

Göring's aides had for some time been anxiously monitoring the enemy's progress with daily calls to Schwedt. But the personal visit came as a surprise to Skorzeny, who was holed up in a cellar in Grabow when informed by divisional HQ that the Reichsmarschall had been waiting at Schwedt 'for hours'.

Skorzeny escorted his portly charge to the front line on foot, occasionally diving for cover from incoming artillery fire in the sodden trenchwork circumvallating the smouldering remains of Grabow. Göring exhibited an almost childlike fascination when exploring the burnt-out Russian tanks littering the way and showered gifts of schnapps and cigarettes on some of the flak crews responsible for knocking them out. Then it was back to Niederkränig, where some very expensive-looking cigars were lavished on Hunke, before Göring returned to his staff car.[43]

In parting, Göring was careful to offer a few words of encouragement to Skorzeny on his 'division conjured out of thin air'. Though diminished, Göring was even now a power to be reckoned with, whose patronage could be invaluable. His practical assistance had already included the transfer to the bridgehead of a newly formed Wachbataillon of redundant fighter pilots and air force cadets, who had been drilling on his nearby Carinhall estate.

These 400 men had no experience of infantry warfare, but Skorzeny made the most of the situation by splitting them into smaller units which were seconded to existing alarm battalions.[44]

Clearly Göring's tour of inspection – and Skorzeny's plea for rapid reinforcement – left their mark. A memorandum sent that very day to Heeresgruppe Weichsel by Göring's adjutant recommended reassigning a section of the Marine Infantry Division stationed near the Küstrin bridgehead to Schwedt.[45] Alas for Skorzeny, the request was ignored.

Several days later Skorzeny's bridgehead was almost overwhelmed by a second Russian tank and infantry assault on Grabow, penetrating as far as Hohenkränig before being stemmed by Schwerdt's armoured force. Four of the original Gran Sasso team were killed in the engagement. Although the bridgehead – including Grabow – was recaptured, from now on Russian pressure became relentless. There were frequent small enemy attacks, supported by tanks, self-propelled artillery and occasionally ground-attack aircraft. Always in the same three places: northwards towards Peetzig/Hanseberg; westwards towards Grabow; and southwards from the direction of Nipperwiese.

'The Russians fought bravely,' Skorzeny commented, 'but they made the mistake of trying to break through with force. All their attempts were stopped at heavy cost to them and beaten back. In each case we counter-attacked immediately.'[46] He was proud of his men: 'we would never have been able to deceive the enemy for so long without the training and without the fighting strength of my own unit, which provided the backbone of the defence, without the mobile anti-aircraft guns mounted on trucks and boats, and without another unit that weakened the enemy considerably: I am referring to the company of snipers from Friedenthal, which was under the command of Odo Willscher.' The snipers operated in no-man's-land, hiding among the great blocks of timber-encrusted ice washed ashore during the thaw. Skorzeny credited a quarter of his success in defence to them.[47] The Heeresgruppe Weichsel daily situation report of 24 February recorded 260 sniper kills since 13 February.[48]

While Skorzeny worked away at his defence and congratulated himself on its success, it never crossed his mind that he was the victim of a grand deception by the Red Army. After initial reconnaissance of the bridgehead, the Russians had lost any interest in making a breakthrough at Schwedt. Under Stalin's personal direction, they focused on smashing Guderian's fragile land corridor to 2. Armee marooned around Danzig. Red Army forces deployed before Schwedt were a screening force for the flank of this assault.

It was an elaborate feint – sustained by relentless small-scale attacks – designed to draw men and resources into the Schwedt bridgehead while the real action was being prepared elsewhere. When, in mid-April, Zhukov's hammer finally struck, it was to be further south, in the Zehden/Küstrin zone, on the Posen/Berlin axis. A second force would punch its own bridgehead across the Oder at Gartz, 20 kilometres north of Schwedt.

By then, the Schwedt bridgehead had been abandoned and its commander had removed himself to another part of the imploding German front.

$$* * *$$

The way Skorzeny tells it, his reassignment came out of the blue: 'On the 28th of February, 1945, I unexpectedly received an order to return to Berlin, with an intimation that it was the wish of FHQ.' That single word 'unexpectedly' neatly glosses over the fact that he had been actively canvassing Jodl for a new role over the past two weeks. The only wonder is that – having thrown his weight about in Berlin – it had taken him so long to get what he wanted.

The defence of Schwedt was to be a model for Skorzeny's post-war thinking on the role of special forces. It is therefore no surprise to find him abridging and embroidering the facts in his memoirs to fit a Cold-War theme. This 'authorised version' depicts the German commando as the heroic leader of a microcosmic 'Euro' force which, under-equipped and undermanned though it was, reduced a Soviet army 15 times its size to stalemate by smart attritional warfare.[49] Towards the end of February, Skorzeny is recalled to Berlin, apparently to discuss a new high-profile role in the forthcoming defence of the capital. Unfortunately for all concerned, he is not allowed to withdraw his units at the same time. Soon afterwards, the Schwedt bridgehead is abandoned by its new commander. Mitte and the SS paratroop battalions are redeployed further south at the Zehden bridgehead where, over the coming few weeks, they are all but annihilated in an increasingly futile struggle.

There is a nugget of truth in these contentions. Skorzeny did command a multinational force of sorts at Schwedt. Besides the Norwegians, Danes, Dutch, French and Belgians that comprised most of Nordwest, he enlisted part of a Cossack regiment (commanded by the son of Cossack general Pyotr Krasnov). On 23 February he received new reinforcements in the form of two companies (400 men) of the Romanian Waffen-SS regiment formerly stationed at Friedenthal. Skorzeny does not mention it, but there were even foreigners fighting for him in the ranks of Mitte: namely the two renegade Irish Royal Fusiliers, James Brady and Frank Stringer.

All the same, these exotic components were hardly the backbone of the bridgehead's defence. By no reasonable yardstick could Kampfgruppe Schwedt be considered a pan-European defence force engaged in an ideological war against the Soviets.

Skorzeny's suggestion that he was being considered for a role in the defence of Berlin also has some foundation. There had certainly been rumours abroad in mid-February that Skorzeny would be transferred to Berlin to take part in its final defence. A BBC broadcast 'amused us greatly', stating that the 'well-known SS-Obersturmbannführer Skorzeny, who carried out the Mussolini rescue, has now been promoted to major-general, and entrusted with the defence of Berlin, thus becoming the most powerful man in the German capital ... He has already made a start with the liquidation of doubtful elements among the civil population of the northern districts of Berlin.'[50]

The unintentional informant was Jodl, who had mentioned Skorzeny's name in discussions on this subject in the Chancellery.[51] On 26 February, an article appeared on the front page of the *Daily Mail* announcing: 'New Dictator in Berlin'. It apparently originated in Stockholm the previous day:

Three of Germany's most desperate men have been given the task of preparing the 6,000,000 people crowded into Berlin to withstand a siege, I am informed to-day from an unimpeachable source.
They are:
The Man Who Saved Hitler after the bomb plot on July 20 – Major [now General] Rehmer [*sic*].
The Man Who Saved Mussolini from his prison in the Abruzzi mountains after the collapse of Italy in 1943 – SS-Hauptsturmführer Otto Skorzeny; and
The Man With A Plan – Lieut-General Ritter von Hauenschildt [*sic*].
These three are answerable only to Himmler and Gauleiter Goebbels, to whom they owe their appointment.[52]

Skorzeny, 'who owes his meteoric rise to ruthlessness' was the 'most powerful of the triumvirate' and had allegedly already begun his grisly task of 'liquidating' 'tens of thousands of people' three weeks previously. It may be that the 'unimpeachable source' the article claimed to rely on was the same one that informed the BBC – British intelligence, which in turn had picked up mention of Skorzeny's name from Ultra intercepts of Jodl's encoded messages at Bletchley Park.[53]

Responsibility for defending Berlin did not fall to Skorzeny. The real explanation for his recall from Schwedt was entirely different. He was fired.

On 21 February, Himmler – no doubt egged on by Bach-Zelewski – relieved Skorzeny of the Schwedt command and appointed SS-Obersturmbannführer Hans Kempin in his place.[54] Skorzeny and Kempin were asked to draw up a joint plan for the withdrawal of Skorzeny's special forces, acknowledging that they could be more usefully deployed elsewhere on tasks for which they had been specially trained. But there was a sting in the tail. Precipitate withdrawal might cause the collapse of the bridgehead. Their disengagement would have to be carefully phased. The jointly agreed plan would therefore require Himmler's personal approval.

So Skorzeny's departure from Schwedt, far from being caused by an 'unexpected' call from Berlin on 28 February, had in fact been decided at least a week earlier and was carefully premeditated. This is the 'when'; the 'why' is a little more complex. Self-evidently, having Bach-Zelewski stabbing him in the back must have made Skorzeny feel he was fighting a war on two fronts. More materially, by 21 February the German military situation had taken a turn for the worse. Himmler's notion of mounting a counter-offensive from Schwedt may have been unrealistic from the start, but he and Guderian continued to harbour grand ideas of a knock-out blow that would stall the Russians and buy time for the defence of Berlin. The counter-offensive that eventually took place on 16 February (known in SS circles as Operation *Sonnenwende*, or *Solstice*) involved over 1,200 panzers in an all-out assault on Zhukov's forces in the Stargard area of Pomerania; it was accompanied by a diversionary pincer attack near Küstrin. *Sonnenwende*, like *Wacht am Rhein*, was dogged by inadequate logistics and a lack of ammunition and fuel. Losses were heavy, the most senior one being the operation's architect General Walther Wenck, who was badly injured in a car accident just after it started. Within two days the operation had to be aborted. The German tanks destroyed were, by this stage of the war, irreplaceable.[55]

Sonnenwende marked the beginning of the end of Himmler's tenure as commander-in-chief of Heeresgruppe Weichsel. Its dismal failure meant the destruction of all his hopes of martial glory. No amount of animal courage bolstered by drumhead repression would now suffice to defeat the Red hordes. Within a month, Himmler had exchanged his sumptuous personal quarters at Prenzlau (described as more like a boudoir than a military camp by one of his officers) for the nearby sanitarium at Hohenlychen – claiming an attack of flu. A week later, on 20 March, he supinely shuffled off his command to Guderian's preferred candidate – Generaloberst Gotthard Heinrici, commander of

1. Panzerarmee – and scuttled back to Berlin, a very different man to the one a few days earlier who had heartily reassured Skorzeny over dinner: 'Believe me, we'll win the war yet!'[56] By the third week of February it must have become blindingly obvious to Skorzeny that he was on a hiding to nothing at Schwedt.

On 27 February[57] – the day before Skorzeny quit the bridgehead – he and Kempin set out their proposals for an orderly disengagement of Skorzeny's Jagdverbände forces and SS-Fallschirmjägerbataillon 600. The plan (which, in the event, was largely ignored) included a meticulous analysis of Division Schwedt and Skorzeny's detailed commentary upon it. Despite his ceaseless requests for reinforcements, the core defence force – a division on paper only – had never risen much above 5,000 men. Skorzeny's commentary reminded Himmler of his personal promises of men and matériel which had either not materialised or been inadequately fulfilled. Skorzeny also noted that Division Schwedt had almost exclusively relied upon the Jagdverbände for arms, ammunition and other supplies, including petrol. This issue would have to be urgently addressed, otherwise the Jagdverbände would no longer be able to perform their proper role.

But in these twilight months of the Third Reich, what *was* the proper role of Skorzeny's SS commando force? At Schwedt one of his worst nightmares – and the reason he, Fölkersam and Radl had done their level best the previous autumn to avoid a conventional regimental structure[58] – had come to pass. Under military pressure, his special forces had been incorporated into front-line combat units. Extracting them was to prove a momentous task.

Skorzeny later admitted that Schwedt was 'just one tiny episode in the closing story of the Second World War'.[59] His achievement was limited, though not insignificant: barring the Soviets from an open goal at what had initially been one of the Oder's most tempting crossing points. In efficiently organising the bridgehead's scratch defence, he showed a flair that had eluded him when he was on the attack at Malmédy, even if it was Milius and his paratroopers who did most of the subsequent fighting.

Skorzeny paid a high price, losing effective control of his commando forces. After 28 February, when he finally received a longed-for summons to Berlin, he would never again command SS-Fallschirmjägerbataillon 600. And despite determined efforts – involving a complicated correspondence between himself, Kaltenbrunner, Schellenberg and OKW[60] – he would succeed in extracting neither Karl Fucker nor the remnants of Mitte from Oderkorps until a month later.

* * *

Once back in Berlin, Skorzeny confessed, 'I was all at sea at first, as I had long lost all taste for staff work at a desk.'[61] By mid-March all but a skeleton staff (which included Radl) had decamped from Friedenthal to a new and safer base at Hof in Bavaria. Then there was the constant drone of Allied bombers. The following month they were to firebomb Skorzeny's staff headquarters complex, utterly destroying it.[62] Even commuting to Friedenthal had become a nightmare, thanks to the progressive destruction of the formerly efficient railway service. Skorzeny therefore spent most of early March hanging around the Reich Chancellery in the hope of a new mission (giving the lie to his later claim that he had been recalled for a specific purpose).

He also paid a visit to Dr Stumpfegger: his eye injury was still troubling him. It was while this examination was being carried out – in the room of one of Hitler's secretaries – that Skorzeny made the acquaintance of Eva Braun, 'of whose existence I had previously been unaware'. He found her 'very simple and extremely likeable' and 'had a long talk with her. She was pleased to meet me and invited me to have dinner another day.'[63] Learning from Stumpfegger that Braun's soirées were invariably attended by Fegelein (married to her sister, Gretl), Skorzeny declined the invitation. Even he, apparently, drew the line at Fegelein's 'boasting and arrogance'.

Time, too, to visit some wounded comrades. Under the massive Zoo Flak Tower (so called because of its proximity to the Zoological Gardens) was Berlin's biggest air shelter. After taking refuge there one evening from the RAF's incessant bombing, Skorzeny decided to do a round of the wards in the 85-bed hospital on the third floor. Hunke, lightly wounded at Schwedt, was among the patients, as was Hanna Reitsch, who had injured her shoulder in an accident; Skorzeny found her 'in a poor frame of mind'.[64] He also encountered the Stuka ace Oberst Hans-Ulrich Rudel, who had destroyed over 500 tanks as well as a Soviet battleship and was the Reich's most decorated war hero. The previous month the apparently invulnerable "Eagle of the Eastern Front" had become a casualty of enemy flak while flying over the Oder Front, and lost his lower right leg. Skorzeny's encounter with Rudel was the foundation of a close post-war relationship; they shared the same brand of extremist political ideology, and much else besides.[65]

* * *

While Skorzeny dodged the bombs in Berlin, the men he had left behind at Schwedt suffered appallingly.

Kempin's command lasted only a few days before the order was given to evacuate the bridgehead. Skorzeny's core Jagdverbände forces – now known as Kampfgruppe Solar – had been placed in the capable hands of Milius. On 3 March, Milius organised an orderly retreat across the Oder, blowing up the bridge behind him. The Kampfgruppe had by now been reassigned to a miscellaneous and depleted unit containing two SS-police regiments. The idea was to withdraw to divisional headquarters at Oderberg for a refit. Only three days later a contrary order came from on high to occupy the bridgehead on the opposite bank of the Oder at Zehden – an enclave that was coming under increasing Soviet pressure.

It was a disaster. The German engineers charged with mining the one and only escape route – the bridge at Alt-Kustrinchen – forgot to temporarily disarm the detonator. A stray Soviet shell managed to blow the bridge away, leaving Milius and his men marooned on the east bank. Though Milius launched a surprise counter-attack that wrong-footed the marauding Russians, they retaliated in such strength that no defence could hold them back.[66] Milius was forced to order a withdrawal. His force had to swim through the icy water by moonlight, leaving many of their weapons behind. The wounded and those who couldn't swim were floated on boards, and a few made it in boats. One of the last men out was Behr.

When Milius roll-called the survivors before withdrawing to Oderberg, only 36 of his paratroopers were fit enough to clamber into the waiting lorries; over 500 – most of his force – were dead, missing or wounded. Mitte had got off more lightly, but only relatively.

It took a massacre of his elite unit for Skorzeny to be given permission, on 31 March, to extract its commanding officer, Karl Fucker, and the 250 remaining Mitte commandos for one last mission.

* * *

On 7 March the Americans managed to pierce the last great natural barrier protecting Germany's western reaches – the Rhine. On arriving at Remagen, south of Cologne, scouts of the US 9th Armored Division were astonished to find the Ludendorff railway bridge intact. Without pause, a motorised platoon, accompanied by engineers cutting every demolition wire in sight, charged across the bridge. There were several minor detonations as the remaining German defenders attempted to blow up the bridge, but the main charge failed to go off. Within 24 hours, 8,000 American troops had poured onto the eastern bank of the Rhine.

Hitler immediately launched a witch-hunt for the incompetents or traitors who had allowed this catastrophe to happen. Then came a comprehensive attempt to destroy the bridge with anything at hand. Yet, despite hundreds of Luftwaffe sorties, nothing could penetrate American defences around it.

Jodl turned to the navy, and Admiral Heye's K-Verbände. Two 12-man teams of naval frogmen armed with torpedo mines were ordered to attack the piers of the bridge. But just as Heye, having overcome problems of manpower and supply, was preparing his attack, Jodl intervened, ordering him to delay the operation until an SS team from Skorzeny's SS-Jagdeinsatz Donau had flown in from Vienna to join them.

The SS team of 11 was headed by SS-Untersturmführer Walter Schreiber, commanding officer of the 60-strong Donau frogmen unit. A young, flaxen-haired Austrian, slight of build and sporting an unmilitary goatee beard, Schreiber's vaguely studious air made him an improbable-looking leader. That appearance was belied by his extraordinary resourcefulness in action – notably a daring attack on the Nijmegen road bridge the previous autumn during Operation *Market Garden*.

Schreiber and his team were undoubted assets but their late arrival compromised their suicidal mission by putting back the timetable to 12 March. Every hour of delay meant more enemy troops debouching across the Rhine. By now, the Americans had erected a formidable battery of defences, with snipers posted on both banks to defend against frogmen. Obsolete tanks had been converted into mobile searchlights that could train 13 million candlepower on anything that moved at night. Moreover, the temperature of the water was near zero, giving the frogmen a matter of minutes to accomplish their mission before succumbing to cold.

Even Skorzeny admitted the operation was a forlorn hope: 'For the first time, I made my acceptance of an assignment conditional ... I said that I saw extremely little prospect, but would rush my best men to the spot and leave it to them to decide whether they would take the risk.'[67]

They would and did, although whether Skorzeny fully spelled out the pointlessness of their mission must be open to doubt. The Americans had now established two pontoon bridges nearby, so even if the mission was successful, the American advance would not be checked.

As it happened, the improbable German objective *was* achieved, without the frogmen needing to get wet. On 17 March, the bridge collapsed of its own accord. Hitler chose to believe that vibration from V2 rockets fired at the bridge from Holland – all of which missed – were responsible.[68]

A seven-strong SS team under Schreiber's direct command undertook a new objective – to destroy the more robust of the two American pontoon bridges, 5 kilometres away at Linz am Rhein. Skorzeny and a group of NCOs staged a diversionary attack while the frogmen, plastic explosives tied in waterproof bags, floated 17 kilometres downstream towards the pontoon bridge. SS-Hauptscharführer Rudi Günter was in Skorzeny's team: 'There were only 6 of us,' he recalled. 'We had synchronised our watches with the frogmen and began our surprise "attack" exactly 45 minutes after they entered the water. By that time Skorzeny thought they would be in the vicinity of the bridge.' The team 'made a sneak raid on the Americans on the east side of the bridge, trying to draw their attention. Just as Skorzeny gave the order to retreat to our jeeps before the Americans caught up with us, I was wounded in the left leg. I couldn't walk. Skorzeny never said a word. He just reached down, picked me up, and carried me on the run to the nearest jeep. We barely got out of the area alive.'[69]

The frogmen were less fortunate. Despite the diversionary tactic, not one of them made it to the target. Two were killed by the racing, icy, water; two more were shot up by the Americans; three, including Schreiber, were captured before they could place their explosives.

14

Skorzeny's Last Stand

Until their crossing of the Rhine, Skorzeny had persisted in the belief that the Allies could be fought to a standstill. It was a common delusion, shared by millions of Germans. Either some miracle weapon would force a negotiated peace, or a way would be found to co-opt the British and Americans into an ideological crusade against Communism.[1] As late as February 1945, Hitler himself was heard exulting over the imminent production of a long-range Messerschmitt jet bomber capable of terrorising New York.[2]

After Remagen the scales fell from Skorzeny's eyes. He returned to his headquarters in Friedenthal one last time and began preparations for a last-ditch defence of the Reich in the Austrian Alps – the so-called Alpine Fortress (Alpenfestung), a proposed network of defended, fortified positions in the Tyrol.

Back in Berlin at the end of the month, 'I received the order from OKW to transfer my headquarters to the Alpine Fortress, where … the Führer Headquarters was also to be set up. Obviously the last battles of the war were supposed to take place in this redoubt. The OKW had confirmed to me that the "fortress" was fully ready to mount a defence.'[3]

While in Berlin, Skorzeny had his last encounter with Hitler: 'I happened to be in the great corridor of the Chancellery as Adolf Hitler emerged from the conference room. I was horrified to see what a tired and bowed old man he had become. When he saw me, he came forward and put out his hands: "Skorzeny, I want to thank you and your men for all you have done on the eastern front.'"[4] Hitler then informed him that he was to be awarded the oak leaves to his Ritterkreuz on account of his defence of Schwedt, and promised to hand out the award personally.[5] The ceremony never occurred; Skorzeny received his award some weeks later, on 9 April, by courier.

* * *

The origins of Otto Skorzeny's final mission are a mystery. There is no record of OKW issuing any such order,[6] though Jodl may have given his tacit blessing. It is probable that Skorzeny, in the chaos now enveloping the command structures of the crumbling Third Reich, took his own initiative and began writing the script as he went along.

Radl – one of those best placed to know – recalled, 'Skorzeny conceived a plan to take five or six groups of people into the Austrian Alps. Each group was to number 400 to 500 men and was to reinforce the Wehrmacht at important passes.'[7] Some time in late February or early March, Skorzeny had rounded on Schellenberg, accusing him of defeatism and telling him 'in a rather condescending manner' (according to Schellenberg) that the Jagdverbände would fight in the Alps 'as Maquis'. 'All who could join would have to place themselves under his orders, everything else was shit. He and Kaltenbrunner were absolutely agreed on that.' Thereafter, Schellenberg 'took no notice' of Skorzeny and 'gave him up as hopeless'.[8]

From Friedenthal, Skorzeny wended his way to Linz via temporary headquarters at Hof, there to collect whatever he could salvage of his Jagdverbände. En route, he received an order from OKW to liaise with Ferdinand Schörner at the headquarters of Heeresgruppe Mitte in Czechoslovakia.

Schörner, known as 'Bloody Ferdinand', was a fanatical Nazi and had been newly appointed Generalfeldmarschall (field marshal) by Hitler. He was in need of some behind-the-lines commando expertise. Accordingly, on 8 April Skorzeny visited the headquarters of Jagdverband Ost II at Janske Lazne in Bohemia. This unit was a reconstructed replacement for Fölkersam's unit, wiped out in January; its new commander was the experienced former Brandenburger and Balt, SS-Sturmbannführer Alexander Auch. Those under his command were mostly Russians.

Two days later, both Auch and Dietrich Kirn (commander of FAK 202 and veteran of Operation *Sonnenblume*) attended a planning meeting with Skorzeny and Schörner. Schörner needed road bridges behind the Russian lines blown up. Skorzeny signed off two operations. Both were successful, and within a matter of weeks, Auch and Kirn had joined him in Upper Austria.

Next stop for Skorzeny was Vienna. The city was only days away from falling to the Red Army forces already pouring across the Hungarian border and fighting their way in through the outskirts. Travelling 'at breakneck speed' the 200 kilometres from Olmütz in a staff car driven by Anton Gföller (a Gran Sasso 'comrade'), Skorzeny and his adjutant Wilhelm Gallent reached Vienna at dusk. They were greeted by an eerie sight. The city was shrouded in darkness illuminated by burning buildings on the skyline. Gunfire and the crump of artillery could be heard to the south and east. By now the Soviet 3rd Ukrainian Front had the city almost surrounded – the Floridsdorf Bridge in the north being the only safe point of access to the historic centre. Skorzeny crossed it.

His main purpose was to establish contact with Jagdverband Südost, based at Krems, west of Vienna, and SS-Jagdeinsatz Donau, based in the city. Both had been forced to quit their headquarters because of the fighting. He also wanted to establish that his family – his mother, wife and child – had been successfully evacuated.

Vienna's defenders consisted of a corps of Sepp Dietrich's shattered 6. SS-Panzerarmee (so named 'because we only have six panzers left', Dietrich joked).[9] They were nowhere to be seen. Skorzeny found their headquarters in the War Ministry deserted; the staff had relocated to the relative safety of the Hofburg Palace.

Destruction was omnipresent. The road to the Danube Canal was blocked at Schwedenplatz, home of Skorzeny's brother Alfred, which had been flattened (Alfred had been called up into the Volkssturm). Their mother's house was also rubble, but Frau Skorzeny herself, along with Skorzeny's wife and daughter, had managed to flee the city. The one person Skorzeny did find was Alfred Schreiber, his partner at the building works in Meidling. They talked by candlelight while Schreiber's secretary made tea over an oil stove.

Next Skorzeny made his way westwards to his home at Peter-Jordanstrasse 37 in the affluent Döbling district. Although intact, it was a picture of desolation: ornaments, pictures, furnishings all untouched, but abandoned and eerie, the clocks all stopped. He took some hunting rifles and left the rest to the Russians and the looters.[10]

The collapse of the city's defences was hours away. But nobody would have guessed it from Skorzeny's bizarre encounter with the city's commandant in his last port of call, the Hofburg Palace. Baldur von Schirach, an effete German aristocrat formerly in charge of the Hitler Youth, had immersed himself in a make-believe world. The palace cellars were converted into a bunker (Schirach lived in mortal fear of air raids), decked out in the decadent style of an 18th-century salon, with 'magnificent carpets, paintings of battles and portraits of generals'. Skorzeny found Schirach poring over a map by candlelight, apparently convinced that two phantom German divisions were about to launch a counter-attack to save Vienna.[11]

After failing to make contact with his own units, Skorzeny decided to get out. At about 5 am on 11 April he went back across the Floridsdorf Bridge. The city fell two days later. Schirach, having vowed eternal defiance, quit the city soon after Skorzeny.

Driving along a devious route through Waldviertel to Linz – to avoid refugees clogging the main route further north – Skorzeny now sought to resume his self-imposed mission of attending to the final defence of the Reich in the Alpine Fortress.

* * *

Skorzeny's reference to collaborating with Kaltenbrunner in his last conversation with Schellenberg was telling. Presumably thinking of his own salvation, Kaltenbrunner had forged a bond with his old friend and fellow-countryman August Eigruber, Gauleiter of Upper Austria,[12] a diehard Nazi and seasoned mass-murderer. In the present turmoil, Eigruber was able to rule Upper Austria – the country's most militarily defensible region – as an autocrat, untroubled by Berlin, with the absolute power to execute anyone suspected of sabotaging the war effort.[13]

But Eigruber had a problem. The Third Reich was now a narrow strip of territory, getting thinner by the day, stretching from Norway and Denmark to Austria, with slivers of northern Italy and Croatia. Upper Austria was filling up with refugees, Jewish and political prisoners, slave workers, Nazis on the run, and deserters from the crumbling Wehrmacht. Skorzeny later claimed that the idea of a Streifendienst – a 'patrol service' to contain these deserters and stragglers – was his own.[14] More likely the suggestion came from Eigruber and was transmitted via Kaltenbrunner,[15] who was making plans to decamp to Upper Austria himself.[16]

On 12 April, Skorzeny attended a meeting in Linz, convened by Eigruber and including a number of high-ranking army and police officials – Kaltenbrunner and Winkelmann among them. On the agenda were defensive preparations, the refugee crisis and the management of food supplies.[17]

The Streifendienst, although real enough, was merely a pretext for a much wider mission. Skorzeny had not returned to Austria merely to act as Eigruber's enforcer. He harboured grander notions of leading a national resistance movement against Bolshevism until such time as the Americans and British aligned themselves against the real enemy.

Initially, he believed this would involve conventional warfare, using tactics adapted to the extremely inhospitable terrain. Like millions of others – including the entire upper echelon of the US military intelligence community – Skorzeny had been duped into believing that the Alpine Fortress (Alpenfestung) was all that Josef Goebbels claimed it to be – a mountainous area of about 300 kilometres encompassing Bavaria, Austria and northern Italy, bristling with sophisticated fortifications reinforced by a military-industrial infrastructure and enough food and ammunition to keep 60,000 men in the field for a further two years. Here, at a specially prepared headquarters in Obersalzberg, the Führer would make his last stand – should Berlin fall – surrounded by diehard Nazi hierarchs.

In fact the Alpenfestung was a myth, as Skorzeny soon realised when he arrived in Linz. Only rudimentary preparations for resistance had been made. The truth was that the Nazi regime had been incapable of envisaging its own demise. Merely to voice the need for contingency plans was to indulge in *Katastrophen Politik* – a policy of despair amounting to treason. This psychosis went to the top of the regime – the monstrous ego of Hitler being its prime exemplar. Compounding this issue was the unexpected rapidity of Germany's military collapse. No one in authority expected the Americans to puncture the Rhine or the Russians the Oder defences with such ease. Even for those with the stomach to contemplate it, there had been too little time to develop a coherent resistance plan.[18]

Only Himmler proved capable of the doublethink required for sponsoring a resistance strategy while simultaneously denying its necessity. As early as September 1944, Skorzeny had been informed by Himmler's private secretary of 'special orders' being carried out on Himmler's behalf by SS-Obergruppenführer Hans-Adolf Prützmann, requiring Skorzeny's assistance.[19] Prützmann had been appointed as General Inspector for Special Defence – the leader of a cellular network of undercover agents perpetrating acts of sabotage and assassination on German territory under Allied occupation. The organisation was nicknamed 'Werwolf', an allusion to a popular novel about a resistance leader during the Thirty Years War. Himmler went public with his scheme in a radio broadcast in October: 'the German will to resist will constantly spring to life again and, like werewolves, death-defying volunteers will damage and destroy the enemy from the rear'.[20] The Americans were only too prepared to believe him.

Skorzeny's reaction to SS-Werwolf was equivocal. On the one hand, it was a logical counterpart to what his Jagdverbände had been doing. On the other, that made Werwolf superfluous. Such tasks were the natural remit of the Jagdverbände, who were professionally trained and properly resourced. Himmler brushed aside Skorzeny's objections, pointing out that he already had too much on his plate.[21] In truth, Himmler wanted Werwolf, essentially a Sipo initiative, to be his very own creature, devoid of responsibility to OKW and military discipline.

Although obliged to cooperate with Prützmann on account of his fealty to Himmler, Skorzeny resented nurturing a rival organisation that was inferior to his own in resources, scale, professionalism and experience. Stealthily, he contrived to thwart Werwolf's ambitions wherever he could, with a view to eventually subsuming its mission in his own.

Werwolf operated through a cellular structure, with groups of three to six operatives directed by an SS-Gruppenführer (major-general) which were to be located in fixed bunkers behind advancing enemy lines. In one of the earlier of five meetings between Skorzeny and Prützmann between September 1944 and late January 1945 (before Skorzeny had become actively involved), the Werwolf leader disclosed that 60 to 70 SS-Gruppenführer from the Rhineland were ready for training and that five or six groups were already operating in East Prussia. In the former, personal conflict had arisen between the local SS police chief and Gauleiter.[22] That was to be the least of Prützmann's problems. It soon transpired that he was wholly dependent upon Skorzeny and his organisation for training and equipment, including rations to survive in the field for 60 days, explosives, light armaments, ammunition and radio sets. Himmler could not persuade Hitler that the project merited separate funding and resources.

Skorzeny's tactic in dealing with Werwolf was to offer grudging cooperation that stopped just short of offending Himmler, telling his supply chief, Gerhard, to 'avoid extravagant promises' and not to compromise Jagdverbände interests. Just one instructor per unit was sent to the Neustrelitz training school.[23] Skorzeny's contempt for Werwolf was fuelled by scorn for the quality of its personnel, which was partly reliant on Hitler Youth and women, the latter of whom he referred to as *Verwelkte Jungfrauen* (frustrated virgins).[24]

Prützmann himself, a former police chief in Latvia and the Ukraine, was steeped in genocide, which, as the war drew to a close, made him a man to shun. His cold, unengaging personality[25] was not an asset in winning over reluctant collaborators. His deputy, Karl Tschierschky, a former SD man heavily implicated in atrocities, was a certified incompetent and 'an intriguer'.[26] In short, the top team in Werwolf were regarded as 'losers'. As 'exorbitant demands' began to pour in from Prützmann's organisation, Skorzeny found little trouble in snubbing them.[27] Schellenberg and Kaltenbrunner were at one with Skorzeny in trying to sabotage Werwolf. Schellenberg thought Prützmann 'a desperado' and that the quality of his organisation corresponded to the mental capacity of its two leaders.[28] Kaltenbrunner resented Prützmann's ability to short-circuit the RSHA by appealing directly to Himmler.[29]

The Werwolf programme thus became bogged down in a proxy war between competing elements of the SS; the result was suffocation. It managed to carry out only one proven high-profile operation: *Karneval*, in which a six-strong commando unit successfully tracked down and assassinated the US-nominated mayor of Aachen, Franz Oppenhoff, on 25 March 1945. Skorzeny had previously been tasked with the mission to kill Oppenhoff, while still at Schwedt. He had protested that he had insufficient resources, and recommended Werwolf.[30]

While its achievements were few, in the hands of Goebbels, Werwolf activity coalesced with the Alpenfestung into a potent myth of a Nazi Last Stand. Faked blueprints and reports on construction, supplies, armament production and troop transfers to the Alpenfestung duly found their way into Allied hands. In the last months of the war Eisenhower gave his full backing to a push by American forces into central and southern Germany, for fear that the Alpenfestung would become a hornet's nest of resistance if it were not summarily snuffed out.[31] While the Nazi elite was incapable of engaging with the *Katastrophen Politik* that would have made effective fortification of the Alpenfestung a possibility, the American intelligence community fervently believed it was a reality.

The appearance of the remnants of Sepp Dietrich's 6. SS-Panzerarmee in the vicinity of Salzburg gave extra potency to the myth.[32] In fact it was simply in retreat after a failed operation to recapture the Reich's last oil resources at Lake Balaton and relieve Vienna. Eisenhower, however, pulled out all the stops to occupy the Alpenfestung before it became a strategic issue. Two armies – General Patch's 7th Army and the French 1st Army under General de Lattre de Tassigny, both of 6th Army Group – raced across southern Germany towards Salzburg. Their progress was scarcely contested, many German soldiers preferring to surrender to the Western Allies than to fall into the hands of the Soviets. (See map on page 16.)

Eisenhower's decision, though based upon a faulty premise, had a useful outcome. While the Red Army was still at the Oder, massing for the Potsdam–Cottbus offensive of 16 April, the Franco-American force was sweeping through the back door. By the end of the third week of April it had taken Stuttgart; by the end of the fourth, Munich had fallen.

So rapid was the collapse of the German front at this stage that Kaltenbrunner – appointed Himmler's plenipotentiary in Austria on 18 April and therefore the chief Nazi civil authority in what remained of German-occupied southern Europe – had no time to improvise suitable defences.

* * *

The Linz meeting of 12 April, attended by, among others, Skorzeny, Kaltenbrunner, Eigruber and Winkelmann, raised more issues than it solved. Skorzeny was doubtful whether supplies and war matériel would be available. 'I imagined from all I had heard in Berlin that the necessary preparations had been completed long before. Yet there seemed to be no single all-embracing plan, and every Gauleiter and Defence Commissioner appeared to be concerned only with his own area.'[33]

Even with Kaltenbrunner appointed plenipotentiary, military personnel – including Skorzeny and his commandos – remained under orders from OKW. The 'single all-embracing plan' was elusive, and improvisation took its place.

Skorzeny's 'security patrols', lending enthusiastic support to Eigruber in the Linz area, created a convenient opportunity for Skorzeny to rally the scattered Jagdverbände under his personal command while keeping his options open. The Jagdverbände headquarters staff (with the exceptions of Radl and Gerhard, who remained in Friedenthal) had been forced to move from its temporary location at Hof in Bavaria to Achthal near Teisendorf, west of Salzburg. By mid-April Skorzeny had won his tussle with OKW over Karl Fucker; and the 250 surviving members of Mitte were dispatched to Friedenthal, which was days away from capture by the Red Army; Radl shut up shop and accompanied them southwards on their march to Achthal,[34] where they arrived around 20 April.

By 15 April the Streifendienst, now primarily concerned with reorganising the military refugees pouring into the Alpenfestung area, had morphed into something much grander: the Schutzkorps Alpenland, or SKA.[35] Skorzeny was drawing up plans for a full-scale guerrilla war should conventional methods fail to halt the Allies.

According to Walter Girg, who mysteriously resurfaced at Achthal around this time, the aim of the SKA, which was to be under Skorzeny's direct command, was to take on the Russians. It incorporated men from the SS Jagdverbände, with recruits to be gathered from the civilian population. 'The mission was to be executed in such a way,' recalled Girg, 'that the enemy was to be forced to recognise the Schutzkorps as an important opponent.'[36]

Skorzeny set out to create eight or more platoon-sized cadres (of 20 to 50 men each) which he planned to send into the mountains, all commanded by stalwarts. The units were strung out in a line west–east which started with SS-Untersturmführer Bihrer's platoon north of Kitzbühlen, Girg's unit at Lofer, and Fucker's at Hochkönig, the latter two just south of the vitally important Berchtesgaden salient. The line then passed through Willscher's group at Mitterberghütten, SS-Hauptsturmführer Streckfuss's at Altenmarkt, Besekow's and SS-Hauptsturmführer Heinz Winter's (a partisan warfare veteran) at Mauterndorf (Rädstadter Tauern), SS-Obersturmführer Hubert Schürmann's at Altaussee, and Benesch's group in the Ennstal Alps region.[37]

To bring coherence to these scattered units, Skorzeny established a new headquarters at the Alpine village of Annaberg im Lammertal (about 20 kilometres north of Eben) whose tiny staff included Radl, Walther, Hunke, and the Jagdverbände intelligence chief SS-Obersturmführer Heinz Graf. Benzine barrels packed with three months' rations were but one small part of extensive preparations. Each well-armed unit had its own 70-watt radio set linked to a central station code-named *Brieftaube* (Carrier-pigeon). At Mitterberghütten Skorzeny had established an enormous munitions dump, consisting of 2,100 boxes of explosive – including several tons of Nipolit – plus 750,000 rounds of ammunition and grenades, which he had been stockpiling since February.[38] Similarly, a supply and procurement centre was set up at Eben.

The 200 or so SKA elite diehards represented a considerable reduction on the hodge-podge of nearly 500 combat swimmers, Mitte and Territorialen Jagdverbände commandos whom Skorzeny had originally summoned to Achthal.[39] The bulk of the less fanatically committed ended up in the service of 6. SS-Panzerarmee, which had now fallen back to the Oberdonau area between Vienna and Linz; a few were simply discharged. Nonetheless, Skorzeny was confident that the sparsely manned SKA platoons would provide the nucleus of a 3,000-strong guerrilla army that would descend, with punishing effect, on any occupying army.[40]

Underwriting his confidence was Kaltenbrunner's discreet sponsorship of SKA. His increasingly interdependent relationship with Skorzeny is best informed by reference to events in Berlin at this time; and Kaltenbrunner's determination to extract whatever advantage he could from them, for himself and his cause.

The Americans had reached the Elbe and the Red Army was encircling the German capital. Allied bombing had redoubled, and on 21 April Soviet artillery pounded the city for the first time. Himmler was the first to flee; having offered perfunctory birthday greetings to the Führer, he left – ostensibly on military business, but in fact to pursue a covert peace initiative with the Western Allies. Göring departed soon afterwards for Berchtesgaden. Only Goebbels, Bormann and Hitler himself remained.[41] Hitler was utterly broken, venting his spleen on the 'treachery' of those around him.[42] His historic destiny had utterly failed. Everyone else could do what they wanted but he was going to die here, in the Berlin bunker. Goebbels announced in a radio broadcast the following morning: 'The Führer will die in Berlin.' Almost needless to say, this was a disappointing departure from Goebbels' earlier script, in which Hitler was to have played a heroic central role in a 'Götterdämmerung' defence of the Alpenfestung. It was all over: every man for himself.

One of the last planes to fly out of Berlin – heading for Salzburg – carried SS-Standartenführer Josef Spacil, head of the RSHA's Amt II and effectively its chief treasurer. Spacil had a highly sensitive assignment, on Kaltenbrunner's behalf: to make caches of some 23 million gold marks of RSHA funds in Austria for the use of Nazi resistance groups.[43] Much of the treasure – in gold, jewellery, watches, rings and foreign currencies as well as Reichsmarks – represented the plunder of the SS. Kaltenbrunner had had the RSHA's sizeable foreign exchange assets (most of which were earmarked for Amt VI) transferred to a secret location in Thuringia. All of this was now supposed to be making its way by truck over the border to Salzburg.

On Kaltenbrunner's express order, a small amount of 'working capital' – about a million marks – that had been left at the Reichsbank in Berlin was removed by one of Spacil's lieutenants and sent to the same destination in a convoy of three cars led by Spacil's adjutant, Kurt Schiebel.[44] Spacil, having arrived at Salzburg, set up quarters in the Schloss Glannegg, along with other prominent RSHA refugees.

All the loot converging on Salzburg during the last week of April was, in the first instance, to create a slush fund to establish Kaltenbrunner as paymaster of the resistance movement in the Alpenfestung. In the slightly longer term, it was intended to be his get-out-of-jail-free card. Kaltenbrunner must have known that, if captured, he would be prosecuted for war crimes.

He had every reason, therefore, to sponsor any stratagem – whether military or political – that would make him a post-war player, or at least a successful escapee. A sociopath, and an austere and conscientious servant of a murderous regime, Kaltenbrunner had almost no interest in personal financial gain.[45]

Accompanied by his mistress, he set up his base in the Villa Kerry in the secluded Styrian mountain resort of Altaussee – as far away from the tightening Allied pincer as possible. Altaussee was the nerve centre of what remained of the SS political intelligence service, a haven for Kaltenbrunner's Vienna Circle chums at VI-E. From here, via a powerful radio, Waneck – ever the conspirator – was able to keep tabs on the few remaining stay-behind networks and maintain contact with Berlin. Nearby were some salt mines containing a priceless trove of stolen art treasures originally destined for Hitler's Führermuseum in Linz.

On 24 April, Kaltenbrunner met Skorzeny and Waneck at the Hotel Österreichischer Hof in Salzburg. What began as a fairly routine discussion of the military and political situation ended dramatically. News had reached Kaltenbrunner of Himmler's initiative to bring the war to a negotiated close, and he roundly condemned Schellenberg as the cause of it.[46] What brought matters to a head was the discovery that Schellenberg's deputy, Dr Martin Sandberger, was seeking headquarters for SD-Ausland at a hotel near Innsbruck.[47] Attempting to cauterise the situation Kaltenbrunner fired Schellenberg, on the grounds that he and Himmler had become 'politically unreliable'.[48]

All the intelligence elements of SD-Ausland were now concentrated in Waneck's hands, while Skorzeny acquired full control of the military elements, which finally included a fused Mil Amt D. The independence of the Frontaufklärung service that Gehlen had covertly championed for the past year was at an end. Schellenberg himself remarked: 'At five minutes to twelve, they take time out for a thing like that!'[49] Skorzeny extracted a promise from Kaltenbrunner to fund his burgeoning guerrilla army.[50]

In charge of the treasure convoy from a secret location in Bad Sulza[51] to Salzburg was SS-Hauptsturmführer Pfeiler, head of the foreign currencies desk of Amt II. Pfeiler had second thoughts about his destination, and refused to go further than a depot at Schliersee just north of the Austrian border. There the loot remained, pending a manageable disposal programme. Meanwhile, the million marks travelling by car had arrived at Salzburg. Kaltenbrunner's reaction was a vague order to distribute supplies, money and weapons 'to the remaining RSHA agents in the Salzburg area'.[52]

Spacil's distribution system ended up a chaotic free-for-all. Only at the beginning of May, with the Americans closing in, was he able to bury the contents of Pfeiler's truck in a secret location at Taxenbach, near Zell-am-See.[53] In the meantime, Spacil was 'besieged by requests for supplies, money, and quarters, most of them impossible to fulfil', he recalled.[54]

Skorzeny was to be one of the lucky few. On 26 April, Spacil ordered one of his colleagues, SS-Hauptsturmführer Schuler, to hand over to Skorzeny about two million marks of Amt VI valuables in cut and uncut diamonds plus a considerable number of dollars – stashed in Schuler's Innsbruck office. Schuler claimed to have made the delivery to Skorzeny's headquarters, but the following day Radl turned up at Spacil's offices, demanding the money, which he said had never arrived. Radl took away at least 50,000 gold francs, stuffed into two jute sacks. Spacil's adjutant, Schiebel, subsequently alleged that Radl was also given 10,000 Swedish Krona, $5,000, 5,000 Swiss francs and five million Reichsmarks.[55] Whether the money was used for pay and supplies, or simply buried in a remote hillside, nobody knows.[56]

Skorzeny needed finance for his final deployment plans in the mountains around Annaberg. On 25 April he reduced his staff – already winnowed on departure from Hof earlier that month – and boarded a 'headquarters' train south of Salzburg at Puch, which he had had the foresight to rent from the Deutsche Reichsbahn (German National Railway) early in March.[57] It was an astute ploy, giving Skorzeny mobility and a degree of cover in sidings at a time when roaming Allied fighters might easily have destroyed a fixed base. Not least, the train could be used to drop off the various group commanders close to their final destinations. The train left Puch for the Pongau area, where it remained for two days, passed through Klammstein, and then terminated at the Radstadt railhead near Eben two or three days later, necessitating a final road-trip to Annaberg.[58]

Somewhere along the line – probably at Puch[59] – Skorzeny ditched the remainder of his female contingent: his secretary of two years, 25-year-old Grete Kopfheiser, and the two Krüger sisters, Annemarie and Lieselotte – who had worked for Besekow's department throughout – as well as Skorzeny's current squeeze, the notorious Berlin film actress Marianne Simson, a Nazi groupie who was close to Goebbels and may have had an affair with him.

While Skorzeny headed for the mountains, Kaltenbrunner began implementing his exit strategy. Whether he and Skorzeny were on the same wavelength is a moot point. Kaltenbrunner had originally poured cold water on Project Herzog, the scheme dreamt up in the winter of 1943 by Göttsch, Höttl and Waneck to create a 'free' post-war Austria, but by April 1945 he was enthusiastically backing the idea. The Allies' declared intention was to treat Austria as a victim of Nazi aggression rather than an accomplice; unlike Germany,

Austria would be a free and independent country after the war was over. However, the declaration was careful not to specify Austria's post-war constitution.

The Soviets, having conquered Vienna, installed a government headed by Social Democrat Karl Renner, who was forced to concede the Ministry of the Interior to the Communists. The Western Allies suspected Stalin of creating a puppet state and Renner of being a stooge. Britain and America withheld recognition of his government. To the Altaussee conspirators, this seemed a perfect opportunity for driving a wedge between West and East; they could offer an alternative regime more to the liking of the Western Allies. Höttl established contact with America's top intelligence officer in Europe – Allen Dulles, the Swiss Director of the US Office of Strategic Services, a virulent anti-Communist with great influence within the US establishment. Dulles intimated to Höttl that the US government did not want strong Soviet influence within Austria,[60] and asked for a personal meeting with the conspirators, who began discussions on setting up a provisional government. Included were Waneck, Höttl, Göttsch and Dr Hermann Neubacher, a Foreign Office Balkans specialist who happened to be a former mayor of Vienna, together with several prominent military and bureaucratic figures. To cloak this Nazi initiative in quasi-legal garb, the Vienna Circle (principally Göttsch and Höttl) had recruited a number of credible pro-Western resistance figures. The general idea was that Kaltenbrunner would use his authority to set up an anti-Bolshevik coalition government, and then fade into the background.

Significantly absent from these discussions was the commander of SKA, Otto Skorzeny. With Wehrmacht resistance withering by the day, Kaltenbrunner had come to prefer a political solution over a military one. Nonetheless, Skorzeny and his SKA remained useful to overcome potential internal resistance to the plan (not least from diehard Gauleiters) through the threat of coercive force. Skorzeny was excluded from the meetings because Kaltenbrunner did not entirely trust him, and wanted to keep 'the Partisan Napoleon'[61] in the dark. He had reservations about the peace mission being derailed by Skorzeny's uncontrollable megalomania and 'political stupidity',[62] and on 20 April had given explicit instructions to Göttsch not to take Skorzeny into his confidence about what was going on.[63] As the infrastructure of the regime dissolved, Skorzeny felt less and less obliged to answer to anyone but himself; he was a loose cannon who might trigger aggression just when it was most impolitic.[64]

Göttsch judged that Skorzeny knew remarkably little about the 'Free Austria' agenda.[65] More surprisingly, he claimed to know little about Werwolf operations, confiding to Göttsch that he had contact with only one Werwolf commander, and that his relationship with the organisation was confined to being a source of supplies and personnel. Göttsch concluded that Skorzeny was, in fact, a fairly minor player and that his one coherent resistance plan amounted to taking loyal followers into the mountains to wait out the war. Keeping an eye on him was going to be difficult, though. Skorzeny stamped on Göttsch's suggestion of a courier service provided by Amt VI-E, lest it betray his position.[66]

* * *

Kaltenbrunner's peace plan and Skorzeny's freelance projects were overtaken by events. Hitler's suicide on 30 April came as a crippling blow to the would-be 'defenders' of the imaginary Alpenfestung.

In truth, the Alpenfestung concept was already redundant. Secret negotiations between Allen Dulles and Karl Wolff – chief of SS police in northern Italy – had brought about the capitulation of all German forces in Italy. Cessation of hostilities would take place on 2 May. The fall of this first card would, within days, bring the rest of the house down.

And yet, the increasing gravity of the situation merely galvanised the Altaussee conspirators. The upshot was to be a gruesome farce. Waneck and Göttsch had hatched elaborate survivalist plans for escaping to the mountains when the Americans arrived, but how were they to stay in contact with each other and Skorzeny's SKA?

Waneck's brainwave was to call upon Adolf Eichmann, primary organiser of the Final Solution. Göttsch (of all people) had described Eichmann as 'a swine and a gangster', yet they thought to exploit his vulnerable position for their own nefarious ends, and then betray him to the Allies as a means of currying favour. The Waneck plan soon revealed an irredeemable flaw when Eichmann and his men, armed to the teeth, turned up unannounced in Altaussee. Kaltenbrunner and his entourage viewed this development with the utmost dismay. Were Kaltenbrunner to be found in the presence of Eichmann by the Americans his chances of survival would be slim indeed. He summoned Waneck and officially trashed the plan. Eichmann was sent packing, complaining bitterly of mistreatment by his 'friends'.

'Herzog' was now a shambles. The proposed assignation with Dulles never took place – the hour-glass sands had run out. The following day, Kaltenbrunner held a final meeting, attended by Neubacher, Waneck and Höttl, as well as the retired Wehrmacht General Edmund Glaise-Horstenau, the last Vice-Chancellor of Austria; Dr Kajuten Mühlmann, an expert on Austrian affairs, who was serving on the staff of Generalfeldmarschall Kesselring; and – on this occasion – Skorzeny.[67] Then it was time to head for the mountains.

Still distrustful of Skorzeny's motives, Kaltenbrunner declined the offer of a shared mountain hut,[68] instead taking refuge in his own, high up at Wildensee in the Totesgebirge, east of Altaussee. The idea was to maintain contact with the rest of his dwindling organisation through a radio transmitter, provided by Skorzeny, that would stay tuned to Waneck, Göttsch and Höttl. That plan went awry when a US Army Counter-Intelligence detail moved into Altaussee on 9 May, arrested the three of them and closed down their transmitter. Only three days later, in a daring early-morning ambush at his mountain lair, they captured Kaltenbrunner himself, with his aide Scheidler and two SS guards.[69]

Meanwhile, on a mountain not far away, Skorzeny was experiencing a moment of uncharacteristic philosophical introspection. Like Adolf Hitler, he was a cod-Nietzsche addict, *Gefährlich leben!* ('Live dangerously!') being one of his favourite sayings. While it is doubtful he ever read *The Joyful Wisdom*, or for that matter any other work of the aphoristic moral philosopher, he had certainly picked an appropriate maxim to encapsulate his life. Skorzeny may not have been on the slopes of Vesuvius, but he was stuck up a mountain, and a volcano of sorts had erupted around him.

On 7 May Skorzeny called a staff meeting at the remote Theodor Körner Hütte, 1,466 metres above sea level, to discuss precisely that. The immediate cause was yet more bad news. Grossadmiral Dönitz, Hitler's designated successor, was arranging an armistice. At the end of April, Skorzeny had reluctantly complied with Kaltenbrunner's wishes by ordering that all fighting cease against the Western Allies immediately. SKA would lend its services to preserving order among the local inhabitants. That had still left plenty of leeway for an anti-Bolshevik crusade; indeed, part of Skorzeny's self-appointed task was 'to prevent the formation of Bolshevik groups'.[70] He considered going underground with his chosen *Kameraden*. Wiser counsels prevailed after someone pointed out that a man of his size with a duelling scar would have difficulty making himself inconspicuous. All the more so as Eisenhower, still smarting from the elaborate 'assassination' prank during the Ardennes offensive, had put out numerous 'Wanted' posters with his likeness. The photograph and description left little to the imagination, as did the words 'Saboteur' and 'Assassin'.

In any case, the Austrians were not proving eager guerrilla recruits. The country had no tradition of partisan warfare. Rough-housing peasant farmers and threatening 'traitors' with summary punishment simply wasn't going to do the trick.

What now for the 'Partisan Napoleon'?

I was attracted by the idea of escaping abroad and also of suicide. It would have been quite easy for me to get away in a Ju 88 from some aerodrome, but that would mean good-bye to everyone and everything – home, family and comrades. As for suicide, many have felt that it was the only way out, but I considered it my duty to stand by my men and share their fate. I had done nothing wrong and had nothing to fear from our former enemies. From our reflections during those days one conclusion clearly emerged – the day of narrow nationalism and nation states was over.[71]

Skorzeny was not exaggerating about a getaway in a German bomber – and one stacked with treasure to boot. The fugitive President of the Reichsbank, Walther Funk, had suggested exactly that when their paths crossed at Berchtesgaden at the end of April.[72] Skorzeny had nothing against taking loot, nor against exile, but he was still hoping against hope that some political opportunity would develop that would allow him to pitch in with the Western Allies against the Soviet Union.

His timing was wrong: the era of bipolar conflict had not yet arrived. But his hunch was right. The Americans would need knowledgeable specialists, experienced in the ways of the Soviet Union. And where better to look than among former German servicemen; even among those who had served in the SS?

$$* \;\; * \;\; *$$

For now, there was no better alternative than surrender. Skorzeny calculated that handing SKA over intact would better impress the Americans than allowing small units of his men to take their own initiative. That way there was a slight possibility they would be redeployed as a local police force.

On 10 May he descended from the clouds to Annaberg, where he encountered a US 15th Infantry Regiment captain and two French officers. Skorzeny proposed that he attach his men to the VI. SS-Panzerkorps under SS-Obergruppenführer Gille to avoid any suspicion that he was planning further operations. To his chagrin, the officers were unimpressed with this suggestion and left without giving instructions.

Two days later, about a hundred American troops moved into Annaberg. Here, surely, was the opportunity Skorzeny had been waiting for. Rather grandly, he submitted a letter which he insisted be delivered to US headquarters in Salzburg, advising the Americans not to bother looking for him because he and his men would be surrendering in a few days' time.

On the appointed morning, 16 May, an American jeep arrived to pick up his party, consisting of himself, Radl, Hunke and SS-Oberjunker Herbert Petter, his interpreter – all in full uniform and bearing side-arms.[73]

15

Trial and Errors

On reaching Salzburg, Skorzeny discovered that the major from the 30th Infantry Regiment charged with taking them into custody hadn't a clue who he was. So much for the ubiquitous 'Wanted' posters.

An intelligence officer present at the initial interview, Lieutenant John McClean, finally made the connection and suggested escorting the would-be captives to a villa at Werfen, near Bischofshofen, where the intelligence section of the 30th Infantry had set up quarters. Skorzeny, anticipating a trap, detached Hunke from the group and gave him orders to scramble the muster arrangements for the rest of his SKA units if he and Radl failed to return within a few hours.

The sequel was humiliating in the extreme. The Americans, from being mind-numbingly complacent about the international terrorist in their midst, now veered into hysterical overreaction. While Radl and Petter were left behind, Skorzeny was led into a dining room, where he was met by four American officers and interpreters who asked him to identify the location of his SKA force:

> Even as I was pointing out on a map where my people were waiting, the three doors and windows were flung open. A dozen submachine-guns were pointing at me and the interpreter asked me to hand over my pistol, which I did ... Then I was frisked and stripped naked. My Mussolini watch was stolen; I had it returned to me but it then disappeared again,

this time for good. Finally, Radl, Petter and I were put into three jeeps, which drove away between two armoured cars. We arrived in Salzburg during the night … I had just lit a cigarette when a pair of MPs grabbed us from behind and handcuffed us behind the back. Then I was shoved into a room where a dozen people sat behind two or three desks. There were several reporters and photographers among them. An officer began interrogating me.[1]

The heavy-handedness of Skorzeny's arrest created exactly the kind of problem the Americans had most sought to avoid. Hunke, deducing that his colleagues had been arrested, was able to scramble Skorzeny's original muster plan for an SKA surrender en masse. Hunke himself – 'a fanatical Nazi' according to the Americans – was arrested at Salzburg on 22 May. The Americans were also able to derive some advantage from passes deviously issued to Skorzeny – before his arrest – that bore the names of ten of his platoon commanders and their approximate whereabouts.

Even so, a number of SKA desperados managed to escape the dragnet – some remaining at large for years. Walther evaded capture until June 1946. Streckfuss, the former Jagdverbände signals chief, having ascertained that Skorzeny was imprisoned at Nuremberg, hatched a hare-brained plot to spring him in March 1946.[2] As for Skorzeny's spymaster, Besekow, he evaded capture altogether and – for a long time – justice as well. In the early 1960s it came to light that he was working for the West German federal police service as a detective superintendent.[3] Only a decade later was he indicted in Hamburg for crimes against humanity.

* * *

From the beginning of his incarceration Skorzeny sought to spin a line on his wartime conduct, in the confident belief that his interrogators would recognise him as a sincere, responsible, but misunderstood commander simply doing his patriotic duty.

Initially this line played well. Concluding their preliminary interrogation report, Special Agents George A. Perper and Peter Regis, of 307th Counter Intelligence Corps, US 7th Army, stated that Skorzeny had been 'sincere in his desire to give all possible information'. Regarding 'the whereabouts and hiding places of his former collaborators … Skorzeny still feels his responsibility as an Army Officer towards his subordinates. Time, however, may mellow certain scruples which he maintains at present.'[4]

The agents noted Skorzeny's advocacy of 'a Western Block [*sic*] against Communism' which had been 'primordial in his voluntary surrender in the hope that he might be given an active part in this undertaking. Due to his Austrian ancestry, he is clear-minded and pliable but politically short-sighted to the point of naivety.'[5] Naive he certainly was, if he believed that he and his new-model Freikorps would stand with the Americans to stem the Red tide in the Alpine passes.

But the Americans got off on the back foot as well by turning the initial interrogation into a media circus. Cross-examined in front of the cameras about his alleged kidnap attempt on Eisenhower, Skorzeny was easily able to refute, or at least cast doubt on, his accusers. Handcuffed, he came across as a victim, and a potentially sympathetic one at that: the caged Lion of Gran Sasso.

Next day he and Radl were driven from the villa at Salzburg to a detention centre at Augsburg for questioning by a wilier interrogator: Colonel Henry Gordon Sheen, chief of US Army Counter-Intelligence at SHAEF. In addition to the Eisenhower affair, Sheen had a new and still more exotic line of inquiry. He had it on very good authority, he said, that the Führer was still alive and that Skorzeny himself had flown him out of Berlin on 30 April.

It is doubtful whether Sheen really believed this story. However, so much had public expectations been hyped by the capture of the fugitive commando that within a week of Sheen's interview with Skorzeny, General Walter Bedell Smith, Eisenhower's chief of staff, had to call a rather humiliating press conference at the Hotel Scribe in Paris, where he admitted that there never had been an Eisenhower 'death plot' and that the whole thing was an inglorious snafu. It was hoped that the Skorzeny myth could be slain before it took flight, but it was too late – Otto Skorzeny was already a legend, capable, in popular imagination, of the most incredible – and the most monstrous – feats.

Skorzeny was moved again on 19 May; this time to a clammy, unventilated wooden hut in Mobile Field Interrogation Unit No. 4, a camp on the outskirts of Wiesbaden. Inside the hut were two beds. There were no pillows and Skorzeny was 'most uncomfortable, but one can get used to anything'. During the night the door opened and, in the darkness, another inmate got into the other bed. In the morning, 'I had a big surprise. The newcomer was none other than SS-Obergruppenführer Dr Kaltenbrunner.'[6]

Managed encounters were as much a feature of Skorzeny's imprisonment as solitary confinement and changes of venue. Clearly, the hut was bugged. A directive explained:

MFIU #4 presently houses at their special installation approximately 25 prisoners of considerable importance. Among these prisoners is Ernst KALTENBRUNNER, Chief of the RSHA and, as such, the most significant CI [counter intelligence] prisoner captured to date. This man possesses information of extreme importance to us with respect to both the CI mission and the overall occupation mission in Germany.

... On 19 May MFIU #4 will receive at the same installation Otto SKORZENY ... SKORZENY is obviously of extreme interest both with respect to his part as Chief of AMT VI S, RSHA, and with respect to the knowledge he possesses concerning underground or guerrilla activities which may take place during the occupation.

... This office wishes to emphasize the need for full utilization of all existing technical facilities to enable maximum information to be extracted from these persons in the shortest period of time.[7]

Skorzeny and Kaltenbrunner – along with other SS men such as Radl – had been captured in the American zone and were to be 'fully interrogated' within American jurisdiction.[8] Under the terms of a four-power agreement, the Allies were able to cross-examine each other's prisoners, yet when two MI5 officers first visited the MFIU, they were barred from seeing either Kaltenbrunner or Skorzeny. Guy Liddell, Deputy Director-General of MI5, considered the Americans 'pathetically ignorant' but since both men were captured by them, felt 'they have got to put up a show ... They have tried milking Skorzeny and Kaltenbrunner together but both of them are clearly well aware of what is going on.'[9]

Kaltenbrunner hadn't given much away, sticking to the line that he was merely a politician and a lawyer and 'did not know anything about the atrocities committed under the orders of [Gestapo chief Heinrich] Müller', and 'is not being drawn into talking about the SD or the planning of the underground movement.'[10]

Eventually the Americans relented. Skorzeny was interviewed by 'a British service colonel'[11] – probably Victor Rothschild, MI5's chief specialist in explosives and counter-sabotage (who had been 'hopping mad' about his previous exclusion). He was under pressure to probe Skorzeny about his relationship with Mil Amt F.

Meanwhile, Kaltenbrunner was interviewed by Captain Stuart Hampshire, an Oxford don who was MI5's expert on the RSHA. Hampshire also gained access to Skorzeny and conducted at least one personal interview in early June. The key intermediary seems to have been Lieutenant-Colonel

Andrew H. Berding, head of OSS/X-2 in Europe.[12] A week later, on 15 June, Berding gave Rothschild access to a highly confidential file on 'Special Activities of the Skorzeny Group (Schwerdt)' – in other words, Operation *Peter* in Denmark.[13]

Skorzeny got off lightly in his encounter with Hampshire. Kaltenbrunner was less fortunate. After a preliminary interview, Hampshire had him hauled back to London for further interrogation. The former RSHA chief was detained at Camp 020 (Latchmere House), on Ham Common near Richmond, Surrey, where he was systematically tortured. Schellenberg was given the same treatment; taken to London, he was shuttled between 020 and the War Room for interrogation, with bouts of torture in between, involving sensory and sleep deprivation, intimidation and immersion in cold water. 'I wanted to kill myself,' Schellenberg said during his interrogation at Nuremberg. 'It was not possible.'[14]

Remarkably, Skorzeny was not whisked back to London. The American military judicial system was relatively patient in extracting the information it needed from him. It may be that, having made Skorzeny such a celebrity, they could not risk any serious mistreatment becoming publicly known. Kaltenbrunner and Schellenberg were, by contrast, shadowy figures whose deeds were known by only a few. Moreover, Skorzeny's asset value as a prisoner was by comparison modest.

* * *

Kaltenbrunner was arraigned in the Nuremberg International Military Tribunal, a show-trial of 22 top-ranking Nazi leaders. Its rulings had important ramifications for all other criminal proceedings lower down the judicial hierarchy. Notably, it criminalised the leadership of all branches of the SS, creating a presumption of guilt by association for all former members.[15]

Below this judicial apex, proceedings devolved individually to the four occupying powers. Within the American zone the next rung was the US Nuremberg Trials, presided over by the Office of Military Government, US. There were 12 trials in all, involving 185 second-tier Nazi leaders, between October 1946 and April 1949. Among the defendants was Schellenberg.[16]

The next tier down in the judicial hierarchy comprised the US Army Tribunals, conducted at the former Dachau concentration camp from June 1946 to early 1948. The venue was deliberately chosen to humiliate the defendants. The tribunals were framed in military law and ultimately the responsibility of the US Joint Chiefs of Staff.

There were 3,887 cases opened, involving 1,672 lower-ranking defendants. The vast majority involved atrocities committed in concentration camps and against Allied airmen. There were, however, some high-profile exceptions, such as the Malmédy massacre, committed by the Waffen-SS in December 1944.

In addition to the trials, there was a Denazification programme, a cleansing procedure that was supposed to provide a passport – known as a *Persilschein*＊ – for people minimally tainted by Nazism back into positions of responsibility within German and Austrian society. The haphazard nature of Denazification could mean years of detention before a verdict was reached.

The Americans and the British had been reluctant converts to the validity of war crimes tribunals. Roosevelt, Churchill and their advisers were determined that the mistakes made at Versailles should not be repeated. Debate on the nature of retributive justice was forced to a hasty conclusion by the unexpected speed of the Third Reich's collapse. The multi-layered judicial system that emerged was a messy compromise. The Dachau Trials, for example, initially lacked any appellate system,[17] which meant many of the verdicts reached were of inconsistent rigour and severity. Standards of justice were nowhere near those of an American civilian court, with no presumption of innocence, and hearsay admitted as evidence. On the other hand, the trials were swift, and the interrogation procedure that preceded them sought, in principle, to get to the bottom of what had happened as a matter of objective historical record.[18]

Otto Skorzeny was suspected of war crimes, making him subject to the Dachau Trials. He would also experience difficulty with Denazification, owing to his membership of a now criminalised organisation, the SS, but he was not a Category A prisoner like Kaltenbrunner, suspected of instigating genocide. Nor was he of such indisputable intelligence value as to make him a Category B prisoner like Schellenberg. Skorzeny apparently imagined that he would soon be cleared when he was moved from Wiesbaden to the lighter, airier conditions of the former Luftwaffe interrogation centre at nearby Oberursel. On 11 August he was released from solitary confinement, and allowed to share a cell with Radl.[19] However, on 10 September 1945 he was put on a plane to Nuremberg, together with Guderian, Dönitz, Schirach and Robert Ley, former head of the Deutsche Arbeitsfront (DAF or German Labour Front). Ley committed suicide on 25 October 1945 after being indicted for crimes against humanity at the Nuremberg Trial.

＊   Clean bill of health

Prison conditions at Nuremberg were harsh. There was calculated humiliation, including the use of African American guards. There was also the regular misery of a military prison, with lights constantly on, minor offences punished with solitary confinement, and perpetual surveillance and denunciations; and when winter came, freezing conditions in the cells – 'all this affected my morale badly', Skorzeny recalled.[20]

In November, Skorzeny was transferred to more relaxed conditions in the witness holding wing, where cell doors were left open and he could freely consort with the 50 other Nazi celebrities confined there. Surely clemency must be just round the corner for a man like himself?

His interrogators didn't share this view. Victor Rothschild of MI5, for instance, had taken an interest in Operation *Peter*, and there were other dark activities for which he might answer. Skorzeny's former supply chief, Reinhold Gerhard, was in a position to reveal damning evidence, and his lukewarm Nazism and truculence towards his former superiors made him a good hostile witness. In addition, he was lucid and university-educated; his arguments would carry weight in a witness box.[21] Gerhard had refused to follow Skorzeny to the Alpenfestung, and was lucky enough to have been picked up by the British in his pre-SS Wehrmacht uniform. He admitted that 'I had been considered "politically unreliable" by the Nazis, which made my colleagues look upon me as a dangerous person.' He was, in his own words, a 'disturbing witness'.[22]

Gerhard was subjected to a managed encounter with Waneck, the former Gruppenleiter of VI-E, who cautioned him to take care under interrogation – 'he felt it was his duty to guide me so that I would discuss and judge only those things which I knew from officially sanctioned sources'. He should deny detailed knowledge of the RSHA, Operation *Greif* and Werwolf, and claim ignorance of the intended use of the matériel he supplied. 'I should maintain complete silence on all persons apparently still at large … I should be particularly careful about statements concerning poisons, falsifications of papers and Skorzeny.' Waneck told Gerhard that Radl had already 'revealed much through his attempts to be diplomatic, and must therefore be considered as something of a traitor, while Skorzeny was stupid and harmless'.[23]

On 1 March 1946, Gerhard was transferred to Civilian Internment Enclosure 91 in Darmstadt, where almost immediately he became reacquainted with Karl Radl himself. It soon transpired that Radl's assessment of Waneck exactly matched Waneck's opinion of Radl: a traitor trying to get in with the Americans. Like Waneck, Radl advised Gerhard to stick to technical details when interrogated; to tell interrogators 'that Skorzeny was a secret service operator, rather than a terrorist or saboteur'; and that Amt VI-S and the Jagdverbände only carried out tasks behind the enemy's lines. Thus Operation *Peter* had nothing to do with their department.

Gerhard noted Radl's 'extreme nervousness' when *Peter* was mentioned, and when the capture of Otto Schwerdt – the leader of *Peter* – by Danish police and US Army military police was reported, Radl was 'unpleasantly moved'. Radl considered *Peter* the big bear-trap for Skorzeny. While the Jagdverbände and their operations were mostly relatively conventional, Operation *Peter* 'might be interpreted as sheer crime'.[24]

As for Werwolf, they should state that Skorzeny had passively resisted it. This rang true for Gerhard, who recalled Skorzeny being 'a little afraid that Werwolf would steal his laurels' and 'unwilling to hand over supplies at the cost of his own units'. Nonetheless, Gerhard later told his interrogators that Skorzeny had 'cooperated quite well' with Werwolf.[25]

Then there was the sensitive matter of the 200 bullets poisoned with aconite supplied to Skorzeny on the eve of *Greif*.[26] Radl counselled Gerhard against so much as breathing the name of Dr Widmann, Head of Section VD-2 (Chemistry and Biology) of the Kriminaltechnisches Institut der Sicherheitspolizei, who had collaborated closely with Skorzeny on the aconite bullets (among other things) and who was still at large. The same applied to Gerhard Hensel, research chemist in the Technische SS- und Polizei-Akademie (Technical SS and Police Academy), and the still fugitive Besekow, Walther and Otto Begus*.

Radl had some tips on interrogation techniques. The key tactic was to reveal a lot of highly secret information in order to win the confidence of the interrogating officers so that one could plausibly feign ignorance of subjects which must be kept secret.[27]

Gerhard received much the same advice from other captive Skorzeny associates, especially concerning Operation *Peter* and the importance of detaching Skorzeny from any blame. The recurring themes indicated to Gerhard 'a type of reasoning peculiar to those who feel the need to justify their past actions by self-deception', and he noted that 'these people have so hypnotised themselves with such reasoning that they almost believe it themselves'.[28]

Skorzeny was clearly legally vulnerable, and his captors were evidently aware of it, manipulating events by inserting *V-Leute* (informants) into prison communities.

By early summer 1947, Skorzeny had spent over two years behind bars and been relentlessly cross-examined by the authorities. One of the

---

* Begas was one of Besekow's operatives, active in Greece and then Italy.

Nuremberg Trial's top interrogators, Lieutenant-Colonel Smith W. Brookhart, had taken over 150 pages of depositions from him, and Major-General 'Wild Bill' Donovan, former head of the OSS (now evolved into the Strategic Services Unit, later indirectly to become the CIA) had interviewed him about Gran Sasso.

Skorzeny had not, in fact, been long detained at Nuremberg, where his role was confined to providing affidavits, without cross-examination,[29] but there followed a seemingly interminable shuffle from camp to camp. The scenery changed, but the wearying questions did not: the use of American uniforms during *Greif*, his precise role in the battle around Malmédy; Operation *Peter*.

It was taking a toll on his health. In winter 1946 Skorzeny was back in Dachau and suffering from dysentery and a recurrence of the colitis and gall bladder complications that had caused his recall from the Eastern Front in 1942. The symptoms were no doubt aggravated by a hunger strike over prison conditions (particularly his long bouts of solitary confinement). The prison authorities consented to hospitalisation on condition that he have his gall bladder removed. In hospital a guard stayed at his bedside round the clock, even though he 'could hardly crawl'. The surgery was done on 6 December, the guard accompanying him into the operating theatre, 'to see that I did not bolt and take the operating table with me'.[30]

His convalescence over, Skorzeny was plunged back into the Dachau interrogation routine. In March 1947, an officer who had exhaustively questioned him on technical aspects of the Ardennes offensive assured him that he had nothing to worry about.[31] The assurance proved false.

∗ ∗ ∗

Three months later, on 23 June, Skorzeny was summoned by the commandant of Dachau's Bunker cell block. There he was brought before a large panel of officials, most of them strangers. Reporters with cameras were on hand. Skorzeny was puzzled at first, but when eight other prisoners were brought in, all veterans of Panzerbrigade 150, he realised that they were about to be charged in connection with Operation *Greif*. Among them he recognised Korvettenkapitän Philipp Freiherr von Behr and the truculent commander of Kampfgruppe Y, Hauptmann Walter Scherf. The other six prisoners 'were wholly unknown' to Skorzeny.[32]

The charges were read out in English and German. Skorzeny 'simply could not understand' one of the charges, which alleged that the prisoners had 'ill-treated, tortured and killed American prisoners of war, whose names and numbers are not known, but were not less than one hundred in number'.[33] It transpired that Skorzeny and his co-defendants were being accused of complicity in the massacre at Malmédy. There was not the slightest doubt that, if they were convicted, they would face the death penalty. The presence of reporters indicated that this trial was going to be conducted in the full glare of publicity.

The men reading the charges were prosecutor Lieutenant-Colonel Abraham H. Rosenfeld, an ambitious Yale Law School graduate, and his assistant, Harry W. Thon.

Skorzeny knew Rosenfeld by reputation – and it was a reputation to be feared. The previous year, he had masterminded the prosecution and conviction of 73 members of Kampfgruppe Peiper and their superior officers – including Dietrich, I. SS-Panzerkorps commander Hermann Priess and the charismatic Jochen Peiper himself. Forty-three of the defendants – including Peiper – had been sentenced to death, the rest to prison terms varying from ten years to life.[34]

As the Law Member of the tribunal panel, which was mostly made up of field officers with little or no experience of judicial matters, Rosenfeld alone decided what evidence was admissible. He was equally influential behind the scenes, in his dealings with the interrogation team. As special prosecutor in the Skorzeny trial (Case no. 6-100), he got to decide the parameters of investigation, including what techniques were acceptable in obtaining the 'truth', and had constantly sifted the affidavits with an eye to the charge-sheet.

Rosenfeld's assistant prosecutor for the trial, Harry W. Thon, despite being employed by the War Crimes Branch, had no legal training. He had formerly been an intelligence officer in the US 104th Infantry Division, which had fought in the Battle of the Bulge, but was now a civilian. As the son of a German Jewish mother who had fled the Nazis,[35] Thon's main value was as a fluent German speaker. Behind closed doors he had been Skorzeny's principal interrogator in the run-up to the trial. Before that, he had been part of the team which had employed mock trials, and the hooding and beating of the Malmédy defendants in preparation for their court appearance.

Thon had been interrogating Skorzeny about all aspects of the Ardennes offensive since May 1946, over a year before the trial. Having failed to get the answers he wanted, he began sharpening his tactics when Skorzeny persistently denied knowledge of any written or oral order to shoot prisoners. Thon had shown Skorzeny a statement by a major in the 1. SS-Panzerdivision 'Leibstandarte-SS Adolf Hitler' which 'was said to contain serious charges against me personally'. Skorzeny would be allowed to keep and destroy the document if he would cooperate with Thon. 'To this offer I replied that I would have nothing to do with so serious a matter as tampering with evidence to be given in court and that, in any event, I was not in the least interested in what had been said by the major, whom I did not know.'[36]

The major in question was SS-Sturmbannführer Gustav Knittel, former commander of the Schnelle Gruppe (Mechanised Group) of the 1. SS-Panzerdivision 'Leibstandarte-SS Adolf Hitler'. In fact Skorzeny *did* formally encounter him at the operational briefing in December 1944, at which he unveiled his battle plan for Panzerbrigade 150 and its Kommandokompanie,[37] though Knittel had in truth learned more about *Greif* from Skorzeny's number two, Willi Hardieck, during an inebriated off-the-record debriefing the same night.

Rosenfeld later admitted that Skorzeny had only escaped joining the other 73 defendants in the previous Malmédy trial by the skin of his teeth – because he hadn't been available at the time.[38] Given the outcome of that trial, Skorzeny had little hope of fair process now. He and his nine co-defendants (one of whom had been absent from the reading of charges) were charged on four counts relating to the violation of the laws and usages of war, according to the 1907 Hague Convention, between 1 October 1944 and 15 January 1945. The charges were:

I.   A conspiracy to adopt the military insignia of the United States with the deliberate intention of 'treacherously firing upon and killing' American troops.

II. A 'common design' involving 'killing, shooting, ill-treatment, abuse and torture' of over a hundred (unidentified) American prisoners.

III. Conspiring to remove uniforms, identity documents, insignia and other effects from American prisoners of war.

IV. Appropriating Red Cross parcels intended for American prisoners of war.

Aside from Behr and Scherf, the other co-defendants were: Leutnant Hans Hass, Scherf's adjutant; Leutnant Wilhelm Maus; SS-Untersturmführer Arendt de Bruin; and Leutnante zur See Dennis Müntz, Günther Fitze, Ralph Bellstedt and Wilhelm Kocherscheidt. All had been involved in aspects of *Greif*.

Already baffled by some of the charges, Skorzeny must have felt still more dismay at the defence team appointed by the court. It was led by Lieutenant-Colonel Robert D. Durst, a hard-bitten lawyer from Springfield, Missouri. His junior counsels were USAF Lieutenant-Colonel Donald McClure, an experienced criminal trial lawyer, and Major Lewis Horowitz. Skorzeny felt that Durst was hostile, insisting on minutely examining the backgrounds of all ten defendants before he and his team would agree to take on the defence. Skorzeny later said his grilling by Durst was the toughest he had experienced.[39] In fact, Durst was merely sharpening his weapons for the courtroom duel that lay ahead.

The course of the Skorzeny trial was affected by a political storm brewing over the previous Malmédy trial. Durst told Skorzeny and the other defendants that 'he could not promise success at the trial unless we worked together as a team with a "team leader"'. They all had to agree that Durst alone should determine the conduct of the defence. Skorzeny would be consulted as 'leader' of the defendants in Durst's decision-making.[40]

Right from the beginning, Durst took control of trial procedure in a way that his counterpart during the Malmédy trial, Colonel Everett, had failed to. Hamstrung by an ignorance of criminal law, Everett had been procedurally outmanoeuvred by Rosenfeld, who had been able to block legitimate cross-examination of prosecution witnesses.[41] The biggest single error by Everett's team had been its failure to impose a coherent narrative by appointing a single spokesman for all of the defendants. As a result, the accused resorted to cut-throat defence tactics once in the witness box, in an attempt to minimise their own culpability.

Durst's total control over defence strategy thwarted the defendants' German lawyers who threatened to undermine his case by attempting to get their clients to sign up to mitigating confessions. Some of them quit, while those who remained agreed to Durst's uncompromising terms.

Although strong, Durst's courtroom strategy was also risky, imposing a huge burden on one man – Skorzeny, who Durst insisted should enter the witness-box alone, as representative of all the defendants. Skorzeny was well aware that this placed 'the fate and, perhaps, the lives of my comrades on my hands'. He consented 'only after long and hard reflection, and with the full approval of my comrades'.[42]

Aside from the burden, there was a risk that Skorzeny – charismatic though he was – might send out the wrong message to the empanelled military judges. Burton Ellis, the prosecutor in the Malmédy case, had been appointed head of the Dachau War Crimes Group, giving him influence in the selection of military panels. Skorzeny believed he 'had not got on particularly well'[43] with Ellis, which was an ill omen. The choice of Rosenfeld as special prosecutor might have been a coincidence, but giving the role of president to Colonel Andrew Gardener – dubbed 'Hanging Gardener' by Durst[44] – was assuredly not. Although Durst managed to get some members of the panel replaced, he could not get rid of Gardener.

* * *

The prosecution opened its case on 18 August 1947. It began by calling Radl and then Hunke to the witness box. What they said amounted to very little, but their mere presence made an impact. Rosenfeld was signalling to the judges that Skorzeny's conduct of *Greif* was that of a maverick, and that even his staff had opposed him.

More damaging was the evidence of Gerhard, who gave compelling testimony on the use of poison bullets. Such weapons, in an offensive capacity, were banned by the 1907 Hague Convention.[45] And yet here was Skorzeny's former quartermaster authoritatively stating that 7.65 mm pistol bullets filled with aconite which exuded through slits in the side had been issued to the Kommandokompanie teams.

Skorzeny could hardly deny that such bullets existed – after all, he was already on record as having had them manufactured with the help of Dr Widmann at the Kriminaltechnisches Institut der Sicherheitspolizei.[46] He took refuge in the rather lame argument that they were 'limited edition' weapons – no more than 50 in number – that had been developed solely for suicide purposes. He told Durst that he had distributed them, via Hardieck, to his commandos as a last resort, should their mission go disastrously wrong. This may have been true, up to a point. Skorzeny apparently kept one of these bullets in the magazine of his own side-arm. ('Be careful, it's loaded,' he told his captors as they disarmed him, 'and the last round is dangerous.')[47] But Stielau's commandos were issued ampoules of cyanide to commit suicide; why would they need bullets as well?

Embarrassingly, this very issue had been raised during the examination of Philipp von Behr. Behr had told the court that Hardieck gave him ampoules of cyanide, plus 'three or four' poison bullets.[48] Why would he need three or four of these bullets for suicide? Any defence would have been further undermined by reference to Skorzeny's admission – to his Counterintelligence Corps (CIC) interrogators two years earlier – that he had borrowed the idea from the Russians, and that the bullets 'were intended for assassinations'.[49]

Skorzeny and Durst therefore developed an elegant diversionary ruse. Gerhard had described the poison bullets as bearing a distinguishing red ring around the casing. Skorzeny managed to obtain an example of a bullet fitting this description (smuggled into his cell in a piece of bread with assistance from an Austrian prisoner-doctor), which he passed on to Durst.[50] Next day in court, Durst subjected Gerhard to a withering cross-examination, alleging that he had lied as a prosecution witness during the Nuremberg International Military Tribunal trials. Then, almost casually, Durst produced the red-ringed bullet from his pocket and asked if Gerhard recognised it as one of the poison bullets. Rather nervously, Gerhard confirmed it was. Thereupon Durst disclosed to the court that the bullet was a waterproof round whose only similarity to the poison version was the red marking.[51]

Though Durst had discredited him, Gerhard's other evidence relating to Charges III and IV was harder to refute. He was, for example, able to tie the defendants Fitze and Müntz to Skorzeny's scheme for seizing American uniforms from the prisoner of war camp at Fürstenberg. Fitze's and Müntz's prior affidavits confirmed Gerhard's story. Another defendant, Wilhelm Maus – an OKW expert on foreign uniforms – not only corroborated this information, but also said that Skorzeny had taken a personal interest in the distribution of American uniforms and Red Cross supplies to Panzerbrigade 150.[52]

However, the point at law here was not whether Skorzeny had done these things, but under whose orders he was acting, and whether he had exceeded them. Defence witness Dr Percy Schramm, who had been in charge of the OKW operational staff diary, stated that Skorzeny 'had absolutely nothing to do' with equipment or supply procurement, which was the responsibility of the quartermaster staff. The American gear had been 'handed over to him because of orders from Hitler himself'. Refusal to comply would have resulted in court martial and execution.[53]

Skorzeny was less concerned about these alleged infractions of the Geneva Convention[54] than about Charge II: the Malmédy killings, which potentially carried the death penalty. And yet, day after day as the prosecution rolled out its case, the sword of Damocles failed to fall on the anxious defendants. Only on 26 August, as Rosenfeld concluded his case, did they discover why. As mysteriously as he had inserted it in the first place, the chief prosecutor now dropped Charge II.

Rosenfeld said that he had two witnesses in the USA, but had failed to get statements from them in time. In truth, he simply did not have sufficient evidence. He had entered Charge II on the basis of a single affidavit. The paucity of his evidence stemmed from the fact that no one in Panzerbrigade 150, not even the Kommandokompanie teams, had been in the area of Malmédy at the time the massacre was committed. The shootings had occurred at the Baugnez crossroads between 1 pm and 2.30 pm on 17 December 1944, according to surviving eyewitnesses. The only *Greif* unit in the area that day had been Behr's jeep team, and that was later in the evening.

In entering Charge II, Rosenfeld might have had a personal agenda, a determination to nail Skorzeny after failing to get him at the Malmédy trial a year earlier. But according to Skorzeny, the principal reason was that Rosenfeld could not have prosecuted the defendants at all without Charge II.[55] By 1947 the United States was becoming impatient with the whole business of war crimes trials; yet the number of cases was increasing. That meant raising the bar on the indictment sheet. Rosenfeld was well aware that he was skating on thin ice with Charge II, but felt its sensationalism would be enough to get the case rolling when it might otherwise have foundered on the complexity of the other three charges. Besides, Charge II was too good to pass up. Evidence might have come to light during the course of the trial to secure a conviction.

Rosenfeld ran out of time, and in the process undermined his own case. The minute he dropped Charge II and rested his case, Durst seized his opportunity. He petitioned the tribunal to dismiss the case and acquit all its defendants on the basis that the prosecution had failed to establish even a prima facie argument against them.[56] The court took Durst's petition seriously, but after deliberating, it ruled that two defendants – Arendt de Bruin and Wilhelm Maus – were acquitted but the rest must continue to stand trial.

The dismissal of Maus weakened still further charges III and IV. The emphasis now moved to the complex and controversial Charge I: that Skorzeny and his brigade had fired on Americans while wearing American uniforms. Article 24 of the Hague Convention permitted 'ruses of war' and necessary espionage, while putting constraints on the definition of legitimate ruses. Article 23f prohibited 'improper use of a flag of truce, of the national flag, or of the military insignia and uniform of the enemy', and 23b amplified this by outlawing the 'treacherous' killing or wounding of enemy individuals.[57] Whether Skorzeny and his men had acted unlawfully revolved around the definition of the words 'improper use' in Article 23f. Active infraction under 23b – 'treacherous' shooting of American troops while wearing American uniforms – was the kind of evidence the prosecution required for a conviction on Charge I.

Such evidence was contained in a prior affidavit by one of the defendants, Leutnant zur See Wilhelm Kocherscheidt, the commander of a jeep team that had set off on the night of 17 December 1944. In the vicinity of Born (near St Vith), their jeep got stuck in mud. An American military policeman came to their aid. The MP's suspicions were raised by the four-up jeep (Americans almost never carried more than two passengers in a jeep). Kocherscheidt, sensing they were in trouble, decided to protect the mission by shooting the MP with his Colt 45. Five shots rang out in the dark and the team fled into the wood. All four eventually made it back to reconnaissance HQ near Born, where Kocherscheidt reported the incident independently to Behr and Knittel, commander of the reconnaissance section of 1. SS-Panzerdivision 'Leibstandarte-SS Adolf Hitler'. Both confirmed Kocherscheidt's account of the incident.[58]

On the face of it, this looked very damning, not only for Kocherscheidt but for all the defendants. But the evidence was flimsy. The incident had taken place not behind enemy lines but in no-man's land. And when the team later went back to recover the jeep, they found no body, leading Kocherscheidt to surmise that he had missed his target in the dark, despite shooting from only 3 metres away.[59] There was, therefore, no firm evidence that Kocherscheidt had breached Article 23f. The prosecution apparently realised this; although the MP shooting was cited in the opening statement ('one of the yellowest incidents of the war'), it was omitted from the charge sheet.

Without corroborative testimony,[60] the prosecution had no evidence that Skorzeny's commandos had shot at Americans while dressed in American uniform. However, it did have an eyewitness account from Lieutenant William J. O'Neill that a Kommandokompanie jeep crew had been killed in an engagement outside Stavelot (implying that they had shot back),[61] and evidence that items of American uniform may have been worn by Kampfgruppe Scherf troops (not part of the camouflage deception) during their assault on Malmédy on 20–21 December.[62]

Rather than resting his case on mere rebuttal, Durst employed a *tu quoque* ('you also') line of defence, seeking to show that the Allies had engaged in exactly the same kind of false flag stratagems. If he could prove his case, the court would have to acquit the defendants or itself be condemned (not least in the international media) for double standards.

The defence had compiled a number of affidavits – some from Skorzeny himself – supporting their case. Both Germans and Russians had commonly carried out such operations on the Eastern Front, but it was harder to demonstrate that the British and Americans had done the same. Former artillery general Walter Warlimont attested that a large number of British aircraft liveried in German camouflage had attacked the battleship *Scharnhorst*. Two statements claimed that Lieutenant Michael Alexander had been wearing a German uniform when captured during the unsuccessful attempt on Rommel's life in 1941. Finally, there were reports that American Rangers had donned German uniforms during the capture of Aachen in 1944 – a suggestion that had so incensed Hitler it became the inspiration of Operation

Greif. At the prosecution's request, General Omar Bradley, former commander of the US 12th Army Group, submitted a letter utterly refuting the suggestion. It was read out in court on 5 September 1947.[63]

There was more anecdotal evidence, but it would have amounted to little had not Durst played a stunningly effective hole card. As his first witness for the defence, he called Wing Commander F. F. E. 'Tommy' Yeo-Thomas GC, one of Britain's top Special Operations Executive agents and most highly decorated war heroes.

Yeo-Thomas, although a master of disguise, had never actually worn a German uniform himself, but in February 1944 he had led an SOE mission codenamed 'Asymptote' to rescue a French intelligence officer from Rennes prison. Accompanying Yeo-Thomas on the mission had been a number of SOE operatives fluent in German. After landing, they acquired SD uniforms, weapons and false papers, then rigged up a van to look like a prison wagon. The plan was to stall the van in the prison gateway so it could not be closed, go to the guard house and present false papers for the prisoner's release. Yeo-Thomas was later betrayed by a double agent and arrested in Paris. Given the appalling treatment he subsequently suffered at the hands of the SS, he was an unlikely witness for the defence in the Skorzeny trial. And yet when Durst, who had done his homework carefully, approached him he volunteered readily enough.[64]

The impact of Yeo-Thomas's testimony was dramatic. Durst had conducted his negotiations in great secrecy. Skorzeny and his co-defendants knew little about the agent's illustrious reputation and nothing at all about his appearance in their defence. Yeo-Thomas made it clear that 'Asymptote' was par for the course in British undercover operations. The other specific example he cited was a false flag operation – ultimately aborted – that involved the kidnapping of Grossadmiral Dönitz.[65] Durst then asked Yeo-Thomas the key question. When wearing a German uniform how far would he – and other secret agents – be prepared to go to protect their mission? 'Bump off the other guy,' was the chilling response.

In retrospect, Yeo-Thomas' testimony was legally doubtful, relying on non-specific and hypothetical statements.[66] Nevertheless, it was enough to muddy the waters. The moral authority of Yeo-Thomas greatly influenced the court. Although the trial had another two weeks to run, its course changed in that moment. Skorzeny noted that, from then on, even Rosenfeld was a good deal more courteous.[67]

The verdict, when it was read out on the morning of 9 September, may have come as a relief to the defendants, but was no great surprise. Every one of them, Kocherscheidt included, was acquitted on all charges.

* * *

The main factor in Skorzeny's acquittal appears to have been the weak prosecution case. At no point did Rosenfeld and his team conclusively demonstrate that Skorzeny and his men had engaged in combat while wearing American uniforms.

Although both sides used forensic tricks to good effect, Rosenfeld's case was ultimately slick but shallow, while Durst – perhaps benefiting from the backlash that was gathering momentum from the slipshod Malmédy trial – managed to sow doubt in the judges' minds. Rosenfeld and Thon had hoped to present Knittel as a star witness. But, not only did he not turn up – it was claimed he was too ill – he also submitted a renunciation of his former statement in a new affidavit which the court received a few days before judgement. Although he did not say that the first affidavit had been beaten out of him (it probably had) he stated that it had been 'written with the intent to deceive and most of it is untruthful'.[68]

The judges may, additionally, have been influenced by Hague Article 31, specifying that when a spy, having rejoined the army to which he belongs, is subsequently captured by the enemy, he should be treated as a prisoner of war and incur no responsibility for previous acts of espionage.[69] In his summing up, Durst leant heavily on the fact that those members of the Kommandokompanie captured alive had been, almost without exception, shot as spies.[70] The survivors could not, therefore, be punished retroactively for their wartime espionage.

Skorzeny's personal contribution to the outcome of the trial was notable. Although Höttl later belittled his performance by suggesting it was all down to coaching from his 'nanny', Radl,[71] Skorzeny in fact performed coolly under pressure as the star, giving testimony which was uncharacteristically 'complete and on the whole truthful'.[72]

The trial was arguably one of the more creditable episodes in Skorzeny's picaresque career. Before it, he was just another Nazi war criminal – albeit a colourful one – awaiting condign punishment. After it, he was able to bask in glowing testimonials on his deeds and character – all from his former enemies.

Foremost in importance was the good opinion of Yeo-Thomas. Skorzeny sent a note of thanks, to which Yeo-Thomas replied: 'You did a damned good war job. I'm sure you will get off. In any case I have a flat in Paris if you should need to lie up somewhere.'[73] It was the beginning of a fitful correspondence – and perhaps friendship – into which Skorzeny may have read more than Yeo-Thomas. When Skorzeny wrote asking his advice on what to do about his increasingly frustrating detention at Darmstadt, the latter suggested he escape. They visited each other in the 1950s, and Yeo-Thomas helped Skorzeny to find a publisher for his memoirs. As late as 1961 Yeo-Thomas was advising Skorzeny on how to fight a libel case in the French courts.[74]

Yeo-Thomas's view on Skorzeny's trial was printed in the *Daily Express* in 1952:

> I have heard German generals and princes at similar trials claim that they were simply carrying out orders from above. But Otto Skorzeny took full responsibility for everything his junior officers had done. He was the only German I knew who had the guts to do so. I take my hat off to him. His trial and acquittal proved him to be a good soldier who pulled off first-class jobs. He fought a good war. I would be glad at any time to have a man like Skorzeny as my commanding officer.[75]

Powerful testimony to Skorzeny's nobility of character – or possibly a sign of the mental and physical deterioration that was gradually engulfing Yeo-Thomas's judgement.[76]

Equally notable was the post-trial behaviour of Rosenfeld. According to Skorzeny, immediately after the acquittal and 'before I could shake my defender's hand', Rosenfeld 'came up to me, shook hands and congratulated me on my success. He said I must know that in instituting the proceedings, he had only done his duty and acted on orders.'[77] Later, however, Rosenfeld told the press corps that he considered Skorzeny 'the most dangerous man in Europe'.[78]

The sobriquet was not designed to flatter, but it soon developed an insidious life of its own. Wherever Skorzeny went, whatever he did in the post-war world, his actions would take on mythic proportions in the Western media. This was a mixed blessing. On the one hand, it enabled Skorzeny to recast his life's narrative as an appealing and popular adventure story. On the other, there would be occasions when media attention was downright unwelcome; when any sighting of the former commando's gigantic frame in an airport departure lounge would be sufficient to trigger an avalanche of media speculation linking him with lurid clandestine activity in the world's most exotic trouble spots.

In their way, the protagonists in Case no. 6-100 – Yeo-Thomas, Rosenfeld and Durst – were no less responsible for creating the legend of Otto Skorzeny than Himmler, Goebbels and the man himself.

16

Escape from Darmstadt

Although cleared of war crimes by the Americans, Skorzeny was not out of the woods yet. Being ex-SS placed him in the 'automatic arrest' category, as a preliminary to Denazification. In the weeks following his acquittal there arose the further possibility that he might be extradited to face criminal charges in Denmark and Czechoslovakia.

The Danish threat appeared the greater. The salient facts of Operation *Peter* were now well established by his CIC interrogators, and they did not make attractive reading. Despite Skorzeny's and Radl's evasions,[1] the real identity of 'Peter' was known: Otto Schwerdt – Skorzeny's bodyguard at Gran Sasso and the man who helped to stem the tide at Schwedt. Another Skorzeny trusty, Anton Gföller, was now also known to have participated. Skorzeny's interrogators had pinpointed Schwerdt as the man who murdered the Danish journalist Christian Damm and resistance leader Kaj Munk in December 1943.[2] The fact that Fölkersam had actually picked the *Peter* team – and that Skorzeny claimed to have been on a skiing holiday at the time – hardly exonerated him.

As for the Prague extradition request, Czechoslovakia was under the control of the Soviet Union – which had a keen interest in getting its hands on Skorzeny. The request referred to unspecified atrocities committed in Czechoslovakia during April 1945. Skorzeny later dismissed this as 'pure myth', relating to events that had taken place while he himself was 'hundreds of kilometres' away. That last part was trivially true: Skorzeny, as we have seen, had only been present in Czechoslovakia for two days in early April, while en route to the Alpenfestung. Which does not mean to say the Czechs had no legitimate interest in linking him to the FAK anti-partisan activities of Thun-Hohenstein or Kirn, who were operating in the area at the time.

Nevertheless, Skorzeny's broader suspicions were probably correct. Like Rosenfeld's Malmédy massacre stratagem, this vaguely worded request was a legalistic cat's-paw designed to hook him in. The Czech extradition ploy was one of a number of tactics – including attempted kidnapping – being used by the Soviet Union to snare Skorzeny.

Luckily for him, the CIC had no intention of relinquishing their prisoner. The Czech request was turned down, while the Danes were fobbed off with Schwerdt, Ludwig Nebel and Alfred Naujocks.

Meanwhile, Skorzeny and Radl were despatched to the US Army Historical Division, based in Neustadt near Marburg, to write up their account of the Gran Sasso raid. In charge of the Operational History (German) Section was Colonel H. E. Potter, and under him, Franz Halder, former OKH chief of staff, coordinating the German contribution. Halder and his aides were given a free rein in selecting the Wehrmacht officers who would participate, allowing these unreconstructed Prussian militarists to mould the historical narrative into a form of apologia.

Halder's team were kept in pampered conditions in the old barracks at Neustadt. Privileges included good rations and cultural and educational activities, plus relatively free access to their families. Some were even allowed to work at home on parole, pending their eventual release from internment.[3]

Skorzeny must have been elated when he learned that he had been co-opted onto this gravy train – and enraged when he and Radl found themselves transported in a caged truck not to some cushy billet at Neustadt but to further solitary confinement under CIC control at the 7707th European Command Intelligence Center at Camp King, Oberursel. Eventually, after a three-day imbroglio with the camp authorities only resolved by Colonel Potter's personal intervention, Skorzeny and Radl were placed in more congenial quarters in a small house just outside the main stockade area.

The atmosphere was intimate, with only five in the house. Skorzeny was with two 'acquaintances' from his 'Italian days', but the more interesting inmate was a woman: Mildred Gillars, an American former model, would-be actress and foreign language teacher. She was one of two women known to Americans as 'Axis Sally', who had broadcast on German State Radio during the war. The 'beautiful blonde' of journalistic hyperbole was actually a husk of her former feisty self, her nerves frayed. Gillars would shortly be returned to the United States to face treason charges. Skorzeny passed 'many a pleasant evening in her room playing bridge and consuming warmed-up breakfast coffee and toast'.[4] She helped improve his 'defective English'.

However cosy his new surroundings, Skorzeny was still under investigation. His American interrogator at that time, Arnold M. Silver, had learned that his brother Alfred Skorzeny was in Soviet captivity in their occupied zone, 'and was to be used to lure Otto into the zone, where the Soviets planned to use him as a rallying point for the youth'.[5]

Silver was tasked with questioning Skorzeny and 'recommending disposition'. In his opinion, Skorzeny had been 'rightly acquitted'. He 'was not a Nazi, and in fact any ideology was alien to him. He was purely and simply a man of action and a patriotic German'.[6] This was a remarkable misreading. Yet Silver was an experienced interrogator and no fool. He'd had little difficulty in unmasking the lies and deceptions of other prominent Oberursel inmates. Hanna Reitsch, for instance, was 'as convinced and unreconstructed a Nazi as we had ever come across'.[7]

Skorzeny got the benefit of Silver's doubt because his status within the American intelligence community was changing. The CIC and their nascent successor the CIA had begun reassessing Skorzeny's value as an intelligence asset, and their conclusion was largely negative. The fact that Skorzeny had no talent for running networks – the real work having been done by Besekow – and rarely kept his opinions to himself, ruled him out as spycraft material. On the other hand, there was no denying his charisma and notoriety.

For this reason, the Americans could not countenance handing him over to the Soviet Union (who might exploit him for propaganda purposes). They were therefore thoroughly alarmed when in January 1948, having been returned to Dachau following completion of the history project, Skorzeny wrote to the American commandant, informing him that he had been 'openly and overtly' invited to collaborate with both German and Soviet Communists.[8] He claimed, during the subsequent interrogation, to have been approached by a fellow prisoner – a former Abwehr Leutnant – at Nuremberg in 1945, and not long afterwards by a Soviet officer. At Regensburg in August 1946, Skorzeny had discovered that many of the SS officers detained there were pro-Soviet. Finally, at Dachau in May 1947 he had been approached by a fellow prisoner, apparently a former Polish officer, several days before that officer escaped.[9]

In revealing these incidents, Skorzeny was probably gaming the system by inflating his asset value to the Americans – who by now suspected the existence of an underground organisation of former SS men plotting to spring

Skorzeny from internment. A CIC operation had been set in motion, to search for evidence of Skorzeny's links with this shadowy organisation. An agent, Karl Albers – who went under cover as 'Peter Holtmann' – had managed to worm his way into Skorzeny's confidence, and found out that there *was* a network operating at Dachau, centring on the prisoner-barber and the prisoner-doctor. Also involved were some of the Polish prison guards who – for a fee – were acting as couriers. Skorzeny had naively confided to 'Holtmann' the existence of a number of boxes containing personal correspondence, valuables and money which he had dispersed among friends and supporters – among them Dr Ferdinand Porsche. One contained 'very valuable jewels' – possibly from Kaltenbrunner's hoard – but Skorzeny would not elaborate on their whereabouts. However, he was persuaded to make 'Holtmann' an intermediary, a role which enabled the CIC to unmask Skorzeny's wife, Emmi – currently living just over the Austrian border at Franking – as one of the network's prime agents.[10]

Evidently, Skorzeny was sufficiently in funds and well enough connected to organise an escape – should he need to. But this was small stuff, hardly on a level with being the mastermind behind a neo-Nazi underground.

For a while, the Americans tried to ensnare Skorzeny in the wider net of Operation *Brandy* – launched in autumn 1946. 'Brandy' – a play on 'Brandenburgers' – was an attempt to bring to heel rogue bands of former Skorzeny commandos, and had been stimulated in part by the arrest of Walther, his former chief of staff, and two others at Annaberg the previous June. The operation was a failure. It found nothing of real substance to place Skorzeny at the centre of a sinister national or international Nazi network and was wound down in late spring 1947 after pressure from above. The cynical thinking behind this decision was that the problem would solve itself: Skorzeny was about to be committed to a war crimes trial that would – it seemed at the time – end with him being hanged. In retrospect, a prime opportunity was lost to accurately gauge the existence of such shadowy Nazi self-help organisations as Die Spinne and ODESSA* at the time they supposedly originated – and before they assumed phantasmagorical post-war proportions.[11]

Despite the failure of *Brandy*, the surveillance continued. Just before Christmas 1947, while still working for the Historical Division, Skorzeny had been granted leave of absence to meet his family. Agents shadowed him,

---

* ODESSA: Organisation der Ehemaligen SS-Angehörigen (Organisation of Former SS Members)

but detected little of interest: a visit to Hanna Reitsch, now residing in the town of Oberursel, trips to Munich and Vienna to meet family and friends, and an encounter with his daughter Waltraut at Berchtesgaden. Skorzeny declined to break his parole and escape. It really did appear he wished to go through the Denazification process and cleanse his name.

By now the CIC's bigger concern, as Arnold Silver noted, was that the Russians might exploit his brother Alfred's plight to lure Skorzeny into the Soviet Zone. As one interrogation report put it, Alfred was 'the exact opposite of his brother'[12] and almost apolitical. His only value to the Russians was his name. The fact that Alfred was being held hostage purely on account of his brother's political sins was surely a source of regret – and perhaps guilt – for Otto Skorzeny. During his interrogation, on being told by Silver about this situation, Skorzeny 'asked for time to think over where he would like to go', and later told Silver that he wanted to move to Spain, a quasi-Fascist safe-haven where he would be relatively immune from Soviet kidnap. Silver made inquiries, and the intelligence officer at US Forces, European Theater in Frankfurt, 'concurred in my recommendation that he be resettled there'.[13]

The American intelligence services were prepared to smooth Skorzeny's passage to Spain, but they couldn't simply release him; by law, he had to pass through the Denazification procedure first. Accordingly, Skorzeny was transferred – together with Radl – to the German-administrated Darmstadt internment camp.

Denazification should have been a formality, since Skorzeny had already been acquitted of major war crimes. The Americans put pressure on the Germans to speed up the process. Skorzeny was technically in Category C – a minor offender who should expect a few years of probation.

Instead, in the early summer of 1948, Skorzeny's hearing was postponed no fewer than six times, leading to suspicions that someone in the judiciary had an agenda. Skorzeny's CIC minders warned him in July that the Czechs, working through the United Nations War Crimes Commission since February, had resurrected their extradition request – and that this time it would go through.

Skorzeny was accused of being the commanding officer of an SS Einsatzgruppe that had massacred 27 people at Ploština, Slovakia, on 19 April 1945. In fact, his only connection was that the actual commander of the unit on that day was a member of Jagdverband Südost.[14] Nonetheless, the best that Skorzeny could hope for, he was told, was a few weeks' delay through bureaucratic prevarication.

Acting quickly, he went straight to Lieselotte Schröter, head of the camp censorship service, with whom he had cultivated a very close relationship. Schröter was easy to access, having an apartment within the camp compound. Using his roguish charm to good effect, Skorzeny was able to send for help.

Critical to his plan was Jacob Gröschner, a colourful, thuggish former SS officer whom Skorzeny had encountered at Dachau, where he was referred to as 'Wild Jacob': 'He was as strong as Hercules,' Skorzeny recalled, 'smashed everything that he could lay his hands on, set his bed on fire, bent the bars in the window, climbed onto the roof and so on … Whenever he saw me, even from a distance, he called out, "Always keep a stiff upper lip, Herr Oberst! Don't give an inch."'[15] Gröschner had been Skorzeny's heavy, severely beating up Gerhard with a stick, for example, after the latter had 'behaved very badly during the trial'.[16]

Told that Gröschner had been approached by Soviet agents who tried to co-opt him into kidnapping Skorzeny,[17] the CIC were sufficiently concerned to allow him to visit Darmstadt, where an uncensored letter in Skorzeny's hand was waiting for him in Frau Schröter's office. It contained details of a breakout plan, plus the whereabouts of certain SS contacts in Hanover who would assist him.

On 27 July, a car containing three US military policemen turned up at the prison gate. They had come to collect Otto Skorzeny, they said, whose services were imminently required at Nuremberg. They produced the requisite papers, entered the camp gatehouse and drove away with their 'prisoner'. That was the last official sighting of Otto Skorzeny for well over a year.[18] The American military policemen were in fact Germans, all former SS men.

The day before, Skorzeny had quite openly told the camp commandant – a former Luftwaffe colonel – of his plans, and had then composed a somewhat hypocritical and self-serving letter justifying his action to the 'Very Honourable Herr Freudell', chairman of the Denazification tribunal.[19]

Skorzeny later claimed the uniforms used by his rescuers were provided by the Americans.[20] The one thing tolerably certain is CIC and CIA collusion. Lieselotte Schröter was caught red-handed passing on Skorzeny's uncensored correspondence and suspended, but eight days later she was reinstated and allowed to go on as before. Jacob Gröschner's key role as a courier would have been difficult without CIC sponsorship. And a man as physically distinctive and indiscreet as Skorzeny could hardly have survived undetected for the best part of the next two years without the protection of an intelligence agency.

17

Apocalypse Soon

Preparing for World War III

Christmas-time 1951. There was a war on in Korea: what began as a localised conflict had morphed into a dangerous international conflagration. A United Nations force – mostly American – was backing South Korea; Communist China had entered on the side of the North, with support from the Kremlin. General Douglas MacArthur had recently been sacked after threatening a nuclear strike against Chinese supply lines, and the Soviet Union had successfully tested its first air-dropped atomic bomb.

Otto Skorzeny, now living in Madrid, was not alone in fearing that the worsening Korean situation would lead to a third world war – a war for which Western Europe was ill-prepared. Soviet forces remained strong – over two million men massed in the Eastern European satellite states. Western forces were weak and vulnerable. An embryonic NATO was hampered by peace-time US politics, shrinking the American military presence. In the event of a Soviet invasion, NATO would be overwhelmed.

It was in America's perceived military and political weakness that Skorzeny saw his opportunity for resurrecting Germany's fortunes and his own. A copy of his so-called Skorzeny Plan – derived from the thinking of former Nazi generals Heinz Guderian, Paul Hausser, Hasso von Manteuffel and Hans Speidel – had come into the possession of Major Robert Bieck, Assistant Air Attaché at the US embassy in Madrid. Bieck was a CIA spook and had made himself Skorzeny's close personal confidant. The Skorzeny Plan rapidly made its way to the CIA, where rumours about its existence were already causing anxiety.

For the past 18 months, reports had been coming in that Skorzeny was plotting a secret German army in exile. Some cited a figure of 200,000 men. Recruits were to be based and trained in the Fascist haven of Spain where, ostensibly, they would be used to blunt a Soviet incursion into Western Europe. Skorzeny was said to be under the protection of the Nazi-leaning Spanish Alto Estado Mayor (Army High General Staff), who were actively sponsoring his proposals. The Spanish generals involved were believed to have dubbed Skorzeny's nascent force 'Legión Carlos V' – an allusion to the all-conquering Habsburg emperor who had ruled most of Europe. General Franco was privy to the plan and, it was said, actively considering sending a high-level delegation to Chancellor Konrad Adenauer, West Germany's leader, to discuss it. Even the Church, in the person of Cardinal Giovanni Montini (who later became Pope Paul VI), was thought to be involved.

The squeaky-clean Adenauer was seriously worried by these rumours, and in January 1951 addressed his concerns to John McCloy, US High Commissioner in Germany and America's top civilian representative in Europe. McCloy immediately wrote to the US Secretary of State that Franco was 'utilizing Skorzeny, former Nazi intelligence chief, for purpose of organising military units in Spain'. Skorzeny was allegedly 'recruiting former Nazi officers and specialists among German refugees'. Adenauer was disturbed by the further information that Skorzeny's project was supported and encouraged by America. If this information became public, 'it would have most serious effects upon opinion, not only in Germany, but elsewhere in Western Europe, as obviously it would result in the creation of revived Nazi force'. McCloy couldn't believe that the scheme had US backing, and asked the Secretary of State for 'any information which could throw light on this report'.[1]

Accordingly, Major Bieck and the US embassy in Madrid had pulled out all the stops in cosying up to Skorzeny to find out more, and now they had a copy of his plan. Evidently, the Most Dangerous Man in Europe was living up to his name.

* * *

The fact that Skorzeny – a penniless fugitive – had made himself a trusted adviser to the Franco regime was remarkable, and somewhat suspicious.

One thing is certain: he didn't achieve it all by himself. On escaping from Darmstadt in July 1948, Skorzeny had followed the principle of hiding in plain sight. It was widely believed that he went straight to South America. But rather than fleeing the country immediately, he took refuge with the ultra-right-wing politician C. Christian Heinz in Wiesbaden in the American Zone.[2] With a police warrant out for his arrest,[3] Skorzeny adopted the first of a series of false identities. A forged ID card, issued in August 1947, identified him as 'Rolf Steinbauer', a journalist from Breslau. The photo showed a sober-suited and bespectacled individual bearing not a trace of the tell-tale scar.[4]

Even with a false ID, a man as conspicuous as Skorzeny could not have skulked about the American Zone without the continued collusion of the CIC and its legatee the CIA. Although they themselves regarded him as having no further intelligence value, the Russians were still extremely eager to get their hands on him. Since there were German officials quite willing to hand him over, and the US was keen to thwart the Soviets, American intelligence agents tried to keep tabs on him and help him as necessary. They were also interested in finding out whom he contacted and where he went.

And a pretty poor job they did of it. The CIC and CIA intelligence files during these months of 1949 are filled with little more than hearsay and newspaper clippings – some of the information palpably wrong and contradictory. In June 1949, sightings of Skorzeny were reported in Barcelona and Andalusia. Yet in April, the CIA heard he was quitting Spain for South America with papers supplied by Spanish state security.[5] The press reported him as heading for Argentina,[6] via Sweden (or was it Italy?) in order to make common cause with air aces Hans-Ulrich Rudel (his wartime friend) and Adolf Galland – both serving as military consultants to the Peronist regime. Confusingly, Skorzeny was also reported to have made a covert visit to Salzburg – where the Austrian authorities claimed he was working with the Nazi ratline organisation, Die Spinne. He was said to have crossed the border to Munich, where he hid in the home of a former girlfriend, Luise Preiss.[7] While there, he and Karl Radl were allegedly approached by the Syrian government, which tried to recruit them as military advisers.[8]

There was just one indisputable Skorzeny sighting during this period – on Saturday, 11 February 1950 in Paris. Skorzeny was recognised (because of his size and unmistakable scar) strolling down the Champs Elysées arm-in-arm with a girlfriend wearing a white scarf. The French Communist newspaper *Ce Soir* despatched a photographer, and an inflammatory exposé appeared in the next edition: 'Skorzeny, No. 1 killer of Hitler's personal guard ... is peacefully sipping a drink in a Champs Elysées café', it reported.[9]

The effect was electrifying. At first *Ce Soir* believed Skorzeny was simply visiting Paris to peddle a far-right journal, *Der Weg*, published in Buenos Aires and part-owned by Hans-Ulrich Rudel. But it soon emerged that Skorzeny had been in Paris for some time. A police raid on his boarding house in the suburb of St Germain en Laye failed to apprehend him, but found his belongings – including evidence of the memoir he was writing – which were immediately seized. It transpired that Skorzeny had struck an exclusive deal to serialise his story in *Le Figaro*, the leading right-wing daily. He had entered France under a false identity (on this occasion 'Rolf Steiner'). As he wasn't wanted for war crimes and was not on any caution list, the authorities shrugged their shoulders, and *Le Figaro* proceeded.

It was a mistake. France was politically polarised and combustible. The *Parti communiste français* (French Communist Party or PCF) had strong electoral support, and many observers believed it was only a matter of time before the PCF – at Stalin's bidding – brought the precarious Fourth Republic tumbling down. A notorious Nazi publishing his memoirs was therefore a highly provocative act. Riots erupted outside *Le Figaro*'s offices in the Champs Elysées. Communists fought running street battles with up to a thousand police officers. Lamp posts were uprooted, cafés smashed up, Claridge's found itself under siege and hundreds were injured and arrested.[10]

The Communists would have been still more incandescent had they known the full truth about Skorzeny's sojourn in Paris. He had been hiding out there for no less than eight months,* nonchalantly hammering away at the typewriter while the smoke and mirrors of the South America rumours kept attention diverted. He had been shielded by France's top *flic*, Pierre Bertaux, head of the Sûreté Nationale[†], and Gilbert Renault (nom de guerre, Colonel Rémy), Charles de Gaulle's wartime head of intelligence and post-war aide and confidant. This astonishing turn of events most likely came about through Skorzeny's friendship with Yeo-Thomas. But a number of sources credit it to Skorzeny's mistress – soon to be his next wife – the young and mysterious Ilse Lüthje, 'Gräfin' Finck von Finckenstein.

---

*　Skorzeny implies eight months (since May 1949, Visa Application CIAS). The eight-month stay is corroborated by Report No. NGF-787, CIAS.

†　In 1949, the French national police force, representing France's major cities but not Paris. It reported to the Ministry of the Interior.

How Skorzeny had first encountered Ilse Lüthje is – like much else surrounding her earlier life – obscure. During the early part of 1949, 'Rolf Steinbauer' had taken refuge as a lodger in a farm in the remote Bavarian hamlet of Sutten, near the Austrian border. It was useful as a base for clandestine meetings with Nazis (such as the former Hitler Youth number two Hartmann Lauterbacher), but also for filing his copious correspondence, practising his writing and taking his first steps in learning Spanish.[11] The farm tenant was Ilse Lüthje, with whom he immediately tumbled head over heels in love. So much so that he would soon begin proceedings to divorce Emmi, who had been reduced to eking out an existence as a clerk in a Salzburg trading emporium.[12] Having loyally supported her husband by providing covert courier services during his internment, she would now find herself abandoned along with nine-year-old Waltraut.

As an arch manipulator and myth-maker in her own right, Ilse Lüthje was an ideal match for Skorzeny. Born in 1918 in Kiel, she was intelligent, charming and attractive, with blue-grey eyes and blonde hair, which she habitually wore combed over her ears and secured in a bun.[13] She had sophisticated manners and spoke English, French and Spanish fluently. Ilse referred to herself as 'Gräfin' (countess) Finck von Finckenstein and claimed to be the niece of Hjalmar Schacht, former head of the Reichsbank and Economics Minister in the early Nazi regime.

Both of these claims were at best half-truths. Ilse had married Graf Adolf Finck von Finckenstein in 1940. The family estates had been lost to the USSR at the end of the war, leaving Adolf and Ilse bereft of a fortune. In 1949 – soon after meeting Skorzeny – she filed for divorce. The title of 'Countess' was therefore a courtesy one – but few questioned it. As for Hjalmar Schacht, Ilse wasn't actually a relative at all. She was, in fact, related to the younger daughter of a university friend of Schacht's father, who had taken Schacht in as a lodger while he was a student. Schacht regarded the friend's daughter as a 'foster sister' with whom he maintained a life-long relationship.[14] Schacht chose not to expose Ilse's fraudulent claim as she was well connected and later helped to advance his business interests.

Despite Skorzeny's past habit of treating women as disposable accessories, Ilse soon came to exercise a mesmeric grip over him. He readily deferred to her superior intellect, organising skill and business acumen. For her part, she tapped into Skorzeny's insatiable vitality and did all she could to exploit – to their mutual advantage – his international celebrity. Together, as a CIA analyst was later to observe, they formed a dangerous team: 'He is extremely active, possessed of tremendous vitality, and willing to try almost anything … She is apparently a clever and intelligent woman who will not stop until she has reached the financial and social position which she believes is her due.' Together, they were 'capable of considerable mischief'.[15] In this sense, Ilse would take over in Skorzeny's life where Karl Radl had left off.

It appears Ilse had worked for German intelligence during the war, and prior to it had spent time in Britain, allegedly on intelligence business.[16] Since the war, the CIA suspected that she had begun working for the French intelligence service, recording that '… the Countess maintains operational connections with the *Sûreté*. Her headquarters in Paris is at the Cabaret de Lido on the Champs Elysées. She has regular contacts with Pierre Bertaux, the former chief of the *Sûreté* in Paris, and Colonel Rémy, General de Gaulle's former G2.'[17] Indeed, Skorzeny and Ilse had actually lived with Bertaux for a time in 1949.[18]

What exactly was the nature of Ilse's relationship with Bertaux and Rémy? Was Wing Commander Yeo-Thomas – who, having been involved with the wartime French resistance at the highest level, returned to live in Paris during the late Forties, and is known to have resurrected his acquaintance with Skorzeny after the trial[19] – in some way involved? The answers are unavailable. The one thing that can be inferred about Skorzeny's relationship with the French intelligence community is that it was not built on the strength of his personal contact with it. The same source that fingered Ilse Finckenstein as the key to unlocking support from Bertaux and Rémy also pointed out that Skorzeny had become evasive and uncomfortable when probed by Radl on this very matter, as if he resented the fact he was not in control. Radl had been tipped off about the Ilse/Bertaux connection while in the pay of a rival French intelligence network, the SDECE (Service de Documentation Extérieure et de Contre-Espionnage). Skorzeny was so upset that his friend had been spying on him that for a while he broke off the relationship. It never fully recovered.[20]

* * *

The French and Americans were not the only ones motivated to shield Skorzeny from the Soviets. Skorzeny had fled to France to evade a Soviet kidnap attempt after a tip-off from Reinhard Gehlen, Skorzeny's collaborator during Operation *Scherhorn* and his rival for control of the Frontaufklärung system on the Eastern Front. Gehlen had contacted Skorzeny at the farm at Sutten. 'Gehlen was marvellous', Isla recalled. 'He and Otto respected each other very much… One of Gehlen's men brought a machine gun to the house and told Otto to be careful.'[21]

What Skorzeny really felt about the man he had once plotted to assassinate (as a potential rival for Allied favour in the last days of the war) is hard to fathom; but if there was any respect, it was far from mutual. Gehlen disliked and distrusted Skorzeny, and was wary of getting involved with him. Nevertheless, he was certainly keeping tabs on him, and may well have tipped him off about the Soviet kidnap attempt.

By 1949 Gehlen was already well on his way to becoming the Cold War's most legendary – and controversial – spymaster. Sacked by Hitler in April 1945, Gehlen had hidden the whole FHO intelligence archive in the Bavarian mountains, foreseeing that the region would fall into American hands. Once captured, he used this unique cache of operational information on Soviet military-industrial capabilities to dazzle his captors. Gehlen played his hand with great skill, and parlayed himself into a unique position in post-war geopolitics.

Gehlen was hardly unique in predicting that the West and the Soviet Union would be at loggerheads, with the German state as a bulwark against Bolshevism. But in peddling his wares to the Americans, he had several advantages, on top of his intelligence trove. His record was relatively clean, and he had been on the right side of the July Plot. Not only that, he was surrounded by a loyal, like-minded and experienced team. All this at a time when the American intelligence agencies were unequipped to penetrate the Iron Curtain. Gehlen manipulated the naive American intelligence establishment into making his off-the-shelf spy organisation – soon to be known as the Gehlen Organisation, or simply the Org – an indispensable European partner in the Cold War, on terms he himself dictated. At American taxpayers' expense, Gehlen rebuilt a civilian equivalent of the Frontaufklärung. 'Rusty', as the Americans initially dubbed the network, developed tentacles stretching from eastern Germany to the French occupation zone, to occupied Austria, Italy, and Soviet-controlled Poland and Romania, with only the most minimal supervision.[22]

Although he had carte blanche to employ whoever he wished, Gehlen had given undertakings not to use war criminals, but it is abundantly clear that he did so.[23] Of his 4,000 or so operatives by 1949, at least 100 came from an SS background, including some real shockers, such as Otto von Bolschwing (an associate of Adolf Eichmann), Horia Sima (the ex-Iron Guard leader) and Dr Emil Augsburg (responsible for massacres on the Eastern Front). This proved an operational error of judgement. Such people were susceptible to blackmail, and what appeared an expedient arrangement for covering an intelligence blackspot would soon become a backdoor by which Soviet intelligence penetrated the Western alliance.

By early 1949, around the time he renewed contact with Skorzeny, Gehlen was walking a political tightrope. The quasi-autonomous Adenauer regime was about to take control, and with the US Army subjected to swingeing budget cuts, its intelligence section was desperate to pass 'Rusty' to someone else. The CIA – now America's best-funded intelligence agency – was invited by Washington to take up the baton.

CIA chiefs were sceptical about the operational limitations of Gehlen's Org, which, while good at tactical field intelligence, lacked high-level assets in the Kremlin or Soviet military. They also expressed doubts about how reliable former German officers would be in promoting Atlanticist policies, as opposed to those of a resurgent nationalist Germany.[24]

Nonetheless, CIA Director Admiral Hillenkoetter signed a contract with Gehlen whose terms were hardly more rigorous than those he had enjoyed under G-2 management. The CIA believed the Org – or 'Zipper' as they called it – simply required reform and better monitoring. War with the Soviet Union was looking imminent, and this was no time to be building a new spy network from scratch. Gehlen was too important to the security of Western Europe for him to be sacked or gelded by the CIA.

They tried a number of ploys to restrain him. A CIA liaison centre was established at Pullach near Munich, but Gehlen soon succeeded in developing a very German agenda, and a nationalist one at that. Initially papered-over, the gap between what the Americans considered their global interest and what Gehlen considered Germany's would become painfully enlarged, but on one matter both remained highly collaborative: spying on the Russians. And that included keeping a watch on one of the Russians' principal targets, Otto Skorzeny.

Gehlen's estimate of Skorzeny's competence and usefulness as an intelligence asset was even lower than the CIA's. In February 1951, he advised the CIA 'to have nothing to do with him'.[25] Nevertheless, the Org was as determined as the CIA to keep Skorzeny under constant surveillance in case he, or his many diehard Nazi associates, created diplomatic embarrassment. The Skorzeny Plan of 1951 was only one such episode. And when need dictated it, Gehlen was not above cooperating discreetly with Skorzeny, who was able to fraternise with the Org through a raft of former SS operatives – precisely that category of people whom Gehlen had promised the CIA he would never employ.[26]

* * *

Rumbled in Paris in February 1950, Skorzeny and Ilse – the girl in the white scarf with whom he had been spotted – made their escape to Germany's Black

Forest. Skorzeny temporarily ditched his Steinbauer alias for that of 'Hans-Rudolf Frey', a bespectacled chemical industry manager.[27] The Black Forest was to be Skorzeny's secret German base over the next year or so.[28]

With France now out of bounds (the authorities being reluctant to risk more trouble with the Communists), Skorzeny's asylum options were slim. He was on a caution list and unlikely to be admitted to the UK or USA. Italy had a left-leaning regime which was unlikely to be sympathetic. Austria was out, due to the matter of three members of the Austrian resistance who had allegedly been eliminated by his commandos in the closing stages of the war; moreover, the Soviet-backed regime there would pass him straight to the Czech authorities. In Germany there was a warrant out for his arrest.[29]

Fear of being kidnapped or assassinated haunted him. He told a friend that since the war there had been no fewer than five attempts on his life.[30] Argentina, Paraguay and Bolivia (all right-wing authoritarian regimes) were possibilities. But they were geographically remote from Germany, where most of the contacts essential to Skorzeny's earning a living were located.

He desperately needed to supplement his limited financial means, largely at this time earned through journalism. Most of Skorzeny's personal assets had been seized after the war by the Russians, and despite some claims by the press, there was no stash of Nazi gold at his disposal.[31] Concerning a rumour about a cache of two million marks, an American diplomat commented that if Skorzeny had ever had it, he must have spent it: 'he is not financially comfortable and is actively trying to unfreeze the royalties on his recent book published in the United States. In France he has also had legal difficulties regarding the royalties which he has indicated he badly needs.'[32]

Franco's Spain was the one place that ticked all Skorzeny's boxes. Many leading German businessmen – Hjalmar Schacht being a prime example – were establishing themselves there, confident that their activities would be shielded from Allied interference. The Francoist elite were still ardent admirers of German military culture. Military heroes with an inconvenient past were welcomed with open arms. Over 10,000 Germans were there, many of them Nazi desperados living under minimal state supervision.[33]

Skorzeny moved to Madrid in September 1950; with few assets, little Spanish, no passport, and almost no contacts, the transition was difficult. His trump cards were a formidable reputation and Ilse, whose Spanish was infinitely better than his.[34] Within a few weeks, Skorzeny's back-slapping bonhomie and networking skills were paying dividends. One of his new friends was Edgar Smith, an American avionics expert working for the Spanish government. He and other friends were treated to sightseeing tours in Skorzeny's Borgward motor car.

Edgar Smith was a fellow engineer, but more importantly he was a well-connected American businessman who might be invaluable in promoting Skorzeny's interests in the States. Posing, in a rather transparent way, as 'Rolf O. S. Steinbauer', Skorzeny explained that he was a consultant industrial engineer working for the impressive-sounding Empresas Reunidas Comercio Exterior, and engaged in the development of domestic solar energy. He also claimed to hold some agencies for German businesses. He had an office at the fashionable Madrid address of Alcala 29, and a flat in the less salubrious Calle Lopez de Hoyas, about 15 minutes away by car. Smith was struck by the 'extremely moderate circumstances' in which Skorzeny and his mistress were living. Eventually, little by little, Skorzeny revealed to Smith his true identity, as the world-famous Liberator of Mussolini.[35]

During his early exile, he continued to live off his earnings as a writer and journalist. Toth Verlag, which first published his memoirs, *Secret Missions*, had paid him 30,000 Deutschmarks (about €50,000); the German magazine *Quick* a further 30,000 Deutschmarks for serialisation rights; and *Le Figaro* six million francs (about €160,000). By the time Skorzeny reached Madrid the proceeds from *Le Figaro* were almost exhausted, leaving him desperately short of money.[36] So much so that, on learning Smith would be returning to the States in mid-November 1950, Skorzeny begged him to act as his representative at E. P. Dutton & Co, his New York publisher. Skorzeny was anxious to funnel any royalties directly to himself, rather than through his French agent, whom he suspected of cheating him. Smith agreed, but the US government sequestered all the proceeds on the pretext that Skorzeny was a fugitive from justice.[37]

Smith did not doubt Skorzeny's sincerity in trying to build an engineering consultancy, but was sceptical of his ability to make a success of it. He considered Skorzeny 'extremely egotistical but not too intelligent' and 'felt that the brains required for any business he might engage in would be furnished by the Countess'. He was also unimpressed by Skorzeny's flights of fantasy. As the friendship deepened, Skorzeny began boasting to Smith that, at the end of the war, he had turned down an offer to fly 8 tonnes of gold to Argentina on behalf of some senior Nazi bankers. He had rejected the proposal because he preferred to face the music back home. He was, after all, a man of destiny and would one day become president of Germany. Not only that, he was on intimate terms with the Prince of Hesse, Hjalmar Schacht and Willi Messerschmitt.[38]

Some of these claims were actually true. Skorzeny *had* turned down an offer from Walther Funk, the Reichsbank president, to fly gold out of

Berchtesgaden. And he was indeed on good terms with Philipp von Hessen, Schacht and Messerschmitt. Before coming to Spain, Skorzeny had worked hard in Germany at building business relations. Among these was the Hesse connection. Skorzeny had met Prinz Philipp while both were in internment after the war.[39] Skorzeny's specific interest in him was his contacts book, including business connections which Skorzeny hoped to develop.[40]

One connection which Skorzeny worked on was with Otto Wolff's steel empire. Wolff had inherited his business at the age of 22 in 1940, and later forged a formidable reputation as a builder of relationships with the Soviet Union and arch-exponent of Ostpolitik', while also being an avowed Atlanticist. He saw nothing contradictory in these objectives: above all, he was a trader. During the war the Otto Wolff company, like most German steel-makers, had placed its resources at the service of the Third Reich. Wolff himself had worked for the Abwehr, one of his tasks being the brokering of precious metals acquired from dispossessed Jews and other enemies of the Reich. After the war, he and his company relied on funds squirrelled away in Spain and Portugal during early 1945.[41] Wolff saw Otto Skorzeny as a useful pair of hands in Madrid, having met him in Germany in 1951.[42]

Schacht, meanwhile, wanted to build a base for his financial interests – primarily banking – in the Iberian peninsula.

Willi Messerschmitt, having been imprisoned for two years for using slave labour, had regained control of his company in 1950. However, he was now prohibited – as were all Germans – from designing and manufacturing aircraft. Messerschmitt turned to prefabricated buildings, sewing machines and bubble cars, making covert trips to Switzerland, where he would draft designs for advanced jet fighters. All of this was part of an agenda he had cooked up with Skorzeny, with whom he spent a good deal of time in the early 1950s, some of it in Madrid.[43] The Americans were under no illusions about the sinister implications of this collaboration. The pair of them were plotting a production plant for military aircraft in Spain.

'This character Messerschmitt frankly worries me,' Major Robert Bieck informed his superiors. 'On the surface it would appear he and his organization arc working for the Spanish, but we know their capabilities toward aircraft production, and it seems entirely logical we will be having the German air industry recreated under our very noses.'[44]

---

*   Neue Ostpolitk: the Federal Republic's post-1969 policy of détente with the Eastern Bloc.

Messerschmitt eventually landed a contract with the Spanish government, and in 1952 began developing the HA 200 jet trainer for Hispano Aviación. What was particularly alarming to the Americans was Skorzeny's participation in the deal. It was an open secret that Skorzeny had for some time been dreaming up a German military strike-force based in Spain, as he unguardedly mentioned on a number of occasions to Edgar Smith.

Smith – who was acting as Skorzeny's unofficial minder on behalf of US intelligence – reported that Skorzeny had asked him 'to put him in touch with the proper US authorities' in the hope of assisting with 'a German group which he professed to control', whose purpose was to 'form a hard core of resistance in case of an invasion of Germany by the USSR'. To prevent these Germans being targeted by the Soviets, Skorzeny was 'anxious to get them organized so that in case of hostilities they could escape from Germany and organize as soon as possible to fight on behalf of the Allies'.[45]

In attempting to curry American support for his plan, in early 1951 Skorzeny was equally indiscreet with Captain Jere Whittington, a language student 'on secondment' to the military attaché in the US embassy, who reported that Skorzeny 'pretends to be fully occupied as an industrial engineer', but was 'much more enthusiastic' about his plans to train German troops 'and return them to Germany for use against the Russians'. Meanwhile, Skorzeny and Messerschmitt were plotting 'the physical transplanting of German industry to Spain'.[46]

Bieck, Whittington's successor as confidant, produced a long list of senior military figures and government figures with whom Skorzeny was linked – one of whom, Major-General Eduardo Iragorri, Minister of Air,[47] was instrumental in securing Messerschmitt permission to visit the Hispano-Suiza aviation manufacturing plant in March 1951. The same year, when a meeting between Skorzeny and Rudel in Lisbon was thwarted by a Portuguese government nervous about having two high-profile Nazis as its guests, Skorzeny complained to his 'friend', Spanish foreign minister Ramón Serrano Súñer, who promptly hauled the Portuguese ambassador in Madrid over the coals. The meeting went ahead at a cocktail reception organised by the Spanish embassy in Lisbon.[48]

Skorzeny's circle of acquaintances ranged from prominent writer and Falangist Victor de la Serna (who remained an intimate of Skorzeny until his death in 1958) to the powerful José Finat y Escriva de Romani, Conde de Mayalde, who had been Spanish ambassador to the Third Reich and was now in charge of the Spanish state security apparatus, albeit in a supervisory role.[49]

The social persona of Otto Skorzeny at this time was gregarious and pleasant. He greeted people with an engulfing bear hug, and loved to talk – especially reminiscing about the war and his own heroic part in it. Robert Bieck described Ilse, his 'alleged wife' (they didn't marry until March 1954), as 'very pretty and extremely well educated … but with very little sense of humour'; she ruled the household and the social environment to the extent that, if Skorzeny's indiscretion went too far, she would bring him up short. Both spoke English very well, with a British accent. Skorzeny liked good Scotch, and was 'very gentlemanly, in fact, almost Victorian in his chivalry'. Crucially, Bieck noted that Skorzeny 'would no doubt give anything to have some kind of a command in another war', although 'he doesn't seem too well informed on strategic matters'.[50]

By cultivating the American intelligence community as well as the Spanish military and government, Skorzeny was manoeuvring to play the honest broker between the Spanish and the Americans. He claimed that the Spanish were 'too proud' to ask for cooperation themselves, and would not join NATO, but were bewildered that America had not approached them.[51] Nervousness over striking a strategic accord with a quasi-Fascist pariah state might be one good reason for American reticence. Skorzeny surely exaggerated when he claimed the Spanish military were 'nearly desperate' to reach a bilateral agreement. But he was not wrong in principle.

His prediction would be proved right within the next two years: the temptation to close off the Iberian end of the Mediterranean to Soviet influence eventually proved too great for the Americans to resist. In September 1953 the two countries signed the Pact of Madrid, which enabled the US to build air and naval bases in Spain, in return for economic and military aid, thus ending Spain's long period of isolation.

* * *

So far, Skorzeny was playing his hand well. Besides his war record and charisma, his hand was stacked with aces, in the form of powerful German contacts who were of use to the Spanish regime and who would form the core of a fully fledged colony of industrial and military specialists, effectively exempt from Allied interference.

The prime example was panzer genius Heinz Guderian, with whom he had become acquainted during internment.[52] In certain right-wing circles, including the Spanish military clique, Guderian was a name to conjure with. His arrogant, maverick personality was no less a problem for the German

Federal Republic than it had been for Hitler. He embarrassed Bonn by publicly declaring that West Germany was defenceless against Soviet attack: NATO forces, he said, would need 100 German divisions.[53] Bonn considered Guderian 'highly unreliable and generally a bad character', and there were concerns about his connection with Skorzeny and his apparently American-approved scheme 'to receive and organize refugees in Spain in the event of a Russian attack upon Western Europe'.[54] Adenauer and his advisers might have been still more alarmed had they known of the other senior Wehrmacht and Waffen-SS figures who had secretly met Skorzeny in the Black Forest in summer 1950 – former generals Hasso von Manteuffel, Paul Hausser and Hans Speidel.[55]

In an early draft of his plan made at around that time, Skorzeny noted that when a 'new German Wehrmacht' was formed, Speidel – former chief of staff to Rommel and one of the inner circle of July plotters – would have 'the highest post' in it and would adopt the Skorzeny Plan.[56] Speidel's near martyrdom in 1944 set him up as the poster-boy 'Good German' in post-war West Germany. By 1951 he had a role in the fledgling Ministry of Defence, where he advised on the formation of the future Bundeswehr*. Adenauer and his aides might have been less enthusiastic about him had they known that, covertly, Speidel and his colleague, former Generaloberst Adolf Heusinger, were sounding out Skorzeny and monitoring with great interest the development of an alternative (and entirely illegal) 'secret' army.[57]

These eminent German militarists could tap into an increasingly powerful constituency: veterans' associations. Mostly made up of former officers and NCOs, they were mushrooming all over West Germany, thanks to the release from internment of nearly two million former servicemen. Their vociferous demands for rights and justice, against what they saw as the defamatory portrayal of their role in the war, created powerful resonance in Bonn. The outbreak of the Korean War galvanised the veterans' movement. The rearmament of Germany became a matter of urgency. Isolated communities of veterans acting at the coffee-shop level began to crystallise into regional and national organisations. Chief of these was the Verband deutscher Soldaten (League of German Soldiers), on whose executive committee were Guderian and Hermann-Bernhard Ramcke, known to Skorzeny as commander of 2. Fallschirmjägerdivision. Ex-Waffen-SS men set up their own organisation, Hilfsgemeinschaft Auf Gegenseitigkeit (HIAG, Mutual Aid Association of Former Waffen-SS Members), co-founded by Paul Hausser, with Otto Kumm as leader.

---

*   West German armed forces

These organisations intended to exploit their political clout by forging a new social contract with the Adenauer administration. *Gleichberechtigung* (equal rights) was their watchword. Skorzeny, who claimed to have made a pact with Guderian on this very principle, explained it as a demand that their opinion should be weighed equally with that of the Allies in determining the future government and defence of Germany, rather than being treated as 'second rate, dominated and vanquished soldiers'. Skorzeny would not, he said, collaborate with the Americans unless his comrades were given *Gleichberechtigung*.[58]

Some – mostly at the extreme end of the neo-Nazi spectrum – felt that Gleichberechtigung would never be forthcoming, and that they should throw in their lot with the Soviets. Skorzeny's friend Rudel typified this view, believing that if the Soviets invaded, they would 'treat the Germans relatively well'. The Bonn government would decamp abroad, and a Nazi organisation could spring to life.[59] Skorzeny, every bit as unrepentant a Nazi as Rudel, was rather more opportunistic. He was prepared to come to an arrangement with his political enemies, even July plotters (Speidel being a key example) if that was what it took to implement his plan for the salvation of Germany.

* * *

The Skorzeny Plan was fluid, subtly mutating with the perceived interests of whomever he was talking to.

While in the Black Forest in 1950 Skorzeny spoke of transferring 200,000 troops to Spain in the event of war, and claimed to have American support.[60] What he actually seems to have had in mind was a small rearguard force of seasoned combatants, stationed beyond the Pyrenees, who would form a training cadre for a bigger professional force, to be manned in the event of war by German refugees spilling across the Spanish border.[61]

Guderian and the other ex-generals steered Skorzeny to a meeting with Speidel, who was most likely to gain the ear of Bonn.[62] Speidel endorsed Skorzeny's blueprint, but within months an enormous row broke out between them which threatened to derail the whole process. In November 1950, Skorzeny found out that Speidel had told two Spanish officials (visiting at Skorzeny's behest to discuss the plan) that he had never had a meeting with Skorzeny, and had never endorsed his plan. They reproached Skorzeny for having misled them. Although Skorzeny surmised that Speidel had got cold feet at the thought of damaging his clean reputation,[63] in fact Speidel had given his endorsement on the strict understanding that it be kept absolutely confidential.[64]

Skorzeny was able to salvage his relationship with the Spanish General Staff by proving Speidel's involvement.[65] Restoring his lustre in Germany proved harder. He managed to talk Guderian round by hinting that his plan had French support. Not only was this untrue; he was actually banned from travelling through France. But Guderian tended to believe him – for the time being – because Skorzeny clearly possessed genuine French documentation, which he could only have obtained with the assistance of the Allied authorities.[66]

The row with Speidel, while having a comic opera aspect, brought to the surface the seething distrust between military cliques: Speidel represented the 'Good Germans' who had risked their lives trying to topple Hitler, while Skorzeny personified the Waffen-SS, which had remained fanatically loyal to the Führer and deemed the former general staff a hive of traitors.

Far from playing the emollient role the situation required, Skorzeny began a hate campaign in the pages of the conservative Madrid daily *ABC*, in which he was uncomplimentary about a number of former Nazi generals, but Speidel in particular, whom he accused of being a traitor.[67] An unseemly war of words ensued with Speidel's representative in Madrid, former Generalmajor Hans Dörr, another July plotter, who was well connected with the Spanish military establishment. Skorzeny suspected Dörr of being an American stooge who was ratting on his Spanish military friends.[68] Dörr in fact worked for the Gehlen Organisation, and the information he sent back did indeed make its way to the Americans.[69] Using information provided by the Org,[70] Dörr portrayed Skorzeny as a bounder who had taken credit for operations planned and led by others. Kurt Student chipped in, suggesting that *he* was the author of Operation *Eiche*, and that Skorzeny's role had been no more than that of a 'young boy with lots of courage and lots of initiative'.[71]

So livid was Skorzeny that he challenged Dörr to a duel. The feud then descended into farce, with Dörr suggesting that Skorzeny was not a real soldier at all but a 'punk', and Skorzeny saying he was going to 'slap' Dörr 'one of these days'. He tried to get Dörr thrown into jail, but nothing came of it.[72]

The Americans chose not to believe Dörr's allegations about Skorzeny, concluding that the old guard Prussian military aristocracy had ganged up on the 'upstart' for refusing to know his place.[73]

In Germany the feud triggered a furious debate over the patriotic merits of the July plotters. Somewhat reluctantly, Guderian, Manteuffel and Hausser backed Skorzeny's position. But misgivings about his relationship with the Americans were creeping in. Hausser was heard to opine that he was 'a pathologically ambitious fellow', who was 'undoubtedly planning some action of a highly undesirable nature'.[74]

In February 1951, Skorzeny went to Germany to meet his associates. According to a hatchet-job report by Gehlen (who opposed Skorzeny playing any significant role in German military reconstruction), it was a tour of double-dealing, in which Skorzeny attempted to set Guderian, Speidel and Hausser against each other.[75] In fact, the prime motive behind Skorzeny's trip was a tip-off that Speidel had hijacked the Skorzeny Plan and was collaborating with an alternative partner, former Oberst Albert Schnez, who had his own plans for a secret army.[76]

Skorzeny held a meeting with Schnez in Stuttgart. It went surprisingly well; while their plans for a secret army had been arrived at separately, on many points they were complementary. Schnez was both better organised and – as a former Wehrmacht transportation officer – less politically controversial than Skorzeny.[77] His idea was to recruit entire staffs of former officers from elite divisions of the Wehrmacht, quickly deployable in the event of an international incident. Schnez had acquired a list of 10,000 volunteers, 2,000 of whom had been inducted into his clandestine enterprise. The target was a force of 40,000.[78] A weakness in Schnez's well-oiled apparatus was his lack of an organisational base outside Germany, at which to muster in the event of a Soviet invasion. He had sounded out the Swiss, but without success.[79]

Enter Skorzeny. Speidel had done him an unintentional favour in alerting him to Schnez's existence. Skorzeny accepted that Schnez was an incomparably better organiser than he was himself, while Schnez appreciated Skorzeny's broad-brush approach and his high-level international contacts. Crucially, Skorzeny offered Spain as a location, a better one than the 'strategic mousetrap' of Switzerland.[80]

The strategic flaw in the Skorzeny Plan was that, in retreating from Germany, the secret army would have to pass through France. Spanish cooperation was conditional upon the Allies agreeing to it first. And this, despite Skorzeny's bluster, was far from assured. Without the nod from the Allies, the Skorzeny Plan was a non-starter.

Nevertheless, with Hausser present, Schnez agreed to fuse his forces with those of Skorzeny and to make Spain the zone where they would regroup.[81] One of the things Schnez particularly valued in Skorzeny was a shared interest in partisan activity and stay-behind operations. Schnez was close to at least two Nazi-connected undercover operations which were preparing for a partisan war against the Russians.

Gehlen, who disliked and distrusted Skorzeny, was nevertheless prepared to put money behind the plan. He would even recommend it to the American authorities as a stop-gap solution to the brewing military crisis in Germany. However, Gehlen had an ulterior agenda. Adenauer became aware of the secret army very shortly after Skorzeny's first meeting with Schnez in mid-February 1951, because Gehlen chose to tell him. Gehlen may have felt that with Schnez having sealed a pact with a loose cannon like Skorzeny, it was time to tip the wink to Bonn about the shadowy paramilitary force in their midst. Adenauer, mindful of the dangers of confrontation with veterans, ordered that no repressive action be taken and that Gehlen should confine himself to monitoring and supervising the secret organisation.[82] Gehlen interpreted this as requiring him to covertly support Schnez and his activities while undermining Skorzeny's standing.

The 'mature' Skorzeny Plan, which Major Robert Bieck presented to the CIA in December 1951,[83] had Schnez's fingerprints all over it. Skorzeny's proposals, in his own somewhat cryptic words, were:

1. The formation of a basic German cadre in Spain, made up of Army, Air and Naval personnel, which could at the same time be used as an organization to absorb the mass of active German forces, the withdrawal of which would have to be organized simultaneously. This latter group would be formed of soldiers, scientists and technicians of the highest quality.
2. The formation of European cadres which would involve the thorough investigation of all European youth prepared to make the sacrifice. This model European organization could be used later in case of war to go into action throughout European territory.
2a. Later on, with the inclusion of Spanish commando units, I would propose the creation of special sharpshooter cadres within the Spanish Army ...
3. I should also like to propose, emphasizing that Proposal 1 requires previous American authorization and subsequent aid ... that an organization be created for an orderly withdrawal from Germany. The seeds of such a group already exist. It would have to be brought into play only in the case of a catastrophe. Included in this group would be these active elements not already incorporated in other military organisms.[84]

Proposal 1 represented Legión Carlos V – the cadre that Skorzeny had sold to an enthusiastic Spanish military elite the previous year. Proposal 2 introduced Skorzeny's pet theme – a pan-European commando force – which he had been working up in the intervening period. It would include a sniper unit, of the type

Skorzeny had deployed with some success at Schwedt. Indeed, its commander and trainer was to be ex-Brandenburger Odo Willscher.[85] The main core of the commando force would be dedicated to sabotage and special operations, and Skorzeny went into considerable details about their objectives, for which 'volunteers must be recruited from all the nations of Europe' knowledgeable of their local terrain.[86] The nations he listed were essentially those of the Third Reich from which Skorzeny had drawn his Jagdverbände units. He had in mind committed anti-Communists – in other words, former Nazis.[87]

Skorzeny had spent much of summer 1951 cultivating the representatives of various shadowy paramilitary organisations – a number of them from behind the Iron Curtain – in a frenetic seven-week, 16,000-kilometre car trip taking him the length and breadth of Germany. It had been a barnstorming performance that also allowed him to patch up his relationship with the former generals (the 'weak sister' Speidel notwithstanding) and boost his business contacts (including those with Messerschmitt and Otto Wolff). He also lobbied on behalf of Joachim Peiper, making clemency for Peiper the price of his cooperation with the Americans.[88]

It is little wonder, therefore, that both the Allied High Commission and the Bonn government came to regard Otto Skorzeny as a man more interested in reversing the verdict of the last war than in fighting for the Allied cause in the next one.[89]

Skorzeny blithely believed he held a trump card that would ease his way towards top-level contacts in Washington – a vital prerequisite for his plan's implementation. In September 1951, shortly after his return from Germany, he told Bieck that he had evidence of a Soviet spy-ring that had successfully planted moles within the Bonn government and the Allied High Commission,[90] sufficiently highly placed to be able to report back to Moscow all important decisions made by the High Commission within 48 hours. If true, this was serious; Bieck promised to get high-level specialists onto the matter as soon as possible.

It soon transpired that the intelligence was not what it was cracked up to be. Gehlen, who was made party to it, was sceptical, not only on account of its unreliable source but because the reports handed to his agency were carbon copies – suggesting that Skorzeny was simultaneously peddling the material to a number of interested parties to maximise its value. Not only the CIA in Madrid but the West German security agency, the Bundesamt für Verfassungsschutz (BfV, or West German Security Agency), had also received the reports. Nevertheless, the material seemed sufficiently detailed and authentic to exclude outright fabrication.[91]

Closer investigation over the coming month uncovered a 'papermill' comprising former SS officers working in and around Hamburg (in the British zone) who had managed to suborn a few minor officials in the Bonn government. The information they were peddling was at best no better than 'the surmises that a reasonably competent journalist could get and make', concluded the CIA.[92] In a security operation involving MI6, the CIA, the CIC, the Gehlen Org and the BfV, the culprits were rounded up.

Skorzeny escaped scot-free – on the grounds that he was incapable of being an intelligence agent and must therefore have been duped into acting as salesman for the papermill. He had got off lightly, but the affair was an egregious error of judgement that damaged any credibility he had with the American intelligence community. From the point of view of the Skorzeny Plan, this was extremely unfortunate.

At this time, a new and improbable conspirator arrived on the scene, giving Skorzeny fresh hope. Father Konrad Simonsen Mackey, sometimes known as Conrado de Hamburgo, had personal access to the very highest echelons of the Vatican (including future pope Cardinal Montini) and the Francoist regime, indeed General Franco himself.[93] Simonsen had been chaplain to the Condor Legion in the Spanish Civil War, and since 1949 had been involved in facilitating Vatican 'ratlines' for Nazis escaping Europe.[94] In 1951 Simonsen was tasked with organising the Madrid chapter of the Verband deutscher Soldaten veterans' group, whose founder members included Guderian and Skorzeny.[95]

Realising that they were never going to gain American support for what was increasingly looking like a neo-Nazi army, Skorzeny and Simonsen began frantically repositioning the Legión Carlos V as simply 'a patriotic Christian and Catholic force' preparing to roll back Communist evil.[96] They were to act in partnership, Simonsen taking charge of the spiritual and ideological welfare of the unit, while Skorzeny (good Catholic boy that he was) dealt with technical and military matters. The idea gained traction in ultra-Catholic Spain, and discussions were held with General Muñoz Grandes (who had commanded the Spanish volunteer Blue Division on the Eastern Front) on the detail of a Hispano-German brigade.

By autumn 1952 it had become obvious that Skorzeny and Simonsen were flogging a dead horse. The Skorzeny Plan ultimately depended on American assent, money and arms, which were not forthcoming. A form of the plan, worked on by Schnez and tacitly backed by Gehlen, was considered by EUCOM[97] (at that time headed by Eisenhower) and rejected. At about the same time the Skorzeny version acquired by Bieck was reviewed by the CIA's Office of Special Operations. Its verdict was also negative.

Skorzeny later blamed the plan's failure on Speidel's slippery double-dealing.[98] Speidel certainly hadn't helped matters by blowing hot and cold, but neither did Skorzeny by picking a quarrel with him which polarised opinion among former servicemen. Speidel, aware of the damage to the rearmament cause, made attempts to patch up the quarrel, but a breathtakingly arrogant Skorzeny was having none of it.[99]

Above all, the Skorzeny Plan failed because its time had passed. By 1952 the geo-political balance had altered. The international situation had stabilised; the Korean War was in stalemate and nuclear confrontation seemed off the table. Adenauer and the Americans had apparently got what they wanted: agreement in principle to a rearmed Germany, which would be carefully integrated within a European-wide defence force, thereby cauterising any resurgent militarism.

Into this new détente Stalin dropped a bombshell – the so-called 'Stalin Note' of March 1952. It promised German reunification with almost no strings attached. The one precondition was that the German army should be neutral and enter into no alliance or coalition with its former enemies. The proposal was promptly dismissed by the Western powers as a gigantic bluff. But as a diplomatic manoeuvre it was indisputably astute. The West offered no possibility of reunification and the best it could put on the table was a 'sanitised' West German army firmly under US control.

The Stalin Note gained traction across German society, not least among Skorzeny's friends on the far right – like Rudel and Otto-Ernst Remer, now heading the Sozialistische Reichspartei Deutschlands (SRP) – who saw it as an opportunity for levering their way back into power. They were forestalled when Adenauer, with the Stalin Note as a bludgeon, was able to cajole the US into an agreement whereby, in return for voluntarily adding 40 German divisions to a European defence force, he greatly enhanced West Germany's sovereignty. The Bonn government stole the far right's clothes, passing a law that would allow former members of the Waffen-SS to join the new West German army, provided they were free of war crimes and below the rank of Oberst. This fulfilled one of the prime demands of HIAG.

* * *

In the end, almost all the principal actors in the Skorzeny Plan got more out of it than the man himself. Speidel went on to play a key role in building the

Bundeswehr and later commanded it. Heusinger became its Inspector General. Gehlen, meanwhile, was appointed head of the Federal Republic's first completely independent intelligence service, the Bundesnachrichtendienst (BND), in 1956. This marked final victory for the plotters of July 1944. Even Schnez came out smelling of roses, reactivated as a Generalmajor in the Bundeswehr.

Willi Messerschmitt initially settled in Spain. But by the end of the decade he was back in business constructing warplanes for the Germans – this time Fiat G91s and Lockheed F-104 Starfighters under licence.

Meantime, Franco and his generals profited from the new tide flowing through international affairs. The Pact of Madrid, a Spanish-American agreement signed in 1953, stopped short of the full bilateral military alliance the Franco regime sought with Washington, but not by much. Spain ended its precarious isolation and received billions of dollars of American military and economic aid in return for the right to construct and run military bases. The pact was symbolic in more ways than one, marking the moment when a somewhat sentimentalised historical admiration for German military culture – with its emphasis upon superior training, meticulous planning and tactical know-how – was finally displaced by the reality of American global power, and its inexhaustible capacity for technological innovation.

The Skorzeny Plan had failed but its chief architect was unbowed. He now turned to alternative political means for bringing about his vision of a regenerated Nazi Germany.

18

Neo-Nazis and Colonel Nasser

Skorzeny's Wilderness Years

On the evening of 14 January 1953 a security detail, working on the personal instructions of British Zone High Commissioner Sir Ivone Kirkpatrick, began rounding up a network of Nazi conspirators based in Hamburg and Düsseldorf. Over the next couple of days, the British arrested seven ringleaders who had been plotting to overthrow West Germany's democracy and replace it with an authoritarian regime.

Otto Skorzeny was not among those arrested, but two of his known associates were. One was Karl Kaufmann, former Gauleiter of Hamburg, who had provided 500 Hamburg dockers as Volkssturm reinforcements for Skorzeny's defence of Schwedt. The other, Werner Naumann, had been understudy to Josef Goebbels. Early in February 1945 he had accompanied Emil Stürtz, Gauleiter of Brandenburg, to Schwedt with an order to organise the assassination of Franz Oppenhoff, the 'turncoat' mayor of Aachen. Naumann had moved in exalted Nazi circles. The assassination order he carried with him came from Himmler or Hitler personally. One of the last escapees from the Führerbunker in May 1945, Naumann had fled to Argentina where he became an editor on the neo-Nazi periodical *Der Weg* and a colleague of Hans-Ulrich Rudel.

Much more worrying for British investigators, sifting through six lorryloads of confidential material confiscated from Naumann during the raid, was his current web of accomplices. Who was he *not* connected to in neo-Nazi circles? The papers revealed not only the usual diehard Nazi suspects, but an international network taking in Britain, France and Belgium, all of whom had helped to finance his organisation.

Although Adenauer threatened a treason trial for the arrested culprits, it never materialised, and the detainees were released. The German view was that the British had overegged the importance of the Naumann conspiracy.[1] However, it left behind questions about Naumann's connections with prominent politicians, such as Kurt Kiesinger, foreign affairs spokesman for Adenauer's Christian Democratic Union party. The Bonn political establishment was keen to bury the whole affair as quickly and quietly as possible.

One of the keys to unlocking the Naumann Circle – and Otto Skorzeny's connection with it – is the nebulous H. S. Lucht Company, an import/export concern set up shortly after the war by Herbert Lucht, former Wehrmacht propaganda officer. Werner Naumann was the general manager of the company. Whatever business was conducted by H. S. Lucht – and, as will become apparent, it had some useful connections with the Eastern Bloc, including an office in Leipzig – seems to have been orchestrated from the Luchts' villa at Lörickerstrasse-33, Büderich-Düsseldorf, into which Naumann was invited to move. The arrangement survived the death of Herbert Lucht in 1951; 'Nau-Nau' and Herbert's widow 'Slicki' Lucht continued to run the business between them. Unfortunately for Naumann, the BfV had penetrated his circle, and one of his closest confidants, former Hitler Youth leader Karl Bornemann, was working for MI6.[2]

Skorzeny's first post-war contact with Naumann took place towards the end of his epic seven-week motor tour through West Germany. He visited the Villa Lucht and met not only Naumann but Bornemann and Herbert Lucht. On the agenda was their shared interest in 'preventing German integration with the Western Powers … with the ultimate objective of re-establishing an authoritarian German State'.[3]

Whether cultivating industrial contacts, building a private army or political machination, Skorzeny's activities in Germany segued neatly into each other and had an underlying coherence. What in his megalomaniac way he imagined he was doing was shaping the destiny of Germany. He liked to think of himself as in control of the network which included Naumann's circle and Rudel's in Argentina. In fact, he was a mere fellow traveller.

More materially, Skorzeny cultivated businessmen such as Schacht, Messerschmitt, Wolff and Krupp – many with a compromising stake in the Nazi past – who needed to find new markets where their activities would be unrestricted. Skorzeny, who was in a position to help them in Spain, could count on their political sympathy, and that meant discreet funding not only for his secret army project but for a clandestine political programme, both of which were calculated to tilt Germany away from its current Atlanticism and towards more independent and assertive statehood.

The political approach that Skorzeny preferred was entryism – infiltration of existing political parties and organisms by like-minded individuals who would, over time, bend them towards the desired end. As early as October 1951 Skorzeny was to be found inviting sympathetic right-wing politicians to Madrid with a view to engaging them in his political programme. Unluckily for him, one such visitor – a German right-wing politician known to the CIA as 'Carotid' – was soon reporting to the Americans that Skorzeny hoped 'to form a rightist coalition movement in Western Germany' and was prepared to 'lend his support to the international ultra-rightist movement'.[4]

Skorzeny had also forged links with the Sozialistische Reichspartei Deutschlands (SRP), Germany's most successful radical right-wing movement of the post-war era. Its dynamic ingredient was its deputy chairman – the sinisterly charismatic Otto-Ernst Remer, Skorzeny's old comrade who had been instrumental in killing off the *Walküre* coup. The SRP's ideology was essentially National Socialism minus Adolf Hitler. Remer railed against what he called West Germany's 'shit democracy' and openly denied the Holocaust, claiming that the extermination camps were faked by the Americans to inflict guilt upon a humiliated and broken Germany. Remer did not much mind how he achieved his aims. If it meant embracing the Russians, then so be it.

Initially the Skorzeny–Rudel–Naumann axis enthusiastically supported the SRP and its policies. At its meeting at Stuttgart on 3 July 1952, Skorzeny and Rudel supplied the security detail. However, at a secret meeting held in August, it was decided that too close an association with the SRP might compromise their own entryist strategy by attracting unwelcome attention.[5] That was prescient. Remer soon found himself tried and convicted for defamatory remarks about the July plotters, and in October 1952, the SRP was outlawed. Remer, facing a prison sentence, fled the country.

Skorzeny's activities in West Germany were typical of the far right's machinations, in which cellular organisations interlocked with business interests, militarism, overt political parties and veterans' associations. In this web Skorzeny and Rudel were important but subsidiary participants. Naumann was the only one with sufficient political nous to make things happen. His interest in Skorzeny and Rudel was surely their iconic status as Nazi war heroes. Either name attached to one's organisation was like having a high-profile recruiting sergeant. Furthermore, their separate power bases in Spain and Argentina were invaluable in tapping international support and funding for causes back in Germany.[6]

How these links worked – and their protean nature – is illustrated by Skorzeny's relationship with Sir Oswald Mosley who, post-war, had become a tireless globetrotter, promoting the cause of international Fascism wherever he went. He and his wife, Lady Diana, were cultivated by Franco, and in Argentina they were soon on intimate terms with most of the senior staff of *Der Weg*, to which Mosley became a contributor. In June 1951 he met Naumann, whose subversive activities he agreed to finance. Following that meeting, Mosley's liaison officer in Italy – the French-Swiss Fascist Jean-Maurice Bauverd – resettled in Madrid. Skorzeny smoothed his way through Spanish officialdom and secured him a job at Agarthis International Features Service. Bauverd was subsequently retained by Skorzeny as a public relations consultant, to persuade European publications to print his articles.[7] Shortly thereafter Bauverd was involved in organising the second ESM* Fascist International at Toledo in September 1951. Among the many invitees were Skorzeny and Mosley.[8]

Mosley's Union Movement was generous with its funds, supporting Naumann's underground movement and various Nazi figures and their families, including Skorzeny's daughter, Waltraut.[9]

Skorzeny acquired an image as a criminal mastermind at the centre of an international web shuttling Nazi fugitives, arms and looted treasure, but the reality was more mundane. In October 1952, Mosley, Naumann and Skorzeny entered into a lengthy correspondence concerning cement prices and the export of cement to the Canary Islands.[10] It involved the mention of a 'Dr van Groede', the alias of René Lagrou, a former Waffen-SS officer living in Argentina who organised Peron-sponsored ratlines for Nazi refugees.[11] Given Lagrou's involvement, this correspondence might suggest a coded language where 'cement' meant 'Nazi refugees' or even 'Nazi gold', but the plain facts are that Skorzeny *was* a dealer in cement, and in the early 1950s there was a burgeoning demand for it in the Canary Isles as the tourist industry took off; and

*   European Social Movement

Skorzeny did later secure his cement deal.[12] Which is a warning not to read 'worldwide neo-Nazi conspiracy' into Skorzeny's every action.

What *can* be inferred is a species of masonic understanding; a loosely filamented self-help web where business and politics worked hand in glove, so long as the price was right. Sometimes politics segued into business. When Remer's political colleague Fritz Dorls – his career in tatters after the dissolution of the SRP and himself a wanted man – quit Germany, it was to Madrid he fled, there to take up a job at H.S. Lucht under the protection of its 'import/export manager', Otto Skorzeny.[13] At this time the company, still under Naumann's central control, seems to have discarded any pretensions to being a political cover in favour of 'pure' enterprise. Just how pure may be deduced from the fact that, a year later, the CIA became convinced that H.S. Lucht was illegally trafficking Spanish nickel to the Soviet Bloc.[14]

All of this is far removed from the popular image of Skorzeny as the criminal mastermind at the centre of a monolithic international organisation dedicated to shuttling Nazi fugitives, arms and looted treasure via carefully orchestrated 'ratlines'. Not that that prevented the press speculating, then and later.

In October 1950 London-based *Reynolds News* carried an item suggesting Skorzeny was the head of the European branch of Die Spinne and was engaged in smuggling Nazi desperados via Rome to Buenos Aires. Skorzeny sued, successfully. A CIA Covert Action Staff report in spring 1953 concluded that Skorzeny 'is an adventurer who is willing to join almost any cause provided it shows inherent possibilities of increasing his fame and fattening his pocketbook'.[15] In truth, Skorzeny was not embraced by Fascist organisations, 'because he is believed to be in close contact with French and American intelligence officers or military attachés, to whom he reports every bit of information he receives on Fascist activities'.[16] It didn't help that he never ceased to boast of his American connections.

On the other hand, he was a celebrity – and a highly gregarious one – who held court (much to Ilse's annoyance) to a ceaseless stream of visitors at his Madrid abode. And he was not that discriminating about whom he entertained or offered a helping hand to – even people he actively disliked, such as the ailing Schellenberg.[17] In time, he would play host to Mossad.

These indiscriminate encounters included some fairly unsavoury characters. With Eichmann he seems to have drawn the line. The arch-war criminal's trial and execution in Israel in 1961–62 inspired speculation about those who had helped him to evade justice in the first place. There was an allegation linking Skorzeny to Eichmann's flight from Austria in 1949.

Skorzeny issued a statement roundly denying both parts of the allegation: 'I, Otto Skorzeny, have never seen or known Mr Eichmann and therefore I could never help him to escape from Austria.'[18] The first part was untrue, and was contested by Eichmann himself; they had met at an SS-organised police conference in Berlin in 1945, in which both were keynote speakers, Skorzeny recounting the rescue of Mussolini, and Eichmann delivering a progress report on the Final Solution. Eichmann also claimed that Skorzeny had aided his escape by supplying some weapons and vehicles.

Nor did the relationship end there. Eichmann recalled that, while in Argentina in the mid-1950s, Skorzeny introduced him to a former Dutch Waffen-SS officer, Willem Sassen, who was working as a journalist and in need of a sensational story. It was Sassen who persuaded Eichmann to confess his role in the Holocaust, on guarantee of anonymity. This confession was what eventually put the gullible Eichmann's head in a noose. Thus Skorzeny not only aided Eichmann's escape but indirectly helped bring about his downfall.

* * *

On Gezira Island, Cairo, stands Egypt's tallest building: the Cairo Tower, the construction of which began in 1954. Its design evokes the pharaohs – suggesting the megalomaniac delusion of the building's sponsor, Egypt's then ruler, Gamal Abdel Nasser. But if it is a monument to anything it is to the folly of American foreign policy. The wily Nasser had Cairo Tower built as a deliberate snub to his would-be master-puppeteers in the CIA and State Department.

The CIA's station chief in Cairo was Miles Axe Copeland Jr, an early master at assisted regime-change in the Middle East. In Cairo in 1952, he played a part in the bloodless coup which brought to power the idealistic Free Officers Movement, whose deputy leader and architect of the coup, Lieutenant-Colonel Gamal Nasser, having abolished the monarchy, soon became president of the new republic of Egypt.[19]

While readily accepting American diplomatic assistance in his efforts to neutralise the British presence in the Canal Zone, Nasser determined not to become an American pawn, refusing point blank to accept an American military mission. When America gave him a 'personal gift' of $3m, Nasser finessed the gesture with a calculated snub, spending the money on the Cairo Tower. According to Copeland, American policy spun out of control in Egypt because third parties were used for the more politically sensitive aspects of

Dachau, 23 June 1947: Skorzeny reads the charge-sheet before his forthcoming war crimes trial. On the left is the prosecutor, Lieutenant-Colonel A. H. Rosenfeld, and in the shadows, Harry Thon, Rosenfeld's assistant. Skorzeny had good reason to believe the proceedings were stacked against him: in an earlier trial, Rosenfeld had played a key role in securing the conviction of both Dietrich and SS-Obersturmbannführer Jochen Peiper. (SZ Photo/Süddeutsche Zeitung Photo)

At the age of 29, Jochen Peiper was a highly decorated SS-Obersturmbannführer and the epitome of the dashing panzer commander. He spearheaded an armoured thrust during *Wacht am Rhein* that was initially successful, but his casual brutality en route was to haunt both him and Skorzeny later. (Bundesarchiv, Bild 183-R65485, Fotograf: Kurt Alber)

Wing Commander F.F.E. 'Tommy' Yeo-Thomas GC was one of Britain's most decorated secret agents. His testimony at the Skorzeny trial was pivotal in securing the defendants an unqualified acquittal. Yeo-Thomas befriended Skorzeny, may have offered him protection in Paris after the war, and visited him in Madrid in 1952. (Central Press/Getty)

Skorzeny during his trial. To his left is the former Kampfgruppe Y commander Walter Scherf. The most serious charges facing both were that they had participated in the massacre of over 80 American servicemen near Malmédy; and that they had opened fire on American soldiers while themselves kitted out with American jeeps, uniforms, papers, guns and ammunition. (Topfoto.co.uk)

Spring 1952, Madrid: The first official photograph of Skorzeny – sharp-suited, scar much in evidence, hair immaculately slicked back – in 7 years. This scoop was the work of Charles Foley, foreign editor of the *Daily Express*, who later wrote a biography that underpinned much of Skorzeny's post-war fame. (Express/Express/Getty)

The dictator Francisco Franco and his army minister, Agustín Muñoz Grandes, 1957. Both were important patrons of Skorzeny during his exile in Spain. They conditionally backed his secret army project. Ritterkreuz holder Muñoz Grandes had commanded a Spanish division during Hitler's Eastern campaign. (Bettmann/Getty)

Heinz Guderian, arch-practitioner of Blitzkrieg. After the war he remained a figure of towering influence, but his maverick personality was no less a problem to Chancellor Konrad Adenauer than it had been to Hitler. His assertion that West Germany needed to recruit 200,000 men to beat back the Russians was the basis of the Skorzeny Plan. (Bundesarchiv, Bild 101I-139-1112-17, Fotograf: Ludwig Knobloch)

Werner Naumann and Hans-Ulrich Rudel: Conspirators in arms. Both were closely connected to Skorzeny. Naumann (left), Hitler's titular heir, was at the centre of a plot to overthrow the Federal Republic in the early Fifties. Rudel, Nazi Germany's greatest air ace, shared Skorzeny's extremist views and was a lifelong friend. (Keystone/Hulton Archive/Getty)

Albert Schnez, seen here in 1968. Independently of Skorzeny, the former Oberst was building his own secret army to defend West Germany should Russia attack. But Skorzeny had the better contacts: Franco's generals and, so he said, American support. Schnez later became a Bundeswehr Generalleutnant. (Bundesarchiv, Bild 183-G1024-0205-007, Fotograf: o.Ang.)

Otto John was a July Plotter and, in the early Fifties, head of West Germany's counter-intelligence agency, the BfV. He was a hate figure to Skorzeny, who tried to frame him as a Soviet spy. John banned him from visiting Germany – an act highly damaging to Skorzeny's business interests. Then, in July 1954, John defected to East Berlin. (Paul Popper/Popperfoto/Getty)

Colonel Nasser and General Naguib after the Free Officers' coup. In 1953 Skorzeny visited 'revolutionary' Egypt in the hope of peddling arms and training Egyptian special forces. He succeeded in neither, but he did gain the friendship of Nasser, who was soon to depose Naguib and become President of Egypt himself. (Ronald Startup/Picture Post/Getty)

The Mufti relaxes with Himmler at the latter's field HQ in 1943. Amin al-Husseini was a pan-Arab nationalist with close links to Amt VI-S. After the war he settled in Egypt, where he was influential at all levels of government. Skorzeny hoped to exploit this leverage for his own political and commercial ends. (Bettmann/Getty)

Eva and Juan Peron, 1950. Skorzeny was certainly close to the dictator of Argentina. He visited the country and met Peron in 1954 as an ambassador for Krupp. But the idea that he slept with Peron's glamorous wife seems to be a myth, possibly cooked up by himself. The dates do not stack up. (Keystone-France/Gamma-Keystone via Getty)

Charles Haughey, three times future Taoiseach. As a young politician on the make, Haughey befriended Skorzeny and his wife. He was broadly supportive of their ambition to settle in Eire. The Skorzenys bought a 168-acre estate in Kildare, but their plan was thwarted by fears that they were outriders of a 'Nazi colony'. (Topfoto.co.uk)

Down but not out: Skorzeny in 1971, less than a year after a difficult operation to remove two tumours from the top of his spinal column. The operation initially left him paralysed from the waist downwards, but within months he was walking again, although he never regained his purposeful, athletic stride. (Len Trievnor/Daily Express/Getty)

Last things, July 1976: Ilse, his wife, and Waltraut, his daughter (right), attend the burial of Skorzeny's ashes at the family plot in Döbling Cemetery, Vienna. The cemetery contains many eminent Jewish intellectuals, but only one SS-Obersturmbannführer. Note Skorzeny's extensive medal collection on display to the left. (AP/REX/Shutterstock)

managing Nasser: for example, building up the notorious Mukhabarat security service. For this task Gehlen's Org was brought in, with its extensive contacts among former SS officers.[20] Allegedly, in 1953, Gehlen – having first consulted Allen Dulles – alighted upon Otto Skorzeny.

Copeland – reputedly a habitual liar[21] – later made grand claims about Skorzeny's involvement in Egypt, describing him with wild inaccuracy as 'a particular favourite of American Counter-Intelligence' who 'was believed to be especially suited, in temperament and personality, for getting along with Nasser'.[22] Skorzeny was supposedly persuaded by Hjalmar Schacht (former president of the Reichsbank), with CIA inducement, to take on the recruitment of hundreds of disreputable Nazis as advisers to Nasser's secret police and special forces. Most remarkable was former SS-Oberführer Oskar Dirlewanger – remarkable mainly because this sadistic mass-murderer had been dead since June 1945.[23] There is a scintilla of truth in Copeland's account, but for decades it has been obscured by the Skorzeny myth.

Skorzeny did visit Egypt twice in 1953, and did meet Nasser. Gehlen's Org was certainly operating there at the time, but there is no evidence the CIA, Gehlen or anyone in his Org recruited Skorzeny for a special mission in Egypt.[24] (Given Gehlen's opinion of Skorzeny's abilities, it would be extremely surprising if they had.) On the contrary, Skorzeny was probably in Egypt under his own steam, and exploited a rapport with certain members of the German mission residing in Cairo at that time. His purpose, ostensibly to build his legitimate business, was actually to dabble in arms trafficking and acquire a role as military adviser to the Egyptian armed forces.

What drew Skorzeny to Egypt in the first place was the presence there of a considerable German diaspora. At its core was the German Advisory Group, led by former SS-Brigadeführer Dr Wilhelm Voss – a friend of Göring, confidant of Himmler and probably the regime's most powerful industrialist – under whose aegis top-secret projects had been developed, from the Me 262 to Hitler's never-completed atomic bomb.[25] Voss was now the most powerful German presence in Egypt – far more so than the official ambassador.[26] The Voss mission had a military and economic remit, involving retraining the Egyptian army along German lines, equipping it with more sophisticated weaponry and eventually creating an Egyptian arms industry. Former Nazis were attractive recruits in Egypt not only on account of their professionalism but because of their visceral anti-Semitism. In the coming confrontation with Israel, such mercenaries could make reliable allies. German technical and military expertise was at a discount, and Egypt was not a wealthy state.

Skorzeny later told a British journalist that 'none of the 34 officials serving in the Egyptian Army as instructors is of outstanding renown', but that sweeping judgement may simply have been sour grapes.[27] And it certainly ignored former Luftwaffe paratrooper Major Gerhard Georg Mertins, who was to become one of the most successful international arms dealers of the later 20th century. Mertins was responsible for training an elite force of Egyptian paratroopers.

Post-war he made no bones about his radical right-wing politics, forging links with HIAG and backing the SRP.[28] In April 1953, Mertins and Voss helped Otto-Ernst Remer find safe haven in Cairo.[29]

Voss operated in a dubious triangular relationship with Joachim Hertslet, former manager of the Third Reich's foreign trade department, and his business partner Wilhelm Beissner, an accomplished SD-Ausland agent whose history included atrocities in Eastern Europe. Beissner had built a critically important personal relationship with Haj Amin Al-Husseini, former Grand Mufti of Jerusalem and Nazi collaborator. Al-Husseini was well known to Skorzeny, having been connected to Amt VI-S; he trained Arabs in intelligence work at The Hague A-Schule.[30] Post-war, Beissner had retained a close association with Al-Husseini, who was now nominally President of the All-Palestine Government at Gaza. This government existed only in principle, but gave the Egyptian army a pretext for continued occupation of the Gaza Strip. Al-Husseini was allowed to live in style, and was a useful contact for Beissner (facilitating, for example, Remer's escape to Egypt).[31] Al-Husseini's All-Palestine Government also provided Otto Skorzeny with yet another of his false identities, in the form of a passport dated 27 July 1952, in the name of 'Hanna Effendi Khoury', Palestinian national and engineer born at Haifa.

Despite vehement denials, then and later, that he had ever dabbled in arms trafficking, this was precisely what Skorzeny had in mind when he made two visits to Egypt in early 1953. Both were 'business trips' on his own initiative, not sponsored by the Egyptian government.[32] Nonetheless, Skorzeny angled for a position as military adviser to the irregular Egyptian special forces then being trained in the Nile Delta for an assault on the British-occupied Canal Zone – and perhaps aspired to become their commander.

Initial contact was set up between Hertslet and Skorzeny; Beissner then acted as Skorzeny's agent in Egypt, arranging the necessary paperwork for both trips with help from Al-Husseini.[33]

Skorzeny's first trip, in January 1953, lasted just over a fortnight. He found that his fame had preceded him. As in Madrid, there was a natural curiosity in Cairo, among even the high and mighty, to rub shoulders with celebrity. He was helped in this by some stage-managing by Beissner and Al-Husseini beforehand. Soon after arriving at his hotel, he was invited to meet the president, General Mohamed Naguib (who would remain in charge until his overthrow by his deputy, Nasser, a few months later). A parade was being held to celebrate the new regime, and Skorzeny was invited to share the dais along with the dignitaries. He sat between Naguib and Al-Husseini, a fact which probably spawned the rumours about his role in Egypt which would persist for decades. In fact, his place there had been arranged by Al-Husseini, and by Skorzeny's own admission, he 'exchanged approximately ten words' with Naguib; that and meeting Nasser, he claimed, was the totality of his involvement with the Egyptian government.[34]

Not everyone in Egypt who mattered was a fan of Skorzeny. The Egyptian Ministry of the Interior warned the Ministry of Foreign Affairs that Skorzeny was an 'American agent' – a self-inflicted wound that was to hamstring his plans right from the start, and no less damaging for being, in the strict sense, untrue.[35]

Skorzeny told NBC Television his visit to Egypt was 'merely to try to develop sales outlets for some Spanish firms', and denied that any were arms companies,[36] and yet he himself wrote to Nasser, offering to sell Egypt arms and ammunition.[37] Moreover, Skorzeny was not only representing a Spanish arms concern but actively promoting the sale of 51mm mortars and 20,000 rounds of compatible ammunition.[38] The arms manufacturer in question was probably Esperanza y Cia, a Basque-based specialist in mortars.[39] Skorzeny had been spotted by an American diplomat spending time with some friends at the Basque holiday resort of Lequeitio ('his tremendous figure and physique, tanned to a dark brown, stood out daily on the beach like a beacon in the night'):

> It was in fact Skorzeny bathing near us one day which apparently prompted my first friend to tell me that he understood the wartime German SS Colonel was involved in Spanish arms sales to Egypt. My friend gave as his source the son of Mr Castor de Uriarte, owner-manager of the Marquina arms firm of Esperanza y Cia, who told him that one day Skorzeny appeared at the factory and told his father that unless he was 'cut in' on the arms contract between Esperanza and the Egyptian Government he (Skorzeny) would use his influence with General Naguib to have the order cancelled.[40]

Skorzeny's offer to supply mortars and ammunition was refused by the Egyptians; what they actually wanted at the time was the versatile MG 42 machine gun. A tender was set up under the auspices of the army's chief supply officer, and among the (unsuccessful) offers received was one from Hertslet, to be sourced via Spain – presumably by Skorzeny.[41]

Skorzeny was no more successful in securing a military command, despite hawking his skills as a commando to anyone on the Egyptian General Staff who would listen. Although Egyptian officers at two commando training centres in the Nile Delta claimed that the overall direction of any guerrilla attack against the British would be carried out by Skorzeny himself,[42] the truth of this is hard to ascertain. Certainly the British were convinced that Skorzeny had given advice on partisan warfare,[43] and there was a rumour that he had scoped out the Canal Zone in a secret visit.[44] However, these freelance initiatives failed to gain traction because Skorzeny could not win over Voss, the man who had the ear of Egypt's rulers. Skorzeny's cordial overtures to senior German military advisers were rebuffed and he had little or no contact with them.[45]

There is little doubt the Germans in Egypt saw Skorzeny as an interloper who might jeopardise their position through reckless behaviour. Voss told the American military attaché that Skorzeny was 'a dangerous man'.[46] He feared that the Egyptians might attack the British in the Canal Zone, and he tried to persuade Naguib to incorporate the 'slightly trained and irresponsible' commandos into the regular army in order to control them.[47] A ruthless maverick like Skorzeny – desperate for a military command of some kind, but lacking a vested interest in the German Advisory Group – presented a threat.[48]

Skorzeny visited Egypt a second time in June 1953, the last stop on a series of long-haul flights taking in Pakistan, Angola and the Belgian Congo.[49] His business affairs in Spain were not going well, and he was considering setting up an alternative base in colonial Africa.

On 12 June he was granted a one-hour interview with Nasser himself,[50] who offered him a position as 'his personal economic and military advisor'. Realising that the job was a poisoned chalice, due to factionalism among the German military advisers, Skorzeny turned down the offer, along with a similar offer of military consultancy from the Syrian government at about the same time.[51] Or so he claimed. The US military attaché in Cairo believed that in fact Skorzeny was in Egypt to sell arms and promote himself as a guerrilla instructor, but failed in both quests. He had asked for '360 Egyptian Pounds a month', which was apparently too steep, and in any case, 'his presence in Egypt would be offensive to the Western Powers'; his mission a failure, 'he left Egypt disgruntled'.[52]

Before meeting Nasser, Skorzeny had visited Voss. When the other Germans protested to Voss about this, he told them he shared their view, and that 'he only accepted Skorzeny's request to see him in order to tell him to keep out of the commando business and to leave the country'.[53] Beissner – now Skorzeny's representative in Egypt – confirmed that Skorzeny had failed to sell a batch of MG 42 machine guns.[54]

In short, Skorzeny's visits to Egypt ended in failure. He was a politically controversial bit-part player in Egyptian politics who emerged bruised from the experience. When, in 1954, the London-based *Daily Sketch* alleged that he had trained Egyptian commandos for deployment against the British, Skorzeny sued the paper, winning £2,000 in damages plus a retraction.[55]

Alongside the arms dealing that never happened and the supposed commando training, it has been alleged Skorzeny later contributed to the reorganisation of Egypt's state security services along Gestapo lines, in collusion with the Gehlen Org and with approval from Allen Dulles.[56] The reorganisation did take place, but the man chosen for it in early 1954 was actually Joachim Deumling, a former Obersturmbannführer in the SD who had worked for the Gestapo. Deumling's engagement was handled, in great secrecy, by Voss. Given that the Ministry of the Interior had earlier called Skorzeny an 'American spy', it is highly unlikely it would then put him in charge of remodelling the state security services.[57]

What Skorzeny does appear to have done is forge an ongoing business association with Beissner, who in 1957 was reported to be working for the largest cement exporter in Egypt. Beissner's business activities extended as far afield as Algeria, Tunisia and Libya – thanks to excellent connections with the Egyptian intelligence service.[58] He himself was deeply engaged in arms trafficking, most notoriously for the brutal Front de Libération Nationale (FLN or National Liberation Front) in Algeria. A CIA report noted Beissner had 'plenty of money, never seems to do any work, and is in immediate contact with all questionable characters arriving in Egypt'.[59] There is no doubt that these 'questionable characters' – who made up much of the '*Kamaradenwerke*' of former Nazis, stretching from Europe and Africa to South America – continued to include Skorzeny.[60] However, when MI6 investigated allegations made in 1956 by the French Deputy Pierre André that Skorzeny himself had been 'the grand master of arms traffic for Algeria', it found no substantiation.[61] A more likely candidate for this shadowy role would be Otto-Ernst Remer, who remained in contact with both Beissner and Skorzeny, and who later collaborated with Beissner in trading arms for the FLN out of Damascus.

Skorzeny's dabbling in Egypt had come to nothing – a recurring theme in so many of his schemes since escaping from German custody in 1948. But he never gave up, and eventually luck started running his way.

19

The Years of Plenty

The year 1952 had been close to a financial disaster for Skorzeny. The fallout from his bogus intelligence-peddling activities the previous year damaged not only his reputation but his business. He became persona non grata in West Germany, and was unable to visit the country for a further two years,[1] effectively cutting his commercial lifeline. Had Ilse not stepped into the breach and maintained a punishing shuttle-schedule he would almost certainly have lost the invaluable business contacts he had built up.

Skorzeny had a theory about the reason for his exclusion. It centred specifically upon Otto John, head of the BfV – at that time, Bonn's home-grown security service and rival to Gehlen's American-sponsored Org. Skorzeny suspected that John was a Soviet mole, and alleged that he had been spying for the Soviet Union since early in the war, as part of the Rote Kapelle (Red Orchestra) spy ring, the most successful Soviet intelligence penetration of the war. Although the RSHA had rolled up much of Rote Kapelle during the war, the identities of some Soviet double agents were never uncovered. The fear post-war – mostly in right-wing German political circles, but shared by the occupying powers – was that these agents had penetrated institutions of the fledgling Federal Republic. Decrypting the stockpile of historic Rote Kapelle radio intercepts, therefore, might unmask a nest of traitors, of which none could be of more sensational interest than the head of West Germany's internal security apparatus.

As head of the BfV John was, to say the least, an improbable candidate. Matinée idol looks, sharp suits, a suave manner and abundant charm shielded a deeply troubled personality that found release in heavy drinking and serial womanising. More controversially, John was a hate figure for the German right, having helped secure the conviction of one of the Wehrmacht's most respected commanders, Generalfeldmarschall Erich von Manstein, for war crimes. He was widely considered a rank amateur in intelligence matters who owed his position not to merit but to the British bending Adenauer's ear. But none of this suggested he was a Soviet mole.

Nevertheless, Skorzeny's claim that he had proof (in the form of decrypts he'd obtained) of John being a traitor who had retained contact with the Russians was not something that his CIA contact, Robert Bieck, felt he could safely ignore. Bieck's colleagues took a more relaxed view. Judging Skorzeny's information 'an example of a ridiculous intelligence report', they passed it straight to John himself for his consideration. Six weeks later, Skorzeny was made aware of his visa prohibition.[2]

John's defection to East Berlin on 20 July 1954, shortly after attending a commemoration of the Stauffenberg plot, seemed to confirm Skorzeny's allegations. And yet his motives remain enigmatic to this day. Despite strenuous efforts, no conclusive evidence has emerged to prove him a member of Rote Kapelle.[3] John claimed later he was abducted by the KGB and forced to denounce Adenauer and the West, but the true reasons probably lie in a disturbed mental state. His job was on the line and he greatly feared the recrudescence of a Nazi state in the Federal Republic. He defected back to the West in December 1955. Arrested and imprisoned for treason, he spent three years behind bars and the rest of his life trying to clear his name.

Skorzeny's impudent denunciation probably played no more than a precipitatory role in his ban from Germany. Skorzeny the unrepentant Nazi, the political agitator, friend of Remer and the SRP, disciple of Naumann and member of his mysterious conspiratorial circle, might seem reasons enough for Otto John, with his uncompromising detestation of scheming old Nazis, to ban him.

It was a grave setback for the Skorzenys, who now weighed up equatorial Africa as an alternative to Spain. Skorzeny was tempted by a large farm in Angola, but the price tag of $40,000 was far too steep.[4] The relocation plan only really began to take off with the appearance of Hjalmar Schacht in Madrid, during May 1952.

After a consultancy stint taking in the ailing emergent economies of Iran, Indonesia and Egypt, Schacht had turned his attention to creating two private banks in Germany. Their specialism was export credit-finance for German businesses seeking to acquire a foothold in underdeveloped markets (such as the aforementioned ones Schacht had been 'doctoring'). This was the main reason for Schacht's visit to Madrid. The plan was to take over a 'sick' Spanish bank and, with the help of German and Spanish capital, put it back on its feet. When the Spanish authorities prevaricated – Schacht still being a controversial figure – the financial wizard turned his attention to Portugal, where he received a warmer reception from its head of state, Dr António Salazar.

The scene was now set for Schacht to open a credit-finance operation in Angola – at that time a Portuguese colony – with Skorzeny as his man on the spot. This segued neatly with a simultaneous offer by the Otto Wolff Steel Trust to make Skorzeny their local representative in Portuguese Africa.[5]

The deal never came off. The Skorzenys visited Central Africa in the summer of 1953 (part of the same tour that took in the failed Egyptian venture) and found it not at all to their liking.

It hardly mattered because business back in Madrid took a dramatic turn for the better when Skorzeny (or more probably Ilse, in all but name) landed his first big steel contract in 1952. The client was RENFE, the Spanish national railway network. The suppliers were a consortium of four of Germany's biggest steel-makers: Krupp, Otto Wolff, Forre Stahl and Klöckner & Co. This was a $6 million contract running over five years, and Skorzeny – as broker – was to receive a commission of $60,000, or 1 per cent (worth about $500,000 in today's money).[6]

There followed deals worth $3 million associated with Brown-Raymond-Walsh, the consortium charged with building American airbases in Spain following the bilateral 1953 Madrid Pact, for whom Skorzeny handled purchases and supplied steel.[7] By the end of the 1950s Skorzeny claimed to represent a portfolio of industries in Spain that included Stolberger Zinck of Aachen, a metallurgy specialist; Coutinho, Caro & Co, a steel manufacturer; Neunkirch and Buderus Iron Works; the steel-maker Hugo Stinnes; Bopp & Reuther, the Mannheim industrial valve specialist, and B&R's consortium salesforce organisation, Vereinigte Armaturen Company. Over eight years these contracts netted Skorzeny approximately $200,000, or $25,000 a year (the equivalent of over $200,000 a year now).[8]

By mid-1954 Skorzeny's lifestyle had undergone a remarkable transformation. His business had moved to new and more spacious premises on Calle Montera, just off Madrid's Gran Via, and he had acquired the services of a secretary, two stenographers and one further employee.[9] He took a second home in San Lorenzo de El Escorial and made frequent appearances in Madrid's Rotarian Club Velasquez, every inch the wealthy, self-confident businessman.[10] By 1957 he had upscaled to a more salubrious apartment at Castellón de la Plana 19.

Not all of Skorzeny's business ventures during this period were successful. In October 1954, the West German and American press were abuzz with speculation about a photograph of Skorzeny in Buenos Aires, consorting with President Juan Perón and a top-level representative from Krupp.

What he was doing, it subsequently emerged, was acting as brand ambassador for a beleaguered industrial conglomerate badly in need of new markets and a new orientation. Krupp had been one of Hitler's principal armourers. Its dynastic owner, Alfried Krupp, was a convicted war criminal[11] who had had his 12-year sentence overturned in 1951 as one of a number of conciliatory gestures aimed at getting the West German economy on its feet. Krupp was allowed to resume control of his company, but at a price. The core of the corporation – all Krupp's steel works and coal-mines within the Federal Republic – was to be forcibly sold off. Making a virtue of necessity, Krupp turned in a big way to engineering consultancy as a means of keeping its geologists, mining engineers, transport and logistics experts on the books.[12] One very attractive market to expand into – from the viewpoint of a German corporation with an undeniable Nazi pedigree – was Argentina, then booming thanks to the so-called 'South American Ruhr' just north of Buenos Aires.

American intelligence agencies had been tipped off about Skorzeny's imminent business trip on Krupp's behalf,[13] although they were wrongly informed that the purpose of his visit was 'munitions'; in fact it was to plan and build a locomotive and carriage factory.[14]

The puzzle, then and now, is why Skorzeny was chosen to represent Krupp at all. Although an engineer with a legitimate interest in a commission, it is likely that he was flown out to Buenos Aires as a piece of wartime exotica, calculated to impress the Naziphile Perón. The real negotiation was to be carried out by Krupp's top foreign-trade expert, Eckhard von Maltzahn.[15] Whatever the reason, it backfired. When informed of Skorzeny's presence in Buenos Aires, the local Krupp representative – concerned for the company's fragile reputation in West Germany and the United States – was forced to deny any foreknowledge and pointed the finger at Essen HQ. Essen admitted his presence in the trade delegation (they could hardly do otherwise) but rather lamely argued that Skorzeny was only there at the request of the Argentinians (which may have been trivially true).[16]

The PR blunder damaged Alfried Krupp's attempts to rehabilitate himself in Germany and the United States. The deal foundered – on account of

Argentinian bureaucratic incompetence, according to Skorzeny. His services were not requested by Krupp again.[17]

This ill-starred incident is the only firm evidence that Skorzeny ever met Perón (before his exile in September 1955 at any rate) or even visited Argentina. Which unfortunately puts paid to one of the most flamboyant elements of the Skorzeny legend: that he met, and slept with, Eva Perón. By the time Skorzeny arrived in Buenos Aires, Eva had been dead for over two years.

The 'Eva narrative' owed much to Oscar Bracker, a financial adviser on Perón's staff, who fabricated it in interviews with two of Skorzeny's biographers.[18] Skorzeny's own insinuations provided fuel; he claimed that, at the time when Eva was touring Europe in 1947, he'd heard a report 'that the only way she could be softened up was to get into bed with her when she was lonely. After being in prison for several months and not able to get near a woman, I replied that I was an ideal man to soften her up.'[19] At the time, Skorzeny was, of course, safely behind bars. What, apparently, provoked this erotic fantasy was the thought that she might be using her tour to 'improperly' stash Nazi gold from Argentina in Swiss numbered bank accounts.

* * *

By 1960, the ageing Lion of Gran Sasso was ten years into his self-imposed exile in Madrid. Otto Skorzeny was 52, greying, a little more jowly, a little less muscle-toned than he had been. No longer the magnetic wartime icon of a few years back, his celebrity nevertheless still drew the curious to his door, where they could expect a hearty welcome. Hard-earned success in business had mellowed him; the incessant meddler in German political affairs, the tireless amateur strategist conjuring up a phantom army of volunteer patriots, had dwindled insensibly into a Madrileño Rotarian given to incessantly retelling his wartime tales.

Skorzeny had all but turned his back on Germany. With the Bundeswehr issue settled, West Germans – now experiencing the seductive benefits of the Economic Miracle – were more preoccupied by consumerism – new cars, television sets and washing machines – than with hurling back the Red Menace. Skorzeny had been sinking into complacency, his thoughts turning more and more to retirement.

A CIA officer in the Madrid embassy, who knew Skorzeny socially, recalled that by 1960 he no longer had much to do with people in Spanish government circles:

Skorzeny has numerous friends among wealthy Spaniards and diplomats of various nationalities as well as with many American officers from the Base. He has an engaging personality, takes pains to be pleasant and courteous and is flatteringly attentive to women, although most of them find him to be excessively boring.

He is a proud and rather vain individual who loves to talk about his wartime experiences; however he does not force them on his audience nor does he monopolize the conversation, but is keenly interested in the opinions of others. In discussions it is evident that he is rather anti-Semitic and violently anti-Communist ...

He is well read, keeps up to date through subscription to West German and French periodicals and considers himself an authority and somewhat of a prophet on world politics. Apparently there is nothing he enjoys more than a bull session with a group of friends on politics and military strategy, both past and future. He indulges in these at great length until his wife is surfeited and turns him off.

Aside from the fact that there is no concrete evidence, it would be difficult to believe that he could be very much involved in intelligence activities because in this sphere he gives one the impression of a bull in a china shop. He talks too much and too vociferously in any group, regardless of privacy.[20]

The report also mentioned that he had bought property in the Balearic Islands and a farm in Ireland, where he now seemed to spend a great deal of his time. The Skorzenys' retirement plans had been greatly accelerated by the recession then gripping Spain. The construction industry was contracting, and the real estate business, into which they had been diversifying, dead in the water. Skorzeny had frankly confessed, at the time of making a US tourist visa application in March 1959, that his income for the previous two months had been precisely nothing.[21]

Expanding into new markets had been the key objective behind applying for the visa. It was not to happen, then or later – for mysterious reasons, never fully disclosed. In 1956, the State Department had declared Skorzeny persona non grata, even as a tourist, due to 'a large amount of unconfirmed reports of intelligence peddling, sale of Spanish arms to Egypt, formation of neo-Nazi groups and planning a coup d'état in Germany', although the CIA, having grilled him in Madrid, recommended that he be allowed a tourist visa; in their opinion 'it strains the imagination that Subject has designs which are prejudicial to the United States'.

However, Washington believed that Madrid was being naive.[22] His visa was denied.

The Skorzenys found the Republic of Ireland considerably more receptive. Shrewdly combining business acumen with her husband's bulging contacts book, Ilse had begun to move into international property development, with a stake in a housing scheme at Cannes. At that time Eire was widely viewed as a scenic backwater, but the country's strict neutrality, mother tongue and favourable geographical position made it the perfect location for a 'new Geneva'. If Ilse could only tempt the diplomatic community there, then business investment would surely follow.[23]

In buying and renovating a dilapidated country estate in Ireland, the Skorzenys not only acquired a highly desirable home for their retirement, but cashed in on a shrewd business investment should they choose to sell.

Skorzeny made use of his relationship with the recently bereaved Mrs Gladys Mooney, whose late husband, Dublin innkeeper Philip Mooney, had been one of the first people to befriend him in Madrid. Through her, he acquired his first tourist visa to the Republic in June 1957. Handily, Mrs Mooney's sister-in-law worked in the Department of External Affairs.[24]

When Mrs Mooney's celebrity guest arrived in Ireland he was treated to all the reverential curiosity he had come to expect in Madrid, Cairo and Buenos Aires. A special reception was held in his honour at the Country Club, Portmarnock, where (to quote the *Evening Press* of 6 June 1957) 'the ballroom was packed with representatives of various societies, professional men ... and, of course, several Teachtaí Dála* including Charlie Haughey and Paddy Burke'. There was much clicking of cameras and popping of flashbulbs as the great man, signing autographs all the while, foregrounded the landing of a helicopter – still an extreme rarity in those days – that had been brought in from an airshow near Dublin to fete the occasion.

Skorzeny and his stylish 'honey-blonde, blue-eyed' 'Prussian' wife attracted favourable comment in the Irish and British media, which made the Irish government's dilemma in dealing with their problematic visitor all the more acute. This was heightened when the visitor, after several years of vacationing, decided he wanted residency.

In June 1959, Ilse Skorzeny signed the title deeds of Martinstown House, a 168-acre estate in the Curragh, County Kildare, which she had acquired for £7,500 (a bargain even by the standards of the day), partly funded by royalties from Skorzeny's latest volume of memoirs, titled *Special Missions*. The

---

* Members of parliament

previous owner was Major Richard Turner, a pillar of the Anglo-Irish gentry whose passions in life were the turf and bagging game-birds; his neglected estate had not been properly farmed for years. The sprawling but homely eight-bedroom mansion, originally a hunting lodge built in the 1830s, was an architectural gem – the only known Irish commission of renowned English architect Decimus Burton.

Skorzeny, soon to be dubbed 'Scarface the quiet farmer' in the press,[25] vowed to restore the estate to its former glory, clearing the pheasant-friendly thickets and replacing them with pasture for cattle and sheep. Horses, he assured interested enquirers, would be joining the livestock, as they were 'a part of my wife's childhood'. Furniture arrived from the Madrid apartment, and even the current family car, a white Mercedes, was imported. In September 1959, Skorzeny's solicitor applied for residency, carefully avoiding any specific date on which it might be taken up.

This looked like adroit blackmail to the Irish authorities – and probably was. Having extracted five or six tourist visas to the country, the Skorzenys were now moving in and, in effect, upping the ante. Awkward questions were beginning to be raised in the Dáil* about Skorzeny's intentions and his murky past. In February 1960 the Minister for Justice, Oscar Traynor, was asked whether he would 'make certain that this man does not intend to use Ireland as a base for furthering any Nazi or neo-Nazi resurgent movements in Germany or anywhere else'. Traynor replied, 'As far as I am concerned, there is no evidence of any activities on the part of this individual such as suggested … Naturally, all these things will be taken into consideration on the granting of such a permit.'[26]

Traynor's reply glossed over the anguished interdepartmental debate about Skorzeny. As Minister for Justice – the ultimate authority on the matter – he could see no good reason for denying the application.[27] The Department of External Affairs took a more nuanced view; they were 'reluctant to authorise permanent residence', on the grounds that Skorzeny was 'a rather controversial character of some notoriety', whose presence could end up being used against the Irish government. The department pointed out 'the tendency in some quarters abroad, when occasion offers, to use any stick to beat us'. The Minister for External Affairs did not feel that the Irish owed Skorzeny any favours.[28]

However, overturning Skorzeny's record as 'a person of good character' – which he had been on the five occasions he had visited Ireland – proved beyond the powers of senior officials. So impenetrable was the case of Otto

* Irish parliament

Skorzeny, and so great their ignorance of the subject, that at one point they had consulted Charles Foley's laudatory biography, *Commando Extraordinary*, in a desperate effort to get on top of matters. After mugging up, an intelligence officer at the Department of Defence felt 'unable to ascertain why he is unacceptable in Britain, but presumably his blacklisting is a relic of the allegations that he committed war crimes'.[29]

In fact, in 1958 the remaining war crimes charge hanging over Skorzeny – concerning atrocities in Czechoslovakia – had been rescinded by Austria. As a token of its good faith, his home country at last issued him a passport.

That left the Irish government grappling with the nebulous rumours about Skorzeny's alleged involvement in arms-trafficking with the FLN. But it was a will o' the wisp that, on closer investigation, had to be discarded, as was the rumour linking Skorzeny to the flight of Eichmann, which bubbled to the surface after the latter's spectacular abduction by the Israelis in May 1960. There were a couple of rumours that Ireland's intelligence service missed. One was a proposed 1958 mission to kill Fidel Castro on behalf of Cuban dictator Fulgencio Batista (Skorzeny's Austrian passport had a visa for Cuba, but it was never stamped – suggesting at most an approach). They also seem to have overlooked an allegation that Skorzeny was assisting Moïse Tshombe's 1961 secession from the newly independent Democratic Republic of Congo by training some 30 Katangan rebels in Spain.[30]

Denying Skorzeny residency, absent any evidence against him, would go against the grain of Ireland's neutrality in international affairs; and the precedent of the Nazi-leaning founding father of the Republic, Éamon de Valera, who had not only sent a note of condolence to the German ambassador commiserating Hitler's death, but refused to hand over suspected Nazi war criminals to Allied custody.[31] On the other hand, Skorzeny had provoked a quite unnecessary international incident in May 1959 by changing flights at London en route for Dublin when he had been specifically advised by the Irish ambassador in Madrid to take an alternative route. Skorzeny, on landing in London, was refused permission to enter Britain and detained by immigration officials, who cross-examined him for over an hour; he was then escorted onto his connecting flight. Predictably, there was a flurry of media activity.

Adding to the Irish government's unease were signs that Ilse's scheme of encouraging wealthy foreigners to settle in Ireland was paying off. In January 1960 the *Daily Express* reported that Madame Ingrid Marbert, a millionairess friend of the Skorzenys who owned cosmetics businesses in Düsseldorf,

Vienna and Madrid, was planning to buy an estate in County Kildare. Later that year the *Sunday Independent* revealed that wealthy German filmmaker Kurt Linnebach had acquired a mansion in County Clare. Were these isolated individuals or outriders of a trend? And if the latter, who else might be visiting or even apply to join the colony? Rudel, Degrelle, Mosley?[32]

Meanwhile, Skorzeny, Ilse and Waltraut, now a young woman, became familiar figures in the Curragh community. They were frequently sighted in a well-known local hostelry, The Hideout, and Major Turner introduced them to the local country set, with whom they proved a hit.[33] Skorzeny was invited to give a talk on his wartime exploits at the Curragh army camp, but it was cancelled when government officials got wind of it.

Skorzeny's aloof attitude made an unfavourable impression on some locals. One recalled, 'I wouldn't say he was particularly friendly. He didn't really mix with local people. Skorzeny liked to drive up to Dublin and park his car outside the Gresham Hotel on O'Connell Street. He considered the parking fines of £1 to be good value.'[34] Former British Army officer H. M. S. 'Dusty' Miller, swapping wartime anecdotes with Skorzeny over dinner, mentioned Hitler's invasion of the Soviet Union and rather wished he hadn't. Surely, he observed naively, the Germans would have had a much easier campaign had they befriended the people they had conquered? 'At that there was silence. Then Skorzeny said, "It's not possible to make friends with them." Why, I asked? "Because they are sub-humans."'[35] Beneath the gregarious, sociable surface and the exciting war stories, Otto Skorzeny was ever the unreconstructed Nazi.

20

Ghosts of the Past

Skorzeny's Last Years

Not only did Otto Skorzeny never abandon Nazi ideology, but his past inevitably caught up with him from time to time. Sometimes it was little more than an embarrassment. On a few occasions, it had irreversible consequences for his and Ilse's future.

On 2 February 1963, the life Skorzeny had built for himself as an international Madrid-based businessman and genial Irish farmer was turned on its axis when the Austrian government – which had recently exonerated him from war crimes and provided him with a passport – suddenly issued a warrant for his arrest and began extradition proceedings.

The charge: that during spring 1944 he had tested an experimental 'poison gas gun' on inmates of Sachsenhausen concentration camp.

That, at any rate, was the story in the international press. Disinformation and muddle clouded the truth of the matter. Skorzeny issued a series of thunderous rebuttals from his Spanish home in Castellón de la Plana.[1] He dared the Austrian government to go ahead and try to extradite him. 'And if they find their stupid accusations don't stand up, they should shut up ... These so-called charges are complete rubbish. I am a pretty good engineer but as far as a poison gas pistol, that's ridiculous. Surely, that was a Russian invention. I was a soldier and an honourable one.'[2]

Skorzeny had a point. The poison gas 'pistol' was indeed a KGB assassination weapon. It worked by spraying cyanide into the victim's face; after death, the blood vessels relaxed, giving the impression of a heart attack. Two prominent Ukrainian nationalists (one of them Stepan Bandera) had died in this way during the late 1950s.

The arrest warrant against Skorzeny had been issued on the strength of documentary evidence produced by the Jewish community in Vienna. The originator was an Austrian Communist Party member, Dr Eduard Rabofsky, who enjoyed close relations with the East German regime. In May 1962 he had walked into Simon Wiesenthal's Jewish Documentation Centre in Vienna and volunteered the information.[3]

Wrapped up with the poison gun charge was a prior accusation that Skorzeny had participated in burning down two Viennese synagogues during Kristallnacht in November 1938.[4] This allegation originated with Tuviah Friedmann, a Nazi-hunter colleague of Wiesenthal, and first surfaced in July 1960, at a time when Skorzeny was also being accused of abetting the escape of Adolf Eichmann. In November 1938 Skorzeny had been an SS-unit commander, but his activities on Kristallnacht have never been pinned down conclusively. Given his position in the SS – which took part in the destruction alongside the SD and SA stormtroopers, on orders from Heydrich – it would be extraordinary if he were not involved in the pogrom in some way.

Ilse Skorzeny dismissed the poison pistol allegation as a trumped-up charge originating in Moscow: 'They resent the fact that my husband is a prosperous businessman … The Communists hate the fact that he is now successful. It is nearly 18 years since the end of the war, and they are still inventing charges against him.'[5] Ilse was right to point to Soviet disinformation; however, the background was not quite the black-and-white issue she claimed it to be.

The premise of the allegation was flawed; Skorzeny would be unlikely to concern himself with testing a non-military weapon. The silenced weapons in which he took a keen interest had a legitimate role in special operations; poison sprays did not.

On the other hand, there was the matter of the aconite-poisoned bullets which had become such an issue during Skorzeny's war crimes trial. Moreover, there *was* a connection between Skorzeny and the testing of secret weapons on Sachsenhausen inmates. SS-Sturmbannführer Dr Albert Widmann – who developed the bullets with encouragement from Skorzeny – had in the earlier part of the war been intimately involved in the T4 euthanasia programme, which murdered disabled patients. Head of Section VD-2 (Chemistry and Biology) of the Kriminaltechnisches Institut der Sicherheitspolizei, he had based a branch of his operations in Sachsenhausen, which was part of the same massive SS complex as Friedenthal. Sachsenhausen inmates provided the slave labour and specialist skills for, among other things, SS weapons workshops, and were also used as human guinea pigs. Besides devising noxious gases to accelerate the Final Solution, Widmann was a special weapons expert. Skorzeny rated him highly in this field – well above his own 'F' branch at Friedenthal, whose chief, Rudolf Lassig, was regarded as rather incompetent.

The purpose of Skorzeny's poison bullets was military: to silence with absolute certainty any enemy who compromised the secrecy of a special mission. While there is no evidence that they were ever used in combat, they were tested on the inmates of Sachsenhausen in Widmann's presence. The victims were 'five persons who had been sentenced to death'. Each victim 'received one shot in the upper part of the left thigh, while in a horizontal position'.[6] Three of the victims died in agony over the course of two hours.

Skorzeny enthusiastically endorsed these aconite bullets, but there is no concrete evidence of his presence during the experiments. There is, however, witness testimony. A prisoner, Ernst Jurasse, who had worked in Friedenthal's special weapons workshop, claimed that Skorzeny 'took prisoners as guinea pigs whenever he needed them'. Another, Paul Pasquier, said that he saw Skorzeny 'emerging from an SS firing range at Sachsenhausen. Skorzeny was armed and dressed in combat uniform, and had just been participating with other officers and NCOs in killing several prisoners – human experiments for sure. I was standing about 10 metres away, holding my broom very tightly.'[7] This is strongly suggestive, but is indirect rather than eyewitness evidence, and doesn't nail him.

It certainly doesn't tie him to the poison gas gun. However, the allegations of Skorzeny's involvement in crimes against humanity at Sachsenhausen – and the press stories which muddied the waters – provided fertile ground for Eastern Bloc intelligence agencies trying to forge a plausible case against him. To an extent, they succeeded. On 12 March 1963, the Irish Minister for Justice, Charlie Haughey, who nearly six years previously had feted Skorzeny's arrival at Portmarnock – was under pressure in parliament to bar Skorzeny from Ireland. He evaded the question.[8]

In the end, the Austrian government was forced into a humiliating climbdown. When queried by a US embassy officer, the Austrian ambassador in Madrid said that the whole affair 'had been a source of constant embarrassment for him and his Government, since there had never been any request for Skorzeny's extradition'.[9] It was all a big mix-up: the warrant had actually been for the arrest of a notorious swindler called Torko, and at the time of his extradition from Spain, 'some Spanish newspaper reports confused Torko with Skorzeny'. (Of course!) The mistake had been parroted by Austrian papers, 'causing the Government some embarrassment'. Skorzeny himself was partly to blame for the furore that followed, the ambassador continued, attracting attention with a press conference to deny the war charges, rather than keeping quiet. An investigation had been made into Skorzeny's alleged complicity in the murder of three members of the Austrian resistance in April 1945, but was too inconclusive to ask for extradition and no action was currently being planned against him.[10]

$$* * *$$

Skorzeny's career as a businessman continued to blossom. It is tempting to believe that his fortune was built on the illicit international arms trade. Certainly he dabbled in arms trafficking; but there is little to indicate he was a significant player. We know that it was his intention to sell arms to Nasser in the early 1950s; and also that he failed in his objective. We know that he was linked to arms sales to the FLN in the late 1950s; but that this was a false claim generated in the French press; the real trafficker was Skorzeny's associate Beissner – possibly aided by Remer.

One nugget of information that does tie Skorzeny to arms trafficking is his association with Gerhard Mertins and his Swiss registered company Merex. Mertins' skill in this department was of a quantum order higher than Skorzeny's. A scandal in the late 1960s – the so-called 'Pakiscam' – revealed that Mertins had been acting with the complicity of the West German government – and Gehlen's BND – in covertly peddling ex-Bundeswehr stock to Third World countries with dubious human rights records. All this with the compliance of Washington (at the time, Mertins was in the CIA's pay), which cynically reasoned that any self-denying ordinance in arming these regimes would be exploited by the even more unscrupulous Soviet Union.

An explicit link between Skorzeny, Mertins and arms dealing is to be found in the person of Fritz Schwend, a former SS procurement specialist who in the later stages of the war had been put in charge of Operation *Bernhard* – the RSHA-inspired Sterling counterfeiting scheme aimed at bringing down the Bank of England. After the war, Schwend fled to South

America, eventually settling in Peru; ostensibly as the manager of a Volkswagen garage in Lima, but in fact working for Peruvian and Bolivian military intelligence. Among the many exiled Nazis with whom he struck up a relationship were Rudel (close to Perón, and subsequently the Alfredo Stroessner dictatorship in Paraguay); Klaus Barbie, the so-called 'Butcher of Lyon',[11] in Bolivia; and Walter Rauff – a protagonist of the Final Solution, who had good connections in Chile. Given their excellent relationship with South American authoritarian regimes, it is easy to see why Mertins might wish to tap into Schwend's network as a conduit for selling arms.

After Schwend's death in 1980, extensive correspondence came to light linking him to Mertins and other Merex officials. In one letter dating to the late 1960s, Mertins tells Schwend that Skorzeny had contacted Merex in the hope of purchasing pistols, machine guns and tanks for a Peruvian general.[12] But the correspondence does not disclose whether Skorzeny's overture paid off.

The key intermediary in this Latin American-based Merex activity was Skorzeny's friend Rudel. It was to him that Merex turned, in summer 1966, when it sent a special envoy, former Wehrmacht Generalmajor Walter Drück – and wartime acquaintance of Rudel – on a fact-finding business trip around Latin America. Rudel was instrumental in introducing him not only to a variety of government and military officials useful in pushing the sale of surplus Bundeswehr stock, but to his well-connected expatriate friends. Among them were Schwend and Barbie (with both of whom he had formed a business venture called La Estrella a few years previously)[13], but also another Skorzeny contact, Willem Sassen, in Argentina. CIA informants had no difficulty in insinuating Skorzeny, despite his residing in distant Madrid, into this spider's web:

> Merex has also been in contact with Otto SKORZENY … for the past several years regarding the arms business. SKORZENY … claims to have excellent contacts in the General Staff of Peru. It has also been revealed that SKORZENY has been involved with RUDEL in a scheme to exploit sulphur deposits in a remote area of Bolivia.[14]

Similarly, there exists in the Skorzeny archive a letter of personal recommendation signed by the Paraguayan dictator Alfredo Stroessner and dated 3 April 1964. In it, Stroessner instructs his ambassador in Madrid to issue Skorzeny a Paraguayan passport immediately. The go-between who has whispered in Stroessner's ear is clearly Rudel. Skorzeny took up the offer (he admits it himself in *My Commando Operations*,[15] and the stamped passport still exists). However, the nature of the business concluded, if any, is unclear. It might have been an arms trade or, just as plausibly, machine tools and 'cement'.

* * *

Shortly after the Austrian extradition fiasco, there occurred one of the most extraordinary episodes in Skorzeny's career, in which he – a prominent, unrepentant Nazi – became involved with Mossad, the Nazis' nemesis.

It began with Egypt. By the early 1960s, Nasser, weary of his overbearing Soviet sponsors, had begun nurturing a new colony of German military advisers, prime among them a dozen rocket scientists at a site known as Factory 333, deep in the Egyptian desert. The aim was to create a missile deterrent against Israel, under the direction of Professor Eugen Sänger, one-time director of the Institute of Research on Jet Propulsion at Stuttgart. Two other factories were overseen by Willi Messerschmitt and engineer Ferdinand Brander with a view to developing an Egyptian jet fighter and building jet engines.[16] Unsurprisingly, the members of this new colony – at one point numbering about 500 Europeans – contained a hard core of ex-Nazi technicians unable to advance their careers in the Federal Republic.

These men, it seemed, were determined to rain down destruction on Israel. That, at any rate, was the conclusion of Mossad, which had infiltrated a double agent into the German colony. 'Wolfgang Lotz' (real name Ze'ev Gur-Arie),[17] plausibly blond and Aryan in appearance, had passed himself off – with help from Reinhard Gehlen – as a former Afrika Korps officer with SS connections. By mid-1962 Mossad had established that over 900 missiles were being built at Factory 333 and that there were plans to tip some of the warheads with radioactive material.

Israel responded with diplomacy. Prime Minister David Ben-Gurion and his consigliere, Shimon Peres, were keenly aware that a more robust approach might jeopardise the goodwill built up with West Germany over the past decade, not to mention the ready flow of economic and military aid to Tel Aviv.

Speaking softly was not something that appealed to Mossad's chief, Isser Harel, organiser of the abduction of Adolf Eichmann; Harel was determined to bring out a big stick. Trusting in his invulnerability to political pressure, he embarked on a covert campaign against the German scientists, known as Operation *Damocles*. Its main instrument was terror, involving letter bombs, targeted assassination and abduction.

Damocles backfired badly. Two of the Mossad agents involved were arrested in Switzerland and brought to trial. Seeking to deflect the coming adverse publicity, Harel launched a smear campaign in the Israeli press, publicising the activities of the German scientists and pointing the finger at the Bonn government as their sponsor. The result was hysteria in Israel, with rumours of deathrays and doomsday machines. The reality was mediocre missile technology incapable of destroying Israel, and Harel knew it. He was fired, and Ben-Gurion stepped down soon afterwards.

But the Egyptian rocket crisis remained undefused. Under the new leadership of General Meir Amit, Mossad tried alternative soft-power tactics for getting rid of the scientists. One of these involved recruiting Otto Skorzeny.

Simon Wiesenthal had discovered that the head of the security detail now guarding the German rocket scientists wherever they went – former SS-Unterscharführer Hermann Adolf Valentin[18] – had once served under Skorzeny. This could be Mossad's way in.

In April 1964, two top Mossad agents were assigned to the task. Rafi Eitan had led the team that kidnapped Eichmann, and his colleague, Avraham Ahituv, was Mossad's station chief in Germany.

Mossad inferred that the Skorzenys' childless marriage was open, and Eitan and Ahituv intended to exploit this situation to the full. Their plan was straightforward – a honey trap involving Ilse Skorzeny. A good-looking German-born Mossad agent, Raphi Medan, was sent to Dublin in July of that year to lure Ilse with the prospect of investment in a Bahamas property scheme in which she was then involved. Ilse found Medan attractive – as his controllers had intended – and it was not long before he was invited back to a party at Martinsdown House and eventually into Ilse's bed.[19] On the night of 7 September, while Medan and Ilse were in Madrid, Medan broke cover. He explained that a friend of his from the Israeli Defence Ministry wanted to meet her husband 'about a very important matter.' That 'friend' was Ahituv and the 'very important matter', it turned out at a meeting in a hotel lobby the following evening, was how Valentin's former commanding officer could put the screws on him.

Despite an obvious personal repugnance at engaging with someone of Skorzeny's reputation[20], Ahituv spent the best part of a week fleshing out the terms of the deal.

Skorzeny was a giant. A hulk of a man. He was obviously remarkably strong physically. On his left cheek was the well-known scar from his pictures, reaching his ear. He was partly deaf in that ear and asked me to sit on his right. Well dressed.

Two moments gave me a shock. Skorzeny was looking for a number in his phone book to give me. All of a sudden, he took a monocle out of his pocket and stuck it into his right eye socket. His appearance then, what with his bodily dimensions, the scar, and his aggressive gaze, made him look like the complete Nazi.

The second incident happened after our meeting, when we were dining together in a restaurant near his office. Suddenly someone came up to us, clicked his heels together loudly, and greeted him in German as 'My General'. Skorzeny told me that this was the owner of the restaurant and he used to be one of the top Nazis in those parts...[21]

I have no illusions about his original opinions. Even his wife didn't try to clear him. She only stressed that he played no part in the Holocaust...[22]

Ahituv and Skorzeny agreed to disagree over the latter's alleged involvement in setting fire to synagogues during Kristallnacht – and then got down to business. The Israeli deal was brutally pragmatic. If Skorzeny, using his influence with Valentin and his excessive contacts in Egypt, could persuade the rocket scientists to abandon their projects and move elsewhere, then the State of Israel would offer Skorzeny 'freedom from fear' – a writ guaranteeing lifetime immunity from retribution, signed by the Israeli Prime Minister, Levi Eshkol.[23]

Skorzeny, faced with this proposition – and fearing the alternative consequences – agreed to act on Mossad's behalf.[24] He met the German security chief, Valentin, who was initially reluctant, but Skorzeny eventually brought him round to Mossad's way of thinking. Who his other contacts were in Egypt at this time remains unknown, although Messerschmitt was likely to have been one of them.[25] In the following months, the Skorzeny connection brought Mossad 'priceless intelligence' detailing the scientists' blueprints – through the simple expedient of having Skorzeny invite them to his Madrid apartment, which Mossad had bugged.[26]

Sensational though this encounter was, an even more extraordinary claim has surfaced suggesting Skorzeny had been collaborating with Mossad as early as 1962, in a plot to assassinate Heinz Krug, the managing director of Intra-Handelsgesellschaft, a front company shipping missile parts to Egypt. On 11 September 1962 Krug stepped out of his Munich office never to be seen again. His car was found abandoned in Munich two days later. Unnamed former Mossad agents claimed that Krug had been taken to a forest outside the city and there shot. The murderer was Otto Skorzeny, assisted by three Mossad agents, who then destroyed the body with quicklime. It was alleged that Krug had summoned Skorzeny to Munich to advise him on security.[27] The claim has effectively been refuted. It now seems likely that Krug was abducted to Israel, exhaustively interrogated by Mossad and then executed, his body disposed of at sea by an Israeli military aircraft. Skorzeny was not in this particular loop.[28]

Even allowing for exaggeration, Skorzeny probably did play a part in dissuading his German contacts from staying on in Egypt. And yet there was no mass exodus. The fact that none of the German projects ever amounted to anything should be ascribed more to low-key diplomacy between Tel Aviv and Bonn than to any encounter between Skorzeny and Mossad – singular though that surely was.

* * *

Skorzeny's political activities, which had been on the fringe since the fall of the Third Reich, moved into the twilight zone during the 1960s. In the first half of the decade he was still hobnobbing with members of the former SRP and other far-right groups.[29] In 1966 he helped to set up Circulo Espagñol de Amigos de Europa,[30] a supposedly cultural organisation dedicated to Wagner. And a rather unlikely initiative for Skorzeny, never known for his musicality. The flimsy pretext was gradually discarded to reveal a neo-Fascist publishing house. Skorzeny's relationship with the organisation was at arm's-length, as a kind of godfather.

He made another characteristically mysterious foray onto the international stage in the late 1960s. On 22 May 1967 the *Daily Express* reported a scoop by its Madrid correspondent.[31] Spain was about to sign a major oil deal with Egypt involving the importation of newly discovered oil reserves near El-Alamein. A British oil company was alleged to be providing technical expertise – controversially, since Britain and Egypt had long since severed diplomatic relations. And who was at the centre of these negotiations, acting as an intermediary between his two 'personal friends' Nasser and Franco? None other than Otto Skorzeny. The deal was scuppered by Israel's Six Day War with Egypt, which broke out weeks after the article appeared. And yet, even at this late date, it seems the old mischief-making magic had not entirely evaporated.

In 1970, Skorzeny set up an Alicante-based 'security consultancy' known as Paladin, which functioned as a training centre and placement agency for mercenaries. Over the years, its clients came to include an eclectic bunch of authoritarian governments and terrorist organisations: the Greek military junta; the South African Bureau of State Security; Colonel Muammar Gaddafi; and Wadie Haddad, leader of the Popular Front for the Liberation of Palestine's armed wing.

Skorzeny's closeness to at least one of its international clients, the apartheid regime in South Africa, is well documented. While visiting in 1965 – ostensibly on a business trip – he met both the prime minister, Hendrik Verwoerd, and his successor, John Vorster.[32] One important contact in South Africa was former Wehrmacht Generalmajor Friedrich Wilhelm von Mellenthin (1904–97). Mellenthin had served in the North Africa campaign and later, in 1944, as chief of staff of 4. Panzerarmee and then Heeresgruppe G. Having lost everything, including his ancestral lands, to the Russians, in 1950 he resettled in South Africa. In 1954, he joined the newly established Trek Airways as sales director and shareholder. Ostensibly a commercial chartered airline, Trek – later Luxair/Luxavia – had close connections with the apartheid regime and undertook covert police and security operations.[33] In 1961 Mellenthin became director of Lufthansa in Africa. Ever the thoughtful strategist, in his spare time he was a keen advocate of a concept called SATO (South Atlantic Treaty Organisation), which was, in essence, a white-supremacist coalition of South Africa, Rhodesia and the Portuguese territories of Angola and Mozambique – linked to NATO and designed to contain the incipient chaos of post-colonial Black African states such as the Congo.[34]

More important, perhaps, was Skorzeny's continuing closeness to senior members of the Francoist regime. Paladin could never have existed on Spanish soil without the tacit collaboration of its government.

From the late 1960s onwards, the regime was under mounting threat from internal subversion, particularly from the Basque separatist movement *Euskadi ta Askatasuna* (ETA). Spain's security chief at the time, General Eduardo Blanco, probably used Paladin as a deniable killing machine for the elimination of political undesirables. The neo-Fascist Aldo Tisei later confessed that he had been recruited by Paladin to assassinate ETA members living in France.[35]

The real mover and shaker in Paladin was a former Goebbels acolyte, Gerhard Hartmut von Schubert, who had spent time in Argentina and Egypt training security personnel. It was one thing for Skorzeny to lend his name, his contacts and his enthusiasm to such a virulently anti-Red organisation, quite another for him to be actively involved in directing it. By 1970 he was a sick man.

* * *

The Austrian kerfuffle had done no lasting damage to Skorzeny's reputation in Francoist Spain, but it had put a severe brake on his retirement plans in Ireland. After 1963 his visits to Martinstown House became rare. Although Ilse continued to be a regular visitor to Ireland, Skorzeny made his last trip in 1969. By that time it was clear that he would never acquire residency.

The final blow had been a sensationalist, inaccurate article in the *San Francisco Examiner* and other papers on 7 February 1965, headlined 'An Escape Web for Top Nazis'. The article, supposedly sourced in Jerusalem, was published against a backdrop of agitation over the West German government's refusal to extend legislation for prosecuting Nazi war criminals still at large. It claimed to expose Skorzeny as the mastermind behind the neo-Nazi organisation Die Spinne. It was alleged that he harboured fugitive Nazi war criminals on his estate in Ireland.

This was a step too far for the Department of External Affairs. As the Irish Consul-General in San Francisco pointed out, the allegation 'tends to place us in an unfavourable light, particularly so far as American Jews are concerned. Such unfavourable references could influence general press comment, business prospects and trading relations, in all of which Jews play a prominent role in this country.'[36]

Martinstown House and its 168-acre estate were eventually sold in 1971, raising £80,000 – more than ten times the amount the Skorzenys had paid for it 12 years earlier. The new owner was an American named Tom Long, a former US Army captain who had fought on the opposite side to Skorzeny in the Battle of the Bulge.

* * *

On a Monday in November 1971, one of Otto Skorzeny's American neighbours in Madrid was greatly surprised to encounter his old friend shambling down the street. It had been well over a year since they had last met. That evening, the neighbour – who was covertly a CIA contract employee – was asked round for drinks at the Skorzenys' apartment, where he discovered why it had been so long. It was quite a harrowing story.[37]

For several years, Skorzeny had been complaining about intermittent soreness in his back. A succession of Spanish doctors had diagnosed it as no more than the onset of arthritis, and prescribed painkillers. The pain got worse and when he began to experience difficulty walking as well, Skorzeny was whisked to Clinica La Paz, where a German specialist identified a lump at the base of his skull. It was probably malignant, and would have to be operated upon immediately.

On 12 November 1970, Skorzeny was admitted to the University Clinic of Hamburg, in conditions of great secrecy. But as in most other episodes of Skorzeny's life, nothing could be accomplished without drama. Fearing attacks from anti-Nazi agitators and intrusions from Nazi-hunters while in hospital, Skorzeny took the precaution of surrounding himself with loyal former Friedenthal comrades – now grizzled 50-somethings – who lurked lugubriously in and around his private ward.

These were the somewhat intimidating circumstances in which his future chronicler, Charles Whiting, first encountered Skorzeny after being elaborately convoyed around the back streets of Hamburg to ensure anonymity. 'He lay in an upper storey hospital bed in a private room … guarded by his ex-commandos who had come from all over Western Europe to guard their old C.O. … He had lost a great deal of weight and had now turned a strange unhealthy light yellow colour. But his broad face … still had that challenging look that I remembered from the wartime photos.'[38]

The surgery was more fraught than the experts had imagined. Two tumours, one above the other, were embedded at the top of Skorzeny's spine. Even with then revolutionary microsurgery, it took over six hours for the surgeons to remove them. The operation left Skorzeny paralysed from the waist downwards.

With indomitable willpower and never-ending physiotherapy, Skorzeny coaxed himself – a couple of months post-operation – from a shuffle to his first hesitant, unassisted steps. By April 1971 he had discharged himself from hospital and was back in Madrid. He recovered his full muscular powers but not, it was clear to those who subsequently encountered him, his purposeful, athletic stride. He was thinner, his American neighbour reported, and 'a bit wobbly on his feet at times, but he was drinking his usual Scotch (albeit only one) … He was completely lucid and opinionated, as in the past', and soon resumed a conversation they had had 18 months previously about Skorzeny's latest pet project: the launch of a chartered airline service in Spain.[39]

In the circumstances, Skorzeny had made a remarkable recovery. But the prognosis was poor, especially given his refusal to submit to the cobalt radiation treatment advised by his clinic in Hamburg.[40] Outwardly life went on as before, Skorzeny attending the office in Calle Montera whenever possible and playing the role of indefatigable correspondent, polemicist and networker to the full. Cancer was never mentioned, although increasingly he was incapacitated by a mysterious 'cold' or 'flu'. A journalist who interviewed him for the 30th anniversary of the Gran Sasso raid recalled his still 'massive bulk', his 'mane of wavy white hair', and 'an amiable smile that masked a volcanic temperament'. The temper came to the fore whenever the interview touched upon doubts about the veracity of his own version of events. Perpetually in play was the trademark lit cigarette, or rather – the one small concession he seems to have made to his degenerative disease – a cigarette-holder bearing a glowing cigarillo.[41]

Almost to the end, Skorzeny continued to attract controversy – and even violence. In February 1975, after completing a live lunchtime interview at the Télévision Française 1 studio in Madrid – in which he had trotted out all the usual Nazi clichés about the Third Reich being brought down by a conspiracy of traitors[42] – Skorzeny was set upon by an assailant who tried to club him to the ground as he left the building. The man, named Legrand, was a former member of the French resistance. According to Skorzeny's own account of the event, he warded off all Legrand's blows with the aid of a briefcase. Other versions suggest the assailant, who was subsequently arrested, managed to draw blood.[43]

Other prominent members of the Waffen-SS men were less fortunate – most notoriously Joachim Peiper, whose body was found a little over a year later in the ruins of his burnt-out home in Traves, France. His assassins, believed to be former members of the resistance, were never caught. Even so, for the now frail and vulnerable Skorzeny the Télévision Française 1 incident served as a reminder that the charmed life he led in Madrid was increasingly under threat.

This creeping sense of insecurity dated back at least a decade to March 1965, when Skorzeny had acquired a firearms certificate after a tip-off that he was going to be door-stepped by Nazi-hunter Simon Wiesenthal. Some months later, that was exactly what happened.[44] There was a tense stand-off at the front door of Castellón de la Plana 19, with Skorzeny toting a loaded rifle and Wiesenthal trading threats. By the 1970s, the open-handed hospitality which had enabled his old comrade Werner Göttsch to look him up in the Madrid telephone directory had long gone. An increasingly suspicious Skorzeny was ex-directory, distributing his personal and business numbers only to those he felt he could trust.[45]

* * *

By late April 1975 Otto Skorzeny's world had shrunk to Room 338 of the Francisco Franco Sanitarium, where he was tended by the best oncological expertise Madrid could offer. Officially, he had a 'few pulmonary complications' and had come in for a rigorous check-up; the story was that he was on the mend. In truth, he was dying of lung cancer.

He lingered for several months. The once Herculean frame had shrivelled to a bag of bones, unrecognisable save for the many scars that covered his body. At about 5 pm on Saturday 5 July 1975, Otto Johann Bapt Anton Skorzeny, aged 67, died. His wife, Ilse, was at his bedside.

At 11.30 on the morning of the following Tuesday, the mortal remains of the former commando leader were cremated at the Almudena Cemetery, Madrid, in the presence of Ilse and Waltraut.[46] The Catholic funeral service preceding the cremation was distinguished less by the mass for the dead than by the glittering display of Skorzeny's military decorations and a profusion of Nazi salutes the like of which had scarcely been seen in public since the end of the war. Among the 225 condolence cards was one from Werner Hunke and another from Karl Radl.

A few days later, the urn containing Otto Skorzeny's ashes was returned to his homeland, and interred at Döbling Cemetery in the heart of upmarket Vienna, after a brief funeral oration by Hans-Ulrich Rudel. Among the 300 guests at the ceremony was former Luftwaffe pilot Oberst Walter Dahle, representing Karl Dönitz, last chief executive of the Third Reich.[47] In one sense it was entirely appropriate that Skorzeny should end up in his family burial plot, not far from the house in Peter-Jordan-Strasse. In another, it is fittingly controversial; at Döbling there are no other SS colonels among Vienna's dead elite, but a significant number of Jews.

Epilogue

Man and Myth

Otto Skorzeny died a very wealthy man. Purely in money terms, his bank accounts in Germany, Switzerland, Spain and the United States yielded $3 million – the equivalent of over $13 million today. With property and shares the estate was worth nearly six times as much, putting him on a par with some of Spain's wealthiest grandees of the era.[1]

This fortune was not derived solely from legitimate consultancy fees, shrewd property deals and stock-market investments. Ilse's itinerary in the years after her husband's death gives an insight into the complexity of his international dealings. Her various passports show that, in addition to 22 entries to the US, two to Rome and one to Bermuda, she visited Egypt, Saudi Arabia, Kuwait, Lebanon, Syria and Athens. Most of these places can hardly be described as holiday destinations or real estate prospects, but would be hot spots for arms trafficking.

Skorzeny was never a major player in the arms trade, but one didn't need to be in order to make a lot of money; and there is also no way of knowing how much Skorzeny made from the Paladin mercenary outfit. Myth and notoriety followed him almost as much in civilian life as it had during his career as Hitler's Commando.

Ultimately, the only certain conclusion about Otto Skorzeny is that he was a supremely accomplished social networker who successfully exploited his iconic martial reputation – and not only among those on the far right. As he told biographer Glenn Infield not long before his death: 'I have in mind to write one day a book about all the political and military persons I have met. You would be astonished to know all the names of kings, presidents of state, dictators, and field marshals I have known.'[2] It was true; and those he hadn't met, such as Adenauer, he had frequently corresponded with. How many other men could claim a personal connection with – to name just a few – Adolf Hitler, Benito Mussolini, Franco, Nasser, Perón and Charlie Haughey?

There were many things that Otto Skorzeny was not. He was no great thinker, his ideas being for the most part received and dogmatic, his opinions assertive rather than thoughtful. Charismatic and reckless in equal measure, the absence of organisational skills makes any suggestion of him being the brains behind an international neo-Nazi web like Die Spinne (assuming it ever existed) frankly laughable. He was an inept intriguer, and would have made a hopeless spy.

As a soldier Skorzeny was unswervingly loyal, unflinchingly courageous even, yet bereft of the qualities of a great general or even brigade commander. Without partners capable of balancing his deficiencies, he floundered. In his military career, these were Fölkersam and Radl; in civilian life, Ilse; in business, a long list of associates. The best that can be said is that he recognised his failings and sought to address them.

One thing Skorzeny did intimately understand was celebrity and how to exploit it. He discovered the knack almost by accident, when Goebbels handed him the microphone in the wake of Gran Sasso. He had many helpers along the way. The Third Reich's propaganda machine gave way after the war to the less disciplined, though hardly less uncritical, American media. Skorzeny was an affable and charming figure; he had a story to tell, and he told it with brio and an unblushing disregard for facts. His media traction was hugely enhanced by his trial; far from convicting him of war crimes, it turned Otto Skorzeny into a misunderstood hero. It was Rosenfeld, not Goebbels, who popularised the sobriquet 'The Most Dangerous Man in Europe'.

Simply being famous was not enough for a man of Skorzeny's ambition. Having moulded his legend, he then curated it. While still in captivity he began this monumental task by supplying American historians with his own self-glorifying version of the Gran Sasso raid. This supposedly confidential account soon leaked into the media, preparing the way for the comprehensive memoirs Skorzeny wrote during his first 18 months on the run.

How he found the time and concentration to tap out over 800 pages of typescript remains one of the minor mysteries of Skorzeny's life. The early manuscript still exists, although it has never been published in unexpurgated form.[3] This original draft was the foundation document for virtually everything autobiographical Skorzeny ever wrote. A cut-down version appeared as *Geheimkommando Skorzeny* ('Secret Commando Skorzeny'), published in 1950, which sold over 10,000 copies,[4] and the original document went on being freely plundered for subsequent books. In a post-war Germany awash with former combatants' memoirs, *Geheimkommando Skorzeny* stood out, and its serialisation in *Le Figaro* triggered riots in Paris. In West Germany, Skorzeny sold the serialisation rights to the illustrated magazine *Quick* and gained kudos with an excerpt on Operation *Greif* printed in *Der Spiegel*.[5]

No one would call Skorzeny a subtle stylist or a connoisseur of human nature; nevertheless, his 'Ripping Yarns' narrative, untroubled by excessive attention to detail or scrupulous accuracy, successfully conveyed the idea that he was but a loyal and politically naive soldier who had performed epic martial deeds.

That tone played well to a German audience, but wouldn't cut the mustard internationally, as Skorzeny soon discovered when a heavily abridged translation was published in the United States in 1951. The *New York Times* called it 'a curious book', and 'due to its author's intellectual and literary limitations, it is much less interesting than it might have been'; damningly, Skorzeny's 'loyalty to Hitler was absolute ... If a new Hitler appeared in Germany tomorrow, one feels after reading this book, Skorzeny would be on his side.'[6]

Nonetheless, the following spring, the *Daily Express* published a series of exclusive interviews with Skorzeny that were to cement his reputation with his Anglo-Saxon reading public. The man behind this scoop was Charles Foley, the paper's long-serving foreign editor and one of its most experienced hacks. Foley had tracked Skorzeny down to his Madrid lair by exploiting a mutual relationship with Hjalmar Schacht. Foley's heroic profile of Skorzeny was accompanied by the first official photograph of him since the war – sharp-suited, scar much in evidence, hair immaculately slicked back.

Foley's initial encounter with Skorzeny successfully conveys what is easily overlooked in the dry written record. That is: powerful charm blended with a hint of controlled menace, capable of mesmerising the most cynical observer. 'I wondered if he would come. Then a shadow darkened the alcove. A huge figure stood over the table.' Skorzeny had 'the air of a man-eating tiger on parole' and 'his mind was as sudden as a club'.[7] After a two-hour lunch, Foley was invited back for a soirée, during which Skorzeny became expansive and intimate about his adventures, showing off the watch[8] given to him by Mussolini: 'He took it off. A fine gold wristwatch and on the back the Napoleonic initial "M" with the date of the famous raid. He laughed.'[9]

Foley clearly admired Skorzeny, a fact which did not escape contemporary critics who described his subsequent biography as 'laudatory'. The sanitised narrative was very much Otto Skorzeny as he would wish us to see him, devoid of ethical complications.

Skorzeny's adventures were sandwiched between a preface written by Major-General Sir Robert Laycock, Earl Mountbatten's successor as Chief of Combined Operations, and a chapter featuring an interview with Colonel David Stirling, co-founder of the SAS. Both these illustrious commandos were beating the drum for a revival of Britain's special forces – criminally (as they saw it) wound down in the immediate aftermath of the war – in light of the growing Soviet menace. Stirling hoped that Foley's book would 'encourage our authorities to reconsider their attitude to special operations of the Skorzeny type'. In Stirling's view, 'there should be set up at the War Office a directorship of strategic assault personnel' which would 'straddle the watershed between the para-military operation carried out by troops in uniform and the political warfare which is conducted by civilian agents'.[10]

Although the War Office politely ignored his advice at the time, in later years this was precisely the route Stirling went down when he set up a private military consultancy – Watchguard International – which operated primarily in the Gulf States and Africa (no doubt with the tacit support of the British government). And of course, Stirling's original unit was revived and became a cornerstone of British special forces; in a sense, Skorzeny might be considered one of the honorary godfathers of the modern SAS.[11]

Laycock and Stirling were not the only members of Britain's wartime military elite to enthusiastically endorse Skorzeny's achievements, and his exploits were not only trumpeted in print.

During the war Skorzeny had proved a confident performer on radio and made several cameo appearances in *Die Deutsche Wochenschau*, the weekly newsreel, including coverage of Gran Sasso and footage of him with Hitler at the Wolfsschanze shortly after. He was naturally mediagenic, and in the post-war years dreamed of enshrining his military achievement in a motion picture. In November 1956 he was courted by the British film producer Roy Rich for the rights to his life story, but nothing came of it.[12] There were more promising dealings with Warwick Films, which specialised in swashbuckling war films and was run by Irving Allen and Albert R. 'Cubby' Broccoli. By January 1959 Skorzeny had written, off his own bat, a script of the Gran Sasso caper in which, as ever, he immodestly took all the credit. Naive and self-aggrandising though the script was (a section still exists), his British publisher, Robert Hale, thought it worth pitching to Harold Huth, then a director of Warwick Films.

A film based on Operation *Eiche* – provisionally entitled *Secret Mission* – would have been ideally suited to Warwick, especially with Skorzeny around to act as consultant. Skorzeny wanted Burt Lancaster to play the lead role. Four unexecuted film rights contracts to Skorzeny's memoirs were afterwards found in his possessions, evidence of how close the film came to being shot. The project foundered on financial disagreements. By 1959 Warwick Films was in serious difficulty, forced to restrict itself to one major film a year, and *Secret Mission* was not to be that film. Skorzeny only made matters worse with some uncalled-for location scouting in Italy, which resulted in a high-profile deportation by the authorities, who became convinced that he was hatching a coup d'état.[13]

More fruitful in promoting the legend were Skorzeny's forays into documentaries. Having made appearances on BBC radio and ITV television during 1958,[14] the following year he was included in a BBC TV series titled *Men of Action*, produced by Huw Wheldon and presented by wartime corps commander Lieutenant-General Sir Brian Horrocks. Despite the awkwardness of his SS pedigree, 'Lieutenant Colonel' Otto Skorzeny was a shoo-in as the subject of one of the five episodes. The other four featured Orde Wingate, Norwegian resistance fighter Odd Starheim, David Stirling, and the Royal Marines, which gives an idea of Skorzeny's perceived stature. The programme aired on 18 March 1959. It has not survived; like many other historic BBC broadcasts, the tape was apparently wiped. There is, however, at least one photograph of Brian Horrocks demonstrating to a BBC camera, with the aid of a scale model, how Skorzeny rescued Mussolini from the Campo Imperatore Hotel.[15]

Skorzeny's own legend limited his horizons. In filming the *Men in Action* episode, he had hoped to be present on location in London, but found his way barred by the Home Office Suspect Control List, on which he featured prominently as persona non grata. The British authorities never gave any official reason for their exclusion order, but they persistently enforced it. Nine months later, en route to Canada to appear on a TV quiz show, Skorzeny planned to visit England, and had to be advised against gratuitously 'twisting the British Lion's tail', which triggered a tirade from Skorzeny on British 'newspapers always telling lies' about him.[16] Canada also refused to admit him on account of his being 'still too pro-Hitler in his outlook', and his appearance on the show was cancelled.[17] The programme, whose theme was the Gran Sasso raid, went ahead, but with a substitute guest, Kurt Czasch, a former Fallschirmjäger captain. Skorzeny – having spurned all advice – was detained by British immigration authorities after landing at Heathrow. After being politely questioned for an hour (and later plied with whisky), he was escorted onto a flight for Dublin.

This apparently trivial episode in Skorzeny's life – at a time when media fixation on him was at its most intense – illustrates a broader truth about the man and the myth. The fact is that three major countries – with not a little hypocrisy on their part – had made it unambiguously clear that he was an unwelcome presence on their soil (while simultaneously acquiescing in the sale of his memoirs). This was a rebuff not only to his self-esteem but to his business interests. In preaching a gospel of unrepentant Nazism, holding open house for Nazi pariahs, and associating with the kind of people he did, Skorzeny was his own worst enemy. He had only himself to blame if the USA, Britain, Canada, France and Italy dropped the shutters whenever he felt inclined to visit them.

But the myth could not be thrust back into Pandora's Box. It eclipsed the man and took on a life of its own. The CIA eventually concluded there was more myth than man. In one of the last reports in his bulging file, dating to February 1969, they noted that his name was 'often used without permission by rebel groups to lend themselves importance', playing on his reputation and exaggerating it further.[18] By the early 1960s, both the CIA and Gehlen's Org were of the opinion that he was a tired old tiger with carious teeth, not worth the expense of surveillance, and certainly not to be trusted in intelligence matters.[19] There is little doubt that Soviet-sponsored intelligence agencies had reached the same conclusion.

Skorzeny was, as with so much else in his life, lucky with the timing of his death (if not in his manner of dying). Within months of passing away, his protector Francisco Franco also died, ushering in a more open, democratic society increasingly ill at ease with harbouring impenitent old Nazis.

Ilse was rather less blessed than her husband. On 27 December 2002, just short of her 85th birthday, she died alone and bankrupt in an old people's home at Tres Cantos, Madrid. The only guests at her funeral were the family of her last benefactor, a businessman to whom she had granted power of attorney in 1998. Over the years Ilse had squandered, or been cheated out of, the stupendous Skorzeny fortune.[20] She handed her benefactor the very last thing of value she owned: a comprehensive archive of Skorzeny memorabilia. For more than a decade the archive collected dust in an attic, its new owner fearful of the consequences of divulging its contents. It was eventually auctioned in 2011, and in the process became public.

* * *

The reputation of Otto Skorzeny weathered the years no better than its widowed custodian. From being regarded as the primary architect of Gran Sasso, he has for the most part been written off as a charlatan who stole the glory of others. And yet Skorzeny *was* a pivotal figure in the operation: in amassing and coordinating intelligence; in following through his special orders from Hitler at a time when others – particularly Student – were being increasingly distracted by military developments in Rome; in executing the mission – even if he did get lucky with the glider sequence, and even if he did disobey orders by forcing a crash-landing.

Admiral William McRaven – probably the world's foremost authority on special ops, theoretical and practical – concluded: 'Whether Skorzeny was a straphanger or the mastermind of the operation is inconsequential. Ultimately success resulted from Skorzeny's action at Gran Sasso and not from Mors's.'[21]

After Gran Sasso the changing balance of forces during World War II increasingly hindered Skorzeny's freedom of action. During Operation *Panzerfaust* he displayed characteristic coolness in action. *Greif* and the defence of Schwedt showed powers of tactical improvisation; even if he was not invariably the innovator, he certainly took executive responsibility. *Scherhorn*, on the other hand, illustrated how remarkably gullible he could be (although, to be fair, he was far from the only one duped).

It is sufficient for most soldiers to be judged on their wartime record. In Skorzeny's case there is the added dimension of his post-war celebrity. Some warriors of renown –Paddy Mayne and David Stirling come to mind – find that nothing in peacetime can match the intensity of wartime experience, and they disintegrate. Skorzeny, despite his volcanic temperament and low boredom threshold, was not one of those. He became a successful businessman, and not only in his black-market operations.

That kind of success was not, of course, his objective. By his own standards he was a failure, in that at no point in the post-war era did he manage to resurrect the legacy of the Führer and the Nazi state to which he remained wedded by a perverse sense of loyalty. Thank goodness for that, we may conclude. And yet, had world affairs mutated ever so subtly during the early part of the Korean War, Skorzeny's future might have been very different. And so might ours.

Glossary

Abwehr	German military intelligence service
AK	Armija Krawoja (Polish Home Army)
Allgemeine	general, as in Allgemeine-SS
Alpenfestung	'alpine fortess', or 'alpine redoubt', the Nazi fortified area, mainly in west Austria, in 1945
Amt	bureau or department
Amt VI	'Department 6', the redesignated name of SD-Ausland, the SS foreign political intelligence service
Anschluss	'union', Germany's annexation of Austria
Ausland	foreign, as in SD-Ausland
BfV	Bundesamt für Verfassungsschutz (West German Security Agency)
Blitzkrieg	'lightning war', manoeuvre warfare involving armoured units and close aircraft support, with the aim of achieving rapid breakthrough and encirclement of enemy
BND	Bundesnachrichtendienst (German Federal Intelligence Service)
Carabinieri	Italian gendarmerie
CIC	Counterintelligence Corps
Die Spinne	web of Nazi contacts post-war; literally 'the spider'
EK I	Eisernes Kreuz 1. Klasse (Iron Cross First Class)
EK II	Eisernes Kreuz 2. Klasse (Iron Cross Second Class)
FAK	Frontaufklärungskommando (front-line reconnaissance units)
Fallschirmjäger	paratrooper
FAT	Frontaufklärungstruppen (front-line reconnaissance troops)

FHO	Fremde Heere Ost (Foreign Armies East)
FLN	Front de Libération Nationale (Algeria)
Freikorps	German paramilitaries, usually veterans
Gauleiter	Nazi regional chief
Gestapo	Geheime Staatspolizei (State Secret Police)
Heeresgruppe	Army Group
Heimwehr	'Home Guard', the most powerful paramilitary organisation in Austria during the 1920s and early 1930s
Jagdeinsatz	Jagdverband company
Jagdverband Mitte	Skorzeny's elite commando unit, overwhelmingly German in composition
Jäger	hunter, commando
Jägerbataillon-502	the predecessor of Jagdverband Mitte
HIAG	Hilfsgemeinschaft Auf Gegenseitigkeit (Mutual Aid Association of Former Waffen-SS Members), Waffen-SS veterans association
Kampfgruppe	ad hoc battle unit up to brigade strength
KdK, K-Verbände	Kommando der Kleinkampfverbände der Kriegsmarine (German Navy special units)
KG	Luftwaffe special unit Kampfgeschwader
Kleinkrieg	'small war'; small scale or guerrilla warfare, including special ops
Kreisleiter	Nazi district chief
Kripo	Kriminalpolizei (Criminal Police/CID); together with the Gestapo was known as Sipo
MFIU	Mobile Field Interrogation Unit
Mil Amt	Militärisches Amt (Military Intelligence Department, formerly the Abwehr)
NKGB	Narodnyi Komissariat Gosudarstvennoy Bezopasnosti (People's Commissariat for State Security). From 1943 to 1946 was responsible for foreign and counter-intelligence, including the Fourth Directorate (sabotage behind enemy lines). Previously, this was the responsibility of the NKVD
NKVD	Narodnyi Komissariat Vnutrennikh Del (People's Commissariat for Internal Affairs). Name of Interior Ministry of the Soviet Union from 1934 to 1946

NSDAP	Nationalsozialistische Deutsche Arbeiterpartei (National Socialist German Workers' Party or 'Nazi Party')
OKH	Oberkommando des Heeres (Army high command)
OKW	Oberkommando der Wehrmacht (Wehrmacht high command)
Org	The Gehlen Organisation
OSS	(US) Office of Strategic Services
Ritterkreuz (des Eisernen Kreuzes)	Knight's Cross (of the Iron Cross)
RSHA	Reichssicherheitshauptamt (the Reich Main Security Office)
SA	Sturmabteilung ('Storm Detachment' – the 'Brown Shirts')
SD	Sicherheitsdienst (Security Service)
SHAEF	Supreme Headquarters Allied Expeditionary Force
Sipo	Sicherheitspolizei, name referring to the Gestapo and Kripo
SKA	the Schutzkorps Alpenland (Alpine Protection Corps)
SOE	(British) Special Operations Executive
Sonderkommando	special unit
SRP	Sozialistische Reichspartei Deutschlands (Socialist Reich Party)
SS	Schutzstaffel ('Protection Squadron')
Stavka	Soviet army high command
Streifkorps	Patrol units, Brandenburger formations
Territorialen Jagdverbände	Skorzeny's four territorial commando units, largely comprising foreign personnel, activated in autumn 1944
Totaleinsatz	Near suicide missions
UPA	Ukrayins'ka Povstans'ka Armiya (Ukrainian Insurgent Army)
Volksdeutsche	ethnic Germans outside the boundaries of the Reich
Volkssturm	Nazi mass militia, recruited from the civilian population
z.b.V.	zu besonderer Verwendung ('on special assignment')

Note on the Waffen-SS

Despite an increasingly gritty performance on the frontline – culminating in the battles of Kharkov and Kursk in 1943 and Normandy the following year – the ambiguous role of the Waffen-SS as a state police force in arms was something the military purists like Hausser and Steiner could never shake off. Nor would the Reichsführer-SS wish them to do so. As chief SS ideologue, Himmler saw no contradiction in the Waffen-SS acting as National Socialist standard-bearer behind the lines as well as at the front. What this meant in practice was that the Waffen-SS had to provide units (about 1,500 men) to assist special SS Einsatzgruppen police squads in the grisly task of exterminating Jews and partisans in the conquered hinterland of the East. Some were to take part in the barbaric suppression of the Warsaw ghetto revolt in 1943. Admittedly these units were drawn from penal brigades and included avowed criminals; nevertheless, they wore Waffen-SS insignia. By then Berger's ceaseless quest for new recruits had changed the organisation's composition out of all recognition to its original Aryan ideal. From the Polish campaign onwards one of the distinguishing marks of the Waffen-SS was its capacity for absorbing heavy losses without yielding in its objectives. In part due to fanatical courage, in part to the Wehrmacht's miserly attitude to supplying its units with armour, these heavy casualties became immeasurably more serious once the invasion of the Soviet Union bogged down into a war of attrition. By 1942, almost all of the first 54 SS officer cadets to graduate from the Bad Tölz school in 1934 had been killed in action. By 1944, the average life expectancy of a frontline Waffen-SS officer was two months.

With conventional replacements increasingly inadequate, Berger – by now an SS-Brigadeführer and Chef des SS-Hauptamtes Erbwesen für Waffen-SS (head of SS Main Office for Waffen-SS Affairs) – began to dismantle

Himmler's ideology and to cast his net outside the Reich's borders. First he trawled the so-called 'racial Germans' (Volksdeutsche), of whom there were over 1,500,000 fit for service in the Balkans and Baltic littoral. Many were ideologically sympathetic to National Socialism, or at any rate to the idea of Hitler winning the war. Then, more controversially, he turned to the so-called 'Germanic' countries – those who, though under occupation, were deemed sufficiently Nordic to count as part of the Aryan family: typically Norway, Denmark, Holland and Flemish Belgium. As early as autumn 1940 the SS-Hauptamt (Waffen-SS HQ) had set up a new training camp at Sennheim in Alsace for European volunteers. By spring 1941 it had created its first non-German SS division, the Wiking division, which performed efficiently under Steiner's command in the Eastern campaign.

The Belgian Rexist leader Leon Degrelle, who rose to SS-Standartenführer (colonel) in the Waffen-SS, was not wrong when he said: 'First there was the German, then the Germanic, and now there is the European Waffen-SS.' Progressively what emerged was a pan-European army – to which was eventually added a Muslim division – allied and motivated not so much by adherence to National Socialist ideology as by a common fear of what would happen if the 'Bolsheviks' finally took control. The bare statistics tell their own tale. By the end of the war, 920,000 men had served with the Waffen-SS – 57% of whom were non-German. Of this total 180,000 were killed, 400,000 wounded and 70,000 missing in action. This multinational, polyglot force was the well from which many – but by no means all – SS commando recruits were to be drawn.

Bibliography

Archive sources

ADN   Arrest of Dr Naumann and his Associates: draft white paper: FO 371/103913: National Archives, Kew

AIR   Reports, Interrogations, and Other Records Received from Various Allied Military Agencies, 1945–8: Otto Skorzeny: RG 238 M1270: National Archive and Records Administration, Washington, DC: available online at www.fold3.com/image/1/231903940 (retrieved 17 September 2017)

ASI   Arthur Scheidler, Final Interrogation Report No. 7, 11 July 1945: WD 208/4478: National Archive and Records Administration, Washington, DC

BAE   Biographical Report, August Eigruber, Office of US Chief of Counsel, 30 October 1945: RG 238/647749: National Archive and Records Administration, Washington, DC

BAM   Heeresgruppe Weichsel, T311/167, Bundesarchiv Militärarchiv, Freiburg

CIAN   CIA name file for Ludwig Nebel: 230/86/24/02, RC Box 110: National Archive and Records Administration, Washington, DC

CIAR   CIA name file for Karl Rudel (*sic*: Radl): 230/86/24/02, RC Box 110: National Archive and Records Administration, Washington, DC

CIAS   CIA name file for Otto Skorzeny: 230/86/24/04, RC Box 121/1 & 2: National Archive and Records Administration, Washington, DC

CIR   Consolidated Interrogation Report no. 4, The German Sabotage Service, Skorzeny and Radl, Headquarters US Forces European

Theater Interrogation Center, APO 655, 23 July 1945: KV
2/403: National Archives, Kew

CIW   Counter Intelligence Report on Werwolf, CIR 4/6, 31 May
1945: KV2/403: National Archives, Kew

FOI   Documents in CIA Freedom of Information Electronic Reading
Room: www.cia.gov/library/readingroom/ (retrieved 19
September 2017)

HAB   Security Service file on Hauptsturmführer Arno Besekow, alias
Felsmark: KV 2/1327: National Archives, Kew

HIR   Interrogation reports on Werner Hunke, 1945–6: CI-PIR/79,
CI-FIR/75: National Archive and Records Administration,
Washington, DC

INA   Department of External Affairs, Republic of Ireland: file P316
on Otto Rolf Skorzeny: Irish National Archives, Dublin

KRI   Interrogation of Karl Radl, 4 June 1945: KV 2/403: National
Archives, Kew

NARA   National Archives and Records Administration, Washington, DC

NBS   Interrogation of Otto Skorzeny by Lt Col Brookhart at
Nuremberg, 6 November 1945: Cornell University Law Library,
Ithaca, NY: available online at lawcollections.library.cornell.edu/
nuremberg/catalog/nur:01898 (retrieved 5 September 2017)

NNS   Interrogation of Otto Skorzeny by Colonel Howard A.
Brundage, Nürnberg, 11 September 1945, JAGD, OUSCC: RG
238 M1270: National Archive and Records Administration,
Washington, DC: available online at www.fold3.com/
image/231904039 (retrieved 5 September 2017)

NTP   Nuremberg Trial Proceedings: Avalon Project, Lillian Goldman
Law Library, Yale Law School: online archive: avalon.law.yale.
edu/subject_menus/imt.asp (retrieved 21 September 2017)

OSA   Otto Skorzeny Archive: privately owned collection of
miscellaneous papers (present owner anonymous): sale handled
by Alexander Historical Auctions, Chesapeake, MD: Sale 46
(various lots), 8 December 2011, viewable online at
www.alexautographs.com (retrieved 15 September 2017)

OSI   Skorzeny Preliminary Interrogation, 19 May 1945 by 307th
Counter Intelligence Corps Detachment, Headquarters Seventh
Army: KV2/403: National Archives, Kew

OSP   Privately owned collection of passports of Otto and Ilse
Skorzeny; owner anonymous, sale handled 20 May 2014 by

passport-collector.com: www.passport-collector.com/skorzenys-passports/ (retrieved 20 September 2017)

OST Records of the Skorzeny trial, July 1945–December 1948: RG 153: National Archive and Records Administration, Washington, DC

RFE Records of the Foreign Exchange Depository Group of the Office of the Finance Adviser, OMGUS, 1944–50, Liaison Visits: DN 1924, Category 940.32: National Archive and Records Administration, Washington, DC

RGI Interrogation of Georg Reinhold Gerhard, May–July 1946: RG 238 M1270: National Archive and Records Administration, Washington, DC

SSR SS record for Otto Skorzeny: Bundesarchiv, Berlin and National Archive and Records Administration, Washington, DC

SWT British intelligence, record of Otto Skorzeny wireless intercepts, KV 2/403 512702: National Archives, Kew

TNH Testimony of Nicholas [Miklós] Horthy before Major John J. Monigan, 27 August 1945, Wiesbaden, Germany. Record name: Horthy, Von Nicholaus. RG 238, Roll 0007: National Archive and Records Administration, Washington, DC

TWH Testimony of Dr Wilhelm Hoettl, taken at Nurnberg, Germany, 4 October 1945, 14.30 to 16.50, pp. 5–6. RG 238 M1270: National Archive and Records Administration, Washington, DC: available online at www.fold3.com/image/231902822 (retrieved 27 January 2018)

TWH2 Testimony of Wilhelm Hoettl, Nurnberg, Germany, 15.50 to 16.30, 5 November 1945, by Lt. Col. Smith Brookhart, p. 3. RG 238 M1270: National Archive and Records Administration, Washington, DC: available online at www.fold3.com/image/231903408 (retrieved 27 January 2018)

WGI Interrogation report on Girg, Walter: S022/USDIC/DC10, 22 January 1946, HQ Intelligence Center 6825 HQ & HQS Company: National Archive and Records Administration, Washington, DC

WGS Statement of Walter Girg, 15 September 1945: RG 238: National Archive and Records Administration, Washington, DC

Published sources

Alford, Kenneth and Theodore P. Savas, *Nazi Millionaires: The Allied Search for Hidden SS Gold* (Havertown, PA: Casemate, 2007).

Amicale d'Oranienburg-Sachsenhausen, *Sachso: Au coeur du système concentrationnaire nazi* (Paris: Terre Humaine/Poche, Librairie Plon, 1982).

Annussek, Greg, *Hitler's Raid to Save Mussolini* (Boston, MA: Da Capo, 2006).

Arad, Yitzhak, Israel Gutman and Abraham Margaliot (eds), *Documents on the Holocaust*, 8th edn, transl. Lea Ben Dor (Lincoln, NE: University of Nebraska Press, 1999).

Ballentin, Günther, *Die Zerstörung der Stadt Schwedt/Oder 1945* (self-published, 2006).

Bar-Zoha, Michael and Nissim Mishal, *Mossad: The Great Operations of Israel's Secret Service*, ebook edn (London: Biteback, 2012).

Bassett, Richard, *Hitler's Spy Chief: The Wilhelm Canaris Mystery*, ebook edn (London: Phoenix, 2010).

Bassiouni, M. Cherif, *Crimes Against Humanity: Historical Evolution and Contemporary Application* (Cambridge: Cambridge University Press, 2011).

Batty, Peter, *The House of Krupp: The Steel Dynasty that Armed the Nazis* (New York: Cooper Square Press, 2001).

Beevor, Antony, *Berlin: The Downfall, 1945* (London: Viking, 2002).

Beevor, Antony, *Ardennes 1944: Hitler's Last Gamble* (London: Viking, 2015).

Berger, Hagen, *Walter Girg, In Hitlers Auftrag hinter den feindlichen Linien* (Munich: Verlag für Wehrwissenschaften, 2014).

Bergman, Ronen, *Rise and Kill First: The Secret History of Israel's Targeted Assassinations* (New York: Random House, 2018).

Bergström, Christer, *The Ardennes 1944–1945: Hitler's Winter Offensive* (Oxford: Casemate, 2014).

Biddiscombe, Perry, *Werwolf!: The History of the National Socialist Guerrilla Movement, 1944–1946* (Toronto, OH: University of Toronto Press, 1998).

Biddiscombe, Perry, *The SS Hunter Battalions* (Stroud: History Press, 2006).

Breitman, Richard and Norman J. W. Goda, *Hitler's Shadow* (Washington, DC: NARA, n.d.).

Carruthers, Bob, *The Waffen-SS in Combat: A Photographic History* (Barnsley: Pen & Sword, 2015).

Christie, Stuart, *General Franco Made Me a Terrorist: The Christie File Part 2, 1964–1967* (ChristieBooks.com, 2003).

CIA, 'The Last Days of Ernst Kaltenbrunner', *Studies Archive Indexes* 4.4 (22 September 1993): available online at www.cia.gov/library/center-for-the-study-of-intelligence/kent-csi/vol4no2/html/v04i2a07p_0001.htm (retrieved 18 August 2017).

CIA, 'The Defections of Dr John', *Studies Archive Indexes* 4.4 (18 September 1995): available online at www.cia.gov/library/center-for-the-study-of-intelligence/kent-csi/vol4no4/html/v04i4a01p_0001.htm (retrieved 31 August 2017).

Committee of the Armed Services, *Malmédy Massacre Investigation* (Washington, DC: Government Printing Office, 1949).

Copeland, Miles Axe, *The Game of Nations: The Amorality of Power Politics* (New York: Simon and Schuster, 1969).

Critchfield, James H., *Partners at the Creation* (Annapolis, MD: Naval Institute Press, 2003).

Doerries, Reinhard R., *Hitler's Last Chief of Foreign Intelligence* (London: Frank Cass, 2003).

Eyre, Wayne D., *Operation Rösselsprung and the Elimination of Tito*, ebook edn (Pickle Partners Publishing, 2014).

Fest, Joachim, *Plotting Hitler's Death* (London: Phoenix, 1997).

Foley, Charles, *Commando Extraordinary: The Spectacular Exploits of Otto Skorzeny* (first publ. 1956; republ. London: Cassell Military Classics, 1998).

Forczyk, Robert, *Rescuing Mussolini: Gran Sasso 1943* (Oxford: Osprey, 2010).

Gehlen, Reinhard, *The Gehlen Memoirs* (London: Collins, 1972).

Gellately, Robert, *The Gestapo and German Society* (Oxford: Clarendon Press, 1990).

Goebbels, Josef, *The Goebbels Diaries, 1942–3*, ed. and transl. Louis P. Lochner (Garden City, NY: Doubleday, 1948).

Goñi, Uki, *The Real Odessa* (London: Granta, 2003).

Greentree, David, *Knight's Move: The Hunt for Marshal Tito 1944* (Oxford: Osprey, 2012).

Hamilton, A. Stephan, *The Oder Front 1945, Vol. 2* (Solihull: Helion & Company 2014, reprinted 2017).

Hammerschmidt, Peter, *Deckname Adler: Klaus Barbie und die westlichen Geheimdienste* (Frankfurt am Main: S. Fischer Verlag, 2014).

Hastings, Max, *The Secret War: Spies, Codes and Guerrillas 1939–1945* (London: William Collins, 2015).

Höhne, Heinz, *The Order of the Death's Head: The Story of Hitler's SS* (first publ. 1967; republ. London: Penguin, 2000).

Höhne, Heinz and Hermann Zolling, *The General was a Spy* (London: Pan Macmillan, 1972).

Horrocks, Sir Brian, *Escape to Action* (New York: St Martin's, 1960).

Horthy, Admiral Nicholas, *Memoirs*, ed. Andrew L. Simon (San Antonio, TX: Simon Publications, 2000).

Höttl, Wilhelm, *The Secret Front* (New York: Enigma Books, 2003).

Hyland, Gary and Anton Gill, *Last Talons of the Eagle* (London: Headline, 1999).

Infield, Glen B., *Skorzeny: Hitler's Commando* (New York: Military Heritage Press, 1981).

Jarkowsky, Major Jeffrey, *German Special Operations in the 1944 Ardennes Offensive*, Master's dissertation, US Army Command and General Staff College, 1994: available online at www.dtic.mil/dtic/tr/fulltext/u2/a284495.pdf (retrieved 20 August 2017).

Kershaw, Ian, *Hitler, 1939–1945: Nemesis* (London: Penguin, 2001).

Kesselring, Albert, *The Memoirs of Field Marshal Kesselring* (London: William Kimber, 1953).

Koessler, Maximilian, 'International Law on Use of Enemy Uniforms as a Stratagem and the Acquittal in the Skorzeny Case', *Missouri Law Review* 24.1 (January 1959), pp. 16–28: available online at scholarship.law.missouri.edu/cgi/viewcontent.cgi?article=1627&context=mlr (retrieved 26 August 2017).

Kumm, Otto, *History of the 7. SS-Mountain Division 'Prinz Eugen'* (Manitoba: J. J. Federowicz, 1995).

Kurowski, Franz, *The Brandenburger Commandos: Germany's Elite Warrior Spies in WWII* (Mechanicsburg, PA: Stackpole Books, 2005).

Lee, Martin, *The Beast Reawakens* (New York: Warner, 1998).

Lehman, Hans Georg, 'Unternehmen Panzerfaust. Der Putsch der SS in Budapest am 15. Oktober 1944', *Ungarn-Jahrbuch* 5 (1973), pp. 215–31.

Longerich, Peter, *Heinrich Himmler: A Life* (Oxford: Oxford University Press, 2012).

Lumsden, Robin, Himmler's Black Order, 1923–45 (Stroud: Sutton, 1997).

Macartney, C. A., *October Fifteenth: A History of Modern Hungary, 1929–1945, Vol. 2* (Edinburgh: Edinburgh University Press, 1956).

Macklin, Graham, *Very Deeply Dyed in Black: Sir Oswald Mosley and the Resurrection of British Fascism* (New York: I.B. Taurus, 2007).

McRaven, William H., *Spec Ops: Case Studies in Special Operations Warfare: Theory and Practice* (New York: Presidio Press, 1996).

Martin, J. R. and Ruth Wodak, *Re-reading the Past: Critical and Functional Perspectives on Time and Value* (Philadelphia, PA: John Benjamins, 2003).

Meyer, Eliah (compiler), *The Factual List of Nazis Protected by Spain* www.scribd. com/doc/209029872/THE-FACTUAL-LIST-OF-NAZIS-PROTECTED-BY-SPAIN-doc (retrieved 27 August 2017).

Mitcham, Samuel W., *Panzers in Winter: Hitler's Army and the Battle of the Bulge* (Westport, CT: Praeger Security, 2006).

Mortimer, Gavin, *The Daring Dozen: Special Forces Legends of World War II* (Oxford: Osprey, 2012).

Mulley, Clare, *The Women Who Flew for Hitler* (London: Macmillan, 2017).

Munoz, Antonio J., *Forgotten Legions: Obscure Combat Formations of the Waffen-SS* (Boulder, CO: Paladin, 1991).

Mussolini, Benito, *The Mussolini Memoirs, 1942–3* (London: Orion Phoenix, 2000).

Naftali, Timothy, 'Reinhard Gehlen and the United States', in *U.S. Intelligence and the Nazis*, eds Richard Brightman and Norman J. W. Goda, pp. 375–418 (Cambridge: Cambridge University Press, 2005).

OKW, *Kriegstagebuch/Oberkommando der Wehrmacht (Wehrmachtführungsstab), 1940–1945, Vol. IV.I*, ed. Helmuth Greinart and Percy Schramm (Königsberg: Bernard and Graefe Verlag, 1961).

O'Reilly, Terence, *Hitler's Irishmen: The Irish Waffen-SS Men* (Blackrock: Mercier Press, 2008).

Ovchinnikova, Lyudmilla, Interview with Lieutenant-Colonel Igor Shchors, 18 January 2002, Russian Federal Security Service (FSB) website: www.fsb. ru/fsb/history/author/single.htm!id%3D10318112@fsbPublication.html (retrieved 16 August 2017).

Pallud, Jean Paul, *Battle of the Bulge, Then and Now* (London: Battle of Britain Prints International, 1984).

Paterson, Lawrence, *Weapons of Desperation, German Frogmen and Midgets of World War II* (Annapolis, MD: Naval Institute Press, 2006).

Pauley, Bruce F., *Hitler and the Forgotten Nazis* (Chapel Hill, NC: University of North Carolina Press, 1981).

Pergrin, Colonel David E., *First Across the Rhine: The 291st Combat Engineer Battalion in France, Belgium and Germany* (Pacifica, CA: Pacifica Military History, 2010).

Petropoulos, Jonathan, *Royals and the Reich: The Princes von Hessen in Nazi Germany* (Oxford: Oxford University Press, 2006).

Poprzeczny, Joseph, *Odilo Globocnik, Hitler's Man in the East* (Jefferson, NC: McFarland, 2003).

Post, Hans, *One Man in His Time* (Otford, NSW: Otford Press, 2002).

Pulver, Murray S., *The Longest Journey* (Freeman, SD: Pine Hill Press, 1986).

Reitsch, Hanna, *The Sky My Kingdom*, transl. Lawrence Wilson (London: Bodley Head, 1955).

Remer, Otto Ernst, 'My Role in Berlin on July 20, 1944', *Journal of Historical Review* 8.1 (Spring 1988), pp. 41–53; available online at www.ihr.org/jhr/v08/v08p-41_remer.html (retrieved 14 August 2017).

Riedel, Durwood, 'The U.S. War Crimes Tribunals at the Former Dachau Concentration Camp: Lessons for Today', *Berkeley Journal of International Law*, 24.2 (2006), pp. 554–609; available online at scholarship.law.berkeley.edu/cgi/viewcontent.cgi?article=1315&context=bjil (retrieved 25 August 2017).

Rohde, Heinz, 'Mit Shakespeare-Englisch', *Der Spiegel*, 10 January 1951, p. 11.

Rudel, Hans-Ulrich, *Stuka Pilot* (Solihull: Black House Publishing, 2012).

Schacht, Hjalmar Horace Greeley, *Confessions of the 'Old Wizard'* (New York: Houghton Mifflin, 1956).

Schadewitz, Michael, *The Meuse First and then Antwerp* (Winnipeg: J. J. Fedorowicz, 1999).

Schellenberg, Walter, 'Affidavit D, 4 January 1946' in *Nazi Conspiracy and Aggression Vol. VIII*, pp. 622–9 (Washington, DC: United States Government, 1946); available online at www.loc.gov/rr/frd/Military_Law/pdf/NT_Nazi_Vol-VIII.pdf (retrieved 11 September 2017).

Schellenberg, Walter, *Walter Schellenberg: The Memoirs of Hitler's Spymaster*, ebook edn, ed. and transl. Louis Hagan (London: André Deutsch, 2006).

Seaman, Mark, *Bravest of the Brave: The True Story of Wing Commander 'Tommy' Yeo-Thomas* (London: Michael O'Mara, 1999).

Segev, Tom, *Simon Wiesenthal: The Life and Legends* (London: Jonathan Cape, 2010).

Sevin, Dieter, 'Operation Scherhorn', *Military Review*, March 1966, pp. 35–43.

Shirer, William L., *The Rise and Fall of the Third Reich* (London: Secker & Warburg, 1971).

Silver, Arnold M., 'Memories of Oberursel: Questions, Questions, Questions', *Studies in Intelligence*, 37.5 (1994), pp. 81–90; available online at www.cia.gov/library/center-for-the-study-of-intelligence/csi-publications/csi-studies/studies/unclass1994.pdf (retrieved 26 August 2017).

Silverstein, Ken, *Private Warriors* (London: Verso, 2000).

Skorzeny, Otto, *Geheimkommando Skorzeny* (Munich: Hansa Verlag, 1950).

Skorzeny, Otto, *Special Missions* (London: Robert Hale, 1957).

Skorzeny, Otto, *My Commando Operations* (Atglen, PA: Schiffer Publishing, 1995).

Smith, Dennis Mack, *Mussolini* (New York: Random House, 1983).

Speer, Albert, *Inside the Third Reich* (London: Sphere, 1977).

Stephan, Robert W., *Stalin's Secret War: Counterintelligence Against the Nazis* (Lawrence, KS: University Press of Kansas, 2004).

Student, Kurt and Hermann Götzel, *Generaloberst Kurt Student und seine Fallschirmjäger* (Friedberg: Podzun-Pallas, 1980).

Sudoplatov, Pavel and Anatoli Sudoplatov, *Special Tasks, The Memoirs of an Unwanted Witness* (Bourne: Warner, 1995).

Summersby, Kay, *Eisenhower Was My Boss* (New York: Prentice-Hall, 1948).

Tauber, Kurt P., *Beyond Eagle and Swastika* (Middletown, CT: Weslyan University Press, 1967).

Thomas, Geoffrey J. and Barry Ketley, *Luftwaffe KG 200* (Mechanichsburg, PA: Stackpole Military History, 2015).

Thompson, Royce L., *Malmédy Belgium Mistaken Bombing, 23 and 25 December 1944*: report for Office of Chief of Military History, 5 June 1952; available online at www.oldhickory30th.com/MalmedyBombingAirReport.jpg.pdf (retrieved 22 August 2017).

Tuohy, William, 'SS Officer Skorzeny Wrongly Credited With Deed, Historian says: Mussolini Rescue: A New Version', *Los Angeles Times*, 26 December 1987.

Vartanyan, Gevork, 'Tehran-43: Wrecking the Plan to Kill Stalin, Roosevelt and Churchill', *Ria Novosti*, 16 October 2007.

Walters, Guy, *Hunting Evil* (London: Bantam, 2009).

Weingartner, James J., *A Peculiar Crusade: Willis M. Everett and the Malmedy Massacre* (New York: New York University Press, 2000).

Weitz, John, *Hjalmar Schacht: Hitler's Banker* (New York: Warner, 1999).

West, Nigel, *Dictionary of World War Intelligence II* (Plymouth: Scarecrow, 2008).

Westphal, Siegfried, *Erinnerungen* (Mainz: Hase und Koehler, 1975).

Whiting, Charles, *Skorzeny: The Most Dangerous Man in Europe* (Barnsley: Pen and Sword, 1998).

Wiegrefe, Klaus, 'Nazi Veterans Created Illegal Army', *Der Spiegel*, 14 May 2014: available online at www.spiegel.de/international/germany/ wehrmacht-veterans-created-a-secret-army-in-west-germany-a-969015.html (retrieved 19 September 2017).

Williamson, Gordon, *German Commanders of World War II (2): Waffen-SS, Luftwaffe & Navy* (Oxford: Osprey, 2006).

Williamson, Gordon, *German Special Forces of World War II* (Oxford: Osprey, 2009).

Wray, Timothy A., *Standing Fast: German Defensive Doctrine on the Russian Front During World War II – Prewar to March 1943*, ebook edn (Pickle Partners Publishing, 2015).

Notes

Prologue

1   Each Wehrmacht regiment had a trained Propaganda Kompanie unit attached to it, whose job was to film, photograph, and write up the regiment's activities. Although under Wehrmacht command, these units existed exclusively to provide Goebbels' Ministry of Propaganda with material. The Waffen-SS had its own equivalent, the SS-Kriegsberichter-Kompanie (SS war reporter company), established in 1940 (Carruthers, *Waffen-SS in Combat*, p. 6). As the Gran Sasso raid was primarily a Luftwaffe operation, the propaganda unit assigned was probably from the Wehrmacht.

2   *Die Deutsche Wochenschau* was the only newsreel in German cinemas from 1940 to 1945; working under the direction of the Ministry of Propaganda, it created its weekly films primarily from footage provided by Propaganda Kompanie units.

3   *Die Deutsche Wochenschau* Nr. 681, 22 September 1943; available online at https://archive.org/details/1943-09-22-Die-Deutsche-Wochenschau-681 (retrieved 22 October 2016).

1. The Knowledge of Pain

1   Skorzeny, *My Commando Operations*, p. 13.

2   Foley, *Commando Extraordinary*, p. 29.

3   Skorzeny, *Special Missions*, p. 7.

4   Skorzeny, *Special Missions*, p. 7.

5   Pauley, *Hitler and the Forgotten Nazis*, p. 6.

6   Quoted in Foley, *Commando Extraordinary*, pp. 29–30.

7   Skorzeny, *My Commando Operations*, p. 13

8   Quoted in Foley, *Commando Extraordinary*, p. 30.

9   Skorzeny, *Special Missions*, p. 8.

10 Skorzeny, *Special Missions*, p. 8.

11 Infield, *Hitler's Commando*, p. 13.

12 Skorzeny claimed (*Special Missions*, p. 8) to have joined immediately after hearing Goebbels speaking to an NSDAP assembly in summer 1932. In fact, his SS record (SSR *Führerkarte*) reveals he joined the Party on 1 May 1932. Goebbels did indeed make a

two-hour speech in Vienna that year, but in September: see Toby Thacker, *Joseph Goebbels: Life and Death* (London: Palgrave Macmillan, 2009), pp. 134–5.

13 Skorzeny claimed that his political activities 'came to an end' with the ban (*Special Missions*, p. 8). They did not.

14 NSDAP membership no. 1083671; SS membership no. 295,979, SSR.

15 Skorzeny, *My Commando Operations*, p. 19. The text is garbled, but clearly indicates May 1934. This first marriage is not well known, but there is evidence that Skorzeny was married not twice (as has been almost universally stated) but three times. Skorzeny's sometime colleague Wilhelm Höttl mentions *three* wives (*Secret Front*, p. 296), while Skorzeny's SS record (Führerkarte and Personal-Bericht, 20 December 1938) indicates a divorce in 1937.

16 SSR.

17 Skorzeny, *Special Missions*, p. 8. Skorzeny was in correspondence with one Alfred Schreiber at Meidlinger Gerüstanstalt as late as 1944 (Skorzeny to Schreiber, January 1944). Clearly Alfred was a member of the family that had originally set up the company. Whether he was the father or brother of Margareta is not known. See also SSR (Lebenslauf des SS-Sturmbannführers Otto Skorzeny).

18 Although he tried to minimise it in his memoirs, Skorzeny's anti-Semitism is documented in CIA dispatch OSMA-11,289, Chief of Station Madrid to Chief Western Europe, 17 August 1960, item 5: Otto Skorzeny CIA name file, NARA.

19 Infield, *Hitler's Commando*, p. 15.

20 Kaltenbrunner moved to Vienna in 1934, based on a listing in Lehmann's Vienna directory for 1934–8; available online at www.digital.wienbibliothek.at/wbrobv/periodical/titleinfo/5311 (retrieved 5 August 2017).

21 Skorzeny (*My Commando Operations*, p. 24) claimed that the propaganda leaflets distributed by the government read 'Down with Hitler! Long live Moscow!' In fact, they said nothing of the sort; they were all about patriotic, Germanic Christian identity and self-determination for the Austrian Fatherland (reproduced in *Die Stimme*, 11 March 1938, p. 1).

22 Skorzeny, *My Commando Operations*, p. 27.

23 Infield, *Hitler's Commando*, p. 14. Skorzeny says that the person who passed on the order was Bruno Weiss (*Special Missions*, p. 10), but Infield identifies him as Anton Dubas. Skorzeny is probably more reliable on this point.

24 Skorzeny, *My Commando Operations*, p. 27.

25 Skorzeny, *My Commando Operations*, p. 27.

26 Skorzeny, *My Commando Operations*, pp. 27–8.

27 Miklas, testimony at Nuremberg, January 1946; *Der Spiegel* 29/1949.

28 Martin and Wodak, Extract 12, *Re-reading the Past*, p. 163. Skorzeny does seem to have put in a good word for him; Birsak was not arrested and later distinguished himself serving the Wehrmacht.

29 Poprzeczny, *Odilo Globocnik*, p. 55.

30 *Jewish Telegraphic Agency*, 4 February 1963. Skorzeny denied an Israeli accusation that he burned five synagogues (O'Reilly, *Hitler's Irishmen*, p. 294). Nazi-hunter Simon Wiesenthal was convinced of the truth of the allegations (Segev, *Simon Wiesenthal*, pp. 163–5).

31 Heydrich, telegram to SD districts, 10 November 1938, reproduced in Arad et al., *Documents*, pp. 102–3.

32   Foley, *Commando Extraordinary*, p. 31.
33   Foley, *Commando Extraordinary*, p. 31. According to *Der Spiegel* 29/1949, Skorzeny won five gold medals in all. The motor section was nominally a police or paramilitary unit, but was in fact mostly involved in sport.
34   SSR (Führerkarte and Personalangaben, 15 March 1939).
35   SSR (*Personal-Bericht*, 20 December 1938).
36   Infield, *Hitler's Commando*, p. 13; SSR (Meldung meiner Heimatanschrift, 13 April 1944).
37   Waltraut Riess, interviewed for the documentary *Hitler's Useful Idols – Otto Skorzeny* (dir. Robert Gokl, 2010).
38   Waltraut Riess, interviewed for the documentary *Hitler's Useful Idols – Otto Skorzeny* (dir. Robert Gokl, 2010).

2. Accidental Soldier

1   Flg.1.Lfw.Nachr.Ers.Rgt.Wien, SSR.
2   Skorzeny claimed (*My Commando Operations*, p. 35) that he was about to take his 'final tests' to be a pilot at this time. There is no independent record of this. Given his sporting background, he may well have trained in gliders, as did many young German men and teenagers.
3   Infield, *Hitler's Commando*, p. 16.
4   SSR (Vorschung für die Verleihung des Deutschen Kreuzes in Gold, 30 January 1945).
5   Felix Steiner, quoted in Höhne, *Order of the Death's Head*, p. 481.
6   See Note on the Waffen-SS, pp. 329–30 of this book.
7   Radl joined the Waffen-SS on 1 August 1940. Born in 1911, he had been a member of the Nazi Party since 1 October 1931 (NS No. 6,175,766), and a member of the SS since 1 December 1933 (SS No. 289591).
8   Skorzeny, *Special Missions*, p. 12.
9   Uscha (Unterscharführer) 1, 5 May 1940, SSR (Vorschung für die Verleihung des Deutschen Kreuzes in Gold, 30 January 1945).
10   Schw.Abt.SS-Art. – Rgt SS-Totenk.: 6 May 1940 to 1 September 1940, SSR.
11   Promoted to Oscha SS-Art. – Rgt.Reich, 1 September 1940, SSR.
12   Jäger, quoted in Infield, *Hitler's Commando*, p. 17.
13   SS-UStuf. II/SS-AR.Reich; backdated to 31 January 1941, SSR.
14   Skorzeny, *Special Missions*, p. 17.
15   SSR (Vorschung für die Verleihung des Deutschen Kreuzes in Gold, 30 January 1945).
16   Foley, *Commando Extraordinary*, p. 36.
17   Skorzeny, *My Commando Operations*, p. 77.
18   Quoted in Foley, *Commando Extraordinary*, p. 40.
19   Foley, *Commando Extraordinary*, p. 42.
20   Skorzeny, *Special Missions*, p. 21.
21   26 August 1941, SSR. For background on the Yelnya Bridgehead see Wray, *Standing Fast*.
22   Skorzeny received the black wound badge, Verwundetenabzeichen schwarz (Verw.ABz. (schw.)), although, curiously, not until 18 August 1943, according to his SS record.
23   SSR (Vorschung für die Verleihung des Deutschen Kreuzes in Gold, 30 January 1945).
24   Infield, *Hitler's Commando*, p. 21.
25   Höttl, *Secret Front*, p. 295.
26   Skorzeny, *My Commando Operations*, p. 127.
27   SSR: 'Beförderung des SS-Ostuf. Skorzeny zum SS-Hauptsturmführer', 30 June 1943.

28   Skorzeny, *My Commando Operations*, p. 138.
29   SS-HStuf RSiHA/VI Führ.d.S Lehrg.Obg. – April 1943, SSR (Vorschung für die Verleihung des Deutschen Kreuzes in Gold, 30 January 1945).

3. Thugs in Field Grey

1   Infield, *Hitler's Commando*, p. 22.
2   Schellenberg, *Memoirs*, ch. 2.
3   Schellenberg, *Memoirs*, ch. 2.
4   Often referred to as the 'managing director' of the German resistance movement.
5   Fest, *Plotting Hitler's Death*, pp. 96–101.
6   Fest, *Plotting Hitler's Death*, p. 212.
7   Even in early 1943 Schellenberg was often referred to as 'General' rather than 'Colonel'. However, his formal promotion to SS-Brigadeführer und General der Polizei appears to have taken place in June 1944.
8   In fact the Kripo – which together with the Gestapo was known as Sipo – was just as much involved as Amt IV with rounding up and deporting enemies of the state to concentration camps.
9   Schellenberg, *Memoirs*, ch. 31.
10   Quoted in Skorzeny, *Special Missions*, p. 32.
11   Schellenberg, *Memoirs*, ch. 33.
12   Waltraut Riess, interviewed for the documentary *Hitler's Useful Idols – Otto Skorzeny* (dir. Robert Gokl, 2010).
13   Schellenberg, *Memoirs*, Introduction.
14   NBS.
15   NBS.
16   April 1943, SSR: SS-HStuf. RSiHA/VI Führ.d. S.Lehrg.Obg, meaning 'SS-Hauptsturmführer. RSHA Amt VI Führer der Sonderlehrgang "Oranienburg"'. No mention here of spy schools; it's quite clearly a military appointment.
17   CIR, p. 6.
18   NNS, pp. 7–10.
19   Höttl, *Secret Front*, p. 295.
20   Interrogation Report S-975, 307th CIC, section 3, p. 2, CIAR.
21   Interrogation Report S-975, 307th CIC, section 3, p. 2, CIAR.
22   While noting Radl's 'sincere convictions' and cooperative attitude, his preliminary CIC interrogator (Interrogation Report S-975, 307th CIC, section 3, p. 2, CIAR) concluded: 'Radl is still a devout Nazi; he has no sense of guilt or shame about Germany's action … He is devoted to his former leaders and in the opinion of this agent will remain so. He is dangerous to the peace and security of Europe.'
23   Interrogation Report S-975, 307th CIC, section 3, p. 2, CIAR.
24   O'Reilly, *Hitler's Irishmen*.
25   O'Reilly, *Hitler's Irishmen*, p. 125.
26   Skorzeny, *Special Missions*, p. 30. Lord Louis Mountbatten was Chief of Combined Operations from 1941 to 1943 and, as such, ultimately responsible for the success of the St Nazaire Raid, as well as the disastrous Dieppe Raid, both in 1942.
27   A German battalion conventionally numbered about 500 men, and was made up of three companies. SS-Jägerbataillon 502 was not, in fact, fully activated until spring 1944.

28   The Totenkopfverbände, formerly an autonomous division, had been transferred to the Waffen-SS at the start of the war, forming the SS-Totenkopf-Division. Many veteran camp guards saw active service on the Eastern Front, and their places were taken in the camp battalions by recruits.

29   According to Radl, Amt VI-F was run by Stubaf Rudolf Lassig, a self-proclaimed expert on bomb fuses, who had compiled a textbook on sabotage which was sent to A-Schule in The Hague for training purposes, but only one copy ever existed (KRI, Technical Development c, p. 18). Skorzeny sidelined Lassig partly by collaborating with Dr Albert Widmann, and through the appointment in 1944 of the proficient Hauptsturmführer Reinhold Gerhard as his weapons procurement specialist.

30   Skorzeny in CIR, p. 6.

31   CIR, p. 6.

32   Later in the war, Knolle was dispatched to Ruma in Yugoslavia – by then the centre of partisan activity – where he temporarily set up a duplicate spy school. Not long afterwards, A-Schule West was relocated to Neustrelitz in eastern Germany, where it was reopened as a 'Kampf Schule' with much more emphasis on military training.

33   Skorzeny, *Special Missions*, p. 33.

34   Skorzeny, *Special Missions*, p. 33.

35   Skorzeny, *Special Missions*, p. 34.

36   Skorzeny, *Special Missions*, p. 34.

37   Misleadingly, Skorzeny refers to it as a 'revolver'. The Welrod had a magazine and a manually operated action, intended to avoid the noise of the slide when firing a semi-automatic pistol.

38   Skorzeny, *My Commando Operations*, p. 144.

39   Skorzeny, *Special Missions*, p. 32. It isn't clear whether 'surveying' means surveillance or studying landscape for tactical purposes.

40   Quoted in Infield, *Hitler's Commando*, p. 26.

41   Schellenberg, in his *Memoirs*, blames the failure of long-distance operations on the Luftwaffe's inadequate provision of transport planes.

42   Quoted in Skorzeny, *My Commando Operations*, pp. 208–9.

43   Foley, *Commando Extraordinary*, p. 53.

44   Skorzeny, *My Commando Operations*, p. 144.

45   Skorzeny, *My Commando Operations*, p. 203.

46   Interrogation Report S-975, 307th CIC, section 3, p 3, CIAR.

47   Typically, Skorzeny fails to acknowledge his debt to Besekow, here and elsewhere in his memoirs.

48   HAB, p. 1.

49   HIR.

4. The Liberator of Mussolini

1   *Hansard*, House of Commons, 21 September 1943, vol. 392, c. 84.

2   Skorzeny, *Special Missions*, p. 41.

3   Skorzeny, *Special Missions*, p. 43.

4   Skorzeny, *Special Missions*, p. 43.

5   Skorzeny, *Special Missions*, p. 43.

6   The last two may well have been Kurt Student's candidates for the job. The ranks, although not the names, of Skorzeny's competitors are listed in his earliest account of the

raid (Dachau deposition, p. 1, CIAS).

7   Skorzeny, *My Commando Operations*, pp. 228–9.

8   Skorzeny, *Special Missions*, p. 44.

9   Skorzeny, *Special Missions*, p. 44. Albrecht Dürer never painted a picture called *The Violet*. It may have been his *Violet Bouquet*. This is one of the small but legion mistakes in his account that mark a cavalier attitude to facts.

10   Skorzeny, *Special Missions*, p. 44.

11   Skorzeny, *Special Missions*, p. 44.

12   Skorzeny, *Special Missions*, p. 45.

13   According to his own account (Dachau deposition, p. 1, CIAS).

14   Skorzeny, *Special Missions*, p. 46.

15   Annussek, *Hitler's Raid*, p. 64.

16   'Controversy between Otto Skorzeny and General Hans Doerr', CIA report no. WSM-543; date of report: 27 March 1951. Otto Skorzeny CIA name file, NARA.

17   Skorzeny, *Special Missions*, p. 47.

18   Skorzeny, *Special Missions*, p. 48.

19   Kesselring, *Memoirs*, p. 171.

20   Höttl, *Secret Front*, pp. 216–7; Schellenberg, *Memoirs*, ch. 18.

21   Höttl, *Secret Front*, p. 210; Skorzeny, *Special Missions*, p. 54; Student and Götzel, *Generaloberst Kurt Student*, p. 410.

22   Dachau deposition, p. 1, CIAS.

23   Student and Götzel, *Generaloberst Kurt Student*, p. 413.

24   Skorzeny, *Special Missions*, p. 56; Student and Götzel, *Generaloberst Kurt Student*.

25   Skorzeny, *Special Missions*, p. 57.

26   Skorzeny, *Special Missions*, p. 58. Some have called this account far-fetched. Forczyk (*Rescuing Mussolini*, p. 15) questions the type of plane Skorzeny flew in. But although Skorzeny's account is highly dramatised (the plane probably developed an unexciting mechanical fault and had to make a controlled emergency landing in the sea), the reconnaissance flight, Skorzeny's presence on it and the crash-landing are indisputable. They are even recorded by Allied intelligence: '21.8.43. Rome-Berlin. Kappler to Grothmann [Himmler's adjutant] … During operations Sk crashed into sea with machine. All the crew were saved. Sk only slightly hurt, still fit for operations … return of Sk on morning of 20/8' (SWT).

27   Skorzeny, *Special Missions*, p. 56

28   Skorzeny, *Special Missions*, p. 59.

29   Skorzeny, *Special Missions*, p. 59.

30   Student and Götzel, *Generaloberst Kurt Student*, p. 414.

31   English transcript of Ultra intercepts, SWT.

32   Skorzeny, *My Commando Operations*, p. 254. Annussek, *Hitler's Raid*, p. 234; also note 51, p.291.

33   Both Student and Skorzeny claimed credit for the Krutoff initiative. In reality, it may have been Gerhard Langguth, Student's intelligence officer, who was responsible (Forczyk, *Rescuing Mussolini*, p. 17).

34   Skorzeny, *My Commando Operations*, p. 254.

35   Skorzeny, *Special Missions*, p. 65. Student (*Generaloberst Kurt Student*, p. 417) records Langguth as taking the reconnaissance photos.

36   Forczyk, *Rescuing Mussolini*, p. 17.

37   Smith, *Mussolini*, p. 300.
38   Skorzeny, *My Commando Operations*, p. 255. There is no independent evidence that a helicopter was ever seriously considered (Hyland and Gill, *Last Talons*, pp. 81–3). The only Fa 223 available would have been production model V12, which later crash-landed during a mountain-rescue mission on Mont Blanc.
39   Student and Götzel, *Generaloberst Kurt Student*, p. 419.
40   Dachau deposition, p. 1, CIAS.
41   Skorzeny, *Special Missions*, pp. 71–2.
42   'Yes, it was the paratroops who planned and carried out the operation,' Mors recalled. 'But for more than 40 years, Skorzeny has gotten all the credit. His version is something of a fairy tale. I'd like to see that remedied by military historians' (Tuohy, 'SS Officer Skorzeny').
43   See Chapter 2.
44   Intercept, 12 September 1943, SWT.
45   Student and Götzel, *Generaloberst Kurt Student*, pp. 419–20.
46   SWT; SSR.
47   Tuohy, 'SS Officer Skorzeny'.
48   Skorzeny, *Special Missions*, p. 75.
49   Skorzeny, *Special Missions*, p. 78.
50   Quoted in Forczyk, *Rescuing Mussolini*, p. 39.
51   Quoted in Forczyk, *Rescuing Mussolini*, p. 39.
52   Annussek, *Hitler's Raid*, p. 225, n.
53   Dachau deposition, p. 1, CIAS.
54   Mussolini, *Memoirs*, p. 133. The glider was probably Radl's, so the time was some minutes after 2 pm.
55   Mussolini, *Memoirs*, p. 134.
56   Skorzeny, *Special Missions*, p. 79.
57   Skorzeny, *Special Missions*, p. 82.
58   Skorzeny, *Special Missions*, p. 84.
59   Student and Götzel, *Generaloberst Kurt Student*, p. 428.
60   Annussek, *Hitler's Raid*, p. 234; Forczyk, *Rescuing Mussolini*, p. 53; Skorzeny, *Special Missions*, p. 84.
61   Skorzeny, *Special Missions*, p. 87.
62   Foley, *Commando Extraordinary*, p. 79. The award is noted in Skorzeny's SS personal file, but oddly the date of the award is recorded as 1 December 1944. It is probably not a clerical error, as the entry appears very deliberately at the bottom of a chronological list.

5. Special Ops and High-Value Targets

1   SWT.
2   Goebbels, *Diaries*, 16 September 1943.
3   Quoted in Tuohy, 'SS Officer Skorzeny'.
4   Exposé of Otto Skorzeny, 10 June 1951, CIAS; Forczyk, *Rescuing Mussolini*, p. 55.
5   Quoted in Tuohy, 'SS Officer Skorzeny'.
6   Skorzeny, *Special Missions*, p. 92.
7   Student and Götzel, *Generaloberst Kurt Student*, p. 429.

8   For example, not sending a team to reconnoitre Gran Sasso (Forczyk, *Rescuing Mussolini*, p. 59).
9   Berger, *Walter Girg*, p. 62.
10 Skorzeny, *Special Missions*, p. 36.
11 Höttl, *Secret Front*, p. 315.
12 Berger, *Walter Girg*, p. 62; p. 71, n.4. My translation from German.
13 Hossfelder, quoted in Mortimer, *Daring Dozen*, p. 223.
14 Post, *One Man*, pp. 155, 167. Skorzeny was close to the Porsche family. The only Porsche sports car then in existence (1944) was the prototype 64, of which there were two, both owned by the family. It is possible that Post meant a (Porsche-designed) Volkswagen.
15 Skorzeny, *My Commando Operations*, p. 215.
16 Forczyk, *Rescuing Mussolini*, p. 12.
17 Skorzeny, *My Commando Operations*, p. 205.
18 Skorzeny, *My Commando Operations*, p. 205. Schellenberg doesn't mention this operation in his memoirs.
19 Sudoplatov and Sudoplatov, *Special Tasks*, p. 130; Vartanyan, 'Tehran-43'.
20 Vartanyan, 'Tehran-43'.
21 Vartanyan, 'Tehran-43'.
22 Vartanyan, 'Tehran-43'.
23 West, *Dictionary*, pp. 140–1.
24 Quoted in Skorzeny, *My Commando Operations*, p. 206.
25 CIR Annex No. IV. Individual Operations, 23 July 1945, p. 33.
26 NBS, p. 11. Skorzeny claimed that when the order for *Peter* came in, he was skiing in Austria (Skorzeny, *Special Missions*, p. 95).
27 CIR Annex No. IV. Individual Operations, 23 July 1945, p. 33.
28 CIR Annex No. IV. Individual Operations, 23 July 1945, p. 33.
29 'Radl, Karl', CIC to Counter Intelligence War Room, London, 22 December 1945. OS file, KV2/403 512702, NAUK.
30 Infield, *Hitler's Commando*, p. 50.
31 Infield, *Hitler's Commando*, p. 52: NNS, p. 122.
32 On 19 January 1950, his death sentence was commuted to 24 years in prison.
33 Infield (*Hitler's Commando*, p. 52) asserts that there are witness statements proving Skorzeny's presence on the night of Munk's murder.
34 The defection from Istanbul of Abwehr agent Erich Vermerhen to the British shortly beforehand was the last straw as far as Hitler was concerned.
35 Doerries, *Hitler's Last Chief*, p. 146. Schellenberg was on holiday at the time.
36 Doerries, *Hitler's Last Chief*, p. 146.
37 When in 1948 Schellenberg was being tried by the American Military Tribunal at Nuremberg, former Swiss intelligence chief Roger Masson swore an affidavit affirming the importance of Schellenberg's action in averting an SS parachute raid (Doerries, *Hitler's Last Chief*, p. 365, n. 81).
38 KRI, p. 17.
39 Skorzeny, *My Commando Operations*, p. 217.
40 According to Skorzeny, the commandant at Fruska Gora – a stop-off en route from Belgrade – told him: 'You'll never make it. There hasn't been a Mercedes along this road in a year. As soon as your car is spotted, the word will be passed and Tito's men will be waiting for you' (quoted in Infield, *Hitler's Commando*, p. 48).

41 There is a mystery about how and when Tetaric's information came into Skorzeny's hands. Skorzeny says he arrived at Belgrade in April. By then, Tetaric was dead, having been recaptured by the partisans and shot on 27 March (Greentree, *Knight's Move*, p. 26). Otto Kumm (*History of the 7. SS-Mountain Division*) suggests Tetaric gave his intelligence to the Germans in mid-March. Skorzeny may have got the dates muddled.

42 Greentree, *Knight's Move*, p. 26.

43 Eyre, *Operation Rösselsprung*, p. 29.

44 Höttl, *Secret Front*, p. 154.

45 Skorzeny, *Secret Missions* (New York: Dutton, 1950 edition), pp.150–1.

46 Skorzeny, *My Commando Operations*, p. 218.

6. Miracle Weapons

1   CIR.

2   CIR.

3   Skorzeny, *My Commando Operations*, p. 174

4   Interrogation of Karl Radl by 307th CIC Det, 19 May 1945, report no. S-980, p. 6, Appendix II. FOI Special Collection, Karl Rudl, document 0005, https://www.cia.gov/library/readingroom/docs/RUDL%2C%20KARL_0005.pdf (retrieved 26 September 2017).

5   Interrogation of Karl Radl by 307th CIC Det, 19 May 1945, report no. S-980, p. 6, Appendix II. FOI Special Collection, Karl Rudl, document 0005, https://www.cia.gov/library/readingroom/docs/RUDL%2C%20KARL_0005.pdf (retrieved 26 September 2017).

6   CIR, p.15.

7   Skorzeny, *My Commando Operations*, p. 174.

8   Paterson, *Weapons of Desperation*, p. 16.

9   HMS *Pylades* and ORP *Dragon*. Paterson, *Weapons of Desperation*, pp. 44–5.

10 Paterson, *Weapons of Desperation*, pp. 52–5.

11 Skorzeny, *My Commando Operations*, p. 174. On suicide missions in general, *Special Missions*, p. 100.

12 Paterson, *Weapons of Desperation*, p. 228.

13 Munoz, *Forgotten Legions*, p. 195.

14 *The Times*, 6 October 1944.

15 Interrogation of Korvettenkapitän Burckhart et al. (officers of KdK), WO 204/12809 UK National Archives.

16 Paterson, *Weapons of Desperation*, p. 37.

17 Interrogation of Karl Radl by 307th CIC Det, 19 May 1945, report no. S-980, p. 6, Appendix II. FOI Special Collection, Karl Rudl, document 0005, https://www.cia.gov/library/readingroom/docs/RUDL%2C%20KARL_0005.pdf (retrieved 26 September 2017).

18 Paterson, *Weapons of Desperation*, pp. 89–90.

19 O'Reilly, *Hitler's Irishmen*, p. 45.

20 CIR, p. 15.

21 Skorzeny, *Special Missions*, p. 100.

22 The only other was test pilot Melitta Schiller.

23 Hein Gerin, cited in Mulley, *Women Who Flew*, pp. 152–3.

24 Reitsch, *Sky My Kingdom*, pp. 194–5. Reitsch described Skorzeny in her memoir as 'the pilot who rescued Mussolini by helicopter', a remarkable feat of false belief in a woman who knew him personally and whose expert knowledge of aircraft was second to none.
25 Reitsch, *Sky My Kingdom*, p. 192.
26 Reitsch, *Sky My Kingdom*, p. 193.
27 Reitsch, *Sky My Kingdom*, p. 195.
28 Skorzeny, *Special Missions*, p. 100.
29 Reitsch, *Sky My Kingdom*, p. 195.
30 Skorzeny, *My Commando Operations*, p. 165.
31 Skorzeny, *My Commando Operations*, p. 34.
32 Skorzeny, *My Commando Operations*, p. 165; Hyland and Gill, *Last Talons*, pp. 324–5.
33 Skorzeny, *My Commando Operations*, p. 165.
34 Reitsch says 'four or five days' (*Sky My Kingdom*, p. 195). Ten days, according to *Special Missions*, p. 103.
35 Hyland and Gill, *Last Talons*, p. 293.
36 Reitsch, *Sky My Kingdom*, p. 196.
37 Reitsch, *Sky My Kingdom*, p. 166.
38 Skorzeny, *Special Missions*, p. 105.
39 Reitsch, *Sky My Kingdom*, pp. 198–9.
40 Hyland and Gill, *Last Talons*, p. 294.
41 Hyland and Gill, *Last Talons*, p. 293.
42 CIR, p. 16.

7. The Stauffenberg Plot – July 1944

1 Skorzeny, *My Commando Operations*, p. 285.
2 Infield, *Hitler's Commando*, p. 58.
3 Skorzeny, *My Commando Operations*, p. 287.
4 Skorzeny says SS-Hauptsturmführer Karl Fucker, but in fact Hunke was in temporary command of 1. Kompanie at this time. See HIR.
5 Although that is exactly what he managed to do in an exchange of fire during the latter stages of the coup. See Fest, *Plotting Hitler's Death*, p. 275.
6 Fest, *Plotting Hitler's Death*, p. 362, n.
7 Fest, *Plotting Hitler's Death*, pp. 263, 272; On Schellenberg's relationship with Thiele, Doerries, *Hitler's Last Chief*, pp. 145–6.
8 Höhne, *Order of the Death's Head*, p. 531.
9 Höhne, *Order of the Death's Head*, p. 532.
10 Remer, 'My Role in Berlin'.
11 Speer, *Inside the Third Reich*, p. 519.
12 Skorzeny, *My Commando Operations*, p. 288.
13 Skorzeny, *Special Missions*, p. 114.
14 Skorzeny, *My Commando Operations*, p. 288; *Special Missions*, p. 115. Most of the Leibstandarte division was on campaign in northern France, but elements were stationed in the Berlin barracks.
15 Skorzeny, *My Commando Operations*, p. 289.
16 Mohnke commanded the Leibstandarte division from 31 August 1944. He was wounded on 17 July (Williamson, *German Commanders*, p. 21) and might conceivably have gone

back to Berlin for treatment. Skorzeny is muddled about Mohnke's rank as well, referring to him as an SS-Oberführer, a rank he was promoted to in November.

17 Skorzeny, *My Commando Operations*, p. 289; Remer, 'My Role in Berlin'.

18 Skorzeny, *My Commando Operations*, p. 290.

19 Skorzeny, *My Commando Operations*, p. 291.

20 Speer, *Inside the Third Reich*, p. 521.

21 Speer, *Inside the Third Reich*, p. 521; Skorzeny, *My Commando Operations*, p. 294.

22 Fest, *Plotting Hitler's Death*, p. 276.

23 But botched the job. He had to be finished off by a sergeant acting under Fromm's direct orders.

24 Himmler arrived in Berlin some time after midnight.

25 The other conspirator arrested by Fromm, tank general Erich Höpner, was spared – presumably because he alone among the six knew nothing of Fromm's complicity.

26 Fest, *Plotting Hitler's Death*, p. 279.

27 Remer, quoted in Skorzeny, *My Commando Operations*, p. 295.

28 Infield, *Hitler's Commando*, p. 57.

29 Skorzeny, *My Commando Operations*, p. 296.

30 Skorzeny, *My Commando Operations*, p. 291.

31 Skorzeny, *Special Missions*, p. 118.

32 Skorzeny, *My Commando Operations*, p. 298.

33 Gestapo records, cited in Shirer, *Rise and Fall*, pp. 1072, 1174, n. 38.

34 Bassett, *Hitler's Spy Chief*, ch. 14; Höhne, *The Order of the Death's Head*, p. 487.

35 Skorzeny, *My Commando Operations*, pp. 298–9.

36 Skorzeny, *My Commando Operations*, p. 299.

37 Stephan, *Stalin's Secret War*, pp. 223–30.

38 Schellenberg, *Memoirs*, ch. 33.

39 Höttl, *Secret Front*, p. 315.

40 Canaris, who never admitted his guilt, escaped a show-trial and certain condemnation, probably through Himmler's intervention. Nevertheless, he was included among the prominent figures imprisoned in concentration camps. In the end he was executed in gruesome and humiliating circumstances on 9 April 1945 – just weeks before the end of the war, when he had outlived any possible utility to the regime. The order came from Kaltenbrunner.

41 Doerries, *Hitler's Last Chief*, p. 159; CIR, pp. 1–5.

42 CIR, p. 5 and Annex No. I, p. 21.

43 CIR, p. 5.

44 CIR, Annex No. I, p. 25.

45 CIR, Annex No. I, pp. 21–6.

46 CIR, Annex No. I, p. 5.

8. The Scherhorn Affair

1 German intelligence summary, quoted in Sevin, 'Operation Scherhorn', pp. 35–6.

2 Gehlen, *Memoirs*, p. 11.

3 Political Information, Research Service East, quoted in Höhne and Zolling, *The General was a Spy*, p. 41.

4   Skorzeny, *My Commando Operations*, p. 389. Also intimately involved in the planning of Operation *Freischütz* was Jagdverband Ost's deputy commander, Wolfram Heinze.

5   Thomas and Ketley, *Luftwaffe KG 200*, p. 234.

6   Stephan, *Stalin's Secret War*, p. 180.

7   Stephan, *Stalin's Secret War*, p. 180

8   Skorzeny, *My Commando Operations*, p. 388. Skorzeny's account of the commando drops differs significantly from other sources.

9   Skorzeny calls Schiffer 'Linder' (*My Commando Operations*, p. 388). However, an earlier account refers to him as 'Sch' and Schiffer is the name favoured in Worgitzky's account, based on radio messages.

10 Sevin, 'Operation Scherhorn', p. 39

11 Sevin, 'Operation Scherhorn', p. 39.

12 Sevin, 'Operation Scherhorn', p. 42.

13 Sevin, 'Operation Scherhorn', p. 42.

14 Skorzeny, *My Commando Operations*, p. 391.

15 Skorzeny, *My Commando Operations*, p. 391.

16 Stephan, *Stalin's Secret War*, p. 181.

17 Stephan, *Stalin's Secret War*, p. 181; Sevin, 'Operation Scherhorn', p. 39.

18 Skorzeny, *My Commando Operations*, p. 391.

19 Skorzeny, *Special Missions*, p. 126. Skorzeny wrote these words in the 1950s.

20 Sudoplatov and Sudoplatov, *Special Tasks*, p. 155.

21 Sudoplatov and Sudoplatov, *Special Tasks*, p. 153.

22 Sudoplatov and Sudoplatov, *Special Tasks*, p. 158.

23 Gehlen, *Memoirs*, p. 72.

24 Sudoplatov's counter-intelligence directorate was moved out of the NKVD and into the NKGB in April 1943.

25 Sudoplatov and Sudoplatov, *Special Tasks*, pp. 167–8.

26 Also known as Rudolf Ivanovich Abel. In 1957 the Scottish-born Soviet spy (1903–71) was sentenced to 30 years' imprisonment for stealing defence secrets in the United States but in 1962 he was exchanged for shot-down U-2 pilot Gary Powers.

27 Ovchinnikova, Interview with Lieutenant-Colonel Igor Shchors, FSB website: www.fsb. ru/fsb/history/author/single.htm!id%3D10318112@fsbPublication.html (retrieved 10 September 2017).

28 Sevin, 'Operation Scherhorn', p. 42.

29 Ovchinnikova, Interview with Lt-Colonel Igor Shchors, FSB website: www.fsb.ru/fsb/ history/author/single.htm!id%3D10318112@fsbPublication.html (retrieved 10 September 2017).

30 Sevin, 'Operation Scherhorn', p. 42.

31 Stephan, *Stalin's Secret War*, p. 180.

32 'Skorzeny's Ghost Army', *Die Zeit*, 19 June 1952.

33 Stephan, *Stalin's Secret War*, p. 287 n. 4.

34 Sudoplatov and Sudoplatov, *Special Tasks*, pp. 168–9.

35 Stephan, *Stalin's Secret War*, p. 149.

36 'Skorzeny's Ghost Army', *Die Zeit*, 19 June 1952.

37 Sevin, 'Operation Scherhorn', p. 39.

38 Sudoplatov and Sudoplatov, *Special Tasks*, p. 168.

9. The SS Changes Tack

1   Himmler to Kaltenbrunner, 16 September 1944; T-175, reel 122, frame 2648214, NARA; Biddiscombe, *SS Hunter Battalions*, p. 386, n. 54.

2   OKH section order, 12 November 1944; T-78/497 NARA.

3   Sudoplatov and Sudoplatov, *Special Tasks*, p. 251.

4   CIR, Annex No. IV. Skorzeny (*My Commando Operations*, p. 372) refers to *Sonnenblume* as Operation *Brown Bear*.

5   Skorzeny, *My Commando Operations*, pp. 371–2.

6   CIR, Annex No. IV.

7   Skorzeny, *My Commando Operations*, pp. 371–2.

8   Sudoplatov and Sudoplatov, *Special Tasks*, p. 250.

9   Doerries, *Hitler's Last Chief*, pp. 298–9. I-Netze were sometimes known as R-Netze.

10 Doerries, *Hitler's Last Chief*, p. 159.

11 CIR, p. 16.

12 CIAN, Vol 2, Preliminary Interrogation of Alice MACKERT @ Antoinette LINSER, OSS/X-2, Paris, 11 May 1945. Casier was also known as 'Yvonne' and Rosita de Villiers.

13 CIR, p. 32.

14 Statement of Walter Girg, CIAS.

15 Statement of Walter Girg, CIAS.

16 Statement of Walter Girg, CIAS.

17 Quoted in O'Reilly, *Hitler's Irishmen*, p. 203.

18 Statement of Walter Girg, CIAS.

19 Statement of Walter Girg, CIAS.

20 Berger, *Walter Girg*, pp. 141–2.

21 WGI, p. 9.

22 Statement of Walter Girg, CIAS; CIR, p. 25.

23 Girg says the 17th (statement in CIAS), but Kolberg fell to the Poles on the 18th, and Girg and his men were imprisoned for a day before their identity could be established.

24 Skorzeny, *My Commando Operations*, p. 409.

25 Statement of Walter Girg, CIAS.

26 His post-war interrogators judged that Skorzeny had 'a limited knowledge of agents employed by Amt VI-S' and 'his greater interest revolved around new sabotage methods, personal leadership of combat missions of Jagdverbände and political action against the Russians insofar as insurrection in the Ukraine and the Balkans could be promoted' (OSI, p. 3).

27 Quoted in Biddiscombe, *SS Hunter Battalions*, p. 39.

28 Alexander Krug, 'The Death Squads of Ostry Grun', *Süddeutsche Zeitung*, 11 May 2010. Available online at http://www.sueddeutsche.de/muenchen/der-fall-niznansky-die-mordkommandos-von-ostry-grun-1.757518 (retrieved 27 January 2018).

29 CIC Final Interrogation Report No. 83, Oberst Buntrock, Georg, 17 September 1945, p. 4.

30 CIA report EGMA-54241, CIAS.

31 CIA, 'Last Days of Ernst Kaltenbrunner'.

32 Schellenberg, 'Affidavit D'.

33 CIR, p. 8.

34 Doerries, *Hitler's Last Chief*, p. 123.

35 For a more comprehensive list of those in VI-E who were allegedly part of this group, see TWH: Testimony of Dr Wilhelm Hoettl, taken at Nurnberg, Germany, 4 October 1945,

14.30 to 16.50, pp. 5–6.

36   TWH2: Testimony of Wilhelm Hoettl, taken in Nurnberg, Germany, 15.50 to 16.30, 5 November 1945, by Lt. Col. Smith W. Brookhart, p. 3.

37   Höttl, *Secret Front*, p. 295.

10. Operation *Panzerfaust*: Budapest, October 1944

1   Skorzeny, *My Commando Operations*, p. 308.

2   Skorzeny, *Special Missions*, p. 128.

3   Skorzeny, *Special Missions*, p. 130.

4   Skorzeny, *Special Missions*, p. 131.

5   Skorzeny, *Special Missions*, p. 131. This document was stolen while Skorzeny was in captivity after the war, and has never resurfaced.

6   Höttl, *Secret Front*, p. 178.

7   TNH, p. 5.

8   Horthy, *Memoirs*, p. 281.

9   Horthy, *Memoirs*, p. 279.

10   Lehman, 'Unternehmen Panzerfaust', p. 218.

11   Höttl, *Secret Front*, p. 197.

12   Skorzeny, *My Commando Operations*, pp. 314–5.

13   As a witness at the Nuremberg trial of Veesenmayer. See Macartney, *October Fifteenth*, p. 389, n. 3. It seems likely that Bach-Zelewski was present to provide Plan B should Skorzeny's mission fail.

14   Skorzeny, *My Commando Operations*, p. 316. Skorzeny probably owed this insight to his parachute battalion commander, Milius.

15   Skorzeny, *My Commando Operations*, pp. 315–6.

16   TNH, p. 13.

17   Winkelmann to Himmler, 25 October 1944, quoted in Lehman, 'Unternehmen Panzerfaust', pp. 222–9.

18   Skorzeny (*My Commando Operations*, p. 312) claims that Fölkersam misheard the name 'Nikki', leading to this hilarious misunderstanding.

19   Höttl, *Secret Front*, pp. 198–9. Clages is often mistakenly referred to as 'Otto Klages', which may have been a rather transparent pseudonym. For more on Clages/Klages see David Bankir (ed.), *Secret Intelligence and the Holocaust* (New York: Enigma Books, 2006).

20   Horthy Senior claims he sent three guardsmen with his son (*Memoirs*, p. 285). Höttl calls the escort 'a powerful security squad … selected men, whom he proceeded to post in all the adjoining rooms and on the roofs of neighbouring houses' (*Secret Front*, p. 199). Skorzeny's account concurs with Höttl's (*My Commando Operations*, p. 313). The figure of two guardsmen is derived from Macartney (*October Fifteenth*, p. 400), who interviewed many of the participants.

21   Macartney, *October Fifteenth*, p. 400; Horthy, *Memoirs*, p. 286.

22   TNH, p. 13.

23   Winkelmann to Himmler, 25 October 1944, quoted in Lehman, 'Unternehmen Panzerfaust', p. 225.

24   Macartney, *October Fifteenth*, pp. 401–2.

25   Skorzeny, *My Commando Operations*, p. 318.

26 Skorzeny claims to have also encountered three Hungarian tanks (*My Commando Operations*, p. 318). Horthy denied that any were in the precinct (TNH, p. 13).

27 Skorzeny, *Special Missions*, p. 142.

28 Skorzeny, *Special Missions*, p. 142.

29 Winkelmann to Himmler, 25 October 1944, quoted in Lehman, 'Unternehmen Panzerfaust', p. 227.

30 Horthy, *Memoirs*, p. 291, n. 19.

31 Horthy, *Memoirs*, p. 291, n. 19.

32 Skorzeny, *My Commando Operations*, p. 320.

33 Winkelmann suggests that the tank idea was originally improvised by Bach-Zelewski (letter to Himmler, 25 October 1944, quoted in Lehman, 'Unternehmen Panzerfaust', p. 226).

34 Horthy, *Memoirs*, pp. 293–4.

35 CIR, Annex No. IV, p. 40.

36 About half of them Hungarian soldiers, the rest mostly Waffen-SS.

11. Everything on One Card: Operation *Greif*

1 Skorzeny, *Special Missions*, p. 146.

2 Skorzeny, My Commando Operations, p. 327.

3 Skorzeny, *My Commando Operations*, p. 327. Skorzeny's account of this meeting is largely corroborated by the OKW war diary. Under the annex 'Unternehmen Skorzeny' it notes the intended use of enemy uniforms, and adds: 'The enemy has tried this tactic out in the East as well as the West and once again just recently during the seizure of Aachen.' Skorzeny's 'successful mission to liberate the Duce proved that he was well qualified to carry out this kind of operation. On 22.10. he received the order to seize a Meuse crossing in full camouflage and to spread confusion among the enemy using small commandos' (OKW, *Kriegstagebuch*, p. 448). General Omar Bradley, commander of the American 12th Army Group, denied the Aachen allegation. In fact, a small unit of US Army Rangers under Office of Strategic Services (OSS) command did mount a false flag operation using German uniforms and papers shortly before the main attack on Aachen. Kendall D. Gott, *Breaking the Mold: Tanks in the Cities*, ebook edn (Pickle Partners Publishing 2014), pp. 23–4.

4 OKW, *Kriegstagebuch*, p. 431.

5 Schadewitz, *Meuse First*, pp. 4–5.

6 Quoted in Schadewitz, *Meuse First*, p. 6.

7 Schadewitz, *Meuse First*, p. 12.

8 Quoted in Schadewitz, *Meuse First*, p. 265.

9 Skorzeny, *Special Missions*, p. 149.

10 Quoted in Schadewitz, *Meuse First*, p. 257.

11 Skorzeny, *My Commando Operations*, p. 334. The Aachen 'false flag' incident was widely believed at the time. During Skorzeny's later trial, Dr Percy E. Schramm, a Kriegstagebuch official at OKW, stated on 22 July 1947: 'I remember very vividly that shortly before Aachen was taken (20.10.1944) High Command received a report that American soldiers had attacked there wearing German uniforms' (quoted in Schadewitz, *Meuse First*, p. 251).

12 Quoted in Skorzeny, *Special Missions*, p. 149.

13 Westphal, quoted in Schadewitz, *Meuse First*, p. 22.

14   Quoted in Schadewitz, *Meuse First*, p. 25.

15   Skorzeny, *Special Missions*, p. 151.

16   Skorzeny, *Special Missions*, p. 151.

17   See for example, 'CI News Sheet No.12. Part 1. Information from Areas Still Under Enemy Control', p. 4. In section 2 a verbatim translation of the order (source: First US Army G-2 Periodical Report No.164) is merely referred to as 'a recently captured German document appealing for recruits for special tasks on the Western Front'. KV2/403 512702, NAUK.

18   Skorzeny, *Special Missions*, p. 151.

19   Skorzeny, *Special Missions*, p. 155.

20   Skorzeny, *Special Missions*, p. 155; *My Commando Operations*, pp. 331–2; Schadewitz, *Meuse First*, p. 27.

21   Schadewitz, *Meuse First*, p. 201.

22   Skorzeny, quoted in Schadewitz, *Meuse First*, p. 29.

23   CIR, Annex No. IV, p. 36.

24   Schadewitz, *Meuse First*, p. 49.

25   Skorzeny, cited in Schadewitz, p. 31.

26   Skorzeny, *Special Missions*, pp. 156–7.

27   See Schadewitz, *Meuse First*, p. 305, n. 107.

28   Not 12 as he reported in his memoirs; Schadewitz, *Meuse First*, p. 305, n. 108.

29   Skorzeny, *Special Missions*, p. 157.

30   Skorzeny, *Special Missions*, p. 157.

31   Skorzeny, *Special Missions*, p. 157.

32   Skorzeny, *Special Missions*, p. 157.

33   Schadewitz, *Meuse First*, p. 282.

34   Scherf, quoted in Schadewitz, *Meuse First*, p. 44.

35   Skorzeny, *Special Missions*, p. 161.

36   Skorzeny, *Special Missions*, p. 158.

37   Skorzeny, *Special Missions*, p. 158.

38   In *Special Missions*, p. 160, Skorzeny claims the officer was 'N', 'a lieutenant in the Commando Company'. In *My Commando Operations* (p. 337) it is 'Hauptmann Stielau' (actually Oberleutnant Stielau at the time). It is possible that 'N' was SS-Untersturmführer Ludwig Nebel. Although Nebel was not a member of the Kommandokompanie, he was a Waffen-SS officer who spoke excellent French. Nebel, through Besekow, was soon to be sent on Operation *Charlie*, a sabotage mission associated with *Greif*. He had previously worked under cover on Operation *Peter*.

39   Skorzeny, *Geheimkommando*, quoted in Schadewitz, pp. 202–3.

40   Skorzeny, *Special Missions*, p. 159.

41   Skorzeny, *Special Missions*, p. 159.

42   Behr, record of his cross-examination, Case 6-100 in the Dachau Trials. These poison bullets would come back to haunt Skorzeny at the time of his trial in 1947.

43   Deputy Judge Advocate's Office 7708 War Crimes Group, 14 April 1948, Otto Skorzeny, et al., Case N.6-100, Review and Recommendations.

44   Behr, record of his cross-examination, Case 6-100.

45   Schadewitz, *Meuse First*, p. 209; Skorzeny, *My Commando Operations*, p. 338.

46   Skorzeny, *Special Missions*, p. 161.

47   CIAN, Vol 1, Ostrich Situation Report, Lt Michaelis to Chief, SCI, 22 December 1944.

48   CIR, Annex No. IV, pp. 34–5.
49   Skorzeny, *Special Missions*, p. 163. Heinz Guderian was then Chef des Generalstabes des Heeres (chief of staff of OKH), with primary responsibility for the Eastern Front.
50   Skorzeny, *Special Missions*, p. 163.
51   Skorzeny, *Special Missions*, p. 163.
52   Schadewitz, *Meuse First*, p. 307, n. 140.
53   Skorzeny, *Special Missions*, p. 163.
54   When Skorzeny introduced Radl to Hitler, 'our Karli was so impressed that he stood at attention as if cast in stone' (*My Commando Operations*, p. 339). Though Radl was happy to publish a bowdlerised version of his military exploits, the post-war textile merchant living quietly in Frankfurt may have been none too pleased to see himself depicted as a sycophantic admirer of the Führer.
55   Skorzeny, *Special Missions*, p. 164.
56   Schadewitz, *Meuse First*, p. 275.
57   Jarkowsky, German Special Operations, pp. 26–8.
58   OSI, p. 2; SWT, Sheet 2.
59   We know this from the timeline. Skorzeny was briefed very early about *Stösser*'s specific objectives, probably no later than 9 December; and certainly earlier than Heydte himself. Heydte learned of Skorzeny's involvement almost casually during a second encounter with Dietrich.
60   Jarkowsky, German Special Operations, p. 49.
61   Sepp Dietrich interrogation transcript, p. 11, AIR.
62   Jarkowsky, German Special Operations, p. 49.

12. Operation *Greif*: Mission and Aftermath

1   The timeline varies in different accounts; the times given by Beevor (*Ardennes*, pp. 111–2) are followed here.
2   Bergström, *Ardennes*, p. 82.
3   Schadewitz, *Meuse First*, p. 71.
4   KRI, p. 9.
5   Built by Henschel, but partially developed by Porsche, the Tiger II entered service in July 1944.
6   Quoted in Pallud, *Battle of the Bulge*, pp. 112–3.
7   Quoted in Pallud, *Battle of the Bulge*, pp. 112–3.
8   Schadewitz, *Meuse First*, map 11, p. 329.
9   Skorzeny, *Special Missions*, p. 171.
10   For instance, the raising of GI helmets during the day; the use of colour-coded Verey flares at night (Schadewitz, *Meuse First*, p. 228).
11   Quoted in Foley, *Commando Extraordinary*, p. 140.
12   Appendix No 2 to G-2 Report No. 151 (22.12.44) German Deception, quoted in Schadewitz, *Meuse First*, p. 231.
13   Summersby, *Eisenhower*, pp. 202–3.
14   Summersby, *Eisenhower*, p. 208.
15   Schadewitz, *Meuse First*, p. 226.
16   Skorzeny, *Special Missions*, pp. 171–2; Schadewitz, *Meuse First*, pp. 209–10.
17   Skorzeny's claims were largely corroborated by Heinz Rohde in an account that appeared in the 10 January 1951 edition of *Der Spiegel*. The fact that both Skorzeny and Rohde

believed these things to be true does not, of course, necessarily mean they were so; merely that they had access to the same source of information.

18 Quoted in Schadewitz, *Meuse First*, p. 213.

19 'Concerning orders! I didn't get any. Hardieck said once ... that I would be ordered to defend the bridge at Huy.' Behr had no contact with Hardieck after 15 December, the day after he drove his jeep to the start zone at Stadtkyll. Behr, record of his cross-examination, Skorzeny court proceedings – Case 6-100, document P-32, RG 153, NARA.

20 Skorzeny, *Special Missions*, p. 171.

21 Skorzeny, *Geheimkommando*, p. 312f.

22 Rohde, 'Mit Shakespeare-Englisch'.

23 Skorzeny, *Special Missions*, p. 174.

24 First US Army, Annex No. 12 Provost Marshal Section Report, p. 229. The following were sentenced and shot at Henri Chapelle during December 1944: Oberfähnrich Günther Billing; Obergefreiter Wilhelm Schmidt; Unteroffizier Manfred Parnass; Leutnant Charles William Wiesenfeld; Feldwebel Manfred Bronny; Stabsgefreiter Hans Reich. All were classified as belonging to Einheit Stielau, stab Solar. Additional defendants were: Leutnant Arno Krause, alias Private Josef Kinsey; Leutnant zur See Günther Schilz, alias Corporal John Weller (executed on 5 May 1945); Unteroffizier Erhard Miegel, alias Private James Smith; Obermachinenmaat Horst Görlich, alias Private Walter Verge; Obergefreiter Robert Pollack, alias Second Lieutenant Charly Holtzmann; Obergefreiter Rolf Benjamin Meyer, alias Second Lieutenant Sammy Rosner; and Obergefreiter Hans Wittsack, alias Private Alfred Rozanski. To be added to this list are Gefreiter Otto Struller, alias Captain Cecil A. Dyer, alias Richard Baumgardner, executed on 11 January 1945, and Obergefreiter Anton J. Morzuck, both of Einheit Stielau, stab Solar. The only Einheit Stielau captive known to have escaped the death penalty is Unteroffizier Heinrich Pipitz. Several other members of Panzerbrigade 150 were also tried and executed. Schadewitz, *Meuse First*, note 352 p. 314.

25 Rohde, 'Mit Shakespeare-Englisch'. Rohde is also referring to the later operation with Skorzeny at Schwedt an der Oder. Rohde himself was awarded the Deutsches Kreuz in Gold for his actions during the Ardennes campaign.

26 Rohde, 'Mit Shakespeare-Englisch'.

27 European Historical Division, European Theater Historical Interrogation (ETHINT) 10 1 SS Pz Regt (11-24 Dec 44) Peiper, Jochen (Freising Germany: September 1945), p. 6.

28 Skorzeny, *Special Missions*, p. 170.

29 Schadewitz, *Meuse*, p. 206. Behr says that he remained at Ligneuville until the 27th, when he was ordered to report to the Kommandokompanie command post at Schloss Wallerode, northeast of St Vith. There is evidence of at least two other jeep commando operations after the 18th. According to Behr: 'Shortly before Christmas an attempt was made by soldiers to penetrate the American lines in the vicinity of Ligneuville ... Oberleutnant Schmidthuber was killed and I saw the corpse the following day' (Behr: record of his cross examination). The other was an expedition in which Rohde and Stielau participated. It took place around 10 January and involved three teams. One team leader, Kapitänleutnant Schmitt, was killed in the action – which was not carried out under Skorzeny's orders (Rohde, 'Mit Shakespeare-Englisch').

30 Some sources claim that up to 1,200 paratroopers were involved. The lower figure is cited both in the Operation Order for the Heeresgruppe B Attack on Antwerp across the Meuse, and by at least one participant in *Stösser*. See Schadewitz, *Meuse First*, pp. 277–9.

31   Skorzeny, *Special Missions*, p. 170.

32   Skorzeny, *Special Missions*, p. 171.

33   Skorzeny claimed falsely that Behr's report dated to the 18th, by which time Behr could have seen clear evidence of the American build-up (*Special Missions*, p.171).

34   Scherf, quoted in Schadewitz, *Meuse First*, p. 145.

35   Scherf, quoted in Schadewitz, *Meuse First*, p. 145.

36   Scherf, quoted in Schadewitz, *Meuse First*, p. 146.

37   Schadewitz, *Meuse First*, p. 154.

38   Pulver, *Longest Journey*, pp. 72–3.

39   Scherf, quoted in Schadewitz, *Meuse First*, p. 149.

40   Scherf, quoted in Schadewitz, *Meuse First*, p. 149.

41   Scherf, quoted in Schadewitz, *Meuse First*, p. 149. Skorzeny's own account of this episode (*Special Missions*, p. 175) omits this confrontation, and glosses over some of his own errors of judgement. Scherf's version is corroborated by American sources.

42   Mandt, quoted in Schadewitz, *Meuse First*, p. 156.

43   Mandt, quoted in Schadewitz, *Meuse First*, p. 156.

44   Pergrin, *First Across the Rhine*, p. 157.

45   Erdmann/Gries, quoted in Schadewitz, *Meuse First*, p. 164.

46   CIR, Annex No. IV, p. 36.

47   Skorzeny, *Special Missions*, p. 177.

48   Thompson, *Malmédy Belgium Mistaken Bombing*.

49   Skorzeny, *Special Missions*, p. 180.

50   Skorzeny, *Special Missions*, p. 180.

51   Wulf, quoted in Schadewitz, *Meuse First*, p. 174.

13. Implosion: The Schwedt Bridgehead

1   Beevor, *Berlin*, p. 6.

2   Skorzeny, *My Commando Operations*, p. 398. It is by no means clear who had previously been in charge of this unit; most likely, the issue was left hanging.

3   Skorzeny, *My Commando Operations*, p. 406.

4   Berger, *Walter Girg*, p. 62. Whether Skorzeny actually knew of Fölkersam's capture and preferred to accord him a hero's death is open to debate. 'Fölkersam had a younger brother who was likewise with the Brandenburg division. As a prisoner in the Soviet Union in 1947, he was said to have learned that Adrian had recovered from his injuries and was being held as a prisoner. I was told that he believes this to this day.' (Skorzeny, *My Commando Operations*, p. 407.) Patrick von Fölkersam, born 1916, survived Soviet captivity and later settled in Cologne. He became a noted Kremlinologist.

5   KRI, p. 9.

6   Skorzeny, *My Commando Operations*, p. 406; Munoz, *Forgotten Legions*, p. 208.

7   Skorzeny, My Commando Operations, p. 406.

8   Wilhelm Walther, interviewed for the documentary *Hitler's Useful Idols – Otto Skorzeny* (dir. Robert Gokl, 2010).

9   Skorzeny, *Special Missions*, p.181. Himmler Command 831, 31 January 1945.

10   Goebbels diary, cited in Longerich, *Heinrich Himmler*, p. 716.

11   Beevor, *Berlin*, pp. 53–4.

12   Hans-Georg Eismann, quoted in Beevor, *Berlin*, p. 53.

13   Beevor, *Berlin*, pp. 69–70.

14 In *My Commando Operations* Skorzeny attributes the command of Nordwest to Appel, the former commander of the Heinrichsburg A-Schule in Yugoslavia (p. 414). The change-over to Hoyer seems to have happened very early during the Schwedt operation. The up-to-90 men is an estimate by Radl – a Flemish company remained behind. Nordwest, all told, probably numbered no more than 140 men (KIR, p. 7).

15 CIAS, Appendix 1 and 2a.

16 Skorzeny, *Special Missions*, p. 180; Rohde, 'Mit Shakespeare-Englisch'.

17 Skorzeny, *My Commando Operations*, p. 414.

18 Skorzeny, *Special Missions*, p. 181.

19 Skorzeny, *My Commando Operations*, p. 416.

20 Skorzeny noted (*My Commando Operations*, p. 418), with slightly smug approval, that many of them were Communists who had now enlisted in the Nazi cause.

21 Skorzeny, *Special Missions*, p. 185; *My Commando Operations*, p. 149.

22 Beevor, *Berlin*, pp. 87–8.

23 SS-Untersturmführer Hans-Joachim Draeger, quoted in Munoz, *Forgotten Legions*, pp. 76–9.

24 Skorzeny, *Special Missions*, p. 183.

25 Skorzeny, *Special Missions*, p. 183.

26 Skorzeny, *My Commando Operations*, p. 421.

27 Skorzeny, *Special Missions*, p. 185.

28 Munoz, *Forgotten Legions*, p. 79.

29 Bolz, Karl Ernst, Obersturmführer SS Jagdverbände, First Detailed Interrogation Report Case no: SO35, 11 January 1946, p. 3, US Military Intelligence Service in Austria. German Intelligence Service (WWII), Volume 2 RC Box 03, RC Collection 230/902/64/1, NARA, www.cia.gov/library/readingroom/docs/GERMAN%20INTELLIGENCE%20 SERVICE%20%28WWII%29%2C%20%20VOL.%202_0003.pdf (retrieved 29 January 2018).

30 Skorzeny, *My Commando Operations*, pp. 421–2.

31 Hamilton, *The Oder Front 1945, Vol. 2*, p. 166.

32 Skorzeny, *My Commando Operations*, p. 423.

33 The Russians were overextended at this point. They had plenty of armour, but much of their infantry lagged behind and was involved in mopping up operations.

34 Skorzeny has been credited with fighting at Malmédy, wishful thinking that seems to have originated in Infield, *Hitler's Commando*, p. 91. He made no such claim in his memoirs, and appears to have spun Infield a yarn.

35 Hamilton, *The Oder Front* 1945, *Vol. 2*, p. 166.

36 Skorzeny, *Special Missions*, pp. 186–8.

37 Skorzeny, *Special Missions*, p. 187.

38 Skorzeny suggests that the services of Sturmgeschützbrigade 210 resulted from this meeting (*My Commando Operations*, p. 421); in fact, it had already arrived at the bridgehead.

39 Skorzeny, *My Commando Operations*, p. 420. Skorzeny blamed Bach-Zelewski for the contretemps over Nipperwiese, but that actually pre-dated his appointment.

40 Though not merely through personal spite. Bach-Zelewski as Korps commander was preoccupied with ensuring all three units under his command were adequately prepared for the upcoming German counter-offensive, Operation *Sonnenwende*.

41 Whiting, *Skorzeny*, p. 83.

42   Günter Prütz, quoted in Ballentin, *Die Zerstörung*, p. 98.

43   Skorzeny, *Special Missions*, p. 190. In *My Commando Operations* (p. 422) Skorzeny implies that the visit took place around 10 February, but Prütz's account places it on 7 February. Skorzeny suggests that the visit took place towards the end of the day; Prütz, at the beginning.

44   Skorzeny, *Special Missions*, p. 189.

45   BAM, 'Vermerk: Reichsmarschall regt an, Teile der Marine-Division "Nord" im Brückenkopf Schwedt...Mitteilung Major Volkmann, Adjutant Reichsmarschall' 7.2.1945.

46   Skorzeny, *My Commando Operations*, p. 421.

47   Skorzeny, *My Commando Operations*, pp. 424–5.

48   BAM, 'Oderkorps: Kampfgruppe Schwedt erzielte am 23., 24.2. 23 Scharfschützenabschüsse, somit seit 13.2 insgesamt von der Kampfgruppe 260 Scharfschützenabschüsse bestätigt.' Tagesmeldung 24.2.45.

49   Skorzeny, *My Commando Operations*, p 418.

50   Skorzeny, *Special Missions*, p. 191.

51   Skorzeny, *My Commando Operations*, p. 426.

52   Of the three, only Ritter actually took charge of the defence of Berlin.

53   The *Mail* cutting is included in Skorzeny's British intelligence file (KV 2/403), among copious intelligence documents. The code-breaking suggested here relates not to Enigma but the Lorenz cipher used by OKW – of which Jodl was operation staff chief.

54   BAM, Der Reichsführer An 1.Kdr. General Oder Korps; 2. SS-Obersturmbannführer Skorzeny; 3. SS-Obersturmbannführer Kempin, 21.2.1945; Hamilton, *The Oder Front 1945, Vol. 2*, p. 167.

55   Although a tactical disaster, *Sonnenwende* did achieve a limited strategic objective. It convinced Stalin to postpone his offensive against Berlin for two months.

56   Skorzeny, *Special Missions*, p. 188.

57   BAM, Vortragsnotiz für Reichsführer-SS, 27.2.45. For a full translation see: Hamilton, *The Oder Front 1945, Vol. 2*, pp. 306–8.

58   Interrogation of Otto Skorzeny by 307th CIC Det, SCI US 7th Army, report no: S-975; date: 23 May 1945, pp. 25–6.

59   Skorzeny, *My Commando Operations*, p. 417.

60   Rudel, Intermediate Interrogation Report, 4 June 1945, p. 6.

61   Skorzeny, *Special Missions*, p. 191.

62   'Vor 70 Jahren im Fadenkreuz der Amerikaner', *Märkische Allgemeine*, 9 April 2015. The Allied raid, which was carried out by American B17 bombers on the afternoon of 10 April 1945, targeted the wider Oranienburg area, primarily the airstrip used for Me 262 jet planes.

63   Skorzeny, *My Commando Operations*, p. 427.

64   Skorzeny, *My Commando Operations*, p. 427.

65   Rudel mentions the encounter in his autobiography: 'Field Marshal Greim, Skorzeny or Hanna Reitsch look in for an hour's chat.' *Stuka Pilot*, ch. 17 – The Death Struggle of the Last Months, ebook edn (Black House Publishing, 2012).

66   Munoz, *Forgotten Legions*, p. 103.

67   Skorzeny, *Special Missions*, p. 192.

68   Paterson, *Weapons of Desperation*, p. 220.

69   Rudi Günter, quoted in Infield, *Hitler's Commando*, p. 108. Günter's account appears to be authentic, but Infield's reconstruction of the raid is faulty. He seems to have believed that the mission was targeted at the Ludendorff Bridge, not the pontoon bridge, and got the date wrong. Skorzeny's own account (*Special Missions*, p. 192) is vague and misleading. He does, however, indicate that the attack was on the pontoon bridge. The confusion may arise from the fact that Schreiber's team was originally tooled up for the aborted joint assault on the Ludendorff Bridge.

14. Skorzeny's Last Stand

1   Note for example Skorzeny's fury over the way Armaments Minister Albert Speer gave him false hope about the emergence of a game-changing super weapon during a visit to FHQ in mid-February: 'In my presence Minister Speer promised the Reichsführer new aircraft and new bombs for the beginning of April. Today Speer assures us that he then considered any hope illusory. However, on one February day I was able to speak with him alone. I wanted to learn more about the famous "secret weapons", which we had been hearing volumes about since October 1944. He could have advised me to give up any hope in this direction. However he contented himself with saying to me, "The decision will soon be made." This was a sentence that all soldiers heard often. I am not surprised that Speer forgot to include it in his memoirs.' *My Commando Operations*, p 425.

2   Speer, Inside the Third Reich, p. 569.

3   Skorzeny, My Commando Operations, p. 428.

4   Skorzeny, *Special Missions*, p. 193. The encounter occurred on or around 29 March.

5   Skorzeny's *Gemeinschaft der Ritterkreuzträger* card (no. 402, 11 April 1956, lot 9, OSA) indicates award of the oak leaves on 18 March 1945, not at the end of the month. However, his last meeting with Hitler may have post-dated the allocation of the award.

6   Biddiscombe, *SS Hunter Battalions*, p. 351.

7   KRI, p. 14.

8   Quoted in Doerries, *Hitler's Last Chief*, p. 250.

9   Quoted in Mitcham, *Panzers in Winter*, p. 166.

10   Foley, Commando Extraordinary, p. 169; Skorzeny, My Commando Operations, p. 431.

11   Skorzeny, *My Commando Operations*, pp. 430–1.

12   BAE.

13   BAE, p. 2.

14   CIR, Annex No. II, p. 28.

15   KRI, p. 5.

16   NBS, p. 15.

17   Ernst Kaltenbrunner, Intermediate Interrogation Report, Annex No. VI, 28 June 1945, p. 23 (Fold 3 image no 232034068) and general report p. 7 (Fold 3 image no 232033974). RG 238, NARA M1270.

18   Doerries, *Hitler's Last Chief*, p. 250.

19   CIW, p. 2.

20   Quoted in Longerich, *Himmler*, p. 714.

21   Skorzeny, *Special Operations*, p. 152.

22   CIW, p. 2.

23   CIW, p. 3.

24   OSI, p. 3.

25 KRI, p. 14.

26 KRI, p. 14.

27 CIW, p. 4.

28 Doerries, *Hitler's Last Chief*, p. 293.

29 Doerries, *Hitler's Last Chief*, p. 292; Testimony of Ernst Kaltenbrunner, p. 18, AIR; Interrogation of Gottlob Berger, pp. 10–13, AIR.

30 Biddiscombe, *SS Hunter Battalions*, p. 345.

31 CIA, 'Last Days of Ernst Kaltenbrunner'; Hastings, *Secret War*, p. 402.

32 Beevor, *Berlin*, pp. 195–6.

33 Skorzeny, *Special Missions*, p. 195.

34 KRI, p. 5.

35 WGS, pp. 9–10.

36 WGS, pp. 9–10.

37 OSI, p. 1; CIR, Annex No. II, p. 29.

38 Biddiscombe, *SS Hunter Battalions*, pp. 351–2.

39 KRI, p. 3.

40 For SKA strength estimates, see KRI, p. 14.

41 Kershaw, *Hitler*, p. 800.

42 Speer, Inside the Third Reich, p. 640.

43 RFE, pp. 1, 4.

44 Alford and Savas, *Nazi Millionaires*, p. 95.

45 ASI, p. 4.

46 ASI, p. 6.

47 ASI, p. 8.

48 Testimony of Walter Schellenberg, Nuremberg Germany, 13 November 1945, pp. 20–1, RG 238 NARA M1270.

49 Quoted in Biddiscombe, *SS Hunter Battalions*, p. 354.

50 Final Interrogation Report No. 8, O/Stubaf Werner Goettsch, 24 July 1945; see attached Special Interrogation Report, 17 July, p. 3. FOI Special Collection, Werner Goettsch, document 19, https://www.cia.gov/library/readingroom/docs/GOETTSCH%2C%20WERNER_0019.pdf (retrieved 15 October 2017).

51 Because of the increasing intensity of Allied bombing, in February 1945 Kaltenbrunner had ordered the RSHA's sizeable foreign exchange assets (most of which were earmarked for Amt VI) to be transferred to a secret location near Bad Sulza in Thuringia.

52 Spacil's diary, quoted in Alford and Savas, *Nazi Millionaires*, p. 95.

53 A motorcycle courier service operated between Fischhorn Castle and the cache – subsequently known as Shipment No. 31 – so giving Spacil a certain amount of notice should the Americans arrive. See RFE, Shipment 31, pp. 1–2.

54 Spacil's diary, quoted in Alford and Savas, *Nazi Millionaires*, p. 96.

55 Interrogation of Kurt Schiebel, quoted in Alford and Savas, *Nazi Millionaires*, p. 112.

56 The loot may have contributed working capital to Radl's post-war textiles enterprise, Otto-Radl.

57 CIR, Annex No. II, p. 27; Biddiscombe, *SS Hunter Battalions*, p. 351.

58 KRI, p. 5. Radl says the departure from Puch took place after 1 May, whereas Skorzeny says 25 April.

59   Memorandum for the Officer in Charge re Otto Skorzeny, 23 May 1945, Section III, p. 2, https://www.cia.gov/library/readingroom/docs/SKORZENY%2C%20OTTO%20%20%20VOL.%201_0029.pdf (retrieved 15 October 2017).

60   CIA, 'Last Days of Ernst Kaltenbrunner'.

61   Höttl, *Secret Front*, p. 294.

62   OSS Mission for Germany US Forces, Subject: Dissension in the German Intelligence Services, Lt-Col. A. H. Berding, Chief of OSS/X-2 Germany, to Chief of OSS Mission Germany, 7 July 1945, p. 7. Donovan Nuremberg Trials Collection, Cornell University Library. Available online at http://reader.library.cornell.edu/docviewer/digital?id=nur:01487#page/6/mode/1up (retrieved 30 January 2018).

63   Testimony of Wilhelm Hoettl, taken at Nurnberg, Germany, from 1430 to 1650, 4 Oct 1945, by Smith W. Brookhart, Lt Col IGD, OUSCC, pp. 13–14. RG 238 NARA M1270. Available online at https://www.fold3.com/image/231903117 (retrieved 30 January 2018).

64   A notable example of this was Skorzeny's espousal of *Regenbogen* (Rainbow), an operation that would have involved linking SKA with SD-Inland's guerrilla organisation, which intended to foment terror throughout liberated Europe. Biddiscombe, *SS Hunter Battalions*, p. 354.

65   Final Interrogation Report No. 8, O/Stubaf Werner Goettsch, 24 July 1945, Special Interrogation Report, 4 July, '8. Skorzeny and the Werwolf' pp. 2–3, https://www.cia.gov/library/readingroom/docs/GOETTSCH%2C%20WERNER_0019.pdf (retrieved 30 January 2018).

66   Final Interrogation Report No. 8, O/Stubaf Werner Goettsch, 24 July 1945, Special Interrogation Report, 4 July, '8. Skorzeny and the Werwolf' pp. 2–3, https://www.cia.gov/library/readingroom/docs/GOETTSCH%2C%20WERNER_0019.pdf (retrieved 30 January 2018).

67   ASI, p. 14; CIA, 'Last Days of Ernst Kaltenbrunner'.

68   Memo Spearhead to Warroom, 8 June 1945, 11 GMT. OS, RG 238 NARA M1270. Available online at https://www.fold3.com/image/232065170 (retreived 30 January 2018).

69   CIA, 'Last Days of Ernst Kaltenbrunner'.

70   KRI, p. 14.

71   Skorzeny, *Special Missions*, p. 196.

72   Infield, *Hitler's Commando*, p. 116.

73   Memorandum, p. 1, OSI.

15. Trial and Errors

1   Skorzeny, *My Commando Operations*, p. 437.

2   Skorzeny, *My Commando Operations*, p. 446; Foley, *Commando Extraordinary*, p. 179.

3   'Westzonenpolizei steckt voller Nazis', *Neues Deutschland*, 1 March 1961, p. 2.

4   Memorandum, p. 5, OSI.

5   Memorandum, p. 5, OSI.

6   Skorzeny, *Special Missions*, p. 202.

7   Memorandum 19 May 1945, AIR.

8   Cable, S18 1100, AIR.

9   Liddell Diaries, Vol. 12, 25 May 1945, p. 346, KV4/196, NAUK.

10   Liddell Diaries, Vol. 12, 25 May 1945, p. 346, KV4/196, NAUK.

11 Foley, *Commando Extraordinary*, p. 177.

12 Spearhead, Amzon to Warroom, London, 7 June 1945; Spearhead to Scarp, undated, AIR.

13 Note, 15 June 1945, AIR.

14 Quoted in Doerries, *Hitler's Last Chief*, p. 47, n. 354. The former Amt VI chief, having voluntarily returned from Stockholm to Germany, surrendered to the American authorities on 18 June 1945.

15 Bassiouni, *Crimes Against Humanity*, pp. 490–1.

16 In the so-called Ministries Trial, which lasted from 6 January to 18 November 1948. Schellenberg was found guilty and sentenced to six years' imprisonment in 1949. He was released in 1951 due to terminal liver disease. He died in Italy on 31 March 1952. Coco Chanel, reputedly his one-time mistress, paid the by-now-penniless Schellenberg's funeral expenses.

17 Riedel, 'U.S. War Crimes Tribunals', pp. 574–5.

18 Riedel, 'U.S. War Crimes Tribunals', p. 567.

19 Skorzeny, *Special Missions*, p. 203.

20 Skorzeny, *My Commando Operations*, pp. 440–2.

21 Preliminary Interrogation Report, pp. 1–2, RGI.

22 Special Interrogation Report, p. 2, RGI.

23 Special Interrogation Report, pp. 3–4, RGI.

24 Special Interrogation Report, p. 4, RGI.

25 Special Interrogation Report, p. 5, RGI.

26 Schadewitz, *Meuse First*, p. 282; Special Interrogation Report, p. 5, RGI.

27 Special Interrogation Report, p. 6, RGI.

28 Special Interrogation Report, p. 7, RGI.

29 Skorzeny, *Special Missions*, p. 209. Under International Military Tribunal rules, witnesses were able to provide affidavits without having to appear in person for cross-examination.

30 Skorzeny, *Special Operations*, p. 211.

31 Skorzeny, *Special Operations*, p. 212.

32 Skorzeny, *Special Operations*, p. 212.

33 Skorzeny, *Special Operations*, p. 212.

34 The conduct of the trial was controversial even at the time. Complaints about abuse of process and a miscarriage of justice brought by the senior defence counsel eventually led to an Army commission of inquiry, US Senate hearings, and some acutely embarrassing revelations about the use of torture to extract confessions. Sentences were gradually scaled back and the defendants released.

35 Testimony of Harry W. Thon, in Committe of the Armed Services, *Malmédy*, p. 1240.

36 Skorzeny, *Special Missions*, p. 208.

37 Knittel, quoted in Schadewitz, *Meuse First*, p. 282.

38 In 1949. Testimony of Colonel A.H. Rosenfeld in Committee of the Armed Services, *Malmédy*, p. 1428.

39 Foley, *Commando Extraordinary*, p. 183.

40 Skorzeny, *Special Missions*, pp. 213–4.

41 Weingartner, *A Peculiar Crusade*.

42 Skorzeny, *Special Missions*, p. 214.

43 Skorzeny, *Special Missions*, p. 214.

44 Testimony of Colonel A.H. Rosenfeld in Committe of the Armed Services, *Malmédy*, p. 1391.

45 Laws and Customs of War on Land (Hague IV), Article 23, 18 October 1907. Available online at http://avalon.law.yale.edu/20th_century/hague04.asp#art23 (retrieved 30 January 2018).

46 CIR, The German Sabotage Service, 23 July 1945, p. 44, Annex No. VI, Poison Bullets, KV2/403 NAUK.

47 Skorzeny, *My Commando Operations*, p. 437.

48 Schadewitz, *Meuse First*, p. 205.

49 CIR, The German Sabotage Service, 23 July 1945, p. 44, Annex No. VI, Poison Bullets, KV2/403 NAUK. However, there was no evidence at that stage that they had ever been used.

50 Infield, *Hitler's Commando*, pp. 136–8; Foley, *Commando Extraordinary*, pp. 188–9.

51 Skorzeny (*My Commando Operations*, p. 447) hints that Gerhard was badly beaten up later for the trouble he had caused during the trial.

52 Schadewitz, *Meuse First*, p. 247.

53 Schramm, quoted in Schadewitz, *Meuse First*, pp. 252–3.

54 Articles 6 and 9 of the Geneva Prisoners of War Convention, 1929. Koessler, 'International Law', p 42.

55 Skorzeny, *Geheimkommando*, p. 409, quoted in Schadewitz, *Meuse First*, p. 245.

56 Koessler, 'International Law', p. 4n.

57 Koessler, 'International Law', p. 6.

58 Kocherscheidt, Case no. 6-100 P33; Behr, Case no. 6-100 P32; Knittel, Case no.6-100, OST. There were two other corroborative hearsay statements, neither exactly matching the alleged facts.

59 Koessler, 'International Law', p. 25.

60 Koessler, 'International Law', p. 13.

61 Judge Advocate's review, Case no. 6-100, 14 April 1948, OST, RG 549 NARA (M1106).

62 Koessler, 'International Law', p. 24.

63 Koessler, 'International Law', p. 14.

64 Foley, *Commando Extraordinary*, p. 194.

65 Koessler, 'International Law', p. 19.

66 Koessler, 'International Law', p. 19.

67 Skorzeny, *Special Missions*, p. 216.

68 Quoted in Schadewitz, *Meuse First*, p. 244. There is evidence that Knittel was severely tortured (Committe of the Armed Services, *Malmédy*, p. 1623).

69 Koessler, 'International Law', p. 7.

70 Schadewitz, *Meuse First*, p. 254.

71 Höttl, *Secret Front*, p. 295.

72 Koessler, 'International Law', p. 18.

73 Foley, *Commando Extraordinary*, p. 198.

74 Seaman, *Bravest of the Brave*, p. 225.

75 *Daily Express*, 7 May 1952.

76 Yeo-Thomas suffered extensive damage, physical and psychological, during the war. Violent headaches were compounded by depression, loss of coordination and motor control, and eventually what appears to have been dementia. Yeo-Thomas died of a massive cerebral haemorrhage in February 1964, aged 62.

77 Skorzeny, *Special Missions*, p. 216.
78 Skorzeny, *Special Missions*, p. 216.

16. Escape from Darmstadt

1 CIR, Annex No. IV, p. 33.
2 Special Activities of Skorzeny Group, pp. 1–2, AIR.
3 It is clear that Skorzeny was angling for this particular privilege from a letter he wrote to Colonel Potter on 16 September 1947 (Infield, *Hitler's Commando*, p. 145).
4 Skorzeny, *Special Missions*, p. 218.
5 Silver, 'Memories of Oberursel', p. 82. Alfred Skorzeny was held in Soviet captivity until 1955. According to his brother, his health was broken when he returned to Austria.
6 Silver, 'Memories of Oberursel', p. 82.
7 Silver, 'Memories of Oberursel', p. 82.
8 Quoted in Infield, *Hitler's Commando*, p. 148.
9 Infield, *Hitler's Commando*, p. 148.
10 Infield, *Hitler's Commando*, pp. 130–2.
11 Operation *Brandy* documents make explicit reference to ODESSA – possibly the first mention of it.
12 Memorandum, p. 1, OSI.
13 Silver, 'Memories of Oberursel', p. 82.
14 UNWCC Case no. 20-e-4095/48-11. The Einsatzgruppe was largely made up of Hlinka paramilitaries and police units, but its commander that day was Werner Tutter of Jagdeinsatz Slowakei, the Slovakian component of Jagdverband Südost. However, the connection with Skorzeny was tenuous. Skorzeny was not the 'commander' of the unit – except in a titular, abstract way. And at the time the massacres took place, his movements are accounted for in the Alpenfestung. It is unlikely that he had any personal knowledge of the Ploština and Prlov massacres. Infield, *Hitler's Commando*, p. 160.
15 Skorzeny, *My Commando Operations*, p. 447.
16 Skorzeny, *My Commando Operations*, p. 447.
17 *Westdeutsche Zeitung*, 26 January 1950; *Stars and Stripes*, 27 January 1950, p. 11.
18 A less colourful account of the Skorzeny escape is that he was stuffed into the boot of a Darmstadt pool car by Radl and a couple of inmates. The obliging driver then dropped him off at the nearest station, where some friends had thoughtfully left a well kitted-out suitcase. Skorzeny took the train to Stuttgart and was in Berchtesgaden the next day. See Foley, *Commando Extraordinary*, p. 200.
19 Letter from Skorzeny to Spruchkammer, 26 July 1948, quoted in Infield, *Hitler's Commando*, pp. 152, 254, n. 9.
20 Infield, *Hitler's Commando*, p. 151.

17. Apocalypse Soon: Preparing for World War III

1 Frankfort to Secretary of State, 26 January 1951, CIAS.
2 Report No. NGF-787, CIAS.
3 Document PA34, CIAS.
4 Deutsche Kenncarte, OSA.
5 Dispatch no. WSM-W-415, 14 June 1949, CIAS.

6   For example *Stars & Stripes*, 15 April 1949, p. 2; 2 June 1949, p. 4; *Der Spiegel*, 14 July 1949. The report was seemingly confirmed by his then wife, Emmi Skorzeny, who had applied for a visa to Argentina.

7   *Stars & Stripes*, 8 October 1949, p. 4.

8   Information Report, 10 June 1951, CIAS.

9   *Stars & Stripes*, 15 February 1950, p. 2.

10   *Stars & Stripes*, 1 April and 6 April 1950, p. 1.

11   His hideout was discovered and published by *Süddeutsche Zeitung*, 8–9 October 1949.

12   Information report no. R-1068-52, p. 2, CIAS.

13   Information report no. 00-B-33806, p. 1, CIAS.

14   Weitz, *Hjalmar Schacht*, p. 339; Schacht, *Confessions*, pp. 36–8.

15   Intelligence Report no. R-359-53, CIAS.

16   Information Report no. 00-B-33806, CIAS.

17   Information Report no. SO 71757, CIAS. The Cabaret de Lido was an entertainment venue, home to the Bluebell Girls.

18   Chief of Station Madrid to Chief Western Europe, 6 March 1959, CIAS.

19   For example, Yeo-Thomas visited Skorzeny in Madrid during February 1952. Seaman, *Bravest of the Brave*, p. 225.

20   Information Report no. SO 71757, CIAS. On the Radl affair, see Chief of Mission, Frankfurt, to Chief of Base, Bonn, 20 November 1952, FOI.

21   Quoted in Lee, *Beast Reawakens*, p. 44.

22   Naftali, 'Reinhard Gehlen', p. 381.

23   Naftali, 'Reinhard Gehlen', p. 377.

24   Naftali, 'Reinhard Gehlen', p. 391.

25   Pullach to Special Operations, 6 February 1951, CIAS.

26   'Concerning his relationship with the Gehlen organization, Subject [Skorzeny] stated he had never been at odds with them. He has many friends in the organization which include former Waffen S.S. officers who are his friends today' (OSMA 9100, CIAS).

27   Deutsche Kenncarte, 21 February 1950, OSA. The card was stamped by the Freiburg police – a district in the French zone – probably indicating that Skorzeny was still being helped by the French intelligence service.

28   Information Report no. 00-B33806, CIAS.

29   Cable PA34/VH1037A 7/2E, 28 July 1951, CIAS.

30   Intelligence Report no. 00-B-33806, CIAS.

31   *Jüdische Rundschau*, Basel, 21 March 1951.

32   American Embassy, Madrid to State Department, 2 July 1951, CIAS.

33   Meyer, *Factual List*.

34   Information Report no. HGF-787, p. 1, CIAS; Chief of Station Karlsruhe to Chief, Foreign Division M, 3 January 1951, CIAS.

35   CIA Information Report no. 00-B-33806, Otto Skorzeny, 5 June 1951; Federal Bureau of Investigation File no. 105-716, 24 September 1951. CIA Otto Skorzeny name file, NARA.

36   Visa Application CIAS.

37   FBI File no. 105-716, p. 2, CIAS.

38   CIA Information Report no. 00-B-33806, 5 June 1951, pp. 1–2, CIAS; FBI File no. 105-716, 9/24/51, pp. 2–3, CIAS.

39   Radl (quoted in Petropoulos, *Royals*, p. 197) states that Skorzeny first came across Prinz Phillip at Führer Headquarters during the summer of 1943. After bad-mouthing the Italians, Skorzeny was taken aside by an SS officer and warned that he was in earshot of the prince, and that everything he said might be relayed to the King of Italy.
40   FBI File no. 105-716, p. 2, CIAS.
41   Records of the Office of Strategic Services, RG 226 NARA, L 53795.
42   Report no. WSM-620, CIAS.
43   Air Intelligence Information Report IR-54-51, p. 4 point 12, CIAS.
44   Reports of the Assistant Air Attaché, 24 September 1951, CIAS.
45   Information Report no. 00-B-33806, CIAS.
46   Report no. WSM-522, CIAS.
47   Air Intelligence Information Report IR-54-51, CIAS.
48   Chief of Station Madrid to Chief Foreign Division W, 1 June 1951, CIAS.
49   'Further Activities of Colonel Otto Skorzeny', 26 September 1951, CIAS.
50   Air Intelligence Information Report no. IR-54-51, CIAS.
51   Air Intelligence Information Report no. IR-54-51, CIAS.
52   Information Report no. 00-B-36178, CIAS.
53   *France-Soir*, 16 November 1950; WDGS-Report R-730-50, CIAS.
54   Memorandum, 7 February 1951, CIAS.
55   Pullach to Special Operations, 6 February 1951, CIAS.
56   Skorzeny Plan, OSA.
57   Information from BND documents leaked to the press in 2014; see Wiegrefe, 'Nazi Veterans'.
58   Visa Application 6 March 1959, p. 5, CIAS.
59   Report no. 00-W-16631, CIAS.
60   Pullach to Special Operations, 6 February 1951, CIAS.
61   Skorzeny Plan, OSA.
62   Skorzeny Plan, OSA.
63   Visa Application, CIAS.
64   Skorzeny Plan, OSA.
65   Memorandum, October 1952, OSA.
66   Information Report no. 00-B-36178, CIAS.
67   Information report no. 00-B-36178, CIAS.
68   Dispatch no. WSMA-J492, CIAS.
69   Critchfield, *Partners*, p. 105.
70   Information report no. 00-B-36178, CIAS.
71   'Controversy between Otto Skorzeny and General Hans Doerr', CIAS.
72   Official Dispatch no. WSMA-J492, CIAS.
73   'Controversy between Otto Skorzeny and General Hans Doerr', CIAS.
74   Dispatch no. MGL-A-5882, CIAS.
75   Exposé of Skorzeny, CIAS.
76   'Informe', 21 March 1951, OSA.
77   Wiegrefe, 'Nazi Veterans'.
78   Gehlen Organisation documents show that several Schnez units were active in Germany at this time, with retired generals heading units in Stuttgart, Ulm, Heilbronn, Karlsruhe and Freiburg. Wiegrefe, 'Nazi Veterans'.

79 'Informe', 21 March 1951, OSA.

80 'Informe', 21 March 1951, OSA. Skorzeny meant that a Spain-based army could fall back to Africa, if necessary.

81 'Informe', 21 March 1951, OSA.

82 'Weltkriegsveteranen bauten geheime Armee auf', *Der Spiegel*, 11 May 2014. Available online at www.spiegel.de/politik/deutschland/veteranen-von-wehrmacht-und-ss-gruendeten-laut-bnd-geheime-armee-a-968727.html (retrieved 19 September 2017).

83 Skorzeny Plan, Dispatch no. WSM-A-1756, CIAS.

84 Skorzeny Plan, p. 5, Dispatch no. WSM-A-1756, CIAS.

85 Skorzeny Plan, Appendix 1, Dispatch no. WSM-A-1756, CIAS.

86 Skorzeny Plan, p. 7, Dispatch no. WSM-A-1756, CIAS.

87 Air Intelligence Information Report no. IR-54-51, CIAS.

88 Report no. WSM-620, CIAS.

89 Air Intelligence Information Report no. IR-54-51, CIAS.

90 'Further Activities of Colonel Skorzeny', CIAS.

91 CIA memo IN 34186, CIAS.

92 Chief of Station Karlsruhe to Chief, FDM, 30 November 1951, CIAS.

93 CIA source evaluation: Father Simonsen etc., 11 June 1956, FOI.

94 Simonsen to Montini, 29 February 1952, OSA.

95 CIA source evaluation: Father Simonsen etc., 11 June 1956, FOI.

96 Simonsen to Vigón, 19 November 1951, OSA.

97 Before 1952, 'European Command (EUCOM)' referred to a single service, United States Army command. The senior US Army administrative command in the European region had previously been designated European Theater of Operations United States Army (ETOUSA) from 8 June 1942 – 1 July 1945; United States Forces European Theater (USFET) from 1 July 1945 – 15 March 1947; and then EUCOM 15 March 1947 – 1 August 1952. After that time, and Eisenhower's return to the United States, EUCOM was restructured as a joint services command – US European Command (USEUCOM). It was headed by General Matthew Ridgeway.

98 Visa Application, CIAS.

99 'Further Activities of Colonel Otto Skorzeny', CIAS.

18. Neo-Nazis and Colonel Nasser: Otto Skorzeny's Wilderness Years

1 *Der Spiegel*, 21 January 1953.

2 The BfV's agent was Richard Gerk, working under the alias Wissmann. Gerk, a former Abwehr officer later employed by the Gestapo, ended his career as head of the BfV's counterintelligence section. On Bornemann, who was arrested later than the others, see *Fourth Reich or Farce? The Origins, Significance and Impact of the Naumann Affair*, by Guy Walters. Available online at http://www.academia.edu/1389394/Fourth_Reich_or_farce_The_Origins_Significance_and_Impact_of_the_Naumann_Affair (retrieved 31 January 2018).

3 'Skorzeny's Neo-Nazi Apparat in Western Germany', CIAS.

4 Report no. MGF-787, CIAS.

5 'Skorzeny's Neo-Nazi Apparat in Western Germany', CIAS.

6 See, for example, *Stars & Stripes*, 28 November 1952.

7 Chief of Station Karlsruhe to Chief, Foreign Division M, 14 June 1951, CIAS.

8   Though neither turned up.
9   Macklin, *Very Deeply Dyed*, p. 94.
10   Walters, *Hunting Evil*, pp. 281–2. See ADN.
11   Goñi, *Real Odessa*, pp. 112–3.
12   Memorandum, 17 September 1953, CIAS.
13   'Fritz Dorls', *Der Spiegel*, 16 September 1953.
14   Skorzeny 201 File. Document control no.6004, 15 July 1954, CIAS.
15   'Activities of Otto Skorzeny', enclosed in Dispatch no. OSMA-476, CIAS.
16   Chief FHB to Chief EE, 7 November 1952, CIAS.
17   Madrid Station to Special Operations, 14 May 1951, CIAS.
18   *Irish Times*, 9 July 1960, quoted in O'Reilly, *Hitler's Irishmen*.
19   Copeland, *Game of Nations*, p. 103.
20   Copeland, *Game of Nations*, p. 103.
21   A fabulist given to 'entertaining and colourful invention', according to Nick Elliott, the MI6 officer who broke Kim Philby and knew Copeland well. Ben Macintyre, *A Spy Among Friends: Kim Philby and The Great Betrayal*, ebook edn (Bloomsbury, 2014), ch. 15, ebook location 3629.
22   Copeland, *Game of Nations*, p. 104.
23   Infield, *Hitler's Commando*, p. 207; Lee, *Beast Reawakens*, p. 130; Tauber, *Beyond Eagle and Swastika*, p. 1114.
24   Naftali, 'Reinhard Gehlen', pp. 404, 417, notes 165, 166.
25   'Dr Wilhelm Voss', CIC Region IV, 25 April 1946, Wilhelm Voss CIA name file, FOI, https://www.cia.gov/library/readingroom/docs/VOSS%2C%20FRIEDRICH%20 WILHELM_0009.pdf (retrieved 16 October 2017).
26   Ambassador quoted in *Der Spiegel*, 10 October 1955.
27   Report no. OSM-175, CIAS.
28   Silverstein, *Private Warriors*, pp. 110–1.
29   Memorandum, 18 May 1953, Wilhelm Voss CIA name file, document 0043, FOI, https://www.cia.gov/library/readingroom/docs/VOSS%2C%20FRIEDRICH%20 WILHELM_0043.pdf. (retrieved 16 October 2017).
30   Doerries, *Hitler's Last Chief*, p. 243.
31   Otto Remer CIA name file, document 18, FOI; and 'Activities of Certain German Experts in Egypt', 16 February 1954, FOI.
32   'Brief file notes on Otto Skorzeny', 14 May 1953, CIAS.
33   Report JX-4307, CIAS.
34   Visa Application, CIAS.
35   NEA-2/F1/CE to WE/Spanish Desk, 14 May 1953, CIAS.
36   R-52-53, CIAS.
37   Skorzeny to Nasser, undated, OSA.
38   NEA-2/F1/CE to WE/Spanish Desk, 14 May 1953, CIAS; Report JX-4307, CIAS.
39   Report JX-4307, CIAS.
40   Memorandum, 17 September 1953, CIAS.
41   'Otto Skorzeny's Efforts to Supply Arms for Egypt', CIAS.
42   'Guerrilla Warfare Training Centers under German Direction', CIAS.
43   Deputy Director Plans to The Secretary of State, July 1953, CIAS.
44   Dispatch no. OBBW-587, 30 June 1953, CIAS.
45   Chief of Mission Cairo to Chief NEA; ref DIR 40127, 25 April 1953, CIAS.

46   Voss, Dr Fritz Wilhelm, October 1956, item 6, FOI.

47   Voss document no. 51, 22 July 1953, FOI.

48   'German Military Experts', RD no. A-5530, 16 April 1953, CIAS.

49   Report no R-182-53, CIAS; Visa Application, CIAS.

50   R-182-53, CIAS.

51   Visa Application, CIAS.

52   Report no R-182-53, CIAS.

53   Jefferson Caffery to Department of State, June 1953, quoted in Infield, *Hitler's Commando*, pp. 208–9.

54   'Skorzeny's Representative in Egypt', 6 August 1953, Beissner CIA name file, FOI.

55   Visa Application, CIAS.

56   Lee, *Beast Reawakens*, p. 125; Infield, *Hitler's Commando*, p. 213; Silverstein, *Private Warriors*, p. 114.

57   Breitman and Goda, *Hitler's Shadow*, p. 27.

58   Chief, Munich Liaison Base to Chief ME, 1966, Beissner CIA name file, FOI.

59   'Beissner, Willi (Dr.) aka Jaeger', January 1959, Beissner CIA name file, FOI, document no. 0053, https://www.cia.gov/library/readingroom/docs/BEISSNER%2C%20 FRIEDRICH%20WILHELM_0053.pdf (retrieved 16 October 2017).

60   A diagram in Beissner's CIA name file shows him at the centre of a web of contacts in the worldwide Nazi diaspora. Among the connections featured is Skorzeny. Beissner document no. 0060, FOI, https://www.cia.gov/library/readingroom/docs/ BEISSNER%2C%20FRIEDRICH%20WILHELM_0060.pdf (retrieved 31 January 2018).

61   Dispatch no. OELA-17, 873, 25 January 1957, CIAS.

19. The Years of Plenty

1   Visa Application, CIAS; Chief of Station, Madrid, to Chief, FDW, 4 January 1952, CIAS.

2   Visa Application, CIAS.

3   CIA, 'Defections of Dr John'.

4   Air Intelligence Report no. IR-54-51, CIAS.

5   Letter quoted in Intelligence Report no. R-1068-52, CIAS. The sender was Hubert Bretsky, an Austrian; the recipient 'Georg Kruger' of Angola Handelsgesellschaft, Hamburg. The latter may possibly be Gerhard Krüger, one of the founders of the SRP. Skorzeny is known to have been a guest at his house near Hamburg during frequent business trips to Germany. Also Chief of Base, Hamburg, to Chief of Station, Germany, 15 July 1960, CIAS.

6   Visa Application, p. 3, CIAS.

7   Specifically, Skorzeny claimed to have handled 20 per cent of all Brown-Raymond-Walsh European purchases for the United States air-bases between 1954 and 1958: value of contracts, $2 million. In addition, he supplied air-base sub-contractors with German steel and other materials: value, $1 million (Visa Application, CIAS).

8   Visa Application, CIAS.

9   Chief of Station, Madrid, to Chief, WE, 20 August 1954, CIAS.

10   Chief of Station, Madrid, to Chief, WE, 20 August 1954, CIAS.

11 In fact, for crimes against humanity committed during the war. The Krupp factories had enthusiastically employed slave labour; most controversially Jews destined for death camps.

12 'The Deadly Symbol', *Der Spiegel*, 30 November 1955.

13 Report no. EGF-578, CIAS.

14 Visa Application, CIAS.

15 *New York Herald Tribune*, Bonn, 18 November 1954.

16 Whoever was responsible for Skorzeny's presence, the button was pressed in great haste. Authorisation from the Argentinian Consul in Madrid was stamped on 16 October 1954, only hours before Skorzeny boarded the plane for Buenos Aires (passport, OSP).

17 Batty, *House of Krupp*, pp. 260–1.

18 Whiting, *Skorzeny*, pp. 110–1; Infield, *Hitler's Commando*, pp. 191–204.

19 Quoted in Infield, *Hitler's Commando*, p. 196.

20 Chief of Station Madrid to Chief WE(?), 17 August 1960, CIAS.

21 Chief of Station Madrid to Chief WE, 15 April 1959, CIAS.

22 Visa Application, CIAS. See also Secret 271555Z, January 1970: 'Despite favorable Consulate recommendation, Subj denied visa in 1959 by Dept, apparently on basis of CS-CI 7856 of 24 August 1956 to Dept. After reviewing Subjs file [Madrid] Station has concluded there really is no current derogatory information info therein. As suggested [in] OSMA-9100, file is largely compilation of allegations, most of which refuted by subsequent investigation.' Whether Skorzeny would have got his US tourist visa in 1970 we shall never know. Shortly afterwards he was stricken with cancer.

23 Chief of Station, Madrid, to Chief, WE, 15 April 1959, CIAS.

24 Philip Mooney had brought Skorzeny into contact with Edgar Smith in Madrid. For Mrs Mooney's sponsorship of Skorzeny's first visit to Eire see INA.

25 *Daily Express*, 18 August 1960.

26 Dáil Éireann Debates, 17 February 1960, INA.

27 Oscar Traynor to Frank Aiken, 8 February 1960, INA.

28 Letter to P. Berry Esq, 10 February 1960, INA.

29 Intelligence Section, Department of Defence to Dr Eoin MacWhite, 26 June 1957, INA.

30 Training 'in paramilitary, anti-Communist activities, and a general political indoctrination', according to the CIA. The programme was sponsored by business interests anxious to garner the rich mineral resources found in Katanga; allegedly in overall charge of the programme was 'a Spanish colonel or general' (Otto Skorzeny -201 file, ESBA-9991, 27 January 1961, CIAS). Skorzeny probably turned the job down. 'He at least considered involvement on Katanguese side in Congo Uprising' (Report no. 180937Z, CIAS). Skorzeny himself claimed never to have met Tshombe until he was exiled to Spain in 1963 (*My Commando Operations*, p. 457).

31 Michael Rynne to Con Cremin, 9 June 1960, INA.

32 Brendan Barry, C.C. Cremin, 27 July 1961, INA.

33 O'Reilly, *Hitler's Irishmen*, pp. 292–3.

34 Reggie Darling, quoted in *Irish Independent*, 24 May 2005.

35 Interview, TV documentary *Ireland's Nazis*, Episode 2, RTE One, 2007.

20. Ghosts of the Past: Skorzeny's Last Years

1 *Sunday Express*, 3 February 1963; *Irish Press*, 4 February 1963; *Daily Mail*, 5 February 1963; INA.

2 *Daily Mail*, 5 February 1963.

3   Report no. CS-3/536,458, CIAS.

4   'Austria Seeks Extradition of Skorzeny; Tested Poison on Jews', *Jewish Telegraphic Agency*, 4 February 1963. Available online at https://www.jta.org/1963/02/04/archive/austria-seeks-extradition-of-skorzeny-tested-poison-on-jews (retrieved 16 October 2017); O'Reilly, *Hitler's Irishmen*, pp. 293–4.

5   Quoted in *Sunday Press*, 17 February 1963.

6   Volume 4, Day 24, NTP.

7   Amicale d'Oranienburg-Sachsenhausen, *Sachso*, pp. 331–2 (author's translation).

8   Dáil Éireann Debates, 12 March 1963, INA file P316.

9   Amembassy Madrid to Department of State, 27 February 1963, CIAS.

10 Amembassy Madrid to Department of State, 27 February 1963, CIAS.

11 Former SS-Hauptsturmführer and head of the Gestapo in occupied Lyon, Barbie (1913–91) was employed as an agent by the CIC after the war. In 1951, it arranged for his flight to South America – where he assumed the identity of Klaus Altmann. Now a 'businessman', he eventually settled in La Paz, Bolivia. His company, Standard Industrial (Bolivia), was to provide cover for his dealings with Merex. Independently of the Schwend connection, the CIA suspected 'some kind of business connection with Otto Skorzeny' though the files do not specify what kind. See 'Klaus Altmann was.', Chief. WH To [redacted], ref HOPW-4732, 6 March 1967, Klaus Barbie CIA name file, Vol I, https://www.cia.gov/library/readingroom/docs/BARBIE%2C%20KLAUS%20%20%20VOL.%201_0035.pdf (retrieved 10 December 2017). In 1966 the BND briefly hired Barbie (known as Agent 43118) as Bolivian representative for Merex. See 'German Intelligence Hired Klaus Barbie as Agent', by Georg Bönish and Klaus Wiegrefe, *Spiegel* Online, 20 January 2011.

12 Silverstein, *Private Warriors*, pp. 124–7.

13 Hammerschmidt, *Deckname Adler*, pp. 254–7.

14 'Former German Intelligence Officer Active with Intelligence Services of Peru and Bolivia', 12 January 1967. CIA Fritz Schwend name file, NARA. FOI document no. 146, https://www.cia.gov/library/readingroom/docs/SCHWEND%2C%20FRITZ_0146.pdf (retrieved 15 December 2017).

15 Stroessner to Paraguayan ambassador, 3 April 1964, file01.lavanguardia.com/2011/12/07/54240808358-url.pdf (retrieved 21 September 2017); Skorzeny, *My Commando Operations*, p. 457.

16 Bar-Zohar and Mishal, *Mossad*, ch. 8.

17 Silverstein, *Private Warriors*, pp. 121–2.

18 Bergman, *Rise and Kill First*, p. 69. Valentin, born circa 1910, had served in the French Foreign Legion and Waffen-SS before being attached to 'Jeanne', Besekow's stay-behind operation in France, during the summer of 1944. CIAN Vol 1, 'Descriptions given by Ostrich', November 1944, FOI document, Vol 1, 0007; Biddiscombe, *SS Hunter Battalions*, pp. 257–63.

19 Bergman, *Rise and Kill First*, p. 78.

20 Bergman, *Rise and Kill First*, p. 79.

21 Probably Otto Horcher – the celebrated Berlin restaurateur whose former clientele had comprised most of the senior figures in the Nazi regime, and notably Hermann Göring. Bombed out, Horcher had quit Berlin near the end of the war and set up an equally fashionable eatery (it exists to this day) in the Calle de Alfonso XII, which Skorzeny used as an informal office.

22 Mossad German Scientists Dossier 136, 14 September 1964, cited in Bergman, *Rise and Kill First*, p. 79.

23 Bergman, *Rise and Kill First*, p. 80. Skorzeny also asked for immediate removal from Wiesenthal's 'Wanted' Nazi list. But despite Mossad's best efforts, Wiesenthal was undeterred.

24 *Matara*, September 1989. A senior Mossad agent confirmed the account in *Yediot Achronot*, claiming 'Skorzeny never worked for Mossad but he was certainly our agent.' See also *Jewish Telegraphic Agency*, 21 September 1989, available online at https://www.jta.org/1989/09/21/archive/former-nazi-was-once-duped-into-working-for-mossad (retrieved 16 October 2017).

25 Skorzeny emphasised his continuing friendship with Nasser and his 'many friends in Egypt' when, a few years later, he was forced to issue a press statement denying involvement with the 'Israeli armed forces'. *La Vanguardia Española*, 22 September 1967, p. 7.

26 Bar-Zohar and Mishal, *Mossad*, ch. 8. Bergman, *Rise and Kill First*, p. 83.

27 The three Mossad agents were allegedly future Israeli Prime Minister Yitzak Shamir, Zvi Malkin and Joe Raanan (the team leader). The newspaper does not explain the English-speaking 'Oriental' man – a 'Mr Saleh' – who was widely reported at the time to have accompanied Krug out of his office on 11 September. Dan Raviv and Yossi Melman, 'The Strange Case of a Nazi Who Became an Israeli Hitman', *Haaretz*, 27 March 2016.

28 Bergman, *Rise and Kill First*, pp. 64–5. According to Bergman, a Mossad agent codenamed Oded ('Mr Saleh' or 'Saleh Qaher') lured Krug, on the pretext of an urgent meeting with Egyptian colleagues, to a house in a Munich suburb. There the actual kidnap took place, under the personal direction of the Mossad chief, Harel.

29 CIA West Europe Division memo to Chief of Operations, DD/P, 25 January 1962, CIAS.

30 See Lee, *Beast Reawakens*, p. 186.

31 See also *ABC*, 24 May 1967.

32 Skorzeny, *My Commando Operations*, p. 457.

33 Lee, *The Beast Reawakens*, p. 431, n. 56.

34 'Friedrich Wilhelm von Mellenthin', *Der Spiegel*, p. 63, 17 August 1960.

35 Christie, *General Franco Made Me a Terrorist*, p. 132. Tisei was not invariably a reliable witness. Many of his accusations failed to pass legal muster. Unfortunately, the Dirección General de Seguridad (DGS) files of the period – which might definitively settle the matter – have never seen the light of day.

36 C. V. Whelan to Department of External Affairs, 8 February 1965, INA.

37 Chief of Station Madrid to Chief European Division, 1 December 1971, CIAS.

38 Whiting, *Skorzeny*, p. 3.

39 Chief of Station Madrid to Chief European Division, 1 December 1971, CIAS.

40 Chief of Station Madrid to Chief European Division, 1 December 1971, CIAS.

41 David Solar, 'El Skorzeny que Yo Conocí', *La Aventura de la Historia*, 27 June 2012, p. 25.

42 *La Vanguardia Española*, 9 March 1975, p. 26.

43 Typescript document written in French, OSA.

44 *La Aventura de La Historia*, 27 June 2012, p. 21.

45 *La Vanguardia Española*, 8 July 1975, p. 8.

46 *ABC Sevilla*, 9 July 1975, p. 34.

47 *La Vanguardia Española*, 17 July 1975, p. 16.

Epilogue: Man and Myth

1   *La Aventura de la Historia*, 27 June 2012, p. 21.

2   Quoted in Infield, *Hitler's Commando*, p. 231.

3   Skorzeny memoir typescript, OSA.

4   *Die Zeit*, 2 October 1964. Toth, the publisher, was a Jew.

5   *Der Spiegel*, 10 January 1951.

6   *New York Times*, 29 December 1951.

7   *Daily Express*, 8 April 1952, p. 1.

8   Almost certainly a fake. The original, as he admitted, had been stolen by American servicemen during his years of detention.

9   *Daily Express*, 8 April 1952, p. 1.

10 David Stirling, quoted in Foley, *Commando Extraordinary*, p. 245.

11 Skorzeny seems to have corresponded with Stirling and claims to have met him, once, at Heathrow Airport. The date cited is incorrect but the background event, which actually took place in August 1958, is authentic. *Skorzeny, My Commando Operations*, p. 147.

12 On the background to the meeting see CIA document S IN 16259, CIAS.

13 *La Aventura de La Historia*, 27 June 2012, p. 20.

14 Visa Application, CIAS.

15 Horrocks, *Escape to Action*, p. 241.

16 Michael Rynne to John Belton, 20 July 1959, INA.

17 *Irish Times*, 4 July 1959.

18 Secret 180937Z, Info Director, 19 February 1969, CIAS.

19 See for example CIA West Europe Division memo to Chief of Operations, DD/P, 25 January 1962 and Chief, Munich Base, to Chief, Western Europe, 12 July 1960, CIAS.

20 *La Aventura de La Historia*, 27 June 2012. The culprits were apparently Skorzeny's former business associates.

21 McRaven, *Spec Ops*, p.192.

Robert & Georgia Shurts
316 SE Oriole Ave
Stuart, FL 34996

Index

Page numbers in **bold** refer to maps

Abwehr (German intelligence)
42, 43–44, 53, 92, 119,
120–21; *see also* Mil Amt D
Academic Legion 22
Adenauer, Konrad 262, 268,
274, 278, 281, 284
Ahituv, Avraham 311–12
aircraft, German 54, 70–71,
271, 282; Fi 103R
'Reichenberg' 106–8;
Fi-156 Fieseler Storch
78–80; Fw 190: 103, 201;
Heinkel He 111: 63, 66;
Ju 88: 103; Me 110: 92;
Me 262A 164
AK (Polish Home Army) 135
Albers, Karl 258
Alexander, Lt Michael 251
Algeria 293–94
Allies 9, 39, 101–2, 134, 240;
and Ardennes 163–64; and
Austria 231–32; and
Hungary 151, 152; and
Italy 58, 61, 62; *see also*
Great Britain; Soviet
Union; United States of
America
Alpenfestung (Alpine Fortress)
(1945) 220, 223–24,
226–29, 233, 233–35; map
16
Alquen, Gunter d' 136
Altaussee conspirators 228,
230, 232, 233

Amit, Meir 311
André, Pierre 293
Angola 296, 297
anti-Hitler movement 110
anti-Semitism 24, 28–29,
289
Antonescu, Ion 152
Anzio, battle of (1944) 101
Ardennes 162–78, 179–96;
and trial 244–46, 247–52
Argentina 263, 264, 286,
298–99
arms trafficking 290, 291–92,
293–94, 308–10, 319
Auch, Alexander 221–22
Augsburg, Dr Emil 267
Austria 18–20, 21–22,
24–29, 147, 231–32; and
Skorzeny 303, 305–8;
see also Vienna

Bach-Zelewski, Erich von dem
153–54, 157, 209–10, 214
Badoglio, Pietro 58, 61, 62,
64, 65, 69, 76
Balkans 58, 93–97, 147, 149
Baltic States 140
Bandera, Stepan 135–36,
137, 138, 306
Barbie, Klaus 309
Batista, Fulgencio 303
Baumbach, Olt Werner 103,
108
Bauverd, Jean-Maurice 286

Beck, GenOb Ludwig 115
Behr, Kapt Philipp Freiherr
von 175, 186–87, 190–91,
202; and trial 244, 246,
248
Beissner, Wilhelm 290, 291,
293–94, 308
Ben-Gurion, David 310, 311
Bendlerblock (headquarters)
111–12, 113, 114, 116
Benesch, Maj Ernst 94, 97,
139
Berding, Lt-Col Andrew H.
239–40
Berger, Gottlob 33–34, 120
Berlepsch, Olt Freiherr Georg
von 70, 72, 73, 77, 78, 83
Berlin 212, 213–14, 229
Bertaux, Pierre 264, 266
Besekow, Arnold 'Arno'
55–56, 139, 176, 237
BfV (West German Security
Agency) 279–80, 284,
295, 296
Bieck, Maj Robert 262, 271,
272, 273, 296; and
Skorzeny Plan 278, 279,
281
Billing, Obfw Günther
183–84
Birsak, Lt Friedrich 27, 28
Blanco, Gen Eduardo 314
Bletchley Park 126, 168, 213
Blume, Walter 49

BND (German Federal
    Intelligence Service) 282
Böhme, Friedrich 102–3
Bolbrinker, GenMaj Ernst
    113, 172
Bolschwing, Otto von 267
Bolsheviks 85, 224, 234
Borghese, Prince Junio Valerio
    99, 100
Bormann, Martin 198, 200,
    206, 207, 229
Bornemann, Karl 284
Bracker, Oscar 299
Bradley, Gen Omar 184, 252
Brady, Pvt James 50, 142,
    212
Brandenburgers 42–43, 51,
    85, 122
Brander, Ferdinand 310
Braun, Eva 216
British Army: 21st Group
    163, 164
Bronny, Fw Manfred 184
Brookhart, Lt-Col Smith W.
    244
Bruin, Arendt de 246, 250
Buchenwald 29
Bulgaria 143
Bundeswehr 274, 282
Buntrock, Ob Georg 139,
    146–47
Bussinger, Hptm Fritz 186

camouflage 165–67, 172
Canaris, Adm Wilhelm 42,
    43, 44, 47–48, 53, 66; and
    Stauffenberg plot 118–19
Casier, Rosita 139
Castro, Fidel 303
Chamberlain, Neville 44
Chlum prison 51, 84
Churchill, Winston 57, 84,
    88, 93, 241
CIA (Central Intelligence
    Agency) 257, 260, 262,
    263, 324; and Egypt 289;
    and Gehlen 268; and
    Skorzeny Plan 278,
    279–81
CIC (Counter Intelligence
    Corps) 255, 256, 257–59,
    260, 263

Circulo Espagñol de Amigos
    de Europa 313
Clages, Gerhard 155, 156
Clissman, Fw Helmuth 50
Cold War 125, 267–68
Communism 220, 232, 238,
    264
concentration camps 34,
    90–91, 241, 285, 305–7;
    see also Dachau
Copeland, Miles Axe, Jr 288,
    289
crimes against humanity 237,
    241, 307
Croatia 93, 139
cyanide 248
Czechoslovakia 44, 255–56,
    259

D-Day landings (1944) 101,
    102
Dachau 29, 240, 241,
    244–52, 257–58
Damm, Christian 90–91, 255
Darmstadt 254, 259–60
De Gaulle, Charles 86
Demianov, Aleksandr
    Petrovich 124–25, 127,
    129–30, 132
Democratic Republic of
    Congo 303
Denazification programme
    241, 255, 259
Denmark 89–91, 242, 243,
    255, 256
Deumling, Joachim 293
Deutsche Wochenschau, Die
    (newsreel) 8, 9, 81, 322
Die Spinne 258, 263, 287,
    315
Dietrich, Joseph 'Sepp' 32,
    168, 178, 188
Dirlewanger, Oskar 289
documentaries 323
Dollfuss, Engelbert 23
Dollman, Eugen 64
Dönitz, GrAdm Karl 58, 66,
    234, 241
Donovan, Maj-Gen 'Wild
    Bill' 244
Dorls, Fritz 287
Dörr, GenMaj Hans 276

Drück, GenMaj Walter 309
duelling 21, 29
Duke, Col Florimond 151
Dulles, Allen 232, 233, 289,
    293
Durst, Col Robert D. 246,
    247–49, 250, 251, 252, 253

East Germany 296
East Prussia 143–44
Eastern Front 57–58, 135; see
    also Schwedt Bridgehead
Eben-Emael raid (1940) 41,
    70, 165
Edelweiss unit 145–46
Egypt 288–93, 294, 310,
    312, 313
Eichmann, Adolf 45, 152,
    233, 287–88, 303, 306;
    and Israel 310, 311
Eicke, Theodor 34
Eigruber, August 223, 224,
    227
Eisenhower, Gen Dwight D.
    174, 184–85, 226, 227,
    234, 238
Eismann, Ob Hans-Georg
    200, 201
Eitan, Rafi 311
Eitingon, Leonid 130
Ellis, Burton 247
enemy uniforms 165–67,
    172, 187, 249, 250–52
Ersatzheer (Reserve Army)
    110, 111, 120, 170
Escriva de Romani, José Finat
    y, Conde de Mayalde
    272
Eshkol, Levi 312
espionage 42, 46, 48, 52–53,
    132, 253; and Besekow
    55–56; and Cold War
    267–68; and Flamingo spy
    ring 124–25, 127, 129;
    and 'Jeanne' network 176;
    and Rote Kapelle ring 295,
    296
ETA (Euskadi ta Askatasuna)
    314

Faiola, Lt Alberto 76–77
Fascism 20, 262, 286, 287

Fegelein, Hermann 168, 200, 216
Figaro, Le (newspaper) 264, 321
film 322–23
Final Solution 152, 288, 307
Finckenstein, Graf Adolf Finck von 265
Finland 143
Fischer, Willie 130, 131
Fitze, Günther 246, 249
FLN (National Liberation Front Algeria) 293–94, 303, 308
Flöter, Kurt 206–7
Foley, Charles 321–22
Fölkersam, Olt Baron Adrian von 84–86, 87, 123, 140, 166, 181; and Ardennes 169, 173–74; and Denmark 90, 91; and Hungary 150, 158; and Malmédy 189, 190, 192–94; and Poland 197, 198–99; and Stauffenberg plot 109, 110, 113, 114, 119; and Yugoslavia 95, 96
Formis, Rudolf 46
France 39, 86–87, 176; *see also* Ardennes; Paris; Vichy France
Franco, Gen Francisco 262, 263, 269, 280, 282, 324
Franz Josef, Emperor 18
French Army: 1st 226
Friedmann, Tuviah 306
Friedrich, Andreas 51
Fromm, GenOb Friedrich 111–12, 114–16
Fucker, Karl 201, 215, 217, 227
fuel 107–8, 128–29, 137
Funk, Walther 235, 270–71

Galland, Adolf 263
Gallent, Wilhelm 222
Gardener, Col Andrew 247–48
Gartenfeld, Maj Karl-Edmund 103
Gaza Strip 290

Geheimkommando Skorzeny (Skorzeny) 321
Gehlen, Ob Reinhard 125–26, 130, 132, 138, 146–47, 197–98; and Cold War 266–68; and Egypt 289; and Mossad 310; and Skorzeny Plan 277–78, 279, 282
genocide 225, 241
Gerhard, Georg Reinhold 204, 225, 242–43, 248, 249
Gerlach, Hptm Heinrich 9, 10, 63, 78–79
German Air Force *see* Luftwaffe
German Army 121; Heersgruppe Mitte 124, 125, 127, 131; 5. Panzerarmee 168, 187; 6. Armee 141, 143; 6. Panzerarmee 13, 168–69, 181, 222, 226, 228; 7. Armee-Oberkommando 168; 15. Armee 169; LXVII Armeekorps 180–81; 1. SS-Panzerdivision 'Leibstandarte-SS Adolf Hitler' 181–82, 189, 246; 2. Fallschirmjägerdivision 69; 3. Panzergrenadierdivision 69; 12. SS-Panzerdivision 'Hitlerjugend' 181, 189; Kommandokompanie Panzerbrigade 150: 174–75, 182–84; Panzerbrigade 150: 169–71, 172, 175–76, 187, 194, 195; Infanterie-Rgt 9: 34; FAK 103: 124, 125, 127; FAK 202: 136, 137; *see also* Brandenburgers; Ersatzheer; Territorialen Jagdverbände; Waffen-SS
German Navy *see* Kriegsmarine
Germany 19–20, 22, 25, 57–58; *see also* Berlin; West Germany

Geschke, Hans-Ulrich 153
Gestapo 29, 43, 44, 155–56, 293; and Stauffenberg plot 112, 118
Gföller, Anton 91, 222, 255
Gillars, Mildred ('Axis Sally') 256–57
Girg, Walter 140–44, 228
Glaise-Horstenau, Gen Edmund 233
Gläsner, Walther 91
Gleichberechtigung (equal rights) 275
Globocnik, Odilo 28
Goebbels, Josef 23, 82, 200, 226, 229; and Stauffenberg plot 112, 113, 116
Göring, Hermann 66, 80, 83, 104, 210–22, 229; and Ardennes 177, 178; and Stauffenberg plot 114
Göttsch, Werner 46–47, 147–48, 232–33
Grabow 204, 206, 207, 208–9, 210, 211
Graf, Heinz 228
Gräfe, Heinz 55
Gran Sasso 8–10, 67–68, 69–78, 83, 325; map 12
Grandes, Gen Muñoz 280
Great Britain 35, 41, 283–84, 322; and Austria 232; and Egypt 313; and Skorzeny 239–40, 303, 323–24; and Ukraine 137–38; *see also* Churchill, Winston; SOE
Greece 143
Gröschner, Jacob 260
Guard Battalion (Wachbataillon Grossdeutschland) 112, 114
Guderian, Heinz 176–77, 197–98, 200, 214, 241; and Skorzeny Plan 262, 273–74, 275, 276–77
Gueli, Gen Giuseppe 67, 72, 76–77, 81
Günsche, Otto 59, 60
Günter, Rudi 219
Gur-Arie, Ze'ev 310

H. S. Lucht Company 284, 287

Häften, Werner von 115

Hague Convention (1907) 166, 246, 248, 250–51

Halder, GenOb Franz 125–26, 256

Hampshire, Capt Stuart 239, 240

Hansen, Lt-Col 184, 190

Hardieck, Willi 172–74, 175, 181, 248

Harel, Isser 310, 311

Hase, GenLt Paul von 112

Haughey, Charlie 301, 307

Hausser, Paul 33, 262, 274, 276–77

Heimwehr (Home Guard) 22

Heinrici, GenOb Gotthard 214–15

Heinz, C. Christian 263

Hensel, Gerhard 243

Herber, Olt Franz 116

Herfurth, Wolfgang 85

Hertslet, Joachim 290, 292

Hessen, Prince Philipp von 270, 271

Heusinger, Adolf 147, 274, 282

Heydrich, Reinhard 29, 32, 43, 45, 47

Heydte, Friedrich August Freiherr von der 177, 178, 189

Heye, Adm Hellmuth 99–100, 102–3, 218

HIAG (Mutual Aid Association of Former Waffen-SS Members) 274, 281, 290

Hillenkoetter, Adm 268

Himmler, Heinrich 21, 24, 41–42, 53–54, 100, 120; and Ardennes 168; and Denmark 90; and *Eiche* 63, 64, 66, 80; and Hungary 150, 152; and Kristallnacht 29; and peace negotiations 229, 230; and Poland 198; and resistance groups 135, 136; and Romania 141; and RSHA

45, 47; and Schwedt 200–1, 208, 209, 214–15; and SS 31, 32–33; and Stauffenberg plot 112, 115, 116, 117–18; and Werwolf 224–25

Hippel, Theodor von 42

Hitler, Adolf 24, 25, 26, 36, 134, 149–50; and Ardennes 162–63, 164, 165, 169, 177; and Berlin 229; and Canaris 44; and Denmark 89, 90; and Hungary 151, 152, 153, 160; and Italy 61–62; and Mussolini 58, 64, 67, 69, 80–81; and Poland 197–98; and Remagen 218; and RSHA 45; and *Scherhorn* 128; and Schwedt 200; and Skorzeny 49, 82, 195–96, 220–21; and special operations 41–43, 53; and SS 31, 32; and Stauffenberg plot 109, 110, 111–12, 113, 117, 118; and suicide 233; and suicide weapons 104, 105; and Tehran Conference 88; and Yugoslavia 93

Hitler Youth 164, 225

Hodges, Gen Courtney 190

Hohensalza 198, 199

Holland 35, 52

Holocaust 285, 288

Holzer, Hans 51

Horowitz, Maj Lewis 247

Horthy, Adm Miklós 150, 151, 152, 153, 154, 156–57, 159, 160

Horthy, Nikki 155–56

Hossfelder, Hans-Dietrich 86

Höttl, Wilhelm 46, 47, 148, 153, 155, 232

Hoyer, Heinrich 201

Hunaeus, Kapt Helmut 65

Hungary 141, 142, 143, 150–61

Hunke, Werner 56, 100, 110, 202, 216, 228; and surrender 235, 236, 237; and trial 248

Al-Husseini, Haj Amin 290, 291

I-Netze 138

intelligence 93–97, 125, 126, 153, 266; and Ardennes 168; and *Greif* 183–84; and sabotage units 121, 123; and Skorzeny Plan 279–80; and Soviet Union 88; *see also* Abwehr; Bletchley Park; CIA; CIC; OSS; RSHA; SIM; SIS; SOE

Iragorri, Maj-Gen Eduardo 272

Iran 54–55, 88–89

Ireland 50, 300, 301–4, 307, 315

Israel 310–13

Italian Army 69, 70

Italian Navy: 10th Assault Vehicle Flotilla 99

Italian Social Republic 81, 99

Italy 35, 58, 61–64, 233; *see also* Mussolini, Benito

Jagdverbände 122–23, 126–27, 221, 222, 225

Jäger, Hans 35

Jews 24, 25, 28–29, 49, 89, 306; and Final Solution 152, 288, 307; *see also* Holocaust

Jodl, GenOb Alfred 66, 117, 141, 149, 150, 218; and Ardennes 165, 167, 169–70; and Skorzeny 212, 213

John, Otto 295, 296

Johnen, Wilhelm 92

Jovanovic, Arso 96

July plotters 267, 274, 275, 276

Jurassc, Ernst 307

Jüttner, Hans 40, 51, 117–18, 120, 122

Kállay, Andreas 159

Kaltenbruner, Ernst 21, 25, 28, 39, 120, 170; and Alpenfestung 223, 227,

228–29, 233–34; and arrest 238–39, 240; and escape 229–30, 231; and peace plan 232; and resistance groups 135; and RSHA 45–46, 47; and Schellenberg 92; and Skorzeny 53, 72; and Stauffenberg plot 114, 118, 119; and trial 241; and Vienna Circle 147, 148; and Werwolf 226
Kampfschwimmer (frogmen) 102, 218–19
Kappler, Herbert 64, 67, 68
Karstensen, Jacob 90, 91
Kaufmann, Karl 283
KdK see Kriegsmarine
Keitel, GenFeldm Wilhelm 42, 66, 80, 112, 150, 170
Kempin, Hans 214, 215, 217
Kesselring, GenFM Albert 61–62, 64, 69
Khrushchev, Nikita 138
Kiesinger, Kurt 284
Kirchner, Olt Hans 94, 97
Kirkpatrick, Sir Ivone 283
Kirn, Hptm see Witzel, Dietrich F.
Kleinkrieg (commando warfare) 41–42
Knittel, Gustav 246, 253
Koch, Erich 140
Kocherscheidt, Lt Wilhelm 250–51, 252
Königsberg 203, 204, 205, 206, 207, 208
Korean War (1950–53) 261, 274, 281
Krappe, GenLt Günther 207, 209
Krebs, Gen Hans 163
Kriegsmarine (German Navy) 99–103
Kristallnacht (1938) 28–29, 306, 312
Krug, Heinz 312–13
Krupp, Alfried 285, 298–99
Krutoff, Lt Leo 68, 70
Kumm, Otto 274
Kuznetsov, Nikolai 88

La Maddalena 65–66, 67
Lagrou, René 286
Lange, Hptm Heinrich 104
Langguth, Hptm Gerhard 64, 68, 69, 70, 73–74, 83
Lawrence, T. E. 36
Laycock, Maj-Gen Sir Robert 322
Lázár, Maj-Gen Károly 158–59
Legión Carlos V 262, 278, 280
Ley, Robert 241
Liddell, Guy 239
Lieppe-Biesterfeld, Bernhard von 35
Linnebach, Kurt 304
Linsen exploding motor-boats 100–1
LLA (Lithuanian Freedom Army) 135
Loos, Dr Roland 138
loot 229, 230–31, 235
Luburić, Col Villa 139
Lucht, Herbert 284
Luftwaffe 9, 10, 30, 58, 204–5, 209; KG 200: 103, 104–8, 127, 128, 137
Lusser, Robert 105

MacArthur, Gen Douglas 261
McClean, Lt John 236
McCloy, John 262
McClure, Lt-Col Donald 246–47
Mackensen, Hans von 61
McRaven, Adm William 325
Maklyarsky, Col Mikhail 130, 131
Malmédy 180, 181, 186–87, 188–95, 241; map 14; and trial 244–46, 247–52
Maltzahn, Eckhard von 298
Mandl, Rupert 94, 139
Manstein, GenFeldm Erich von 296
Manteuffel, Hasso von 262, 274, 276
Marbert, Ingrid 303–4
Marcus, Joachim 'Macki' 205, 206

Markomannia Student Society 21–22
Maus, Wilhelm 246, 249, 250
Mauthausen 146, 156
Mayer, Franz 88, 89
Medan, Raphi 311
Mellenthin, GenMaj Friedrich Wilhelm von 314
Men in Action (TV series) 323
Menzel, Ulrich 76
Merex 308, 309
Mertins, Maj Gerhard Georg 290, 308–9
Messerschmitt, Willi 270, 271–72, 282, 285, 310, 312
Meyer, Lt Elimar 74–75
MI5 239
Miklas, Wilhelm 27–28
Miklós, Gen Béla 156
Mil Amt D 121, 136, 138–39
Milch, GenFeldm Erhard 103–4, 105, 107, 108
Mildner, Rudolf 89–90
Milius, Siegfried 122, 150, 201, 217
Model, Walter 165, 168
Mohammed Reza Shah 54
Mohnke, Wilhelm 113, 188, 189–90
Mooney, Gladys 301
Mors, Maj Harald 69, 70, 71, 78, 79, 83
Mosley, Sir Oswald 286
Mossad 287, 310–13
Müller, Heinrich 45, 112, 118, 119, 120
Munk, Kaj 91, 255
Müntz, Lt Dennis 246, 249
Mussolini, Benito 58, 61, 62; and rescue 8–10, 57, 64–81, 82–83

Naguib, Gen Mohamed 291, 292
Nasser, Gamal Abdel 288–89, 291, 292, 308, 310
NATO 261, 273
Naujocks, Alfred 42, 256
Naumann, Maj Fritz 138

Naumann, Werner 283–84, 286, 287
Nazi Party 22, 23, 24–26, 110, 207, 283–84; and denazification 241, 255; and Egypt 289–90; and hunters 306; and the Vatican 280; and Werwolf 224–26
Nebe, Arthur 45, 112
Nebel, Ludwig 176, 256
Nedić, Gen Milan 93
Neger torpedo 101–2
Neubacher, Dr Hermann 232, 233
Ney, Karoly 154
Night of the Long Knives (1934) 24, 31, 32, 42
NKGB 130, 131, 132, 137
NKVD 88–89, 129–31
nuclear weapons 261
Nuremberg International Military Tribunal 240–42, 244

Oberg, Carl 87
ODESSA (Organisation of Former SS Members) 258
Ohletz, Werner 145
OKW see Wehrmacht
Olbricht, GenOb Friedrich 111–12, 114–15
O'Neill, Lt William J. 251
operations 62; Achse (Axis) (1943) 9; Bagration (1944) 120, 124, 130; Barbarossa (1941) 35–38, 93, 125–26; Berezino (1944) 126–33; Bernhard (1942–45) 308; Brandy (1946) 258; Damocles (1962) 310–11; Eiche (Oak) (1943) 61–81, 276, 323; Fischadler (Osprey) (1942) 50; Forelle (Trout) (1944–45) 160–61; Franz (1943) 54–55; Greif (1944) 165–76, 179–88, 243, 244–52, 325; Karneval (1945) 226; Landfried (1944) 141–43; Margarethe (1944) 152;

Market Garden (1944) 102, 218; Mickey Maus (1944) 155–56, 159; Panzerfaust (1944) 153–60, 325; Peter (1943) 89–91, 240, 242, 243, 255; Rösselspring (Knight's Move) (1944) 94–97; Scherhorn (1944) 124–25, 126–33, 325; Schlange (1944) 176; Sonnenblume (Sunflower) (1944) 136–38; Sonnenwende (Solstice) (1945) 214; Stösser (1944) 177–78, 188–89; Toto (1944) 176; Ulm (1943) 53–54; Wacht am Rhein (Watch on the Rhine) (1944) 162–65, 176; Walküre (Valkyrie) (1944) 110–20; Weitsprung (Long Jump) (1943) 88–89; Zeppelin (1941–45) 126
Oppenhoff, Franz 226
Org 267–68, 276, 289, 293
OSS (Office of Strategic Services) 146, 176, 232
Ostafel, Gerhard 110, 113, 158, 199
Oster, GenMaj Hans 44

Pact of Madrid (1953) 273, 282
Paladin 313–14, 319
Palestine 290
Paris 263–65, 266
Parnass, Uffz Manfred 183–84
Pasquier, Paul 307
Paul VI, Pope 262
Pavelić, Ante 93
PCF (French Communist Party) 264
Pechau, Manfred 139–40
Peiper, Joachim 181–82, 187, 190, 191, 195, 245; and assassination 317; and Skorzeny Plan 279
Peres, Shimon 310
Perón, Eva 299
Perón, Juan 298, 299
Perper, George A. 237

Pétain, Philippe 86, 87
Petter, Herbert 235, 236
Pfeffer-Wildenbruch, Karl 153, 157
Pfrimer, Walter 22
Phleps, Artur 141, 143
Pius XII, Pope 64
poison gas pistol 305–6
Poland 42, 135, 196, 197–98
Porsche, Ferdinand 105–6, 258
Portugal 297
Post, Hans 86
Potter, Col H. E. 256
Preiss, Luise 263
Pridun, Olt Karl 116
Priebke, Erich 68
Priess, Hermann 245
prisoners of war 130, 131, 172, 244–45
Propaganda Kompanie 8, 9, 78
Prützmann, Hans-Adolf 224, 225–26
psychological warfare 136, 173–74, 186

Qashqai rebellion (1942–43) 54–55
Quirnheim, Ob Mertz von 115

Rabofsky, Dr Eduard 306
Radl, Karl 34, 49, 51, 56, 109, 263; and Alpenfestung 221, 227, 228; and Ardennes 177; and arrest 238, 239, 241; and Denmark 90, 91; and Eiche 64, 65, 66, 68, 75–76; and Gerhard 242–43; and Gran Sasso 256; and Himmler 54; and loot 231; and Mussolini 59; and Skorzeny 98, 138, 266; and special forces 122; and surrender 235, 236; and trial 248; and Yugoslavia 94
Rahn, Rudolph 153, 157
Ramcke, Hermann-Bernhard 274

Rauff, Walter 309
Red Army 142, 197, 198, 222; and Schwedt 201, 205, 206, 207–8, 211–12
refugees 135, 203, 223
Regis, Peter 237
Reich, Stabsgfr Hans 184
Reitsch, Hanna 104–5, 106–7, 216, 257, 259
Remagen, battle of (1945) 217–19
Remer, Col Otto-Ernst 112–13, 114, 116, 281, 285; and Algeria 293–94; and Egypt 290
Renault, Gilbert (Col Rémy) 264, 266
Rendulic, Genob Lothar 94, 95, 96, 97
RENFE 297
Renner, Karl 232
resistance groups 135–40
Reza Shah Pahlavi 54
Rhine River 217–19
Ribbentrop, Joachim von 66, 150
Rich, Roy 322
Rohde, Fw Heinz 182–83, 186, 187
Röhm, Ernst 24
Romania 141–43, 152
Rommel, Erwin 64, 166
Roon, Maj Arnold von 69, 83
Roosevelt, Franklin D. 84, 88, 89, 241
Rosenberg, Alfred 140
Rosenfeld, Lt-Col Abraham H. 245, 246, 247, 248, 249–50, 253, 254
Rote Kapelle (Red Orchestra) spy ring 295, 296
Rothschild, Victor 239, 240, 242
Royal Air Force (RAF) 58
Royal Navy 99
RSHA (Reich Main Security Office) 44–47, 112, 126
Rudel, Ob Hans-Ulrich 216, 263, 264, 275, 281; and arms trade 309; and far right activities 285, 286; and Skorzeny 318

Rumohr, Joachim 160, 161
Runstedt, Gerd von 165, 168
Russia see Soviet Union
Russian Revolution 85

SA (Sturmabteilung) 24, 26, 27, 32
sabotage 52, 99, 121, 123
Sachsenhausen 305–7
St Germain, Treaty of (1919) 22
Salazar, Dr António 297
Sandberger, Dr Martin 230
Sänger, Eugen 310
Sassen, Willem 288, 309
Schacht, Hjalmar 265, 269, 270, 271, 285; and banking 296–97; and Egypt 289
Schellenberg, Walter 43, 44–46, 47–48, 92, 139; and Abwehr 120–21; and arrest 240; and Denmark 91; and Gehlen 126; and Mussolini 63; and peace negotiations 230; and Skorzeny 54, 221; and Stauffenberg plot 109–10, 111, 118–20; and Tehran Conference 88; and trial 241; and Werwolf 226
Scherf, Hptm Walter 172–73, 181, 189, 190–92, 244, 246
Scherhorn, Olt Heinrich 124, 125, 126, 127–28, 129, 130–31, 132
Schiebel, Kurt 229
Schiffer, Ob 127, 128, 129
Schilz, Lt Günther 184
Schirach, Baldur von 222–23, 241
Schmidt, Ogfr Wilhelm 183–84
Schnez, Ob Albert 277, 278, 282
Schörner, GenFeldm Ferdinand 221–22
Schramm, Dr Percy 249
Schreiber, Alfred 222
Schreiber, Walter 102, 218, 219
Schröter, Lieselotte 260

Schubert, Gerhard Hartmut von 314
Schuschnigg, Kurt von 25, 26, 27
Schwedt Bridgehead 200–13, 214–15, 216–17; map 15
Schwend, Fritz 308–9
Schwerdt, Otto 51, 75, 77; and Denmark 90, 91, 243, 255, 256
SD (Sicherheitsdienst) 43–44, 46, 92
Serbia 93, 139
Serebryansky, Yakov 130
Serna, Victor de la 272
Serrano Súñer, Ramón 272
Seyss-Inquart, Arthur 26, 27, 28
Sheen, Col Henry Gordon 238
Silver, Arnold M. 257, 259
SIM (Servizio de Informazione Militari) 65
Sima, Horia 267
Simonsen Mackey, Father Konrad 280
SIS (Secret Intelligence Service) 137
Six, Franz 45
SKA (Schutzkorps Alpenland) 227–29, 232, 233, 236–27
Skorzeny, Alfred (brother) 257, 259
Skorzeny, Anton (father) 18–19, 23, 29
Skorzeny, Emmi (2nd wife) 29, 49, 80, 258, 265
Skorzeny, Ilse (3rd wife) 264–66, 268–69, 273, 295, 324; and Ireland 301, 303–4; and Mossad 311
Skorzeny, Margareta (1st wife) 23–24
Skorzeny, Otto 18–19, 20–22, 23–24, 216, 230, 315–18; and Abwehr 121; and acquittal 253–54; and Alpenfestung 221–22, 223–24, 227–29, 231, 234–35; and Ardennes 162–63, 176–77, 178; and arms trade 308–10; and

arrest 236–40; and Austria 305–8; and 'automatic arrest' 255–56; and *Barbarossa* 36, 37–38; and BfV 295, 296; and Denmark 90, 91; and Egypt 289, 290–93, 294; and Eichmann 287–88; and enemies 144–47, 148; and escape 260; and espionage 52–53; and exile 263–67, 268–69; and far right activities 284–87; and Fölkersam 199; and France 86–87; and *Greif* 165–68, 169–74, 179–81, 182, 183, 184–87, 188; and Hitler 58–61, 134–35, 149–50, 195–96, 220–21; and Hungary 150–51, 153–55, 156, 157–60; and Ireland 301–4; and Jews 28–29; and legend 319–25; and Malmédy 189–90, 191, 192, 194–95; and mercenaries 313–14; and Miklas 27–28; and Mil Amt D 138–39; and Mossad 311–13; and Mussolini 8–10, 57, 62–63, 65–67, 68, 71–72, 74–75, 76, 77, 78–84; and the navy 99–100, 102–3; and Nazi Party 25–27; and Remagen 218, 219; and resistance groups 135, 136, 137, 140; and RSHA 45, 46, 47, 48–51; and Schellenberg 92; and *Scherhorn* 125, 126, 128, 129, 131, 132, 133; and Schwedt 201, 202–11, 212–14, 215; and Skorzeny Plan 261–62, 273–74, 275–79, 280–81; and Spain 269–71, 272–73, 299–300; and special operations 42; and SS commandos 84, 85; and Stauffenberg plot 109–10, 113–14, 116–20; and steel 297–99; and Tehran

Conference 88–89; and Territorialen Jagdverbände 122, 123; and trial 241, 242, 243–49, 252; and USA 256–59; and Vienna 222–23; and Waffen-SS 30–31, 34–35, 39–40; and weaponry 98–99, 104, 105–8; and Werwolf 225, 226, 232–33; and Yugoslavia 94–95, 96–97
Skorzeny, Waltraut (daughter) 29, 259, 265, 286, 304
Slovakia 143, 145–46
Smith, Lt-Col Baldwin B. 185
Smith, Edgar 269–70, 272
Smith, Gen Walter Bedell 238
SOE (Special Operations Executive) 52, 252
Soleti, Gen Fernando 72, 73, 75
Sonderkampf (special warfare) 98
South Africa 314
South America 308–10; *see also* Argentina
Soviet Union 22, 35–38, 54, 267, 268; and Austria 232; and Germany 275; and Hungary 143, 151, 152–53, 156–57, 160; and nuclear weapons 261; and Romania 141, 142; and Rote Kapelle spy ring 295, 296; and *Scherhorn* 124–25, 126–33; and Skorzeny 255, 256, 257, 259, 263; and Ukraine 135, 136, 137; *see also* NKVD; Red Army; Stalin, Joseph
Spacil, Josef 229, 230–31
Spain 259, 262, 263, 269–70, 271–73, 296–97; and Egypt 313; and ETA 314; and steel 297–98; and USA 282
special operations 41–43
Speer, Albert 54, 108, 114
Speidel, Hans 262, 274,

275–77, 281–82
spies *see* espionage
SRP (Socialist Reich Party) 285, 290
SS (Schutzstaffel) 23, 24–25, 26, 31–33, 257–58; and Mussolini 82; and special operations 42; and Stauffenberg plot 112; and trials 240, 241; *see also* RSHA; Waffen-SS
Stalin, Joseph 37, 84, 88, 89, 137, 281; and Austria 232; and France 264; and *Scherhorn* 129, 130, 132; and Schwedt 205
Stalingrad, battle of (1942–43) 39, 83, 132
Starhemberg, Prinz Ernst Rüdiger von 22
Stauffenberg, Ob Claus Schenk Graf von 110, 111, 112, 114, 115, 116, 117; *see also* operations: *Walküre* (Valkyrie)
steel industry 297–99
Steiner, Felix 33
Stielau, Olt Lothar 175
Stirling, Col David 322
Streif Korps 122, 123
Streifendienst (patrol service) 223–24, 227
Stringer, Pvt Frank 50, 212
Stroessner, Alfredo 309
Strong, Sir Kenneth 89
Struller, Otto 170
Student, GenOb Kurt 9, 61, 83, 113–14, 276; and Mussolini 62, 63, 65, 66–67, 69, 70–71, 72, 73
Stumpfegger, Dr 195, 216
Stürtz, Emil 207
Sudoplatov, Lt-Gen Pavel 129, 130, 131, 138
suicide missions 100, 102, 104–5, 106–8, 122
Summersby, Kay 185
Süsskind-Schwendi, Ob Hugo von 138
Switzerland 92
Szálasi, Ferenc 153, 157, 160
Sztójay, Gen Döme 152

tanks 171–72, 181, 191, 193
Tehran Conference 88–89
Territorialen Jagdverbände
  122–23, 126–27
Thiele, GenOb Fritz 111
Thon, Harry W. 245–46, 253
Thun-Hohenstein, Maj
  Erwein Graf von 145–46,
  256
Tisei, Aldo 314
Tito, Josip Broz 93, 94,
  95–96, 109, 155
Traynor, Oscar 302
treasure convoy 229,
  230–31
Tschierschky, Karl 226
Tshombe, Moïse 303

Ujszaszi, Maj-Gen István
  151, 153, 155
Ukraine 135–38, 140
uniforms *see* enemy uniforms
United States of America
  (USA) 50, 69, 232, 261,
  273, 282; and arms deals
  308; and Cold War 267,
  268; and Egypt 288–89;
  and Skorzeny 236–39,
  240, 257–59, 263, 300–1;
  and Soviet Union 235; and
  Ukraine 137–38
UPA (Ukrainian Insurgent
  Army) 135–38
US Air Force (USAF) 58
US Army 164, 188–89, 234,
  256, 268; 7th Army 226,
  237; 1st Infantry Dvn 186;
  2nd Infantry Dvn 180; 9th
  Armored Dvn 217; 84th
  Infantry Dvn 186; 15th
  Infantry Rgt 235; 30th
  Infantry Rgt 236; 285th
  Field Artillery Btn 182
Ustaše 93, 139

Valentin, Hermann Adolf
  311, 312
Valera, Éamon de 303
Vartanyan, Gevork 88–89
Vatican, the 44, 280

Veesenmayer, Edmund 152,
  153, 156, 159
vehicles 171–72
Venlo incident (1939) 41, 47
Verband deutscher Soldaten
  (League of German
  Soldiers) 274, 280
Verwoerd, Hendrik 314
Vessem, Pieter van 50
veterans' associations 274–75,
  280
Vichy France 39, 86–87
Victor Emmanuel III of Italy,
  King 58, 61, 62, 65, 69
Vienna 18–19, 21–22,
  24–28, 26, 222–23; and
  Circle 46–47, 147–48,
  232; and Jewish
  community 306
volunteers 169–70
Vorster, John 314
Voss, Dr Wilhelm 289, 290,
  292, 293

Waffen-SS 30–31, 33–35,
  38–40, 120, 329–30;
  Jägerbataillon 502: 48,
  51–52, 53; SS-
  Fallschirmjägerbataillon
  500: 84; SS-
  Fallschirmjägerbataillon
  600: 122, 215; SS-
  Sonderlehrgang
  'Oranienburg' 50; and
  veterans 274, 281
Walther, Olt Wilhelm 97,
  140, 199, 228, 237, 258
Waneck, Wilhelm 46, 47,
  141, 147, 230, 232; and
  Alpenfestung 233; and
  Gerhard 242
war crimes 240–41, 249–50,
  259, 296
Warche Brück 193–94; map
  14
Warger, Robert 65–66, 67, 75
Warlimont, Gen Walter 251
Warwick Films 322–23
weaponry, German 53,
  98–99, 101–2, 104–5,

153–54, 172; poison
  bullets 248–49, 306–7;
  V-1 flying bomb 103–4,
  105–7
Wehrmacht 42, 48, 51,
  121–22, 138–39
Weichs, GenFeldm
  Maximilian von 93, 95
Weiss, Bruno 26–27, 28
Wenck, Gen Walther 153,
  157, 214
Werwolf 224–26, 232–33,
  243
West Germany 262, 273–75,
  281, 295–96, 299, 315
Westphal, GenLt Siegfried
  163, 164, 167–68, 171,
  186
Whiting, Charles 316
Whittington, Capt Jere 272
Widmann, Dr Albert 99,
  243, 248, 306–7
Wiesenfeld, Lt William
  184
Wiesenthal, Simon 306, 311,
  317
Willscher, Odo 202, 211, 279
Winkelmann, Otto 152, 153,
  155, 156, 157, 159; and
  Alpenfestung 227
Witzel, Dietrich F. 136–37,
  221–22, 256
Wolff, Karl 233
Wolff, Otto 271, 285, 297
Wolfsschanze (Wolf's Lair)
  59, 66–67, 80, 110, 111
Worgitzky, Ob Hans-Heinrich
  125, 132
World War I (1914–18)
  18–19, 31–32
Wulf, Oblt Hermann
  172–73, 181, 189, 195

Yeo-Thomas, WC F. F. E.
  'Tommy' 252, 253–54,
  264, 266
Yugoslavia 35, 36, 93–97,
  139, 143

Zhukov, Georgy 212, 214